ECONOMIC ISSUES, PROBLEMS AND PERSPECTIVES

FINANCIAL ASSET PRICING: THEORY, GLOBAL POLICY AND DYNAMICS

ECONOMIC ISSUES, PROBLEMS AND PERSPECTIVES

Additional books in this series can be found on Nova's website under the Series tab.

Additional E-books in this series can be found on Nova's website under the E-books tab.

ECONOMIC ISSUES, PROBLEMS AND PERSPECTIVES

FINANCIAL ASSET PRICING: THEORY, GLOBAL POLICY AND DYNAMICS

PAUL E. SCHULZ
AND
BARBARA P. HOFFMANN
EDITORS

Nova Science Publishers, Inc.
New York

For permission to use material from this book please contact us:
Telephone 631-231-7269; Fax 631-231-8175
Web Site: http://www.novapublishers.com

LIBRARY OF CONGRESS CATALOGING-IN-PUBLICATION DATA

Financial asset pricing : theory, global policy and dynamics / editors, Paul E. Schulz and Barbara P. Hoffmann.
p. cm.
Includes index.
ISBN 978-1-61122-803-8 (hbk.)
1. Capital assets pricing model. I. Schulz, Paul E., 1955- II. Hoffmann, Barbara P.
HG4636.F56 2010
332'.041--dc22
2010042607

Published by Nova Science Publishers, Inc. + New York

CONTENTS

PREFACE

In finance, the capital asset pricing model (CAPM) is used to determine a theoretically appropriate required rate of return of an asset. This book presents current research in the study of financial asset pricing, including monetary policy and boom-bust cycles in asset pricing; migration dynamics of stock movements between portfolios; return calculation in international mutual funds; risk premium, market price of risk, and stochastic price models for commodities; computation finance for stochastic volatility and correlation; and consumption-based asset pricing model (CCAPM) in Latin America.

Chapter 1 - In this paper, a general overview regarding asset prices and monetary policy is given. First, the role for asset prices in the objective function of monetary policy is discussed. In this context, a short overview concerning the possible inclusion of asset prices in the inflation measure is given and the role of financial stability in the objective function of monetary policy is analyzed. Second, the development of research and literature regarding the topic of whether and how monetary policy should respond to asset price misalignments and boom-bust cycles is presented. After the classic discussion of exogenous bubbles and linear rules is laid out, the development to a middle ground with endogenous bubbles and non-linear rules is put forward. Third, since the worldwide financial crisis 2007-2009 has led to a thorough re-evaluation of related research, respective developments are surveyed.

Chapter 2 - This chapter uses monthly UK stock market data sorted into a two-dimensional set of portfolios to establish the year-on-year migration dynamics of stock movements between portfolios. The system of (monthly re-balanced) portfolios comprises six dividend yield strata (including a separate zero-dividend category) each of which is further subdivided into market capitalisation quintiles. Monthly re-balancing ensures that portfolios are constantly populated by stocks having similar dividend yield and size characteristics; the movement of stocks, year-on-year, between portfolios provides information about the relationship linking returns behaviour to yield. Simply stated, the analysis of migration patterns provides additional insights into the phenomenon of the much-quoted 'U' shaped characteristic which purports to relate risk-adjusted returns to dividend yield; it does so by drawing attention to the *similarities* between high-yielding and zero-dividend stocks, a linkage which is de-emphasised when these are conventionally viewed as being at opposite ends of a yield spectrum. This leads to the notion of 'adjacency', and implies a circular, rather than linear, relationship between returns and yield; a notion supported by the relatively high levels of *direct* migration between these two (high- and zero-yielding) groups; and by the observation, both in this chapter and in the supporting literature, that smaller firms with high average returns are concentrated in the two groups. The analysis here of direct migration also takes account of stocks distinguished by year-on-year expansion versus year-on-year contraction; it emerges as being both robust to, and consistent with this separation. A plausible explanation for such direct migration would be one associated with 'distress', whereby declining price levels among such stocks tends to inflate the yield metric (implying migration toward the 'high dividend' stratum) as firms struggle to maintain dividend levels; ultimately, firms fall directly, upon virtually inevitable dividend cessation, into the zero-dividend category. A similar analysis applies when growing firms commence paying dividends for the first time. Finally, the analysis examines the dynamics of the process in terms of a long-run equilibrium and a speed of adjustment, treating the transition matrix as a Markov process; it finds plausible values for these parameters in the context of the UK stock market.

Chapter 3 - The authors study the methodology of return calculation in international mutual funds with investment in emerging markets particularly those with short market history. Besides daily and monthly returns they introduce a new procedure: the daily recalculated monthly returns (*DRMRs*) and investigate which is the adequate method for testing market efficiency and measuring fund performance. DRMR represents the log returns of the previous month (assuming 21 trading days in a month) and is recalculated day by day for the studied period. The authors show that DRMR is effective for all assets and markets for which there is no suitably long time series available.

Chapter 4 - Commodities are not financial assets, yet futures contracts on commodities are financial instruments which have been traded for over 100 years. The most relevant features in these contracts include the convenience yield, mean reversion, the risk premium, changing volatility, and seasonality, among others. The stochastic price models developed over time usually try to account for these characteristics. The choice of a particular model will depend on the specific features of the commodity and the particular purpose of the model.

The aim of this paper is twofold. First, the authors analyze the modelling of the market price of risk in different stochastic dynamic models. Then they derive the corresponding equation for the risk premium, and the dynamics of futures prices (both in the physical world and under the risk-neutral probability measure). They use several models with mean reversion; the standard Geometric Brownian Motion is also considered as a particular case of one of them. They explore different specifications for the market price of risk in these models. One of them allows for the possibility that the market price of risk is stochastic and correlated with the commodity price.

Second, they estimate the market price of risk for two commodities, namely coal and carbon dioxide, using the surface generated by daily futures prices for different maturities. From the stochastic models for the spot price and the equations for the futures price they obtain the stochastic dynamic models for the behaviour of futures prices in the physical world, which are used to estimate the market price of risk.

Their results allow identify the sign and size of the market price of risk for these commodities. The authors check whether futures prices are biased estimators of expected spot prices in both cases. They also compute the necessary correction factor to get a better estimate of the expected spot price.

Chapter 5 - A recent study comparing international housing affordability finds Australia has three of the five most unaffordable housing markets in the world. One reason for Australia's ranking is that the house price bubble in Australia unlike elsewhere has not yet burst. Demographia believes it will burst eventually, but this is a controversial view in Australia. Many analysts claim Australia did not build as many houses during the boom as were built in other markets, and therefore we will not see the massive price declines that other countries have experienced. In this research the authors forward several reasons why Australia's house prices are unlikely to succumb to the price falls experienced in the US, UK and Europe generally. Based on historical and current data the paper provides a comparative analysis of the determinants of house prices in Australia and the US, including an analysis of housing affordability. From the evidence presented, the factors, which played the most significant roles in creating the conditions for the US house bubble, were not evident for the Australian housing market. In fact, the growing demand push factors combined with the constrained supply factors in providing new housing stock in particular for the major cities of Melbourne and Sydney appear to have anything but abated.

Chapter 6 - Risk inhomogeneously changes through time, which gives rise to important impact on derivative securities pricing theory. In past two decades, in either industry or academics, it is gradually realized that the factor, i.e., the volatility, stochastically changes over time. Consequently, a lot of models have been developed to explain the empirically observed deviations from Black-Scholes formula. In this chapter, to figure out another unnoticed stochastic factor, the authors check the historical correlation in several exchange rates, and find that the correlations vary more violently than their volatilities. On the other hand, based on the market price of index option, its implied correlation is investigated, which can not coincide with the realized one at all. This fact means the pricing of options in market is not based on same measure. Therefore, they introduce a more sophisticated scenario, namely, stochastic correlation, to describe such a phenomenon. As a stochastic process with two bounds is highlighted to describe the time-varying correlation, they can build up the partial differential equation for pricing multi-asset option. Meanwhile, the authors also incorporate the random correlation in the stochastic volatility model, and give its solution. Finally, the correlation risk in interest rate product is analyzed. This work is helpful for hedging risk better.

Chapter 7 - This study investigates whether the Consumption-based Capital Asset Pricing Model (CCAPM) is consistent with the data from four Latin-American countries: Brazil, Chile, Colombia, and Mexico. Empirical results showed that there is a statistically significant relationship between mean excess returns and consumption betas in the countries cited above, with the exception of Mexico. Such results are, in part, similar to the results reported in previous studies for the United States of America.

Chapter 8 - In this chapter the authors consider a simple financial market model following the pioneering works by R. Day, described by one-dimensional piecewise linear maps, either being continuous or discontinuous. They shall see how rich the related dynamics are, with sequences of stable cycles and chaotic intervals. Their results explain, among other things, the emergence of intricate bull and bear markets dynamics, as observed in many actual financial markets. Due to its simplicity, the model allows both a useful analytical study and a qualitative interpretation of the dynamic outcomes. The authors describe bifurcation sequences with both period increment by one and by two, and they illustrate the wide regions of chaotic behavior.

In: Financial Asset Pricing
Editors: P. E. Schulz and B. P. Hoffmann

ISBN 978-1-61122-803-8

Chapter 1

MONETARY POLICY AND BOOM-BUST CYCLES IN ASSET PRICES: A LITERATURE SURVEY

Rolf Knütter** and Helmut Wagner
University of Hagen, Department of Economics,
Hagen, Germany

ABSTRACT

In this paper, a general overview regarding asset prices and monetary policy is given. First, the role for asset prices in the objective function of monetary policy is discussed. In this context, a short overview concerning the possible inclusion of asset prices in the inflation measure is given and the role of financial stability in the objective function of monetary policy is analyzed. Second, the development of research and literature regarding the topic of whether and how monetary policy should respond to asset price misalignments and boom-bust cycles is presented. After the classic discussion of exogenous bubbles and linear rules is laid out, the development to a middle ground with endogenous bubbles and non-linear rules is put forward. Third, since the worldwide financial crisis 2007-2009 has led to a thorough re-evaluation of related research, respective developments are surveyed.

Keywords: Monetary Policy, Asset Prices, Boom-Bust Cycles.

1. INTRODUCTION

Should policymakers adjust interest rates when they observe rapidly rising asset prices and to what extent? Is it optimal to adopt a proactive policy of raising short term real interest rates during an asset price boom to prevent the build-up of a financial market crisis scenario, or is it optimal to follow a reactive policy that ignores its impact on the likelihood of a future downward financial cascade? A pre-emptive interest rate hike may involve unnecessary high

* E-mail: rolf.knuetter@fernuni-hagen.de and helmut.wagner@fernuni-hagen.de

welfare losses in terms of inflation and output deviating from their targets during the boom-phase, while a reactive strategy may be associated with a bust-induced economic recession in the aftermath of the boom.

Whereas contributions of the classic discussion often remain skeptical about both the feasibility and the desirability of the pre-emptive monetary policy strategy (Bernanke and Gertler 1999, 2001, Greenspan 2002), more recent studies, however, emphasize that there is no clear-cut answer to the optimal policy choice. Rather, the optimal policy response to an asset price boom may depend in a complex way on various economic determinants, such as the probability of a bust-induced credit crunch and the degree of 'market exuberance' (Bordo and Jeanne 2002a, b), the extent of the private sector's forward-looking behavior (Berger, Kißmer and Wagner 2007) or the time lags of monetary policy (Gruen, Plumb and Stone 2005).

Academic research has devoted considerable efforts in exploring this monetary policy trade-off.[1] The contributions of the reactive strategy often expressed general skepticism about both the feasibility and the desirability of the pre-emptive monetary policy strategy. For example, Bernanke and Gertler (1999), (2001) argue that central banks should take asset prices only insofar into account as they influence inflation and output. Furthermore, a reactive strategy seems to be synonymous in many cases to a policy of 'benign neglect', in the sense that central banks do not react pre-emptively in the boom phase but rather ease monetary policy reactively if and when an asset price crash occurs. The advocates of the reactive strategy point to three issues justifying their approach. First, central banks may not be able to identify asset price misalignments. Second, monetary policy is often regarded as a blunt tool. A small interest rate increase could even further fuel the boom – the increase necessary to slow the boom or prick the bubble may lead to a severe recession. Third, monetary policy behaving in an active manner may raise credibility problems: central banks with the primary objective of stabilizing inflation might have problems in communicating to markets a monetary tightening, especially in the case of low inflation.

In contrast, the proponents of the proactive strategy (e.g. Cecchetti et al. 2000, 2003) argue that monetary policy should raise interest rates in a proactive manner in order to prevent bubbles from growing. Using the (modified) model of Bernanke and Gertler (1999), (2001), Cecchetti et al. (2000) show that the inclusion of asset prices in the Taylor rule may enhance macroeconomic performance. Regarding the identification problem, they argue that other variables used in conducting monetary policy, like the output gap, are hard to assess too.

Following this debate, several studies show that there are no simple rules for solving this problem. Rather, the optimal policy response to an asset price boom may depend in a complex way on various economic determinants, such as the probability of a bust-induced credit crunch and the degree of 'market exuberance' (Bordo and Jeanne 2002a, b), the extent of the private sector's forward-looking behavior (Berger, Kißmer and Wagner 2007) or the time lags of monetary policy (Gruen, Plumb and Stone 2005). Furthermore, following the subprime and financial crisis 2007-2009, the topic of whether and how monetary policy should take asset price developments into account, is currently being re-evaluated with

[1] Bernanke and Gertler (1999, 2001), Cecchetti et al. (2000), Cecchetti, Genberg and Wadhwani (2003), Kent and Lowe (1997), Bordo and Jeanne (2002a, b), Filardo (2003), Gruen, Plumb and Stone (2005), Berger, Kißmer and Wagner (2007). See also the discussion between Roubini (2006) and Posen (2006).

several authors arguing for a stronger role of financial factors and for the "leaning against the wind" approach.[2]

In this survey, an overview regarding boom-bust cycles in asset prices and monetary policy is given. In chapter 2, the role for asset prices in the objective function is discussed. First, a short overview regarding the possible inclusion of asset prices in the inflation measure is given. Second, the role of financial stability in the objective function of monetary policy is analyzed in detail. In this context, the classic discussion of exogenous bubbles and linear rules is presented, including the models of Bernanke and Gertler (1999), (2001) and Cecchetti et al. (2000), (2003). Then, the development to a middle ground with endogenous bubbles and non-linear rules is discussed. In this regard, several important models are referred to: Kent and Lowe (1997), (1998), Gruen et al. (2005), and Bordo and Jeanne (2002a, b). Since the worldwide financial crisis 2007-2009 has led to a thorough re-evaluation of related research, recent developments are surveyed in chapter 3. Chapter 4 concludes.

2. Should Asset Prices Be Included in the Objective Function?[3]

In the last decade or so there has been an intense debate among policymakers and scientists regarding asset prices and monetary policy. During boom-bust cycles like the New Economy bubble and the 2007-2009 subprime and financial crisis in the U.S. this discussion was regularly amplified. There is consensus that central banks should watch asset price developments since they may have an impact on economic variables such as output and inflation and on financial stability. However, what is far from clear is the question of whether asset prices should be part of the central bank's objective function and whether and how central banks should respond to asset prices. Policymakers can take account of asset prices by integrating them in the inflation measure and by considering financial stability in the objective function. In the following sections an overview on the different problems discussed in this context is presented.

2.1 Asset Prices and the Inflation Measure

Usually, the objectives of monetary policy are the stabilization of output and inflation with the latter regularly perceived as the most important objective. Inflation is the increase of the level of prices of goods and services in a certain period. Since assets are an important part of the transmission mechanism of monetary policy, it has been discussed whether asset prices should be included in the measurement of inflation (see the seminal paper by Alchian and Klein 1973). In the context of monetary policy and asset prices this can be viewed as the most extreme proposal (see ECB 2005). Since price stability is typically defined as holding constant a consumer price index given by the costs of consuming goods and services in a year

[2] See for example Yellen (2009), Trichet (2009), White (2009), Weber (2009), Cúrdia and Woodford (2009), de Fiore and Tristani (2009), Adrian and Shin (2008), Lipsky (2008) and Wagner (2010). Even Svensson (2009) can be interpreted in a way that leaning against the wind can be synonymous with flexible inflation targeting.

[3] The structure of this section is based in part on Funke, Kißmer and Wagner (2004).

relative to the costs in a base year, the focus of the inflation measurement lies on current consumption. However, sometimes it has been argued that consumers care about future consumption as well. Therefore, Alchian and Klein (1973) argue that a price index should follow an intertemporal approach, thus including asset prices. The reason is that asset prices can be viewed as claims on future consumption. Hence, the authors argue that conventional consumption baskets are incomplete and that a proper consumption basket should not only include current, but also future consumption. However, there are various practical barriers. For example, prices for future goods are not always available. For that reason Alchian and Klein (1973) suggest the use of asset prices as proxies for future consumption. Following their work, several authors have dealt with that issue. Pollack (1989) shows in a theoretical analysis that asset prices can be used for the measurement of inflation. Employing a dynamic equilibrium price index, Shibuya (1992) shows how the proposal of Alchian and Klein (1973) can be interpreted as a weighted sum of consumer and asset price inflation. Concerning the weights, Shibuya (1992) is using 3% for the weight of the current price index and 97 % for the weight of asset prices. In addition, Shiratsuka (1999) employs the dynamic equilibrium price index by Shibuya (1992) and tests the information contents of assets prices regarding inflation. He concludes that the forecasting reliability of asset prices is relatively low and the weight of asset prices too large.[4]

In this context, Bryan, Cecchetti and O'Sullivan (2002a) argue there will be a so-called "excluded goods bias" in the calculation of the inflation statistic. In their analysis, they find that the exclusion of asset prices from the CPI has caused a downward bias of approximately 0.25% annually. Considering three types of assets (equities, bonds and houses), it turns out that the non-consideration of houses leads to the largest error. Furthermore, Bryan, Cecchetti and O'Sullivan (2002b) argue that in periods with a fluctuating real interest rate the exclusion of asset prices from the measurement of inflation can even deform the inflation of all goods. However, Filardo (2000) argues that inclusion of housing and stock market prices in the inflation index does not necessarily lead to an increase in economic performance (of the U.S.). He finds only weak empirical evidence for a link of house price and stock market developments for consumer price inflation with the latter being smaller. There are several authors arguing for an inclusion of house prices at least in the inflation measure. Goodhart (2001) and Goodhart and Hofmann (2001) show that in particular house prices are closely linked to the development of inflation. Moreover, Goodhart and Hofmann (2000) find that house prices are the most informative asset price for making inflation prognoses, whereas equity prices and the yield-spread provide less information. In this context, it should be stressed that the inclusion of house prices into a price index is being discussed at Eurostat. This should be done by including the actual costs of living in houses. In the first two stages (2002-2004 and 2006-2007) the construction of price indices for newly built and old houses has been developed. From the third stage on (since 2008) all EU member states are participating and a price index for reconstruction and renovation is displayed. Finally, there should be a price index for housing and real estate, which may in the future be integrated in the Harmonised Index of Consumer Prices (HICP) of the EMU (see Cournède 2005).

[4] Moreover, Stock and Watson (2001) analyze the role of asset prices for output and inflation. They obtain mixed results: there are asset prices which predict output and inflation growth in some periods, but there are ambiguous results as well. Sometimes a good indicator in one period turns into a useless indicator in another period.

Furthermore, Eurostat aims at preparing an International Handbook on Residential Property Price Indices.

However, despite the reasons for including asset prices in the inflation measure there are several arguments against the inclusion of asset prices. Already, Alchian and Klein (1973) put forward some arguments. First, it might not be possible to obtain all the prices necessary for such an index. Since an appropriate asset price should theoretically include all assets (e.g. human capital), it would be disadvantageous when some assets are not covered. Second, a change in asset prices might be hard to interpret. The reason is that not only a change in private sector's inflation expectations, but a lot of different possible underlying reasons can be responsible for the volatility and variability of asset prices (Gilchrist and Leahy 2002). Hence, the link between asset price changes and future price changes is quite weak (Shiratsuka 1999). There might be situations of asset prices moving in directions completely unrelated to future inflation. For example, a decline in stock prices can be due to impairment in expected profits, whereas future consumption may not be affected. In addition, although house prices are a good indicator for future consumption, this is not true for stock prices.[5] Moreover, when central banks aim at measuring and reacting to asset price inflation, they need to know the fundamental value of all assets, an assumption which is strongly doubted (Smets 1997, Filardo 2000).[6] Third, since current consumption is just a small fraction of lifetime consumption, taking account of asset prices in the sense of Alchian and Klein (1973) would give asset prices a weight far too high and central banks would possibly target asset prices (see Goodhart 2001). Fourth, when monetary authorities are targeting asset prices, moral hazard might be the result. Investors may increase their risk taking when a stabilization of asset prices by monetary policy is anticipated (ECB 2005). Fifth, the appropriate weight of asset prices needs to specified. As stressed by ECB (2005) the weight of asset prices could reach 90%, which would result in a very volatile monetary policy.[7] [8] Sixth, inflation indeterminacy could arise. Since monetary policy is usually forward-looking and asset prices are in part built from expectations regarding the future monetary stance, inflation expectations might become self-fulfilling and highly volatile (ECB 2005, Bernanke and Woodford 1997). Finally, when central banks successfully stabilize current consumer price inflation, this will stabilize inflation expectations as well, so there might be no need to take future inflation rates into account.

To sum up, including asset prices in the inflation measure appears to be an unrealistic task. The only exception is the inclusion of house prices in a price index.

---

[5] There is, however, even some evidence for a negative relationship of equity prices and future inflation, see Filardo (2000).

[6] King (2002) states that no one really knows the equilibrium level of asset prices, because, amongst other things, they are driven by private sector's expectations. Therefore he concludes that targeting asset prices directly is not possible. However, he proposes to extend the time horizon of monetary policy beyond the usual two-year-horizon.

[7] Bryan et al. (2002a, b) use similar approaches: For example, they are weighting asset prices in dependence to their inflation forecast ability and are relating the weight inversely to the volatility of the asset (hence, stocks and bonds get a very small weight). Other approaches are those of Cecchetti et al. (2000) who weigh asset prices according to their empirical relationship with prices of goods and services, and of Goodhart and Hofmann (2000) who relate the income spent on assets to total income.

[8] The volatility of asset prices (in particular equity prices) is a problem per se. As is argued by Cecchetti et al. (2000), the extremely high variance of stock returns may just add noise.

2.2 Financial Stability and the Objective Function

The second issue of the topic of asset prices and the objective function of monetary policy is the question of whether asset prices should enter the objective function in an independent way, for example by considering financial stability as a second objective beside price stability. The term financial stability has not been exactly defined yet (see Goodhart 2004). Rather, authors often define financial instability. However, following Issing (2003) there are two approaches of a positive definition. The systemic approach stresses that financial stability is associated with a functioning financial system being able to ensure an efficient allocation of capital on markets (Mishkin 1991, Schinasi 2004). The second approach links financial stability to a situation without a banking crisis and stable asset prices (Foot 2003, Ferguson 2002). There is a broad consensus that financial stability is considered an important target for central banks. However, it is usually not given the same weight as price stability which is part of the objective function. Furthermore, there is broad conviction that a high volatility of the inflation rate may induce financial instability. In turn, some authors see price stability as a sufficient condition for financial stability (Schwartz 1995) or as help ensuring financial stability, see Bordo and Wheelock (1998).

However, financial stability is often viewed as a constraint rather than a target (Svensson 2004). Financial stability will affect monetary policy only in the case of financial crises, hence in rare cases. In addition, Issing (2003) argues that although there might be a short run trade-off between price stability and financial stability[9], this trade-off cannot be exploited. Policymakers should rather focus on the long run where monetary and financial stability assumingly reinforce each other. This finding is supported by empirical evidence.[10]

Furthermore, the chosen monetary policy strategy is important for financial stability (Issing 2003). If central banks employ a simple inflation targeting strategy with a limited policy horizon (one to two years), the costs of financial instability (e.g. deflation following a bust) might not get the appropriate weight. In this regard, one can imagine a situation where the deviation of inflation from target in the short run might be optimal in order to ensure price stability in the medium and long run (Kent and Lowe 1997, 1998). In addition, if financial instability is associated with asymmetric risks (very large losses of a crisis, relatively small losses of a deviation of monetary policy objectives from target), it might be optimal to have lower inflation and output in the short run due to an interest rate hike (Bordo and Jeanne 2002a, b and Berger, Kißmer, Wagner 2007). Moreover, there is rather a short-term conflict than an exploitable short-run trade-off between price stability and financial stability. The reason is that an interest rate hike could indeed stop bubbles from growing, but, as already mentioned, this induces a movement below target of the near-term inflation. Since the time horizon for price stability includes future periods which might lead ex post to a possible crisis, the conflict is due to the fact that financial stability must be so important that a long-

---

[9] The trade-off can be imagined as a situation where low and stable inflation can foster non-fundamental developments on asset markets. Hence, in turn, less price stability might generate more financial stability (see Issing 2003). But, as Issing (2003) stresses, the only situation where lower inflation can generate financial instability is a situation of significant disinflation. But, to come into a situation of disinflation, there has been usually a period of high inflation in advance.

[10] Bordo, Dueker and Wheelock (2000), (2008) show that financial crises were often accompanied by large changes in inflation and unanticipated changes in inflation have played a major role in large movements in the U.S. stock market. The authors conclude that one policy lesson is that central banks should aim for minimizing unanticipated fluctuations in inflation in order to support stock market stability.

run deviation from price stability is justified by policymakers. As Issing (2003) stresses, this does not imply that price stability should not be the most important objective for monetary policy.

Monetary stability - defined as low and stable inflation (Borio and Lowe 2002) - may contribute to financial stability. This at least is the conventional view in literature (see Bordo et al. 2000). However, this wisdom was challenged even before the financial crisis 2007-2009. Borio et al. (2003) call it the "new environment view". It is characterized by liberalized financial markets and low inflation even during booms, with monetary policy fuelling booms in an unintended way. The low inflation of the recent decades is the result of better anchored inflation expectations, higher competition and a higher credibility of monetary policy.[11] This, in turn, together with a more successful stabilization of output, decreases the perceived risks and may encourage financial market participants to take higher risks, maybe resulting in boom-bust cycles on asset markets. In an environment of low inflation and better anchored inflation expectations, it can be expected that there is – in contrast to the conventional view mentioned above – financial turmoil in a low-inflation-environment. An empirical validation is the increased number of boom-bust cycles, often preceded by rapid credit growth.[12] Since central banks are now characterized by a higher anti-inflation credibility, it may take longer for booms showing up in increased inflation which is labeled by Borio et al. (2003) "the paradox of credibility".

Should central banks integrate financial stability in their objective function? This question is not answered definitely, not even by the proponents of the "new environment" view. Most of the time this question is negated, in particular in the conventional part of the literature. As already mentioned, some authors argue that financial stability can be obtained by focusing on the monetary policy objectives, inflation and output gap. Furthermore, when using a new objective, there might be pressure by the public when there is a deviation of the other target. Since it cannot be excluded that asset price misalignments lead to permanent deviations of inflation and output from their targets, some authors and policymakers call for a longer policy horizon (see White 2006, Bean 2003 and Borio et al. 2003). Carney (2009) argues that flexible inflation targeting can be the right approach to ensure price and financial stability through different time horizons. However, the time horizon should not be stretched too far since the credibility of the central bank can be impaired. This may in particular be a problem with the occurrence of longer term shocks.[13]

There are several empirical analyzes dealing with the role of financial stability for monetary policy. Mishkin and White (2003) analyze 15 stock market crashes in the U.S. and conclude that monetary policy should focus on financial stability rather than on stock markets alone, because there may be situations where a stock market crash does not induce financial instability. Adrian and Shin (2009a) show that the fluctuations in leverage are linked to periods of financial booms and busts. Furthermore, Adrian and Shin (2008) demonstrate that there is a tight link between the central banks instrument, the overnight rate, and credit growth (broker dealer asset growth) by short-term interest rates, yield spread and risk measures. Funds are passed by broker dealers to other leveraged institutions investing in short and longer terms. Hence, the cost of borrowing is closely associated with monetary policy. As

[11] See Wagner (2002).
[12] A stronger role for credit in the conduct of monetary policy is claimed by Borio and Lowe (2004).
[13] For a formal analysis of the extension of the policy horizon see Roi and Mendes (2007).

Adrian and Shin (2009a) point out, this result of giving financial intermediaries a role in the transmission process through credit supply and making short-term rates directly important for monetary policy stands in contrast to the current policy stance of many central banks assuming that short-term interest rates are only important for determining long-term interest rates. This conclusion is rooted in the assumption of financial amplifications due to frictions in the lending sector (in contrast to Bernanke and Gertler 1989 and Kiyotaki and Moore 1997). The authors point to the papers of Bordo and Jeanne (2002a, b) who focus on balance sheets (like Adrian and Shin) and argue that these balance sheets should enter a monetary policy rule in order to reduce the probability of financial crises. Hence, they argue that there is a "case for rehabilitating a role for balance sheet quantities for the conduct of monetary policy" (Adrian and Shin 2009a, p. 604). The reason is that balance sheet dynamics makes monetary policy important in ensuring financial stability. Furthermore and regarding the meaning of credit booms, during the financial crisis 2007-2009, Yellen (2009) admitted that credit booms fuelling house and bond prices are potentially more dangerous than other bubbles since they are able to generate "powerful adverse feedback loops between financial markets and real economic activity" (Yellen 2009, p. 5). Although she argues that basically policymakers are better off when avoiding a pre-emptive tightening, Yellen (2009) acknowledges that she "can now imagine circumstances that would justify leaning against a bubble with tighter monetary policy" (Yellen 2009, p. 5). See also Walsh (2009), who admits that allowing the bubble in house prices to continue to rise was a "serious policy mistake" (Walsh 2009, p. 32).

2.3. Monetary Policy and Asset Prices: The Classic Discussion and the Middle Ground

2.3.1. The Classic Discussion

The question of whether and how central banks should respond to boom-bust cycles in asset prices has very controversially been debated during the last decade or so. Whereas there seems to be consensus that central banks should react to a bursting bubble or a bust, it is less clear how monetary authorities should behave during asset price booms. The discussion mainly focuses on two positions: the reactive and the proactive strategy.

The proponents of the reactive strategy stress that central banks should take asset prices only insofar into account as they influence inflation and output.

Furthermore, in many cases a reactive strategy can be equated to a policy of 'benign neglect' (easing of monetary policy in the bust phase but never tightening in the boom phase). Main proponents of this strand of literature are Bernanke and Gertler (1999), (2001). Bernanke and Gertler (1999) use a dynamic New Keynesian model with sticky prices. It differs from the standard models in assuming frictions on the credit market which lead to a so-called "financial accelerator" influencing output. In their model, using flexible inflation-targeting ensures both economic and financial stability. Therefore, responding to asset prices is only necessary when they have an impact on inflation. Furthermore, Bernanke and Gertler

(2001) find no significant additional benefit of a response to asset prices.[14] Rather, trying to influence asset prices can be detrimental.

The authors conclude that an aggressive inflation-targeting rule stabilizing inflation and output is sufficient for achieving both macroeconomic and financial stability.[15] There are several other authors arguing for a reactive policy stance. Gilchrist and Saito (2006) stress the role of information and identification. Using a New Keynesian model with a financial accelerator they show that responding to the asset price gap delivers the largest gains when policymakers can correctly identify the growth of technology. Svensson (2004) argues for consideration of asset prices only insofar as they have an impact on the objectives of monetary policy. The central bank should not have asset prices as additional target. He proposes a financial stability report. Financial stability works as a constraint on monetary policy, but is binding only in a crisis situation. Goodfriend (2003) stresses that monetary policy should not directly respond to asset prices since there is no positive correlation between interest rates and equity prices. Moreover, there might be situations in which monetary policy should move in the opposite direction or not react at all. According to that, he argues that monetary policy in Japan in the late 1980s and in the U.S. in the late 1990s could not have been improved by reacting directly to asset prices. Goodfriend (2003) presents arguments why monetary policy should not directly respond to asset prices:

- there can be no theoretical assumption linking interest rate decisions positively to equity price movements,
- there are situations where interest rates should move in the opposite direction,
- for the central bank of a large economy with a low level of openness and a conservative inflation objective it might be not beneficial to target exchange rates.

In central banking practice, policymakers have usually advocated the reactive approach. Greenspan (2004) stresses that central banks should not target asset prices or lean against the wind but should "...mitigate the fallout when it occurs and, hopefully, ease the transition to the next expansion". In this regard, the "risk-management approach" is referred to. Since many risks are not quantifiable and central bank actions might affect these risks, "...risk management often involves significant judgment as we evaluate the risks of different events...".

Yellen (2005) stresses that the central point is not whether central banks should react at all while referring to the taking-account-of wealth effects of assets (e.g. house prices) on consumption, but rather if monetary policy should prick the bubble. Yellen (2005) refers to three issues to be fulfilled before responding in a proactive manner: first, the effect of the deflating bubble on the economy would be very large if the central bank does not act at all, second, it could not be expected that the central bank is able to "mitigate the fallout..." and third, monetary policy is viewed as the best instrument in order to deflate a bubble. Many

---

[14] The authors find that the small gains due to the reduced variability of output gap are likely to be outweighed by the respective increased variability of inflation.

[15] For somehow related analyses see Gilchrist and Leahy (2002) and Faia and Monacelli (2007). The latter find that a strong anti-inflationary stance is associated with the highest welfare when considering asset prices. Furthermore, they conclude that monetary policy should respond to rising asset prices by lowering interest rates. The reason is that in their model an increase in asset prices is related to an increase in the price of capital relative to consumption goods, which in turn, works as an implicit tax on investment.

authors would argue that it is very unlikely that all three issues are fulfilled, so that monetary policy should respond to asset prices only insofar as they influence target variables like inflation and output. In a similar vein, Posen (2006) argues against taking asset prices into account since there is only a weak link between monetary policy and the development of bubbles. Bubbles are caused by irrational exuberance, technological jumps and financial deregulation. The damage generated by bubbles depends on the financial structure of the economy: if there is a functioning banking system, the transmission of a shock will only be weak. However, in the case of financial instability, the possible costs of recession rise significantly. So Posen (2006) concludes there is no substitute for financial stability and the central bank should not directly respond to asset price bubbles, unless they are the cause for fluctuations in inflation and output. Blinder and Reis (2005) examine the question of whether central banks should burst bubbles and look therefore at the Fed's policy under Greenspan. They defend the policy conducted by Greenspan, a strategy what they call "mop up after" strategy.

In general, the position of favoring the reactive approach brings forward the following arguments against the proactive strategy[16]:

- The problem of identification of asset price misalignments,
- The problem of the adequate instrument: monetary policy is regarded as a blunt tool in order to deflate bubbles (a small interest rate increase could even further fuel the boom; the increase necessary to slow the boom or prick the bubble may lead to a severe recession),
- The problem of credibility: central banks with the primary objective of stabilizing inflation might have problems in communicating a monetary tightening, especially in the case of low inflation, thus risking their credibility.

The main proponents of the other policy choice are Cecchetti et al. (2000) and (2003). These authors argue that monetary policy should raise interest rates in a proactive manner in order to prevent bubbles from growing. Using the (modified) model of Bernanke and Gertler, Cecchetti et al. (2000) show that integrating asset prices in a Taylor rule may improve macroeconomic performance. In addition, Cecchetti et al. (2003) argue for reacting to (not targeting) asset price changes as well. Considering an inflation-targeting central bank, they stress that the monetary response should differ depending on whether asset prices changes are driven by fundamentals or not. However, Cecchetti et al. (2003) are aware of their proposal raising communication problems. Furthermore, although they argue that the proactive strategy can lead to smaller probability of asset price bubbles occurring, they in fact employ only an exogenous bubble process.

General arguments in favor of the proactive strategy are[17]:

---

[16] Arguments are mentioned in: Bernanke and Gertler (1999), (2001), Dillén and Sellin (2003), Cogley (1999), Posen (2006), Rudebusch (2005), Greenspan (2004), Issing (2004), Yellen (2005) and Blinder (2006). Schwartz (2002) stresses that central banks should be aware of the effects of asset price inflation on financial stability. In this regard, however, she argues against a monetary policy trying to deflate asset price bubbles.

[17] Arguments are mentioned in: Cecchetti et al. (2000), (2003), Kent and Lowe (1997), Filardo (2000), (2001), (2004), Crockett (2001), Mussa (2003), Dupor (2002), Roubini (2006), Akram et al. (2006), Akram and Eitrheim (2006) and Blinder (2006). Roubini (2006) presents several arguments in order to show why central banks should burst bubbles and responds to arguments brought forward by opponents of a proactive strategy (like Posen 2006).

- regarding the identification problem, other variables used in conducting monetary policy, like the output gap, are hard to assess too,
- a tighter policy in the run-up phase of a bubble is expected to lead to macroeconomic costs lower than those arising if the bubble bursts, even if the central bank fails in achieving the goals in the short run,
- moral hazard: if market participants know that monetary policy will offset the consequences of a bursting bubble, they might even be stimulated to invest during the boom period,
- monetary policy known for acting preemptively might help to prevent bubbles from occurring and growing, respectively,
- central banks are responsible for maintaining financial stability which is threatened by asset price bubbles.

It should be stressed that the recommendations differ somewhat from the usual Taylor-type reaction functions. Cecchetti et al. (2003) and Smets (1997) argue that central banks should not respond to all asset price misalignments in the same way, but rather depending on the underlying source - in the case of Cecchetti et al. (2003) only when financial shocks are the source of bubbles.

Furthermore, the argumentation of Cecchetti et al. (2003) implies that a response is only justified in the case of a misalignment, which means the central bank is able to distinguish between asset price movements based on fundamentals and irrational movements. This is one of the main fields of controversy between reactive and proactive strategy.

Again, there are several other authors proposing this policy stance. Crockett (2003) stresses that without an early monetary response further imbalances and larger future costs might be the result. The unwinding of such imbalances may hinder the effectiveness of monetary policy. Although the author refers to the problems (identification, political-economic constraints) associated with such a strategy, he proposes two changes in the conduct of monetary policy: a longer policy horizon and a greater weight on the balance of risks to the outlook. Regarding the identification problem, Dillén and Sellin (2003) stress that not this is the main problem, but rather the high degree of uncertainty regarding the link between monetary policy and asset prices. There are several approaches dealing with (or abstracting from) the identification problem. Employing a model with asset prices driven by irrational shocks regarding expectations of capital returns, Dupor (2005) shows that there is a trade-off between price stabilization and non-fundamental asset-price movements. When the central bank has full information regarding asset-price movements (fundamental or non-fundamental), it responds more aggressively than in the case of limited information. The same applies if the central bank acts under discretion (compared to the case of commitment). Filardo (2004) assumes no information problem. In his backward-looking linear stochastic control model the central bank should systematically respond to asset prices. Moreover, the central bank should only take the non-fundamental part into account. In addition, implementing uncertainty (about the existence of bubbles), Filardo (2004) shows that the central bank still responds to asset prices, albeit in a different way (different from the Taylor rule). However, if paradigm uncertainty is introduced, it turns out that a monetary response can be detrimental.

One important feature of the classic discussion about the optimal stance of monetary policy during boom-bust-cycles is the fact that linear rules are used for setting monetary policy, for example the Taylor rule which is based on Taylor (1993). This framework is often associated with a (flexible) inflation targeting framework and is used, amongst others, by Bernanke and Gertler (1999), (2001) and Cecchetti et al. (2000), (2003). The use of linear (instrument) rules like the Taylor rule in the early debate about the optimal stance of monetary policy during asset price booms is characterized by using only a limited set of variables. This has been criticized by several authors, for example by Bordo and Jeanne (2002a, b), Gruen et al. (2005) and by Svensson (2002), (2004). Svensson (2002) argues that flexible inflation targeting should not be interpreted as an instrument rule, but rather as a specific targeting rule in the sense that the objectives have to fulfill a specific condition. However, the results of Svensson (2002), (2004) are pretty similar to those of the proponents of the reactive strategy. Using the targeting rule, asset prices would only be taken into account if they affect the target variables inflation and output. This can be described as a procedure of two steps. In the first step, policymakers would try to identify the underlying source and nature of the respective shock. In the second step, they would estimate the possible consequences of the shock for the expected future path of inflation and output (not only a fixed horizon), conditional on an interest rate path. If they conclude that the (asset price) shock has consequences for inflation and output conditional on the chosen interest rate path, they would adjust the interest rate and revise their interest-rate plan. In addition, Disyatat (2005) argues that preemptive policy cannot be motivated in the standard inflation targeting framework; for such a policy stance either the targeting rule or the model have to be altered. Similar to Bernanke and Gertler (1999), (2001) and Cecchetti et al. (2000), (2003), he assumes a linear Taylor rule and explicitly considers asset prices. Disyatat (2005) constructs a monetary reaction function that reacts to asset prices insofar as they bear information for inflation and output now and in the future. However, he argues that a tighter stance can not be justified to prevent a bust since this policy would be motivated by "something that is not within the model". Consequently, financial stability should become part of the loss function.

However, this view has not remained undisputed. One objection is that central banks usually set monetary policy for fixed horizons (two to three years), whereas the argumentation of Svensson assumes that there is an infinite time horizon. Thus, monetary rules in practice might be much simpler than Svensson's optimal rule. Hence, developments on asset markets might not be considered adequately and there may be reasons for an extra response to asset prices. The argumentation of Cecchetti et al. (2000), (2003) for a proactive behavior of monetary policy is based on a fixed time horizon forecast. However, as will be argued below, there is a discussion to extend the typical two year horizons in order to be able to better assess developments on asset markets. Monetary policy should have the long run consequences of asset price shocks for output and inflation in mind. In addition, the second pillar of the ECB strategy is justified with the link between credit and money growth and developments on asset markets: strong growth of money and credit aggregates are reliable indicators for boom-bust-cycles and financial instability in the medium to long run, see the findings of Bordo and Jeanne (2002a, b) and Borio and Lowe (2002).

2.3.2. The Middle Ground Position

As already mentioned, there has been a development towards a "middle ground" position (Richards 2003): neither should monetary policy respond aggressively to asset prices nor should it act according to the benign neglect approach. Rather it should take asset price fluctuations into account when they contain information about shocks or have implications for monetary policy within a longer than the usual policy horizon. If the analysis of asset prices delivers information that there are risks of financial instability, this will have implications for economic activity and inflation. Consequently, inflation-targeting central banks should watch asset prices and their implications for the risks that an economy is facing in the medium term (see Bean 2003 and Disyatat 2005). In this regard, it should be stressed that in practice the reactive and the proactive strategy might be not so far away from each other: the reactive strategy may have to respond to asset price fluctuations (Dillén and Sellin 2003). The new view is characterized by two features: there are no longer linear rules employed (like the Taylor rule) and the bubble or asset price development is, at least partly, modeled endogenously. The non-linearities can be interpreted in the sense that the possible negative effects of an asset price bust are significantly larger than the positive effects during an asset price boom.[18] [19]

In contrast to Cecchetti et al. (2000), (2003), there are several studies adopting the “middle ground” position and, in part, model the bubble or asset price process endogenously, for example Kent and Lowe (1997), (1998). Employing a model in which the central bank is able to affect the probability of bubble bursting, the asset price bubble is assumed to grow exponentially. The consequence of a bursting bubble is a reduction in inflation which is larger the longer the bubble has survived. The authors show that an increase in interest rates at an early stage can be the optimal strategy. Yet, the proactive stance is associated with immediate costs due to deviations from target inflation and these costs are larger the longer the bubble has survived.

Kent and Lowe (1997) propose a tighter monetary policy in some cases, naming three reasons for that:

- A tighter policy increases the probability of a bubble bursting,
- Once the bubble bursts it does not grow again for a certain time,
- Although inflation will be in the short term below target, the central bank tightens its policy in order to avoid extreme deviations of inflation from its target.

Furthermore, they draw an important conclusion. They show that boom-bust cycles in property cycles are often accompanied by cycles in credit growth. This result is similar to the results in the analysis of Kent and Lowe (1998), Bordo and Jeanne (2002a, b) and several other papers.[20]

---

[18] Note that in the wake of the financial crisis (and even before) there has been a development in the New Keynesian literature towards the inclusion of limited asset market participation. Galí et al. (2004) and Bilbiie (2008) allow for non-asset holders. They show that, if the share of non-asset holders becomes large, the Taylor principle is weakened and even changed completely, see also Stehn (2009). However, one of the implications is that higher real interest rates raise aggregate demand (violation of the Taylor principle in the ‚non-Keynesian’ region).

[19] An interesting approach is delivered by von Peter (2009): his work is linking banking with asset prices in a macroeconomic model. He shows in an overlapping generation and non-linearized model that falling asset prices have via borrower default indirect, non-linear feedback effects from the banking system by constraining credit.

[20] See for example Igan et al. (2009), IMF (2009c) and Schularick and Taylor (2009).

In a similar vein, Gruen, Plumb and Stone (2005) allow for endogenous bubbles and non-linearities. Assuming two different policymakers, a skeptic (using the current price to forecast asset prices) and an activist (using stochastic implications of the bubble), the authors show in their model that the optimal monetary response depends on the stochastic properties of the bubble. If information is not available sufficiently, a robust approach used by the skeptic might be the best alternative. Sometimes the activist recommends tighter, sometimes looser policy. Therefore, the activist might need to use a judgment of the process behind the bubble. Due to the lag structure of monetary policy the proactive policy might already be associated with a loosening of monetary conditions during the boom. Hence, it is not longer clear that the proactive policy always implies looser policy than the reactive strategy during an asset price boom. Similar to Gruen et al. (2005), Kontonikas and Montagnoli (2006) are using an extension of the Ball (1999) and Svensson (1997) model and show that in the case of non-fundamental developments of asset prices as well as wealth effects and inefficient markets, policymakers should respond to asset price misalignments.

A seminal paper in this context is the analysis of Bordo and Jeanne (2002a, b). They show that the desirability of a proactive policy depends in a rather complex way on economic conditions. It is therefore not easy to obtain a simple policy rule for acting proactively. Rather, the central bank has to solve the trade-off of immediate losses today (proactive strategy in order to prevent a credit crunch by raising interest rates) and possible losses in the future due to a credit crunch with decreasing output. Following the classic discussion of Bernanke and Gertler (1999), (2001) vs. Cecchetti et al. (2000), (2003) the authors show that there is no clear-cut answer for central banks to behave reactively or proactively, since there is no linear solution in the form of a simple Taylor rule. Rather, there is a non-linear solution, depending on various parameters. Hence, there is no clear answer to the question of whether a proactive strategy of curbing asset price inflation in the boom phase or a reactive strategy of dealing only with the consequences of an asset price bubble crash is always the optimal choice. The latter option is usually known as 'benign neglect': never tighten monetary policy in the run-up phase, only react in the aftermath of a bust.

Bordo and Jeanne (2002a, b) try to solve the identification problem by looking for indicators of boom-bust cycles in house prices. For example, they find that in the run-up phase of boom-bust cycles credit growth has been particularly strong and boom-bust cycles on property markets are more likely to be associated with detrimental consequences for the economy than boom-bust cycles on equity markets. Furthermore, the authors do not focus on bubbles per se, but rather on developments on asset markets which might end in serious consequences, irrespective of the question of whether asset prices are justified by fundamentals or not. In this regard, their analysis differs from the work of Bernanke and Gertler (1999), (2001), Cecchetti et al. (2000), (2003) and many others. For these reasons Bordo and Jeanne (2002a, b) focus on firms' property used as collateral for new credit which is necessary for production and not on bubbles per se. Rather, they use the empirical evidence that during booms on property markets there is a strong credit growth to model the boom-bust cycle as the occurrence of a boom on property market and a possible credit crunch. In addition, the empirical evidence shows that busts on housing markets have larger wealth effects on consumption than busts on equity markets.

Extending the analysis of Bordo and Jeanne (2002a, b) in the New Keynesian direction, Berger, Kißmer and Wagner (2007) find that due to a forward-looking behavior of the private sector even the reactive strategy has to adjust monetary policy during the boom phase. The reason is that private agents know that a credit crunch may appear in the future if the central bank pursues a reactive strategy. The possible response is therefore contained in the private expectations, leading to lower output and higher inflation today. Therefore, 'benign neglect' is not a sensible option for central banks in the case of forward-looking private agents, see also Berger and Kißmer (2008). The proactive strategy is not affected by the forward-looking expectations in welfare terms, whereas the losses of the reactive strategy increase. In addition, Berger and Kißmer (2009) stress that empirical studies show that policymakers often "lean with the wind" during asset price booms. See Berger, Kißmer and Knütter (2007) and Knütter and Wagner (2011) for the impact of globalization on the policy trade-off for central banks during boom-bust cycles in asset prices.

To sum up, all studies arguing for a proactive strategy assume (at least under certain circumstances) that the interest rate is a proper instrument to influence asset prices. However, as mentioned above, doubts regarding this issue are raised regularly. First, the models often assume only one asset price, whereas in reality central banks face a multitude of asset prices. In the case of a misalignment on one asset market (say the stock market), developments on other asset markets (say housing market) can be justified by fundamentals. A bursting bubble on one market may induce or fuel another bubble on a different market (see Filardo 2006 for theoretical evidence and Detken and Smets 2004, Funke et al. 2004, Kent and Lowe 1998 for empirical evidence). Second, it is doubtful whether an increase in interest rates has the desired effects. It might even be possible that a small interest rate increase amplifies the boom because the private subjects assume that the central bank is able to control the situation and is ahead of the curve.[21] To obtain the desired result, it may be necessary to increase interest rates significantly. In turn, the central bank risks raising the interest rates in a way that causes a recession. However, as recently stressed by Trichet (2009), the instrument problem might not be that large: Recent research shows that even a small change of the policy rate might be sufficient. Adrian and Shin (2008) show that in case of financial institutions borrowing short and lending long (like in the run-up of the recent subprime crisis) even a small change in the policy rate can significantly affect the profits of these institutions. Moreover, when small interest rate changes split up the private herding behavior and reveal the central banks intentions, then they might have great impact on asset prices, see Hoerova et al. (2009).

3. RECENT DEVELOPMENTS

The subprime and financial crisis 2007-2009 has led to a thorough reevaluation of the topic of whether and how monetary policy should take boom-bust cycles in asset prices (and credit growth) into account. For the causes of the recent crisis and the particular role of central banks see Wagner (2010). During the last decade or so, there has been a development towards inflation targeting frameworks aiming at relatively strict price stability objectives. While central banks all over the world were successful in achieving these objectives, they might have neglected developments in credit growth and, somewhat consequently, asset

[21] Bernanke and Kuttner (2003) argue that a small interest rate increase may boost asset prices further since private agents believe that the central bank takes the inflation target serious and is able to steer the economy, hence is ahead of the curve. For example, during the New Economy Boom, the Fed increased interest rates up to 6 %, but stock prices increased further. Hence, a small interest rate increase may not be sufficient to curb asset price inflation.

prices. In some countries, like the U.S., the result was an unsustainable degree of leverage and debt in the financial system. However, there were some warnings which stressed the link between credit growth and increasing asset prices, often used as collateral, and fuelling consumption and investment, see Borio (2006), Borio and White (2004), Borio and Shim (2007), Borio et al. (2003), White (2006), (2008). Moreover, there is empirical evidence that financial crises were preceded by rapid credit growth (see above, e.g. Bordo and Jeanne 2002a, b). Furthermore, in the past, it has been argued that only a "leaning against the wind"-strategy is associated with costs. However, as has been shown, the reactive (benign neglect) strategy is not necessarily costless. Costs could be rooted in a loss of credibility of the banking system, as in Japan's lost decade and the current financial crisis. Moreover, if the zero lower bound is reached, monetary policy might fall into a liquidity trap. In both situations, the only solution might be a fiscal bailout. Further costs could be the deviation from monetary policy objectives which regularly occur in the case of financial imbalances.

Since the financial crisis 2007-2009 it has become obvious that the standard macroeconomic modeling had not considered the financial sector in an appropriate way. As stressed by Walsh (2009), the largest part of the literature concluded that central banks should ignore asset price developments and just focused on the stabilization of inflation and the output gap. Researchers should rather have put the focus on the question of whether and how financial frictions can generate distortions in itself and should have considered to put these frictions into the target rule (interest rate rule).

In the following, some important theoretical contributions of the recent past focusing on the topic of monetary policy, asset prices and integration of financial markets are presented.

Employing the model of Kiyotaki and Moore (1997), Miller and Stiglitz (2009) show that the integration of an asset price bubble can lead to a serious downward spiral. Since they take additional channels into account (e.g. high leverage, overvalued collateral, balance sheet effects), it turns out that interest rate cuts by monetary policy alone are not sufficient. Rather, the authors argue that the purchase of assets and the restructuring of capital are important features of a crisis solution. Fukunaga and Saito (2009) base their analysis on the Bernanke, Gertler and Gilchrist (1999) model (BGG) and Gilchrist and Saito (2008) framework. In their analysis, the financial accelerator plays an important role. Shocks to the economy affect the balance sheet of borrowers and induce countercyclical movements of the external finance premium. They consider financial market imperfections by allowing the external finance premium to rise when the net worth of the borrower is decreasing. Following BGG, the authors include asset prices in the monetary policy rule and show that when movements in asset prices are associated with inefficiencies in the economy it can be beneficial (in terms of the variance of output and inflation and a welfare function weighting the variances of output and inflation) to include asset prices in the Taylor rule. However, the benefits decrease when policymakers possess only limited information about the relation between financial distortions and asset price movements. Fujiwara and Teranishi (2009) show in a New Open Economy Macroeconomic model that central banks aim at achieving financial stability, meaning in integrated financial markets to minimize fluctuations of loan rates.

IMF (2009) is focusing on the potential lessons for monetary policy from asset price fluctuations. Using a New Keynesian model, the authors argue that it can be beneficial when monetary policy reacts stronger to imbalances on credit and asset markets. In addition, it is shown that a macroprudential instrument which dampens credit spreads can be useful in dealing with credit and asset price imbalances. As in Bordo and Jeanne (2002a, b), the authors focus rather on house prices than stock prices since housing wealth is more important than stock market wealth and housing almost always requires issuing debt for a bank credit. They focus on two shocks: a positive productivity shock and a financial shock that is associated with a relaxation in lending standards. Similar to Bordo and Jeanne (2002a, b) they do not focus on bubbles or irrational exuberance. The macroprudential instrument can mitigate fluctuations in credit spreads which arise through changes in collateral and financial shocks. This instrument should have the same impact on the financial sector like a regulation that requires banks to hold more capital reserves (and therefore increasing the rate which banks charge over funding costs).

IMF (2009), based on Kannan et al. (2009), employs a credit accelerator mechanism, which is similar to the financial accelerator mechanism of the BGG model, but is working through housing finance rather than firms' capital. The credit accelerator is characterized by lower lending rates when collateral is rising. Subsequently, lower rates lead to an increase in housing demand, which feeds into higher house prices. Therefore, collateral value is rising which leads again to lower lending rates and induce households to take out even more loans. The authors analyze several policy rules in reaction to the shocks. Regarding the financial shock, they show that a positive financial shock (modeled as reduction in lending standards of 100 basis points) induces increasing investment and house prices. IMF (2009) shows that enhancing the standard Taylor rule by an additional term reacting directly to credit can produce greater stability in terms of smaller output and inflation variability. Furthermore, additionally integrating the macroprudential instrument into the Taylor rule improves the results even more.[22] The results of the IMF (2009) indicate that policymakers should take risks of macrofinancial developments into account and possibly react to it.

As in Bordo and Jeanne (2002a, b) central banks should not focus too much on asset prices themselves, but rather on developments that are associated with them: lax lending standards, excessive credit growth, overinvestment and deteriorating balances. One way is that the objective function of central banks can be extended, another way could be macroprudential supporting monetary policy. The problem with the modeling of the macroprudential instrument is that it is ad hoc and should be only interpreted as the intention to act as a regulatory instrument (see IMF 2009).

Adrian and Shin (2009b) analyze a model containing a friction in the credit supply. Assuming that monetary policy and, in turn, the supply of credit, can affect the risk-taking of central banks, the short term interest rate becomes an important price variable in its own (in contrast to the usual assumption that central banks are primarily interested in steering long-term interest rates by managing expectations).

Adrian and Shin (2008) argue that policymakers should ask the following questions:

- Do you know for sure there is a bubble in real estate prices?
- Could the current benign funding conditions reverse abruptly with adverse consequences for the economy?

They argue that even if the first question has been answered with no, it is still possible to answer the second question with yes. This, in turn, means that it is not necessary to identify bubbles, but rather recognize critical situations in terms of leverage and credit growth.

---

[22] When focusing only on productivity shocks, the simple Taylor rule turns out to be the best.

Furthermore, they show that the short term interest rate and expectations of the future policy path are important determinants of asset growth (broker dealer asset growth). In particular, they stress that variations in the policy rate change short term rates, which in turn have a direct impact on the profitability of the banking sector and the credit supply. Hence, central banks are able to curb excessive credit growth and short term interest rates matter directly for monetary policy. Adrian, Moench and Shin (2010) analyze the meaning of financial intermediaries for macroeconomic fluctuations. In particular, they focus on the link between the macro risk premium and the growth of balance sheets of financial intermediaries. They assume that the capacity of their balance sheets is linked to their risk taking and credit supply. They show that a macro risk premium (consisting of a combination of financial market spreads) is related to credit spreads. Adrian et al. (2010) extend the model by two variables and two equations: first, they extend both the IS and the Phillips curve by the macro risk premium which is defined in an extra equation. The second variable is the risk appetite, which determines, amongst others, the macro risk premium. Hence, it is assumed that monetary policy is able to affect the credit supply of banks via the risk-taking channel. The risk appetite itself is determined by macroeconomic conditions (inflation, output, interest rate). The Taylor rule is extended by the macro risk premium and the risk appetite as well. As stressed by the authors, their approach differs from the financial accelerator literature focusing on credit demand by analyzing the effects of financial frictions on credit supply. One of their findings is that interest rate and credit spreads are more important than the level of interest rates for macroeconomic fluctuations.

There are several models integrating financial market frictions in the New Keynesian model (Cúrdia and Woodford 2009a, b, de Fiore and Tristani 2009, Christiano et al. 2007, 2008, Hülsewig et al. 2009, Teranishi 2008, Sudo and Teranishi 2008, Cohen-Cole and Martinez 2008, Meh and Moran 2008, Gertler and Karadi 2009, Dellas et al 2010 and Gerali et al. 2010).[23] Using the proposal of McCulley and Toloui (2008) and Taylor (2008), Cúrdia and Woodford (2009a, b) present a formal analysis of the problem. Assuming an intermediation technology, which implies that for real lending an intermediary is necessary, the total amount of lending consists of the funds that the intermediary lends to its borrowers and a cost of loan origination and monitoring. Due to this technology, there will be a credit spread in the banking sector. A negative financial shock leads to higher costs of intermediation between borrowers and savers, inducing an increase in the credit spread. The mere existence of a credit spread does not have a significant influence on the path of different policies. However, variations in the credit spread are more important in that it influences the equilibrium relation between the policy rate and expenditure and the output-inflation tradeoff. Cúrdia and Woodford (2009a, b) show that a response to variations in a credit spread (a rising spread would imply a reduction of the policy rate) can improve results stemming from disturbances in the financial sector. When variations in credit spreads occur, the total cost-push term is a combination of the usual cost-push shock and a cost-push term due to financial

[23] For empirical evidence of financial shocks, see Jermann and Quadrini (2009). The authors define a financial shock as a shock which affects the firms' capacity to borrow. They show that the inclusion of financial shocks (shocks to firms' ability to borrow in combination with rigidities in the adjustment of their financial structure) makes the model better fit the data. Muellbauer (2010) shows that the assumption that in DSGE models without financial frictions asset prices play no separate role is in contrast to data from U.K. consumption evidence. However, by using an Ando-Modigliani consumption function which is able to capture features like liquidity, wealth and housing collateral effects the author can explain the data.

frictions. In case of a change in credit spreads the policy rate is shifted (the rate should be lowered when credit spreads rise). Consequently, Cúrdia and Woodford (2009a, b) find evidence that the credit spread moves the simple Taylor rule in the right direction and that the simple Taylor rule is too tight when the credit spread is increasing and too loose when the credit spread is decreasing. See for the cost push effects of financial frictions also Demirel (2009).

A similar analysis is the one by Fiore and Tristani (2009). It differs from Cúrdia and Woodford (2009a, b) in the source of the underlying financial friction. The microfounded friction arises due to optimal debt contracts and reflects in the Phillips curve in form of a credit spread. Since a higher credit spread implies a higher external finance costs, resulting in pressure on inflation, the financial frictions act as a cost-push term like in the paper by Cúrdia and Woodford (2009a, b). In addition, the financial shock has a negative impact on output. Real wages are falling since firms try to offset the negative effects of the increase in financing costs. As Fiore and Tristani (2009) show, an aggressive easing is the optimal response to a financial shock increasing the credit spread.

Furthermore, and in contrast to Cúrdia and Woodford (2009a, b), Teranishi (2009) analyzes a New Keynesian model with financial frictions working through the cost channel. Teranishi (2009) includes terms for loan interest rates in the New Keynesian Phillips curve so that they act like a cost-push shock. He shows that the (optimal) Taylor rule also includes a credit-spread term. However, the optimal reaction of monetary policy to a rise of the credit spread can be positive or negative.

Conclusion

In this paper, a general overview regarding asset prices and monetary policy was given. In the chapters 2.1 and 2.2, important policy questions were analyzed and discussed: whether asset prices should be included in the inflation measure and whether they should enter the objective function of monetary policy. It turned out that these topics have been intensively discussed. The development of academic research and discussion was presented in chapter 2.3. The classic discussion of exogenous bubbles and linear rules was laid out, followed by the development to a middle ground with endogenous bubbles and non-linear rules. Here, empirical findings flow into the models of the middle ground. Since the financial crisis 2007-2009 has led to a thorough re-evaluation of related research, recent developments were surveyed in detail in chapter 3. In particular, an overview about recent developments in theoretical and empirical literature was delivered.

It turned out that this topic is a very important issue for both policymakers and researchers, not only since the recent subprime and financial crisis. This is true when looking at the monetary policy transmission channels and several historic boom-bust cycles. Concerning typical patterns associated with boom-bust cycles, the empirical evidence regarding economic conditions during and before boom-bust cycles is striking. In particular, money, credit growth and private debt played a crucial role. This is one reason why future research should aim at taking some of these variables and developments into account.

REFERENCES

Adrian, T. and H. S. Shin (2008), Financial Intermediaries, Financial Stability, and Monetary Policy, Staff Report No. 346, September 2008, Federal Reserve Bank of New York.

Adrian, T. and H. S. Shin (2009a), Money, Liquidity, and Monetary Policy, *American Economic Review*, Vol. 99 (2), pp. 600-605.

Adrian, T. and H. S. Shin (2009b), Financial Intermediaries and Monetary Economics, Federal Reserve Bank of New York Staff Reports No. 398, Federal Reserve Bank of New York, Handbook of Monetary Economics (forthcoming).

Adrian, T., E. Moench and H. S. Shin (2010), Macro Risk Premium and Intermediary Balance Sheet Quantities, Staff Report No. 428, Federal Reserve Bank of New York.

Akram, Q. F. and O. Eitrheim (2006), Flexible inflation targeting and financial stability: Is it enough to stabilise inflation and output?, Working Paper ANO 2006/7, Norges Bank.

Akram, Q. F., G. Bardsen, O. Eitrheim (2006), Monetary Policy And Asset Prices: To Respond Or Not?, *International Journal Of Finance and Economics*, Vol. 11 (3) pp. 279-292.

Alchian, A. A. and B. Klein (1973), On a Correct Measure of Inflation, *Journal of Money, Credit and Banking*, Vol. 5 (1), pp. 173-191.

Ball, L. (2006), Has Globalization Changed Inflation?, NBER Working Paper No. 12687, Cambridge, MA.

Batini, N., B. Jackson and S. Nickell (2005), An Open-Economy New Keynesian Phillips Curve for the U. K., *Journal of Monetary Economics* 52, pp. 1061-1071.

Bean, C. (2003), Asset Prices, Financial Imbalances and Monetary Policy: Are Inflation Targets Enough?, BIS Working Paper No 140, Bank for International Settlements, Basle.

Bean, C. (2006a), Comments on Ken Rogoff: “Impact of Globalization on Monetary Policy”, Paper prepared for the 30th Annual Economic Symposium, Federal Reserve Bank of Kansas City, Jackson Hole, Wyoming, 26 August 2006.

Bean, C. (2006b), Globalisation and Inflation, Speech given to the LSE Economics Society, London School of Economics on 24 October 2006.

Berger, W., F. Kißmer and H. Wagner (2007), Monetary Policy and Asset Prices: More Bad News for ‘Benign Neglect’, *International Finance* 10 (1), pp. 1-20.

Berger, W., F. Kißmer and R. Knütter (2007), Monetary Policy and Asset Prices: The Impact of Globalization on Monetary Policy Trade-Offs, In: A. N. Kendall (ed.), International Business and Finance Issues, pp. 133-148, New York 2007.

Berger, W. and F. Kißmer (2008), Optimal Interest Rate Policy During Asset Price Booms: The Mirage of 'Benign Neglect.' *Economics Letters*, Vol. 101 (3), pp. 265-267.

Berger, W. and F. Kißmer (2009), Why Do Monetary Policymakers Lean With the Wind During Asset Price Booms?, *Frontiers in Finance and Economics*, Vol. 6 (1), pp.155-174.

Bernanke, B. S. and M. Gertler (1989), Agency Costs, Net Worth, and Business Fluctuations, *American Economic Review*, Vol. 79 (1), pp. 14-31.

Bernanke, B. S. and M. Woodford (1997), Inflation Forecasts and Monetary Policy, *Journal of Money, Credit and Banking*, Vol. 29 (4), pp. 653-84.

Bernanke, B. S. (2007), Globalization and Monetary Policy, Speech at the 4th Economic Summit, Stanford Institute for Economic Policy Research, Stanford, California, March 2, 2007.

Bernanke, B. and M. Gertler (1999), Monetary Policy and Asset Price Volatility, Federal Reserve Bank of Kansas City (ed), New Challenges for Monetary Policy, Proceedings of the 1999 Jackson Hole Conference, Kansas City, pp. 77-128.

Bernanke, B. and M. Gertler (2001), Should Central Banks Respond to Movements in Asset Prices?, *American Economic Review Papers and Proceedings* 91, pp. 253–257.

Bernanke, B. and K. Kuttner (2003), What Explains the Stock Market's Reaction to Federal Reserve Policy?, Staff Report No. 174 , Federal Reserve Bank of New York, October.

Bilbiie, F. O. (2008), Limited Asset Markets Participation, Monetary Policy and (inverted) Aggregate Demand Logic, *Journal of Economic Theory*, Vol. 140 (1), pp. 162-196.

Blinder, A. S. and Reis, R. (2005), Understanding the Greenspan Standard, In: The Greenspan Era: Lessons for the Future, Federal Reserve Bank of Kansas City symposium, Jackson Hole, Wyoming, August 25-27.

Blinder, A. S. (2006), Monetary Policy Today: Sixteen Questions and about Twelve Answers, Paper presented at the Banco de Espana Conference on "Central Banks in the 21st Century", Madrid, June 8-9, 2006.

Bordo, M. D. and O. Jeanne (2002a), Boom-Busts in Asset Prices, Economic Instability, and Monetary Policy, NBER Working Paper No. 8966, National Bureau of Economic Research, Washington DC.

Bordo, M. D. and O. Jeanne (2002b), Monetary Policy and Asset Prices: Does 'Benign Neglect' Make Sense?, *International Finance* 5, pp. 139-164.

Bordo, M., M. Dueker and D. Wheelock (2000), Aggregate Price Shocks and Financial Instability: an Historical Analysis, NBER Working Paper 7652, National Bureau of Economic Research.

Bordo, M., M. Dueker and D. Wheelock (2008), Inflation, Monetary Policy and Stock Market Conditions, NBER Working Paper No. 14019, National Bureau of Economic Research.

Borio, C. and P. Lowe (2002), Asset Prices, Financial and Monetary Stability: Exploring the Nexus, BIS Working Paper No. 114, Bank for International Settlements.

Borio, C. and P. Lowe (2003), Imbalances or 'Bubbles'? Implications for Monetary and Financial Stability, in: W. Hunter, G. G. Kaufmann and M. Pomerleano (eds.), Asset Price Bubbles: The Implications for Monetary, Regulatory, and International Policies, Cambridge, Mass (MIT Press), pp. 41–50.

Borio, C. and A. Filardo (2006), Globalisation and Inflation: New Cross-Country Evidence on the Global Determinants of Domestic Inflation, mimeo, Bank of International Settlements, Basle.

Bryan, M. F., S. G. Cecchetti and R. O'Sullivan (2002a), Asset Prices in the Measurement of Inflation, NBER Working Paper No. 8700, National Bureau of Economic Research.

Bryan, M. F., S. G. Cecchetti and R. O'Sullivan (2002b), A Stochastic Index of the Cost of Life – an Application to Recent and Historical Asset Price Fluctuations, Paper prepared for the joint Federal Reserve Bank of Chicago, World Bank Group Conference "Asset Price Bubbles: Implications for Monetary, Regulatory and International Policies," 22-25 April 2002.

Calvo, G. (1983), Staggered Prices in a Utility-Maximizing Framework, *Journal of Monetary Economics* 12, pp. 383-398.

Carney, M. (2009), Some Considerations on Using Monetary Policy, Remarks to a Symposium sponsored by the Federal Reserve Bank of Kansas City, Jackson Hole, Wyoming, 22 August 2009.

Cecchetti, S. G., H. Genberg, J. Lipsky and S. Wadhwani (2000), Asset Prices and Central Bank Policy, London (CEPR).

Cecchetti, S. G., H. Genberg, and S. Wadhwani (2003), Asset Prices in a Flexible Inflation Targeting Framework, In: Asset Price Bubbles: The Implications for Monetary, Regulatory, and International Policies, Eds. W. Hunter, G. G. Kaufmann and M. Pomerleano, Cambridge, Mass (MIT Press), pp. 427–444.

Christiano, L., R. Motto and M. Rostagno (2007), Two Reasons Why Money and Credit May Be Useful In Monetary Policy, NBER Working Paper No. 13502, National Bureau of Economic Research.

Christiano, L., R. Motto and M. Rostagno (2008), Monetary Policy and Stock Market Boom-Bust Cycles, ECB Working Paper No. 955, European Central Bank.

Ciccarelli, M. and B. Mojon (2005), Global Inflation, ECB Working Paper No. 537, European Central Bank, Frankfurt.

Cohen-Cole, E. and E. Martinez-Garcia (2008), The Balance Sheet Channel, Quantitative Analysis Unit Working Paper QAU08-7, Federal Reserve Bank of Boston.

Clarida, R., J. Galí and M. Gertler (2001), Optimal Monetary Policy in Open versus Closed Economies: An Integrated Approach, *American Economic Review Papers and Proceedings*, Vol. 91 (2), pp. 248-252.

Cogley, T. (1999), Should The Fed Take Deliberate Steps To Deflate Asset Price Bubbles?, Economic Review pp. 42-52, Federal Reserve Bank of San Francisco.

Cournède, B. (2005), House Prices and Inflation in the Euro Area, Economics Department Working Paper No. 450, OECD.

Crockett, A. (2001), Monetary Policy and Financial Stability, Speech by Andrew Crockett, General Manager of the Bank for International Settlements and Chairman of the Financial Stability Forum, given at the Fourth HKMA Distinguished Lecture, held in Hong Kong, 13 February 2001.

Crockett, A. (2003), International Standard Setting in Financial Supervision, Institute of Economic Affairs Lecture, Cass Business School, London, 5 February.

Cúrdia, V. and M. Woodford (2009a), Credit Frictions and Optimal Monetary Policy, unpublished, Columbia University, May 2009.

Cúrdia, V. and M. Woodford (2009b), Credit Spreads and Monetary Policy, Prepared for the FRB-JMCB research conference "Financial Markets and Monetary Policy", Washington, DC, June 4-5, 2009.

De Fiore, F. and O. Tristani (2009), Optimal Monetary Policy in a Model of the Credit Channel, ECB Working Paper No. 1043, European Central Bank.

Dellas, H., B. Diba and O. Loisel (2010), Financial Shocks and Optimal Policy, Documents de Travail 277, Banque de France.

Demirel, U. D. (2009), Optimal Monetary Policy in a Financially Fragile Economy, *The B. E. Journal of Macroeconomics, Contributions*, Vol. 9 (1), pp. 1-35.

Detken, C. and F. Smets (2004), Asset Price Booms and Monetary Policy, Working Paper No. 364, European Central Bank, Frankfurt.

Dillén, H. and P. Sellin (2003), Financial Bubbles and Monetary Policy, Economic Review 3/2003 pp. 119-144, Sveriges Riksbank.

Disyatat, P. (2005), Inflation Targeting, Asset Prices and Financial Imbalances: Conceptualizing the Debate, BIS Working Paper No. 168, Bank for International Settlements.

Dupor, W. (2002), Nominal Price Versus Asset Price Stabilization, Paper prepared for the Bank of Finland/CEPR Annual Workshop "Asset Markets and Monetary Policy", 25/26 April 2002, Helsinki.

Dupor, W. (2005), Stabilizing Non-fundamental Asset Price Movements Under Discretion and Limited Information, *Journal of Monetary Economics*, Vol. 52, pp. 727-747.

European Central Bank. (2005), Asset Price Bubbles and Monetary Policy, European Central Bank, Monthly Bulletin, April, pp. 47-60.

Faia, E. and T. Monacelli (2007), Optimal Interest Rate Rules, Asset Prices, and Credit Frictions, *Journal of Economic Dynamics and Control*, Vol. 31, pp. 3228-3254.

Ferguson, R.W. (2002), Should Financial Stability Be an Explicit Central Bank Objective? Paper presented to an International Monetary Fund conference on Challenges to Central Banking from Globalized Financial Markets, Washington, D.C., September 17.

Filardo, A. (2000), Asset Prices and Monetary Policy, Federal Reserve Bank of Kansas City Economic Review, third quarter.

Filardo, A. (2001), Should Monetary Policy Respond to Asset Price Bubbles? Some Experimental Results, In: G. Kaufman (Ed.), Asset Price Bubbles: Implications for Monetary and Regulatory Policies, Amsterdam: Elsevier Science.

Filardo, A. (2003), Should Monetary Authorities Prick Asset Price Bubbles?, Preliminary draft, Bank for International Settlements.

Filardo, A. (2004), Monetary Policy and Asset Price Bubbles: Calibrating the Monetary Policy Trade-Offs, BIS Working Paper No. 155, Bank Of International Settlements.

Foot M. (2003), Protecting Financial Stability - How Good Are We at It?, Speech at the University of Birmingham, Birmingham, June 6.

Fujiwara, I. and Y. Teranishi (2009), Financial Stability in Open Economies, IMES Discussion Paper No. 2009-E-9, Institute for Monetary and Economic Studies, Bank of Japan.

Fukunaga, I. and. M. Saito (2009), Asset Prices and Monetary Policy, IMES Discussion Paper No. 2009-E-21, Institute for Monetary and Economic Studies, Bank of Japan.

Funke, N., F. Kißmer and H. Wagner (2004), Asset Price Booms, Recessions, and Monetary Policy, Mimeo.

Galí, J. and T. Monacelli (2002), Monetary Policy and Exchange Rate Volatility in a Small Open Economy, CEPR Discussion Paper No. 3346, London.

Galí, J., D. López-Salido and J. Vallés (2004), Rule of Thumb Consumers and the Design of Interest Rate Rules, *Journal of Money, Credit and Banking*, Vol. 36 (4), pp. 739-763.

Gertler, M., S. Gilchrist and F. Natalucci (2003), External Constraints On Monetary Policy And The Financial Accelerator, NBER Working Paper No. 10128, National Bureau Of Economic Research.

Gilchrist, S. and J. V. Leahy (2002), Monetary Policy and Asset Prices, *Journal of Monetary Economics*, Vol. 49, pp. 75-97.

Gilchrist, S. and M. Saito (2006), Expectations, Asset Prices and Monetary Policy: The Role of Learning, IMES Discussion Paper No. 2006-E-18, Institute for Monetary and Economic Studies, Bank of Japan.

Goodfriend, M. (2003), Interest Rate Policy Should Not React Directly to Asset Prices, In Asset Price Bubbles: The Implications for Monetary, Regulatory, and International Policies, William Hunter, Georg G. Kaufmann, Michael Pomerleano (Eds.), pp. 445–457, Cambridge, Mass: MIT Press.

Goodhart, C. (2001), What Weight Should be Given to Asset Prices in the Measurement of Inflation?, *The Economic Journal*, Vol. 111, pp. 335-356.

Goodhart, C. (2004), Per Jacobsson Lecture: Some New Directions for Financial Stability?, FMG Special Papers, No. sp158, Financial Markets Group.

Goodhart, C. and B. Hofmann (2000), Do Asset Prices Help to Predict Consumer Price Inflation? *Manchester School Journal*, Vol. 68, pp. 122-140.

Goodhart, C. and B. Hofmann (2001), Asset Prices, Financial Conditions, and the Transmission of Monetary Policy, Paper prepared for the Conference on "Asset Prices, Exchange Rates, and Monetary Policy", Stanford University, 2-3 March 2001.

Greenspan, A. (2002), Opening Remarks, in: Rethinking Stabilization Policy, A Symposium Sponsored by The Federal Reserve Bank of Kansas City, Jackson Hole, pp. 1-10.

Greenspan, A. (2004): Risk and Uncertainty in Monetary Policy, American Economic Review, Vol. 94, pp. 41-43.

Greenspan, A. (2005), Testimony before the Joint Economic Committee, November 3, http://www.federalreserve.gov/boarddocs/testimony/ 2005/20051103/default.htm.

Gruen, D., M. Plumb and A. Stone (2005), How Should Monetary Policy Respond to Asset Price Bubbles?, *International Journal of Central Banking* Vol. 1 (3), pp. 1-31.

Helbling, T., F. Jaumotte and M. Sommer (2006), How Has Globalization Affected Inflation?, World Economic Outlook, Chapter III, International Monetary Fund, Washington, DC., April, pp. 97-134.

Hoerova, M., C. Monnet and E. Temzelides (2009), Money Talks, ECB Working Paper No. 1091, European Central Bank.

Hülsewig, O., E. Mayer and T. Wollmershäuser (2009), Bank Behavior, Incomplete Interest Rate Pass-Through, and the Cost Channel of Monetary Policy Transmission, *Economic Modelling*, Elsevier, Vol. 26 (6), pp. 1310-1327.

Igan, D., A. Kabundi, F. N. De Simone, M. Pinheiro and Natalia Tamirisa (2009), Three Cycles: Housing, Credit, and Real Activity, IMF Working Paper 09/231, International Monetary Fund.

IMF (2009), Lessons for Monetary Policy from Asset Price Fluctuations, In: World Economic Outlook, October 2009, pp. 93-120, International Monetary Fund.

Issing, O. (2003), Monetary and Financial Stability: Is There a Tradeoff? BIS Paper No. 18, Bank for International Settlements, pp. 16-23.

Issing, O. (2004), Financial Integration, Asset Prices And Monetary Policy, Dinner speech held on Monday, 10 May, at the Hotel "Frankfurter Hof" (Symposium concluding two years of the ECB-CFS research network on "Capital Markets and Financial Integration in Europe").

Jermann, U. and V. Quadrini (2009), Macroeconomic Effects of Financial Shocks, NBER Working Paper No. 15338, National Bureau of Economic Research.

Kannan, P., P. Rabanal and A. Scott (2009), Monetary and Macroprudential Policy Rules in a Model with House Price Booms, IMF Working Paper No. 09/251, International Monetary Fund.

King, M. (2002): The Inflation Target Ten Years On, Bank of England, Quarterly Bulletin 2002, Vol. 42 (4), pp. 459-474.

Kiyotaki, N. and J. Moore (1997), Credit Cycles, *Journal of Political Economy*, Vol. 105 (2), pp. 211-248.

Kent, C. and P. Lowe (1997), Asset Price Bubbles and Monetary Policy, Research Discussion Paper 9709, Reserve Bank of Australia, Sydney.

Kent, C. and P. Lowe (1998), Property-Price Cycles and Monetary Policy, In: The Role of Asset Prices in the Formulation of Monetary Policy – BIS Conference Paper No. 5, Bank for International Settlements, Basle.

Knütter, R. and Wagner, H. (2011), Optimal Monetary Policy during Boom-Bust Cycles: The Impact of Globalization, *International Journal of Economics and Finance*, Vol. 3 (2), May 2011.

Khan, H. (2005), Price-Setting Behaviour, Competition, and Mark-Up Shocks in the New-Keynesian Model, *Economics Letters* 87, pp. 329-335.

Lipsky, J. (2008), Remarks on "Financial Intermediaries, Financial Stability and Monetary Policy" (by Tobias Adrian and Hyun Song Shin) at the Federal Reserve Bank of Kansas City's Annual Economic Symposium in Jackson Hole, Wyoming.

Loungani, P., A. Razin and C.-W. Yuen (2001), Capital Mobility and the Output-Inflation Tradeoff, *Journal of Development Economics* 64, pp. 255-274.

McCulley, P. and R. Toloui (2008), Chasing the Neutral Rate Down: Financial Conditions, Monetary Policy, and the Taylor Rule, Global Central Bank Focus, PIMCO, February 20, 2008.

Mishkin, F. S. and E. N. White (2003), U.S. Stock Market Crashes And Their Aftermath: Implications For Monetary Policy, In Asset Price Bubbles: The Implications for Monetary, Regulatory, and International Policies, William Hunter, Georg G. Kaufmann, Michael Pomerleano (Eds.), pp. 53–79, Cambridge, Mass: MIT Press.

Muellbauer, J. (2010), Household Decisions, Credit Markets and the Macroeconomy: Implications for the Design of Central Bank Models, BIS Working Paper No. 306, Bank for International Settlements.

Mussa, M. (2003), Asset Prices and Monetary Policy, In Asset Price Bubbles: The Implications for Monetary, Regulatory, and International Policies, William Hunter, Georg G. Kaufmann, Michael Pomerleano (Eds.), Cambridge, Mass: MIT Press, pp. 41–50.

Pollack, R. A. (1989), The Theory of the Cost-of-Living Index, Oxford University Press, Oxford.

Posen, A. S. (2006), Why Central Banks Should Not Burst Bubbles, *International Finance*, Vol. 9 (1), pp. 109-124.

Razin, A. and P. Loungani (2005a), Globalization and Disinflation: The Efficiency Channel, CEPR Discussion Paper No. 4895.

Razin, A. and P. Loungani (2005b), Globalization and Inflation-Output Tradeoffs, NBER Working Paper No. 11641.

Razin, A. and C.-W. Yuen (2002), The "New Keynesian" Phillips Curve: Closed Economy Versus Open Economy, *Economics Letters*, Vol. 75, pp. 1-9.

Richards, Anthony (2003) "Introduction", In Asset Prices and Monetary Policy, Anthony Richards and Tim Robinson (Eds.), Reserve Bank of Australia 2003 Conference, pp. 1-7.

Rogoff, K. (2003), Globalization and Global Disinflation, Paper prepared for the Federal Reserve Bank of Kansas City conference on "Monetary Policy and Uncertainty: Adapting to a Changing Economy", Jackson Hole, Wyoming, August 28-30, 2003.

Rogoff, K. (2006), Impact of Globalization on Monetary Policy, Paper prepared for Symposium sponsored by the Federal Reserve Bank of Kansas City on "The New Economic Geography: Effects and Policy Implications", Jackson Hole, Wyoming, August 24-26, 2006.

Roi, M. B. and R. R. Mendes (2007), Should Central Banks Adjust Their Target Horizons in Response to House-Price Bubbles?, Discussion Paper 2007-4, Bank of Canada.

Romer, D. (1993), Openness and Inflation: Theory and Evidence, *Quarterly Journal of Economics*, Vol. 108, pp. 869-903.

Rotemberg, J. J. (1982), Monopolistic Price Adjustment and Aggregate Output, *Review of Economic Studies* 49, pp. 517–31.

Rotemberg, J. J. and M. Woodford (1997), An Optimization-Based Econometric Framework for the Evaluations of Monetary Policy, in: B. Bernanke and J. J. Rotemberg (Eds.), NBER Macroeconomics Annual, Cambridge, Mass. (MIT Press), pp. 297-346.

Roubini, N. (2006), Why Central Banks Should Burst Bubbles, *International Finance*, Vol. 9 (1), pp. 87-107.

Rudebusch, G. D. (2005), Monetary Policy and Asset Price Bubbles, Federal Reserve Bank of San Francisco Economic Letter, No. 2005-18, pp. 1-3.

Schinasi, G. J. (2004), Defining Financial Stability, IMF Working Paper Series, WP/04/187, International Monetary Fund.

Schularick, M. and A. M. Taylor (2009), Credit Booms Gone Bust: Monetary Policy, Leverage Cycles and Financial Crises 1870-2008, NBER Working Paper No. 15512, National Bureau of Economic Research.

Schwartz, A. (1995), Why Financial Stability Depends on Price Stability, *Economic Affairs*, Autumn 1995, pp. 21-25.

Schwartz, A. (2002), Asset Price Inflation and Monetary Policy, NBER Working Paper No. 9321, National Bureau of Economic Research.

Smets, F. (1997), Financial Asset Prices and Monetary Policy: Theory and Evidence, CEPR Discussion Paper No. 1751, Centre for Economic Policy Research.

Stehn, S. J. (2009), Optimal Monetary and Fiscal Policy with Limited Asset Market Participation, IMF Working Paper No. 09/137, International Monetary Fund.

Stock, J. H. and M. W. Watson (2003), Forecasting Output and Inflation: The Role of Asset Prices, *Journal of Economic Literature*, Vol. 41 (3), pp. 788-829.

Svensson, L. E. O. (2002), Monetary Policy and Real Stabilization, In: Rethinking Stabilization Policy, A Symposium Sponsored by the Federal Reserve Bank of Kansas City, Jackson Hole, Federal Reserve Bank of Kansas City (eds.), pp. 261-312.

Svensson, L. E. O. (2004), Asset Prices and ECB Monetary Policy, Briefing Paper for the Committee on Economic and Monetary Affairs (ECON) of the European Parliament, www.princeton.edu/~svensson.

Svensson, L. E. O. (2009), Flexible Inflation Targeting: Lessons from the Financial Crisis, Speech given at the workshop "Towards a New Framework for Monetary Policy? Lessons from the Crisis", organized by De Nederlandsche Bank, Amsterdam, September 21, 2009.

Taylor, J. B. (1993), Discretion versus Policy Rules in Practice, Carnegie-Rochester Conferences Series on Public Policy, Vol. 39, pp. 195-214.

Taylor, J. B. (2008), Monetary Policy and the State of the Economy, Testimony before the Committee on Financial Services, U.S. House of Representatives, February 26, 2008.

Teranishi, Y. (2009), Credit Spread and Monetary Policy, IMES Discussion Paper No. 2009-E-14, Institute for Monetary and Economic Studies, Bank of Japan.

Tootell, G. M. B. (1998), Globalization and U. S. Inflation, Federal Reserve Bank of Boston, New England Economic Review (July/August), pp. 21-33.

Trichet, J.-C. (2009), Credible Alertness Revisited, Intervention at the Symposium on "Financial Stability and Macroeconomic Policy", sponsored by the Federal Reserve Bank of Kansas City, 22 August 2009, Jackson Hole, Wyoming.

von Peter, G. (2009), Asset Prices and Banking Distress: A Macroeconomic Approach, *Journal of Financial Stability*, Vol. 5 (3), pp. 298-319.

Wagner, H. (2002), Implications of Globalization for Monetary Policy, SUERF Studies No. 2002/17.

Wagner, H. (2010), The Causes of the Recent Financial Crisis and the Role of Central Banks in Avoiding the Next One, *International Economics and Economic Policy*, Vol. 7 (1), pp. 63-82.

Walsh, C. E. (2009), Using Monetary Policy to Stabilize Economic Activity, Paper prepared for the Jackson Hole Symposium on "Financial Stability and Macroeconomic Policy", August 20-22, 2009.

Weber, A. (2007), A Central Banker's Interest In Phillips Curves, Speech held at the Symposium on "The Phillips Curve and the Natural Rate of Unemployment" at the Kiel Institute for the World Economy Kiel, Sunday, June 3, 2007.

White, W. (2006), Is Price Stability Enough?, BIS Working Paper No. 205, Bank of International Settlements.

White, W. R. (2009), Should Monetary Policy "Lean or Clean"?, Working Paper No. 34, Globalization and Monetary Policy Institute, Federal Reserve Bank of Dallas.

Woodford, M. (2003), Interest and Prices: Foundations of a Theory of Monetary Policy, Princeton and Oxford (Princeton University Press).

Yellen, J. L. (2005), Housing Bubbles and Monetary Policy, Presentation to the Fourth Annual Haas Gala San Francisco, October 21, 2005.

Yellen, J. L. (2006), Monetary Policy in a Global Environment, Federal Reserve Bank of San Francisco Economic Letter (June), pp. 1-7.

Yellen, J. L. (2009), A Minsky Meltdown: Lessons for Central Bankers, FRBSF Economic Letter No. 2009-15, May 1 2009, Federal Reserve Bank of San Francisco.

In: Financial Asset Pricing
Editors: P. E. Schulz and B. P. Hoffmann

ISBN 978-1-61122-803-8

Chapter 2

DYNAMIC MIGRATION BETWEEN STOCK PORTFOLIOS BASED ON DIVIDEND YIELD AND FIRM SIZE

Ian McManus,[1] Owain ap Gwilym[2]* and Stephen Thomas[3]

[1] School of Management, University of Southampton,SO17 1BJ. UK
[2] Bangor Business School, Bangor University,Wales, LL57 2DG. UK
[3] Cass Business School, City University,London, EC1Y 8TZ. UK

ABSTRACT

This chapter uses monthly UK stock market data sorted into a two-dimensional set of portfolios to establish the year-on-year migration dynamics of stock movements between portfolios. The system of (monthly re-balanced) portfolios comprises six dividend yield strata (including a separate zero-dividend category) each of which is further subdivided into market capitalisation quintiles. Monthly re-balancing ensures that portfolios are constantly populated by stocks having similar dividend yield and size characteristics; the movement of stocks, year-on-year, between portfolios provides information about the relationship linking returns behaviour to yield. Simply stated, the analysis of migration patterns provides additional insights into the phenomenon of the much-quoted 'U' shaped characteristic which purports to relate risk-adjusted returns to dividend yield; it does so by drawing attention to the *similarities* between high-yielding and zero-dividend stocks, a linkage which is de-emphasised when these are conventionally viewed as being at opposite ends of a yield spectrum. This leads to the notion of 'adjacency', and implies a circular, rather than linear, relationship between returns and yield; a notion supported by the relatively high levels of *direct* migration between these two (high- and zero-yielding) groups; and by the observation, both in this chapter and in the supporting literature, that smaller firms with high average returns are concentrated in the two groups. The analysis here of direct migration also takes account of stocks distinguished by year-on-year expansion versus year-on-year contraction; it emerges as being both robust to, and

* Corresponding author. owain.apgwilym@bangor.ac.uk

consistent with this separation. A plausible explanation for such direct migration would be one associated with 'distress', whereby declining price levels among such stocks tends to inflate the yield metric (implying migration toward the 'high dividend' stratum) as firms struggle to maintain dividend levels; ultimately, firms fall directly, upon virtually inevitable dividend cessation, into the zero-dividend category. A similar analysis applies when growing firms commence paying dividends for the first time. Finally, the analysis examines the dynamics of the process in terms of a long-run equilibrium and a speed of adjustment, treating the transition matrix as a Markov process; it finds plausible values for these parameters in the context of the UK stock market.

1. INTRODUCTION

Well-established portfolio formation methods (e.g. Keim (1985), Morgan and Thomas (1998), McManus (2001), McManus, ap Gwilym and Thomas (2004), Fama and French (2007)) provide for a large spread of characteristics in terms of the explanatory variables featuring in a typical characteristics-based regression model. This type of construction favours estimation efficiency; and to some extent mimics the behaviour of investors 'tilting' their portfolios to suit particular investment styles. This chapter examines the aggregate information implied in the patterns of migration, over time, of the individual stocks within such a portfolio structure.

A common portfolio formation methodology is based upon a two-dimensional arrangement involving firm size (market capitalisation) and a measure of firm 'value';[1] here, the value measure is based upon dividend yield. In much of the literature, the term 'U' shaped characteristic has been applied to the distribution of returns across dividend yield groups, when a dedicated zero-dividend group is included in the structure. The effect is evident in the results presented here (Table 1). Keim (1985), using US data, identifies his overall result as being driven primarily by effects which occur in January. Christie (1990), using a different (portfolio matching) methodology for assessing excess returns, also finds the non-linearity to be a feature of January returns, but finds the effect absent for other months.

Table 1. Average Monthly (%) Compound Returns (Jan. 1958 - Dec. 1997)

	Large	2	3	4	Small	(All Caps)
High Divd.	1.94	1.87	1.92	2.23	2.88	2.19
2	1.60	1.51	1.72	1.83	2.25	1.80
3	1.26	1.44	1.34	1.46	2.10	1.54
4	1.14	1.18	1.19	1.34	1.83	1.36
Low Divd.	1.02	1.02	0.95	1.01	1.98	1.22
Zero Divd.	1.09	1.05	1.67	2.31	5.47	2.41

The concept of the 'U' shaped relationship is, however, predicated upon the notion that zero-dividend and high dividend-paying stocks are at opposite extremities of a continuum

[1] The 'value' dimension may also be regarded as being indicative of 'relative distress', in which distressed stocks (which are marked down by the market in consequence) exhibit high values of those measures which feature price in the denominator.

along the yield axis. Whilst in a strict sense this has some validity, since the otherwise monotonic relationship between returns and yield for positive yields is breached when zero-dividend stocks are included, there would seem to be room for an alternative interpretation. This finds strong links between the categories of zero- and high-yielding stocks, therefore suggesting that, in a different sense, the two categories are 'adjacent'. Indeed, in terms of the growth and perhaps later decline of companies toward cessation of trading (or alternatively, merger / take-over),[2] the typical life-cycle characteristics of firms may well carry them through the stages of initial zero-dividend payment as they retain cash for growth, followed by a period of high dividend payment as early product lines mature to 'cash cow' status; concurrent to this phase, firms may be seeking to appeal to the investment community through good dividend performance. Declining firms, on the other hand, may relegate themselves through the capitalisation 'league tables' as the onset of poor earnings, profit warnings, etc. engenders a fall in the share price, sufficient in itself to give rise to high dividend yield (assuming a constant dividend stream, at least in the short term). Thus yield may be as much a 'price' effect in the denominator, at least as much as an earnings effect in the numerator, of the yield equation. Eventually, as pointed out by Morgan and Thomas (1998) (hereafter, MT(1998)), when declining high-yielding companies are no longer able to sustain the payment of dividends, they fall naturally into the zero-dividend category.

Following the notion of re-positioning zero-dividend firms (this may be viewed in terms of a re-ranking of Table 2, risk-adjusted returns), it is clear that linearity / monotonicity may be established by placing small zero-dividend firms *above* high dividend firms in the two smallest capitalisation quintiles. In the case of capitalisation quintile 3, a suitable ranking would reverse the ordering of the high- and zero-dividend stock portfolios, but leave them still adjacent. Only for the largest capitalisation zero-dividend stocks would the ordering place them near the 'conventional' position - even then they would remain above the 'low' dividend paying stock portfolios in the ranking.

Further evidence in support of the contention of 'adjacency' is that of Table 3. While dividend-paying categories 5 (low) to 2 (second-highest yielding) share broadly similar market capitalisation distributions, these are markedly distinct from the distributions of both zero- and high-yielding stocks. Whilst the latter pair differ one to another (zero-dividend stocks are clearly smaller, on average, than high-yielding stocks), their market size distributions nevertheless do set them apart from the remaining groups. Keim (1985), pp. 478 highlights his finding, in relation to US stocks:

> "the smallest firms on the NYSE (those firms with the largest average returns) are concentrated in the zero dividend yield group and the highest dividend yield group."

In order to further test the 'adjacency' hypothesis, i.e. that the relationship between the zero- and high-yielding categories is one of 'closeness' rather than separation across a continuum, and that their constituent stocks share common characteristics, a study of the migration patterns of stocks between categories over time is carried out.

---

2 The average 'lifetime' of individual stocks in the London Share Price Database is 141 months, or 11¾ years.

Table 2. Mean and Standard Deviation of Net Simple Returns

	(Including Mean of Dividend Yield) - by Dividend Strata and Capitalisation Quintile						
		C_Quintile					
D_Quintile	Data	1	2	3	4	5	Grand Total
1	Average of NRET	0.0210	0.0202	0.0205	0.0234	0.0298	0.0230
	StdDevp of NRET	0.0571	0.0551	0.0516	0.0489	0.0448	0.0518
	Average of Div_Yld	0.1099	0.1127	0.1136	0.1201	0.1382	0.1189
2	Average of NRET	0.0177	0.0167	0.0187	0.0196	0.0236	0.0192
	StdDevp of NRET	0.0596	0.0565	0.0550	0.0509	0.0470	0.0540
	Average of Div_Yld	0.0720	0.0727	0.0729	0.0733	0.0735	0.0729
3	Average of NRET	0.0143	0.0159	0.0149	0.0158	0.0221	0.0166
	StdDevp of NRET	0.0595	0.0553	0.0536	0.0489	0.0481	0.0533
	Average of Div_Yld	0.0564	0.0565	0.0567	0.0568	0.0570	0.0567
4	Average of NRET	0.0132	0.0135	0.0133	0.0148	0.0195	0.0149
	StdDevp of NRET	0.0604	0.0591	0.0545	0.0529	0.0494	0.0555
	Average of Div_Yld	0.0427	0.0427	0.0429	0.0429	0.0428	0.0428
5	Average of NRET	0.0121	0.0121	0.0112	0.0116	0.0212	0.0136
	StdDevp of NRET	0.0635	0.0612	0.0592	0.0537	0.0532	0.0584
	Average of Div_Yld	0.0254	0.0250	0.0246	0.0240	0.0236	0.0245
6	Average of NRET	0.0131	0.0127	0.0190	0.0259	0.0580	0.0257
	StdDevp of NRET	0.0667	0.0663	0.0673	0.0756	0.0861	0.0747
	Average of Div_Yld	0.0000	0.0000	0.0000	0.0000	0.0000	0.0000
Total Average of NRET		0.0152	0.0152	0.0163	0.0185	0.0290	0.0188
Total StdDevp of NRET		0.0613	0.0591	0.0572	0.0562	0.0582	0.0586
Total Average of Div_Yld		0.0511	0.0516	0.0518	0.0529	0.0558	0.0526

Table 3. Maximum capitalisation (£M) of companies in each of 30 portfolios (December 1997)

	Large	2	3	4	Small
High Divd.	29088.2	203.6	46.4	22.9	9.4
2	25838.8	532.5	106.1	40.4	16.8
3	48743.0	475.8	130.6	46.6	22.2
4	17952.7	460.6	163.5	66.6	21.5
Low Divd.	32271.8	535.7	150.9	53.2	21.0
Zero Divd.	2999.4	55.3	12.4	6.2	2.8

In summary, rather than being an open-ended linear spectrum, the universe of stocks may possibly be regarded as forming a closed system which places zero- and high-dividend stocks adjacently. As indicated above, firms may frequently effect the transition directly from one category to the other, in either direction. The possibility of subsequent recovery of previously 'failing' firms may signal the start of a further 'revolution' around the closed circle. These considerations form the basis for a hypothesis of firms' characteristics which will be investigated in this chapter, through the medium of examining the ways in which, through time, firms position themselves within this classification structure.

2. Data and Methodology

The empirical analysis begins with an examination of stock returns over the period of January 1958 to December 1997, and in particular with the relationship of monthly total returns to dividend yield and market capitalisation. This (40-year) span of complete calendar years makes use of data from the London Share Price Database (LSPD).

Initially, the methodology of MT(1998) is closely followed, albeit in the context of the period of interest here, extending their 1975-93 time frame with both earlier and later data. In addition, in order not to exclude a disproportionate number of small capitalisation and zero-dividend stocks (see, in addition, Christie (1990)), the pre-qualification period is reduced from the 60 continuous months of Keim (1985) to 24 months.[3] Additional tests in MT(1998) showed this reduction to be methodologically acceptable. In view of the importance attached in this chapter to zero-dividend stocks, however, the incorporation of market capitalisation information differs from that of earlier papers. The method of sorting used by Keim (1985) avoids the imposition of a 'hierarchy of sorts' as between dividend yield and market capitalisation. Rather, two separate sorts are carried out, enabling individual stocks to be 'tagged' with their quintile identifiers; the two 'tags' then functioning as co-ordinates in assigning stocks to their appropriate portfolios within a 2-dimensional dividend yield / market capitalisation matrix. The 'even-handed' approach avoids *a priori* 'favouring' of either factor, but suffers from the problem of engendering a highly asymmetric assignment to certain portfolios; thus in MT(1998, Table 3) 60.9% of all zero-dividend stocks were assigned to the smallest capitalisation / zero-dividend portfolio, and only 3.3% of zero-dividend stocks were assigned to the largest capitalisation / zero-dividend portfolio. Quite simply, the majority of zero-dividend firms are small; and, amongst small firms (those in the lowest size quintile), zero-dividend firms are the largest grouping, standing at almost one-third of the total, twice the number of the next nearest dividend yield group. This co-incidence of measures results in the asymmetry described. (In contrast, Table 4 (below) shows the numbers of samples assigned to each portfolio by the method of formation described in the following paragraphs. Apart from the unavoidable numerical imbalance between zero-dividend stocks and individual quintiles of dividend-paying stocks[4] due to the differing selection criterion, the portfolios within the matrix are closely similar in size).

Given that an implied 'hierarchy of sorts' derives from the above discussion, the question now posed is as to which, of dividend yield or market capitalisation, should form the basis of the primary sort, and which the secondary.

Three reasons are given for the choice of dividend yield as the primary sort candidate. Firstly, the hypothesis that dividend yield is the more dominant effect is plausible, and supported by some evidence (Keim (1985)); secondly, dividend yield is (at least in part) a policy parameter under the control of firms, in a way in which size clearly is not.

---

[3] It is the case that each additional 12 months of pre-qualification, up to 5 years, reduces the number of companies featuring in the data set by over 8%. This figure, compounded, would result in over one third of UK returns records being excluded from consideration by the 60-month rule; at 24 months, the reduction is less than one sixth.

[4] Only chance would engender perfect balance here, but the relaxation of the qualification period to 24 months does serve to admit a proportionately larger complement of zero-dividend stocks, thus militating toward parity.

Table 4. Two-way classification of stocks by 1) Dividend Yield Group and 2) Market Capitalisation Quintile (Jan 1958 - Dec 1997)

	Large	2	3	4	Small	Totals	%
High Divd.	23441	23324	23342	23334	23723	117164	17.499
2	23579	23459	23475	23461	23849	117823	17.597
3	23572	23462	23452	23450	23849	117785	17.592
4	23575	23441	23456	23475	23829	117776	17.590
Low Divd.	23753	23631	23646	23647	24014	118691	17.727
Zero Divd.	16123	15959	15964	15965	16297	80308	11.994
Totals	134043	133276	133335	133332	135561	669547	100
%	20.020	19.905	19.914	19.914	20.247	100	

The units above are 'Company x Month' sample records falling into particular portfolios across the entire (480 month) period.

Thirdly, methodological compatibility with the literature quoted earlier facilitates comparison of results, at least up to the point of divergence of method.

Thus portfolio formation by (initially) dividend yield closely follows Keim (1985), Christie (1990) and MT (1998), except that the 'dividend announcement' criterion favoured by Christie (1990) is rejected as impractical in the UK context, due to lack of data; (only 55% of company data incorporates the information necessary to implement this scheme). Rather, the 'usual' computation,[5] based upon the sum of dividends DIV_T, paid in the months t_{-12} to t_{-1}, divided by the price of the stock at time t_{-13}, (P_{t-13}) :

$$DY_t = 1/\, P_{t-13} * \Sigma_{t-13}\, DIV_T \qquad (1)$$

Using this measure, the population of firms is ranked each month, and subdivided into six groups; non-zero-dividend firms being formed into quintiles, with zero-dividend firms remaining as a distinct group. Certain preliminary analysis was carried out using the six equally-weighted portfolios deriving from the above scheme; however, for much of the remaining work, the additional, separate subdivision based on market capitalisation was necessary. Thus, each of the six dividend yield groups was further subdivided, being ranked, internally, according to size; 30 portfolios, summarised in Table 4 were formed.

In order to develop a responsive, dynamic measure of market capitalisation of the sort recommended by Christie (1990), (see below), the market capitalisation data presented in the Returns file of the LSPD was rejected in favour of an alternative measure. The (Returns File) market capitalisation data suffers from poor resolution, both in terms of magnitude and of time; amounts are given to the nearest integer £1M, too crude a measure to rank smaller firms in a fashion smooth enough to result in balanced quintiles; and the data is annual, which precludes the rapid re-classification required in order to take account, in particular, of firms announcing dividend cuts and suffering rapid changes in share price as a result.

The measure of market capitalisation used here is based upon the product of share price (at the end of the preceding month) and the number of shares outstanding. The latter figure is

5 It has been argued by some that a 'fresher' measure of dividend yield is afforded by division by P_{t-1} rather than P_{t-13}; however, Keim (1985) claims to have used both measures with little influence on his results.

given each year in explicit form for the beginning of January; this information is factored (if necessary) through the year, using the 'Adjustment Factor' which is provided to take account of capital changes (e.g. scrip, rights issues, etc.). Thus in the months February - December, the number of shares outstanding is taken as being unchanged from the previous month, unless an Adjustment Factor is quoted; however, each January, the 'annually updated' figure is taken as definitive.[6]

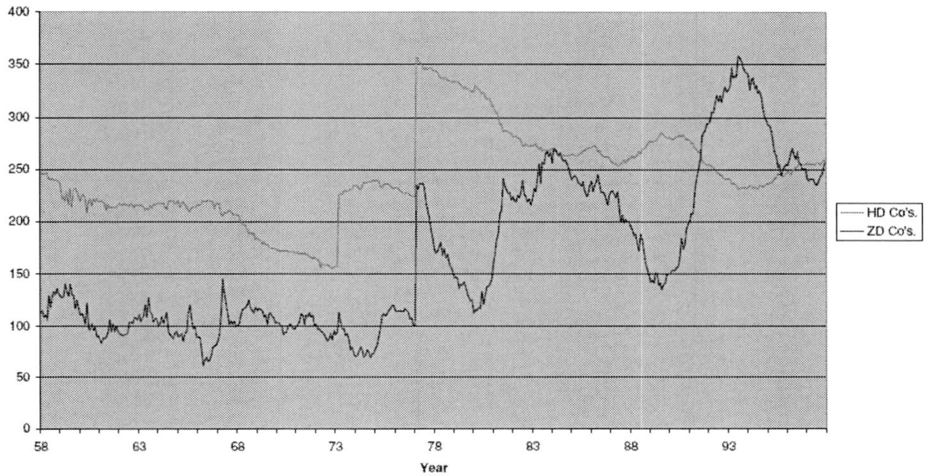

Figure 1. Numbers of HD & ZD Firms in sample (by Year).

The result of these manipulations is the system of 30 (6x5) portfolios, ranked primarily by dividend yield and secondarily (i.e. within dividend category) by market capitalisation, as indicated in Table 4. Portfolios are dynamically re-balanced on a month-by-month basis on both criteria. This ensures that each portfolio remains populated by 'like' firms through time. For each portfolio, there exists a time series of 480 monthly observations. Figure 1 shows the variation, with time, of the number of samples in the zero-dividend category (across all firm sizes), and, arbitrarily chosen as typical, the corresponding number of firms in the highest yield category. (Numbers in the other dividend-paying yield categories are closely similar, differing only because the system of ranking leaves occasional 'N^{th} = ' samples grouped together). Thus numbers of firms in the zero-dividend category approximate to 100 in the first half sub-period, fluctuating and rising to 250 by the end of the second sub-period. Numbers in the dividend paying quintiles both begin and end at 250, but with declining trends punctuated by two 'step' increases between February and March 1973 and between January and February 1977, due to significant new admission changes to the LSPD Database which had occurred two years previously to these dates, and which (firms) had now emerged from the 24- month qualification period.[7] Only the latter of these step increases, however, significantly affects the zero-dividend stock numbers. The subdivision of these stocks by capitalisation is

[6] Discrepancies are in any case small, and are ascribed to the timing of the measurements; however, using the above scheme, potential errors are not allowed to cumulate beyond 11 months.

[7] In 1971, the largest companies (by market value in 1976) and "Times Top 1000" 1976 (quoted companies only) were added to the LSPD database, and in 1975, "All British quoted companies" were included. Other, smaller samples were added at various other times, but these two tranches represented the major additions.

substantially equal; thus, at the end of the period, the number of firms in each of the 30 portfolios approximates to 50.

Table 5 shows a summary of the number of firms in the total sample during each month throughout the period. It shows that the minimum number of firms in any one monthly sample was 877, (January 1973) shortly before the 'step' increase of that year from 880 to1246 (Feb/Mar). The maximum, 2022, occurred in February 1977 following the step increase (of qualified firms) for *that* year, having stood at 1224 during the previous month. The opening figure (Jan 1958) was 1353, the closing (Dec 1997) 1554. The whole-period average was 1395.

Table 5. Number of firms in sample (by Year / Month)

Sum of Count	Month												
Year	1	2	3	4	5	6	7	8	9	10	11	12	Grand Total
58	1353	1351	1348	1346	1345	1344	1342	1339	1336	1334	1333	1325	16096
59	1319	1314	1311	1304	1306	1301	1299	1292	1286	1281	1275	1267	15555
60	1257	1252	1241	1231	1229	1220	1214	1213	1211	1207	1202	1199	14676
61	1193	1187	1182	1181	1178	1177	1175	1174	1173	1179	1181	1179	14159
62	1180	1178	1176	1179	1180	1181	1183	1191	1187	1189	1190	1190	14204
63	1189	1187	1188	1183	1178	1179	1186	1193	1194	1192	1193	1195	14257
64	1191	1195	1196	1195	1196	1193	1194	1193	1192	1190	1189	1190	14314
65	1192	1186	1183	1185	1179	1170	1170	1175	1174	1176	1174	1169	14133
66	1176	1174	1174	1167	1164	1167	1168	1172	1176	1179	1179	1178	14075
67	1177	1179	1181	1182	1183	1172	1163	1159	1155	1147	1146	1140	13984
68	1134	1134	1127	1111	1103	1103	1089	1081	1075	1067	1060	1050	13134
69	1044	1034	1033	1022	1015	1004	997	995	990	987	983	983	12087
70	974	966	964	962	954	956	957	961	958	957	958	957	11524
71	961	960	955	964	960	957	960	957	946	943	936	932	11431
72	928	917	909	900	895	887	882	883	882	881	878	881	10723
73	877	880	1246	1244	1242	1245	1244	1243	1241	1238	1241	1247	14188
74	1246	1244	1242	1245	1250	1257	1263	1267	1270	1266	1275	1290	15105
75	1291	1288	1288	1296	1287	1289	1292	1296	1298	1291	1289	1296	15471
76	1284	1281	1277	1267	1261	1260	1256	1257	1251	1239	1235	1226	15094
77	1224	2022	2016	2005	1996	1985	1972	1962	1944	1941	1935	1913	22915
78	1902	1899	1890	1881	1873	1866	1862	1860	1850	1840	1833	1825	22381
79	1819	1822	1816	1806	1801	1793	1793	1788	1770	1770	1758	1753	21489
80	1747	1772	1765	1763	1753	1750	1747	1742	1732	1733	1732	1721	20957
81	1718	1712	1707	1700	1690	1682	1675	1673	1674	1666	1657	1650	20204
82	1644	1637	1635	1631	1628	1618	1613	1601	1597	1591	1584	1588	19367
83	1586	1609	1606	1605	1604	1598	1603	1607	1610	1610	1610	1614	19262
84	1609	1618	1615	1595	1594	1599	1586	1581	1580	1577	1573	1571	19098
85	1571	1568	1566	1560	1563	1564	1575	1581	1579	1578	1583	1592	18880
86	1600	1596	1604	1600	1587	1580	1560	1550	1544	1537	1529	1533	18820
87	1526	1519	1514	1504	1500	1490	1487	1495	1500	1494	1499	1506	18034
88	1511	1511	1502	1504	1503	1510	1518	1533	1525	1521	1529	1532	18199
89	1534	1528	1529	1540	1545	1557	1564	1567	1560	1555	1558	1557	18594
90	1562	1555	1556	1564	1573	1572	1589	1599	1596	1589	1594	1596	18945
91	1594	1589	1586	1592	1593	1586	1590	1593	1578	1577	1568	1570	19016
92	1574	1573	1572	1570	1561	1559	1556	1546	1541	1537	1538	1533	18660
93	1536	1533	1529	1524	1518	1513	1515	1520	1521	1512	1512	1508	18241
94	1509	1500	1507	1500	1494	1495	1488	1499	1492	1478	1481	1483	17926
95	1483	1481	1474	1475	1476	1478	1485	1486	1479	1471	1475	1492	17755
96	1498	1493	1501	1520	1526	1525	1538	1542	1536	1529	1528	1533	18269
97	1528	1521	1520	1523	1520	1512	1522	1523	1517	1535	1550	1554	18325
Grand Total	55231	55965	56231	56116	56003	55894	55872	55890	55720	55584	55543	55498	669547

Table 3 indicates the 'typical' capitalisation spread within portfolios by showing the transition thresholds of capitalisation (for each dividend Yield category) between adjacent market capitalisation portfolios, for the end of the period (December 1997). These are considered to be more insightful than nominal values averaged over a period during which inflation averaged some 6½ %.

3. Initial Results for Raw Returns

Following MT (1998), average returns and dividend yields are tabulated for each of the 6 dividend yield portfolios; in this case, with the benefit of the greater number of samples in the extended full period, it becomes feasible in addition to do likewise for the 30 dividend yield / market capitalisation portfolios. These results are firstly presented (Table 2) in the form of (averaged) net simple returns, appropriate for the aggregation, cross-sectionally, of individual stocks within portfolios (each month). In addition, (Table 1) they are also shown as equivalent monthly compounded portfolio returns, in order to reflect the performance of each of the portfolios longitudinally over the full time period. In each case, the rightmost column shows the results for the 6 dividend yield portfolios.

Referring to Table 2, viewing horizontally (with 'constant' dividend yield), the characteristic is one of 'flat' returns performance among the larger companies (overall 1.52% per month), followed by a rising trend as company size decreases, particularly within capitalisation quintile groups 4 and 5, up to an overall 2.9% per month among dividend-paying stocks. Vertically, the 'U' shaped curve identified by other researchers (Keim (1985); Christie (1990)) is apparent, with returns generally declining with decreasing dividend yield from quintile 1 to 5, followed by an upturn into the zero-dividend category. An exception to this 'rule' is the case of the smallest capitalisation quintile, where the upturn commences in the low dividend-paying quintile. Returns for the zero-dividend / smallest capitalisation portfolio (portfolio 30) are over twice that of any other, excepting the high dividend / smallest capitalisation portfolio, where the ratio is just under 2. However, this high return may be largely due to the compensation required by investors to invest in illiquid, thinly-traded sub - £3M (1997 values) stocks, with larger bid-ask spreads relative to (generally) low price levels per share, many of them 'penny' stocks.

3.1. Adjustment for Risk

Following established practice (e.g. MT(1998)), the one-period Sharpe-Lintner CAPM is used to generate abnormal returns, by estimating the relation:

$$R_{pt} - R_{ft} = \alpha_p + \beta_p(R_{mt} - R_{ft}) + u_{pt} \qquad (2)$$

where p = 1,2,...,6 (for dividend yield categories); p = 1,2,...,30 (for dividend yield / market capitalisation portfolios); t = 1 - 480.

R_{pt} is the rate of return for portfolio p in month t, R_{mt} is the market return for month t, an equally-weighted average of all stocks in the sample, R_{ft} is the monthly risk-free rate for month t, based on the 3-month Treasury bill rate, and u_{pt} is the vector of residuals.

According to the CAPM, abnormal returns are identified by statistically significant, non-zero values of α_p .[8] Table 6 (rightmost column for dividend yield categories) shows that high abnormal returns are associated with high dividend yields. Returns decline monotonically with decreasing dividend yield through to the lowest, non zero-dividend paying category,

[8] This parameter is commonly referred to as 'Jensen's Alpha'.

though not including zero-dividend stocks; here, positive abnormal returns are once again in evidence. Negative abnormal returns are associated with the three lowest yield categories, with the value for category 5 being -0.54%, in contrast with category 1, at 0.55%. The corresponding figure for the zero-dividend category is 0.69%.

Observation of the within-category subdivisions (by market capitalisation) reveals the profound influence of the smaller stocks on the above figures; this is particularly the case for the extreme categories (highest and zero) of dividend yield. Thus the abnormal return of portfolio 30 is 4.19%, that of portfolio 5 (the highest yield / smallest capitalisation portfolio) is 1.52%. Examination, as before, of the 'horizontal' (within dividend category) characteristic reveals a similar pattern; largely constant abnormal returns across the 3 largest size quintiles (2 largest in the case of the zero-dividend category), but with rapidly increasing abnormal returns with decreasing size thereafter. Vertically, the 'U' shaped characteristic is in evidence across all size quintiles, but becomes greatly pronounced as size decreases.

Table 6. Market Model (for 30 portfolios, summarising DY & CAP subtotals)

		C Quintile				Small Co's.	
D Quintile	Data	1	2	3	4	5	Overall (by Div)
1	ALPHA Coefficient	0.0019	0.0013	0.0026	0.0065	0.0152	0.0055
	t-value (Alpha)	1.76	1.39	2.76	6.11	10.84	9.80
High Divd.	BETA Coefficient	1.04	1.03	0.95	0.87	0.67	0.91
	R Squared	0.84	0.88	0.85	0.79	0.56	0.94
2	ALPHA Coefficient	-0.0016	-0.0026	-0.0005	0.0016	0.0074	0.0009
	t-value (Alpha)	-1.29	-3.02	-0.65	1.86	6.40	2.18
	BETA Coefficient	1.07	1.06	1.05	0.95	0.80	0.99
	R Squared	0.81	0.89	0.92	0.88	0.73	0.97
3	ALPHA Coefficient	-0.0047	-0.0032	-0.0040	-0.0017	0.0054	-0.0016
	t-value (Alpha)	-3.53	-3.93	-5.39	-2.06	4.97	-4.12
	BETA Coefficient	1.04	1.05	1.02	0.91	0.84	0.97
	R Squared	0.78	0.90	0.92	0.87	0.77	0.97
4	ALPHA Coefficient	-0.0059	-0.0064	-0.0056	-0.0037	0.0026	-0.0038
	t-value (Alpha)	-4.19	-7.12	-7.05	-4.50	2.28	-7.40
	BETA Coefficient	1.04	1.12	1.03	1.00	0.86	1.01
	R Squared	0.76	0.90	0.90	0.89	0.76	0.96
5	ALPHA Coefficient	-0.0078	-0.0081	-0.0087	-0.0069	0.0044	-0.0054
	t-value (Alpha)	-5.49	-7.78	-9.38	-6.95	2.94	-9.61
Low Divd.	BETA Coefficient	1.11	1.14	1.11	0.99	0.85	1.04
	R Squared	0.78	0.87	0.89	0.85	0.65	0.95
6	ALPHA Coefficient	-0.0073	-0.0073	0.0004	0.0070	0.0419	0.0069
	t-value (Alpha)	-4.66	-4.39	0.20	2.66	11.64	5.03
Zero Divd.	BETA Coefficient	1.15	1.12	1.00	1.03	0.80	1.02
	R Squared	0.75	0.72	0.56	0.47	0.22	0.75
Overall ALPHA Coeff. (by Cap)		-0.0042	-0.0044	-0.0026	0.0005	0.0128	0.0004
Overall BETA Coeff. (by Cap)		1.08	1.09	1.03	0.96	0.81	0.99

Examination of the beta (covariance risk factor) characteristic is revealing, particularly with decreasing size. Looking first at the largest size quintile, beta increases, as might be expected, as dividend yield drops into the 'low' and 'zero' categories. However, from a peak of 1.15 (portfolio 26, the large capitalisation, zero-dividend portfolio), beta drops sharply to a value of 0.8 in the case of portfolio 30. What appears to be a paradox here (low beta in spite of the high 'own variance' of portfolio 30) is resolved by observing the low value of R^2 (0.22); in fact, the variance of the returns of this portfolio is apparently somewhat 'de-coupled' from market variance[9]. An isolated, but 'telling' example of this fact is given by the response of portfolio 30 to the 37.2% (equally-weighted) market increase which took place in a single month in January 1975; the small-cap zero-dividend portfolio responded by only 4.4%. Clearly, this 'extreme' portfolio, carrying relatively little market weight, is frequently ignored by a large part of the market as a whole. However, a caveat is in order here - these exploratory observations are based upon a simple, non-robust estimation technique (OLS). In other work, this is extended using estimators robust to heteroscedasticity and autocorrelation, such as that induced by infrequent (thin) trading (see McManus, ap Gwilym and Thomas (2004)).

The portfolio 30 beta, however, is not the lowest. Portfolio 5 (high dividend / small capitalisation) is only 0.67; here, the value of R^2 is higher, at 0.56. This apparent further anomaly is resolved, at least in part, by observing that the standard deviation of portfolio 5 returns is the *lowest* of all portfolios, at 4.48% (see Table 2). In contrast, that of portfolio 30 is the *highest*, at 8.61%.

4. The Migration Study (Methodology)

4.1. Data

The data held in the individual 'Year' files constructed for the preceding analyses (above) provides the basis for the migration study, since the process of sorting stocks into positive yield quintiles and into the zero-yield sub-category is already complete. A total of 655,770 valid[10] records are available in the 40 'Year' files covering the period January 1958 to December 1997. These are brought together in a single, dedicated database file, and are then split into records for particular months (e.g. all files for the month of January, etc.).

This facilitates the comparison of records exactly one year apart, in terms of their migration behaviour. The choice of this interval is based upon two considerations:

1) The calculation of dividend yield is based upon the application of a 12-month rolling average; this effectively imposes a 'low-pass' filter upon the data. Using an interval of commensurate length in order to monitor migration, ensures consistency in terms of the frequency characteristics of the 'filters' through which the data are viewed.
2) Over a 12-month period, the effects of seasonal variation present in migration patterns tend to be attenuated by the process of integration.[11]

[9] MT(1998, footnote 9) note that i) "beta estimates …do not rise as dividend yields fall", and ii) "the beta for the zero-dividend portfolio is by far the highest". The effects described (above) may have been masked in the earlier study by virtue of the asymmetric 'crowding' of zero beta stocks largely into a single yield / size portfolio. As is shown here, with a sufficiently populated 'portfolio 26', the rising beta in the 'large-cap' / zero-dividend portfolio does in fact emerge, as does that of the 'large-cap' / *low* dividend portfolio (and also the distinction between these and the lower beta in portfolio 30).

[10] 'Validity' in this context implies the application of the inclusion criteria discussed earlier.

[11] Nevertheless, a distinct non-random pattern remains, in terms of the month to month interval chosen versus the calendar year. This is addressed in detail below.

The data in the newly-constructed 'Month' files includes a column holding the dividend category identifier (1 - 6). To this is added a new data column which places, on each record, a cell containing information as to the location (dividend yield category) of the *stock exactly one year previously* (where this datum exists for that time). An additional category identifier (0) is included to cater for the first entry for a particular firm, or for non-continuous records (breaks in the monthly returns series).[12] If both of these tests are passed, the cell is loaded with the previous year's dividend category identifier.

The effect of the above is to create records which embody both the source (previous) and destination (current) dividend categories for each stock over each (12-month) interval.

The migration information contained in the source and destination fields is summarised by cross-tabulation; a matrix of 7 columns (including the '0' category) x 6 rows is formed, with individual cells containing the count of the number of migrations from a particular source to a particular destination. Thus the number of migrations along a particular path, e.g. from dividend yield category '6' (the zero-dividend category) to category '1' (the 'high' yield category), is indicated by the data at the intersection of the *column* headed '6' and the *row* headed '1'. Inclusion of the '0' category, which is not used further, serves to provide a 'checksum' on the total number of records scanned. In this way, transitions may be regarded as *entering* via columns, and *exiting* via rows, with a count being maintained at the intersection.

Table 7(a) shows the matrix as described, containing the raw numbers of transitions, together with row and column totals. Table 7(b) shows the data normalised to reflect a correspondence between the 593,338 valid records (excluding 62,432 records in the '0' category),[13] expressed as 100% in the 'Corner Total' cell.

Tables 7(c) and 7(d) re-express the data as percentages of the column and row totals, respectively. This presentation assists the interpretation of the proportion of migrations *from* a given dividend yield category (Table 7(c)), and *into* a given dividend yield category (Table 7(d)). The need for this distinction arises for two reasons. Firstly, and most importantly, the table represents a transition process not yet in equilibrium; the differences between the percentages in 7(d) vs. 7(c) largely arise out of the one-period differences along a (corrective) path toward equilibrium. This form of presentation also assists in handling the imbalance between the number of stocks (and therefore migration samples) in the zero-dividend-paying category, compared to the number of stocks in each of the other categories. (The latter are approximately balanced (one to another) by construction, since they represent fractile subdivisions of their class). Here, the zero-dividend-paying category comprises approximately 11% of the migration sample count, as compared to 17.8% for each of the (quintile) groups.

---

[12] For example, the first record in a new block will have a 'current' dividend category associated with it, but not a migration path from a 'previous' category. The latter is therefore assigned the designator 'zero'.

[13] Approximately 9.5% of samples are not associated with a prior migration path. This figure is consistent with the average company lifetime of 11¾ years, which would account for 8.5%, to which must be added a proportion to account for discontinuous returns records.

	ALL Stocks									
Count of NRET	Mig_FROM									
D_Quintile	0	1	2	3	4	5	6	Grand Total		
1	10667	52761	25888	10879	5726	5493	3883	115297	51869	-831
2	9811	25191	37887	25032	10178	5596	1979	115674	67976	-473
3	10160	11044	23264	35491	24679	9086	2027	115751	70100	-596
4	10415	6208	10196	23021	40772	22489	2615	115716	64529	-918
5	11834	6166	6502	8912	21351	56059	5704	116528	48635	-1213
6	9545	4091	2599	2852	3513	7184	47020	76804	20239	4031
Grand Total	62432	105461	106336	106187	106219	105907	63228	655770		0
		52700	68449	70696	65447	49848	16208			

Table 7b

Overall %	Mig_FROM							
Mig_TO	0	1	2	3	4	5	6	Grand Total
1	1.80	8.89	4.36	1.83	0.97	0.93	0.65	17.63
2	1.65	4.25	6.39	4.22	1.72	0.94	0.33	17.84
3	1.71	1.86	3.92	5.98	4.16	1.53	0.34	17.80
4	1.76	1.05	1.72	3.88	6.87	3.79	0.44	17.75
5	1.99	1.04	1.10	1.50	3.60	9.45	0.96	17.64
6	1.61	0.69	0.44	0.48	0.59	1.21	7.92	11.34
Grand Total	10.52	17.77	17.92	17.90	17.90	17.85	10.66	100.00

Table 7c

			% of departures from groups (Columns)				
Count of NRET	Mig_FROM		(Expressed as % of its own group)				
Mig_TO	0	1	2	3	4	5	6
1		50.03	24.35	10.25	5.39	5.19	6.14
2		23.89	35.63	23.57	9.58	5.28	3.13
3		10.47	21.88	33.42	23.23	8.58	3.21
4		5.89	9.59	21.68	38.38	21.23	4.14
5		5.85	6.11	8.39	20.10	52.93	9.02
6		3.88	2.44	2.69	3.31	6.78	74.37
		100.00	100.00	100.00	100.00	100.00	100.00

Table 7d

			% of arrivals into groups (Rows)					
Count of NRET	Mig_FROM		(Expressed as % of its own group)					
Mig_TO	0	1	2	3	4	5	6	
1		50.43	24.74	10.40	5.47	5.25	3.71	100.00
2		23.80	35.79	23.65	9.61	5.29	1.87	100.00
3		10.46	22.03	33.61	23.37	8.60	1.92	100.00
4		5.90	9.68	21.86	38.72	21.36	2.48	100.00
5		5.89	6.21	8.51	20.39	53.55	5.45	100.00
6		6.08	3.86	4.24	5.22	10.68	69.91	100.00

Table 7e

		99% Confidence Intervals based on Table 1(c)					(+/- %)	
D_Quintile	0	1	2	3	4	5	6	Z(a/2)
1		0.396	0.339	0.240	0.178	0.175	0.246	2.575
2		0.338	0.378	0.335	0.233	0.177	0.178	
3		0.243	0.326	0.373	0.334	0.222	0.180	
4		0.187	0.233	0.326	0.384	0.324	0.204	
5		0.186	0.189	0.219	0.317	0.395	0.293	
6		0.153	0.122	0.128	0.141	0.199	0.447	

Table 7f

		99% Confidence Intervals based on Table 1(d)					(+/- %)
D_Quintile	0	1	2	3	4	5	6
1		0.398	0.344	0.243	0.181	0.178	0.150
2		0.337	0.379	0.336	0.233	0.177	0.107
3		0.243	0.328	0.374	0.335	0.222	0.109
4		0.187	0.235	0.328	0.387	0.325	0.123
5		0.187	0.192	0.222	0.321	0.397	0.181
6		0.237	0.191	0.200	0.221	0.307	0.455

Secondly, there exists a further complication in that, uniquely for zero-dividend stocks, there is (over the full period) a net *positive* migration (i.e. an excess of *arrivals* over *departures*) into the zero-dividend category amounting to 4,031 samples. All *dividend-paying* categories experience negative net migrations, individually and collectively, the absolute total of which, of course, equals 4,031. The two effects combined account for the differing relative size of zero-dividend category *arrivals* (11.34%, Table 7(b) versus *departures* (10.66%), and in turn therefore, affects normalisations based upon these two values which appear in subsequent tables.

Tables 7(e) and 7(f) present confidence intervals (at 99%) corresponding to the (point estimate) percentages in corresponding cells of Tables 7(c) and 7(d), expressed in the same units (%). Thus they should be interpreted as +/- additions to the values presented in the Tables 7(c) and 7(d). The calculation of these intervals is based upon the (large sample) normal approximation to the underlying binomial distribution which results from a proportion (p) of a sample of (n) observations *leaving* a given category (column) of Table 7(c), or, similarly, *arriving* in a given category (row) of Table 7(d). Proportions are obtained from the percentage values in the individual cells of 7(c) and 7(d), while the values of (n) are derived from the column totals of Table 7(a) (departing) or the row totals of Table 7(a) (arriving); in the latter case, these *exclude* the non-valid sample 'migrations' from column heading '0'.

The +/- intervals are computed as:

Population proportion (P) {lies in the range} Sample proportion (p) +/- :
$Z_{\alpha/2} . \sqrt{(p(1-p)/n)}$

where $Z_{\alpha/2}$ is the critical value corresponding to $Prob(Z > Z_{\alpha/2}) = \alpha/2$, $\{100(1-\alpha)\% = 99\%\}$

$= 2.575$

4.2. Analysis of Results (Presented in Table 7 (a-f))

The principal diagonal of the 6x6 matrices (which tabulate valid migration paths) reflects data associated with non-transitioning samples. Among these, the zero-dividend category stands out as being the most 'isolated', since approximately ¾ of migration samples in this group indicate no movement out of the category. The next-ranked groups in this regard are the 'low' and 'high' dividend yield categories, situated at the extremities of their class, where approximately one-half remain and one half migrate. The middle three yield groups are seen to be the more fluid, with just over one third remaining in place, the majority migrating. However, in all cases, the proportion of samples remaining 'in place' is greater than the proportion migrating to any one particular alternative category - as indeed would be expected.

The second significant observation is that, in all cases, the *second highest* proportion of samples indicate migration to their *next-highest* dividend yield category, excepting, of course, category 1, which is not dominated in this regard. The *third-highest* proportion of samples indicate migration to their *next-lowest* dividend yield category. Expressed alternately, it is the *adjacent* categories to which 'out of category' migration preferentially takes place. Again, this is what might reasonably be expected.

Turning attention now to the 'extreme' categories - highest- and zero-yield; how do these fit the pattern which is being suggested by the data? If the 'continuum' concept holds, they have only a single adjacent category, and the description above largely suffices. However, the alternative concept, that of 'Adjacency' between these extreme categories, is substantially supported by the (full-sample)[1] migration data as well as by the market capitalisation distribution (see Table 3).

Considering the migration to and from the zero-dividend category; in both of these cases, the second-highest migrating proportion (i.e. excluding those remaining 'in category') are those which are associated with the highest yielding group. Thus 6.14% of samples leaving the zero-dividend group are destined for the high-yield category; and 6.08% of samples arriving in the zero-dividend group are from the high-yield category. As a proportion of the 'movers', these represent almost one quarter, in each case.

Viewed from the perspective of the high-dividend category, there would appear to be a monotonic relationship between the migrating proportions (both arriving and leaving) and the linear 'distance' between the categories, along the supposed continuum. However, it should be stressed that the normalisations which give rise to these proportions do not take account of the smaller size of the zero-dividend group relative to each of the individual quintiles. For this reason, the evidence presented in the previous paragraph is considered to be the stronger, in terms of the probability (relative frequency) of events occurring in relation to the zero-dividend category.

4.3. Expanding versus Contracting Companies

The above form of analysis lends itself to the examination of a further dimension to the investigation. The 'valid' samples may be subdivided into two classes, namely those which exhibit strictly positive year-on-year size (i.e. market capitalisation) increases (Expanding companies) versus those which demonstrate either decreasing, or no change in (nominal) size ('Contracting' companies).

A simple extension to the methodology described above suffices to implement this supplementary investigation. Two additional columns are generated alongside the previously added column in the 'Month' files. The logic associated with these are as follows:

1) 'Expanding' stocks: if the new field for the record was previously invalid ('0'), then it remains so. If the market capitalisation field indicates year-on-year expansion, then the category data in the new field is copied; otherwise '0' is inserted into the field.
2) 'Contracting' stocks: the logic here differs only in terms of the inequality; thus the treatment of 'invalid' data is identical in that '0' entries are transferred as above; however, the treatment of 'valid' data is, by contrast, the *complement* of that in the above case. Therefore, 'Contracting' samples' category data is transferred.

---

1 This conclusion is weaker for more recent data.

Table 8a

	Expanding Stocks							
Count of NRET	Mig_ FROM							
D_ Quintile	0	1	2	3	4	5	6	Grand Total
1	40633	36360	18704	8164	4355	4178	2903	115297
2	46976	15352	24537	16733	6853	3843	1380	115674
3	50600	5770	13962	22599	15604	5892	1324	115751
4	53159	2969	5237	13488	25206	13843	1814	115716
5	59987	2762	2897	4230	11339	31854	3459	116528
6	42161	1592	993	1150	1382	2962	26564	76804
Grand Total	293516	64805	66330	66364	64739	62572	37444	655770
		28445	41793	43765	39533	30718	10880	

Table 8b

Overall %	Mig_ FROM							
Mig_TO	0	1	2	3	4	5	6	Grand Total
1	11.22	10.04	5.16	2.25	1.20	1.15	0.80	20.61
2	12.97	4.24	6.77	4.62	1.89	1.06	0.38	18.96
3	13.97	1.59	3.85	6.24	4.31	1.63	0.37	17.98
4	14.67	0.82	1.45	3.72	6.96	3.82	0.50	17.27
5	16.56	0.76	0.80	1.17	3.13	8.79	0.95	15.61
6	11.64	0.44	0.27	0.32	0.38	0.82	7.33	9.56
Grand Total	49.47	17.89	18.31	18.32	17.87	17.27	10.34	100.00

Table 8c

			% of departures from groups (Columns)			
Count of NRET	Mig_ FROM		(Expressed as % of its own group)			
Mig_TO	0	1	2	3	4	5	6
1		56.11	28.20	12.30	6.73	6.68	7.75
2		23.69	36.99	25.21	10.59	6.14	3.69
3		8.90	21.05	34.05	24.10	9.42	3.54
4		4.58	7.90	20.32	38.93	22.12	4.84
5		4.26	4.37	6.37	17.51	50.91	9.24
6		2.46	1.50	1.73	2.13	4.73	70.94
		100.00	100.00	100.00	100.00	100.00	100.00

Table 8d

Count of NRET	Mig_ FROM		% of arrivals into groups (Rows) (Expressed as % of its own group)					
Mig_TO	0	1	2	3	4	5	6	
1		48.70	25.05	10.93	5.83	5.60	3.89	100.00
2		22.35	35.72	24.36	9.98	5.59	2.01	100.00
3		8.86	21.43	34.69	23.95	9.04	2.03	100.00
4		4.75	8.37	21.56	40.29	22.13	2.90	100.00
5		4.88	5.12	7.48	20.05	56.34	6.12	100.00
6		4.60	2.87	3.32	3.99	8.55	76.68	100.00

Table 8e

		99% Confidence Intervals based on Table 8(c)					(+/- %)	
D_Quintile	0	1	2	3	4	5	6	Z(a/2)
1		0.502	0.450	0.328	0.254	0.257	0.356	2.575
2		0.430	0.483	0.434	0.311	0.247	0.251	
3		0.288	0.408	0.474	0.433	0.301	0.246	
4		0.211	0.270	0.402	0.493	0.427	0.286	
5		0.204	0.204	0.244	0.385	0.515	0.385	
6		0.157	0.121	0.130	0.146	0.219	0.604	

Table 8f

		99% Confidence Intervals based on Table 8(d)					(+/- %)
D_Quintile	0	1	2	3	4	5	6
1		0.471	0.408	0.294	0.221	0.217	0.182
2		0.409	0.471	0.422	0.294	0.226	0.138
3		0.287	0.414	0.480	0.431	0.289	0.142
4		0.219	0.285	0.423	0.505	0.427	0.173
5		0.233	0.239	0.285	0.434	0.537	0.260
6		0.290	0.231	0.248	0.271	0.387	0.585

From this point, the treatment of the data is similar to that of the earlier investigation; the effect of these latter manipulations is to channel the 'unwanted' data (i.e. 'Contracting' samples in (1), 'Expanding' samples in (2)) into the 'invalid' group (0). Tables 8 (a-f) show summary data for the 'Expanding' set, Table 9 (a-f) show that for the 'Contracting' set.

Table 9a

	Contracting Stocks							
Count of NRET	Mig_ FROM							
D_ Quintile	0	1	2	3	4	5	6	Grand Total
1	85331	16401	7184	2715	1371	1315	980	115297
2	78509	9839	13350	8299	3325	1753	599	115674
3	75311	5274	9302	12892	9075	3194	703	115751
4	72972	3239	4959	9533	15566	8646	801	115716
5	68375	3404	3605	4682	10012	24205	2245	116528
6	44188	2499	1606	1702	2131	4222	20456	76804
Grand Total	424686	40656	40006	39823	41480	43335	25784	655770

Table 9b

Overall %	Mig_ FROM							
Mig_TO	0	1	2	3	4	5	6	Grand Total
1	36.93	7.10	3.11	1.17	0.59	0.57	0.42	12.97
2	33.97	4.26	5.78	3.59	1.44	0.76	0.26	16.08
3	32.59	2.28	4.03	5.58	3.93	1.38	0.30	17.50
4	31.58	1.40	2.15	4.13	6.74	3.74	0.35	18.50
5	29.59	1.47	1.56	2.03	4.33	10.47	0.97	20.84
6	19.12	1.08	0.69	0.74	0.92	1.83	8.85	14.11
Grand Total	71.58	17.59	17.31	17.23	17.95	18.75	11.16	100.00

Table 9c

			% of departures from groups (Columns)			
Count of NRET	Mig_ FROM		(Expressed as % of its own group)			
Mig_TO	0	1	2	3	4	5	6
1		40.34	17.96	6.82	3.31	3.03	3.80
2		24.20	33.37	20.84	8.02	4.05	2.32
3		12.97	23.25	32.37	21.88	7.37	2.73
4		7.97	12.40	23.94	37.53	19.95	3.11
5		8.37	9.01	11.76	24.14	55.86	8.71
6		6.15	4.01	4.27	5.14	9.74	79.34
		100.00	100.00	100.00	100.00	100.00	100.00

Table 9d

			% of arrivals into groups (Rows)					
Count of NRET	Mig_ FROM		(Expressed as % of its own group)					
Mig_TO	0	1	2	3	4	5	6	
1		54.73	23.97	9.06	4.58	4.39	3.27	100.00
2		26.47	35.92	22.33	8.95	4.72	1.61	100.00
3		13.04	23.00	31.88	22.44	7.90	1.74	100.00
4		7.58	11.60	22.30	36.42	20.23	1.87	100.00
5		7.07	7.49	9.72	20.79	50.27	4.66	100.00
6		7.66	4.92	5.22	6.53	12.94	62.72	100.00

Table 9e

		99% Confidence Intervals based on Table 9(c)					(+/- %)	
D_Quintile	0	1	2	3	4	5	6	Z(a/2)
1		0.627	0.494	0.325	0.226	0.212	0.307	2.575
2		0.547	0.607	0.524	0.343	0.244	0.242	
3		0.429	0.544	0.604	0.523	0.323	0.261	
4		0.346	0.424	0.551	0.612	0.494	0.278	
5		0.354	0.369	0.416	0.541	0.614	0.452	
6		0.307	0.253	0.261	0.279	0.367	0.649	

Table 9f

		99% Confidence Intervals based on Table 9(d)					(+/- %)
D_Quintile	0	1	2	3	4	5	6
1		0.469	0.402	0.271	0.197	0.193	0.168
2		0.433	0.471	0.409	0.280	0.208	0.124
3		0.340	0.425	0.470	0.421	0.272	0.132
4		0.272	0.330	0.429	0.495	0.414	0.140
5		0.278	0.285	0.321	0.439	0.541	0.228
6		0.368	0.299	0.308	0.342	0.464	0.669

4.3.1. Analysis of 'Expanding' and 'Contracting' Data

Before discussing the direct comparisons between corresponding parameters *within* the three sets of tables, it is useful to examine an additional parameter which describes a relationship which exists *between* the tables. This concerns the percentages of 'Expanding' (valid) samples (in each category) relative to 'All' (valid) samples. Here, an interesting finding emerges. There is indeed a monotonic relationship between the dividend Yield category and the percentage of 'Expanding' samples. This remains the case, moreover, even when zero-dividend samples are included. This is expressed in Table 10.

The implications of this table are interesting. While the characteristic of increasing returns with increasing dividend Yield may be partially explained by the increasing proportion of 'Expanding' stocks,[2] the implication for the (previously determined) high returns of zero-dividend stocks, given the fact that these comprise only 51.5% of 'Expanders', is that the latter subdivision deliver *exceptional* returns performance. This is so since they must compensate for an almost equal number of 'Contracting' samples before contributing to the positive returns performance of their overall category. For investors, the value of a 'reliable' measure capable of identifying 'Expanding' stocks is clear.

Returning to the comparison within the three tables, the overall findings are similar to the case of 'All' (valid) samples, in that the migration patterns are ranked 1) to remain in place, 2) to migrate to the adjacent category with higher dividend yield; and 3) to migrate to the adjacent category with lower dividend yield. The main differential finding to emerge is seen most markedly in relation to the migration from zero-dividend category 6 to high-yield category 1, which is now more pronounced, at 7.75% (vs. 6.14%), and from 1 to 6, at 4.60% (vs. 6.08%). (N.B. both sets of figures are expressed in relation to the column / row totals for category 6, as before).

Table 10. Percentage of 'Expanding' samples

D_Quintile	% Expanding
(High) 1	71.36
2	64.89
3	61.70
4	59.41
(Low) 5	54.01
(Zero) 6	51.51
Overall	61.05

The above result is to be expected among 'Expanding' samples; more expanding companies will initiate dividend payments, many of which will therefore migrate from 6 to 1. Fewer will cease dividend payments, moving from 1 to 6. Nevertheless, the concept of 'Adjacency', developed in the last section, continues to apply; as evidenced by the figures presented here.

Finally, Table 9 ('Contracting' samples) is considered. The equivalent percentages to those presented in Table 8 are not shown; trivially, they are represented as (100-a) %, where (a) % is the corresponding value in Table 8. For all categories excepting 5 (lowest dividend-paying quintile), the rankings 2) and 3) (above) are reversed, such that the most frequent tendency among declining 'migrators' is to move to the adjacent category with *lower* dividend yield[3].

---

[2] Among dividend paying stocks, it is possible for 'Contracting' cases to deliver positive returns if the dividend component over-compensates for the capital loss. It is also the case that (for all stocks) the simple market capitalisation measure implies that a minority of samples are influenced by capital changes as well as by returns.

[3] For this to be the case, mathematically, the proportional reduction in the dividend payment must be greater than any reduction in share price brought about by the contraction (on average).

As to the zero-dividend category, there are fewer 'departures' (20.66%), and more 'arrivals' (37.28%). Again, however, the hypothesis of 'Adjacency' to the high-yield category is supported; whilst migration from 6 to 1 is reduced to 3.80% (vs. 6.14%) and that from 1 to 6 increased to 7.66% (vs. 6.08%), these values remain the second highest among 'movers', after category 5 (low yield).

5. Long-Run Equilibrium and Speed of Adjustment

5.1. The Transition Matrix as a Markov Process

Table 7(c) represents historical data over the 40-year period, expressed in terms of the relative frequencies of transition of stocks between categories in a 12-month period. The following section addresses the question of the future patterns of migration, based upon the assumption that the relative frequencies (m) may provide an estimate of transition probabilities in the future. Before proceeding in this direction, however, it is prudent to verify the extent to which the relative frequencies over the entire sample period are sufficiently stable to be taken as reliable estimates of current probabilities.

In order to motivate this particular line of inquiry, a time dimension is appended to the data represented in Table 7(c), to allow the consideration of temporal variation. The number of transitions in each calendar year (from 1959 - 1997) along each transition path involving the zero-dividend category is computed, and plotted as Figure 2.

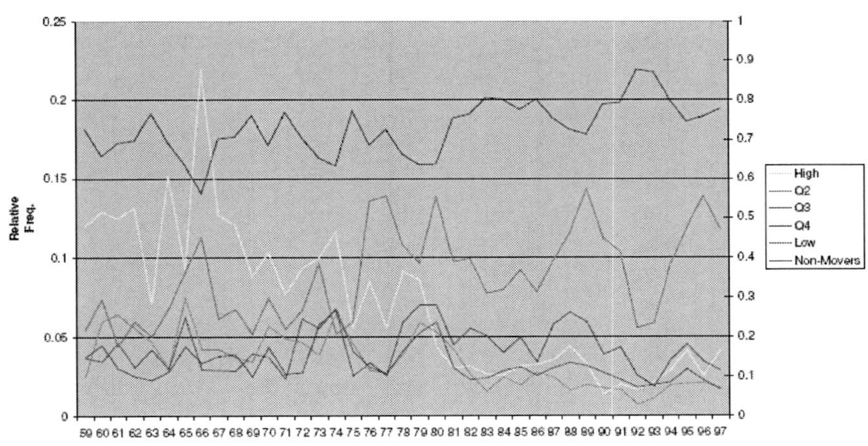

Figure 2. Proportions of Stocks leaving the Zero Dividend category.

From this, it is apparent that an assumption of stationarity prior to 1981 would be difficult to justify; the transition path directly from the zero-dividend category to the high-dividend category, in particular, is volatile in the first decade, and shows a consistent downward trend in the second decade.[4] Only after the second oil price shock of 1979[5] does the characteristic settle sufficiently for reasonable estimates to be made.

As a consequence of the above, the assumption is made that the best estimate of future probabilities derives from the 17-year period 1981-1997, following the 'regime shift' implied by the second oil price shock. The transition matrix is re-computed, restricted to this period.

In this form, the table constitutes a Markov matrix, i.e. a system of equations defining a Markov Process:

$$\begin{Bmatrix} x^1_{t+1} \\ . \\ . \\ x^6_{t+1} \end{Bmatrix} = \begin{Bmatrix} m_{11} & \cdots & m_{1k} \\ \cdots & \cdots & \cdots \\ \cdots & \cdots & \cdots \\ m_{61} & \cdots & m_{66} \end{Bmatrix} \begin{Bmatrix} x^1_t \\ \\ \\ x^6_t \end{Bmatrix}$$

i.e. $x_{t+1} = M\, x_t$

where $\mathbf{x}_{t+1}$ is a (6x1) vector defining the population states of the six yield categories at time (t+1), as a function of the equivalent vector $\mathbf{x}_t$ for time (t) and the Markov matrix (M).

As the process continues into a second period (year), the following equation applies:

$x_{t+2} = M\, x_{t+1} = M.M\, x_t$, i.e. $M^2\, x_t$

and, in general, over n periods, $x_{t+n} = M^n\, x$

In order to ascertain the long-run equilibrium state brought about by the current transition probabilities (as expressed by M), we require to examine the state as $n \rightarrow \infty$. This is facilitated by factoring M , using the non-singular transformation matrix P to create a diagonal matrix D, using the relation:

$M = PDP^{-1}$, (whence $D = P^{-1}MP$)

Here, the factorisation is such that the matrix P is a matrix formed from the *eigenvectors* of M, and D is the diagonal matrix of *eigenvalues* of M.

Also, $M^n = PD^nP^{-1}$

The elements of D^n are such that they are formed directly by raising each of the individual (diagonal) elements of D to the nth power. Since it is a property of a Markov matrix that its largest eigenvalue is unity (Simon and Blume (1994, p. 581)), the structure of D^n is such that it retains the unit eigenvalue, but its remaining eigenvalues tend to zero as n tends to infinity.

The long-run proportions associated with each of the six categories may be determined by examination of the eigenvector associated with the unit eigenvalue. The former is

---

[4] There is a significant transient occurring shortly after the 1965 imposition of Capital Gains Tax in the UK, which is discussed more fully later.

[5] This particular 'time marker' also post-dates the two large step increases in the number of companies in the database, which have the effect of re-defining the constitution of the database to its 'current' composition.

determined up to a scale factor; since the proportions inherently sum to unity, scaling may be performed to accord to this restriction. As an alternative, the matrix multiplication

PD^nP^{-1} may be evaluated (for $n = \infty$), whereupon any of the (identical) columns provides the solution. Table 11 summarises the computations.

Table 11. Computed and Modelled Time Traces of Migration

Number of Years	Computed value m_{66}	Modelled value m_{66}	Error (%)
0	1.00000*	1.00000*	
1	0.78671*	0.78671*	
2	0.63164	0.62820	-0.55
3	0.51737	0.51040	-1.37
4	0.43238	0.42286	-2.26
5	0.36872	0.35780	-3.05
6	0.32080	0.30945	-3.67
7	0.28460	0.27351	-4.05
8	0.25716	0.24681	-4.19
9	0.23633	0.22696	-4.13
10	0.22049	0.21222	-3.90
Long Run	0.16954*	0.16954*	

5.2. The Dynamics of the Process

Table 11 provides an introduction to the dynamics of the process in that it displays proportions of the aggregated sample in the various categories initially, one year later, and finally, projected toward the long run. The more detailed analysis that follows seeks to quantify the speed of adjustment of the process toward that long run. It does so by measuring the time trajectory of the cell 'm_{66}' in the Markov Matrix M, which exhibits the widest dynamic range and which relates specifically to the category of primary interest in this context, namely the zero-dividend Category. Table 11 (Column B) lists the values of this quantity as computed by evaluating $M^n = PD^nP^{-1}$ for a range of values of (n). Column (C) models the trajectory with an exponential function (see below), and column (D) displays the (%) error expressed as 1- (Computed / Modelled).

5.2.1. Model Design

The functional form of the required model was expected to be exponential in nature, given the nature of the process by which the computed values (Column B) were generated. This was verified by evaluation of the following function relating successive computed values:

$$a = \mathrm{Ln}((x_{t+2} - x_{t+1}) / (x_{t+1} - x_t))\, t = 0,1,\ldots,8.$$

The value of (a) was found to be substantially constant at a mean value of -0.289, which confirmed the expectation of an exponential function with an exponent coefficient of this magnitude. Rather than arranging for a 'best fit' based on this value, the coefficient was chosen to drive the fitted exponential curve through the (measured) co-ordinate (1, 0.7867), the implied co-ordinate (0, 1) and the computed long-run co-ordinate (LR, 0.1695). This resulted in an exponent value of -0.297, which was accepted as definitive, based as it was on the chosen co-ordinates, and producing acceptably small errors, albeit all negative (Column D).

The model equation was derived as follows:

$$e^{a} = (0.7876 - 0.1695) / (1 - 0.1695) \Rightarrow a = -0.297$$

from which: $f(t) = e^{-0.297t}(1 - 0.1695) + 0.1695$, the equation of the model generating the values of Column (C).

5.2.2. Interpretation of the Exponent

The exponent (at) is dimensionless, implying that the multiplier (a) has the dimensions of T^{-1} (inverse Time). Taking the (negated) reciprocal of (a) as T = 3.37, this is interpreted as the exponential time constant (expressed in years) required for the process to complete 63% ($1 - e^{-1} = 0.63$) of its transition from any arbitrary point along its trajectory toward the long-run asymptote. This parameter therefore summarises the speed of adjustment towards the long-run equilibrium.

6. Extending the Analysis to Include the 'Time' Dimension

The above analysis has largely treated the migration data as being 'time homogeneous',[6] in the sense that the samples have been hitherto considered without regard to their temporal ordering. The next part of the analysis will utilise this information in order to study the way in which the pattern of migration varies with time. Of primary interest in this context is the relationship between the zero-dividend and dividend-Paying categories. Figure 3 shows the proportions of stocks *arriving in* the zero-dividend category, as a function of both time[7] and of destination category (L/h scale), and the proportion of non-migrating stocks (R/h scale). Figures 4 and 5 show the *monthly* migration patterns between the zero- and high dividend categories (zero to high, and high to zero respectively), expressed as percentages of the whole (valid) sample. Figure 6 indicates the net (difference) migration between the same two categories, on the same basis.

After the 1981 'regime shift', the proportion of stocks leaving the zero-dividend category in favour of the HD category is not dissimilar to the migration from the zero-dividend category to the 'middle' categories (3) and (4). Only the migration to the low yield category dominates. The same conclusion is true of the 'arriving' stocks (Figure 3); however, the volatility of the 'arriving' stocks pattern is clearly higher, and may be seen to follow the pattern of the business cycle, with local maxima coinciding with the recessions of 1981/2 and 1991/2. The net migration characteristic (Figure 6) indicates a positive mean migration of 0.107% from the HD to the zero-dividend category over the period Jan. 1981 to Dec. 1997. In

6 Except for the subdivision of the period into an earlier and a later sub-period, for the purposes of the estimation of migration probabilities.

7 Data is aggregated by calendar year.

effect, the stocks 'captured' by the zero-dividend category during periods of recession were not fully relinquished in periods of economic 'boom'.

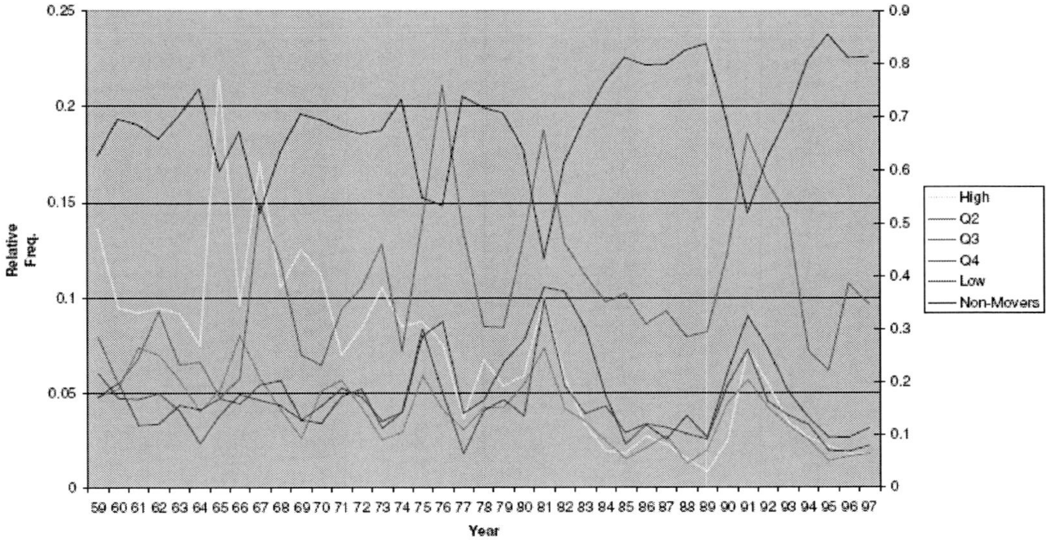

Figure 3. Proportions of Stocks arriving in the Zero Dividend category.

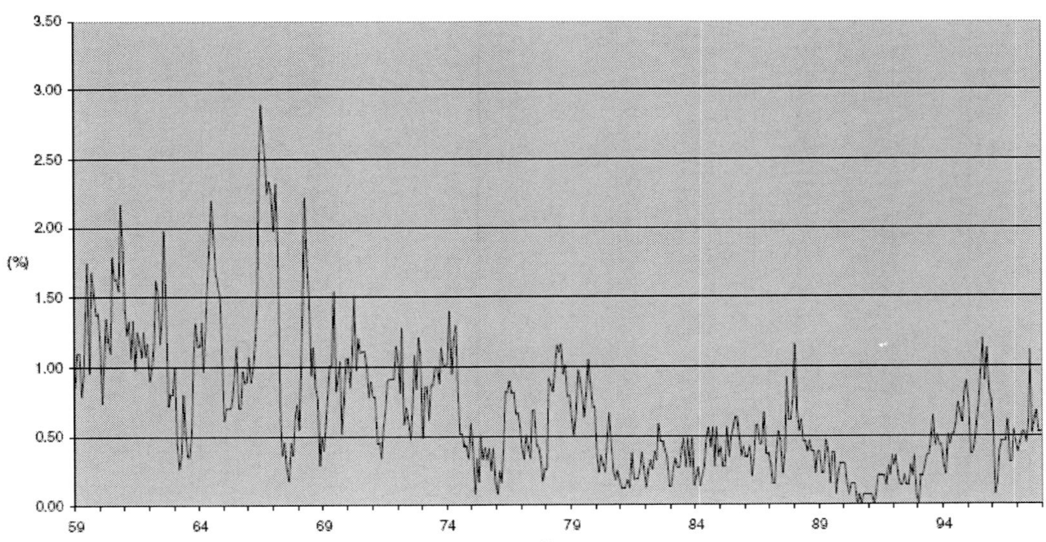

Figure 4. Monthly Migration; Zero-Dividend -> High-Dividend categories (1959-1997).

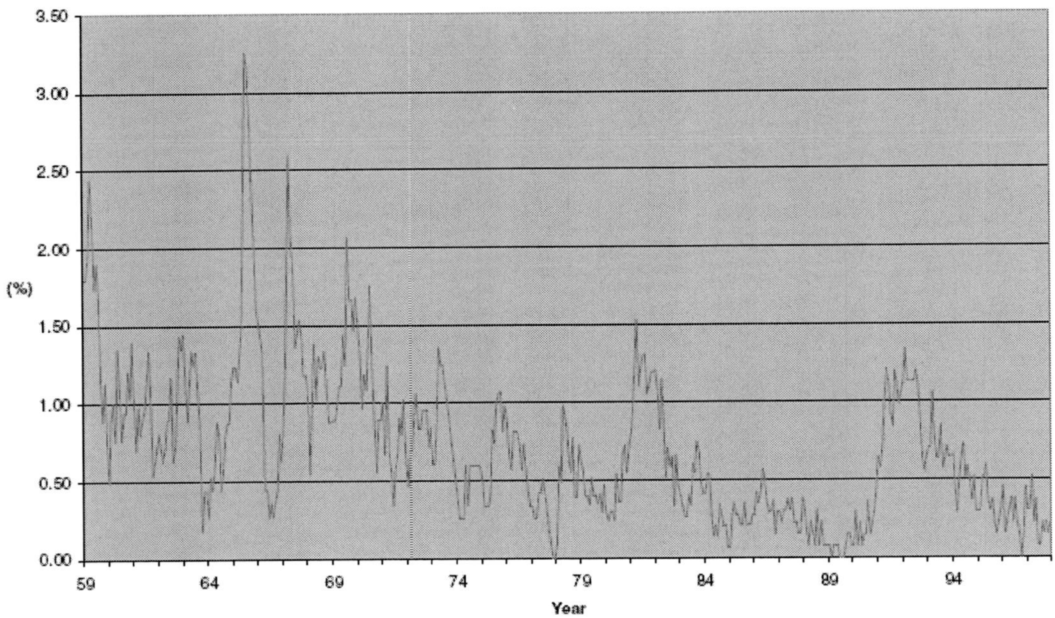

Figure 5. Monthly Migration; High-Dividend -> Zero-Dividend categories (1959-1997).

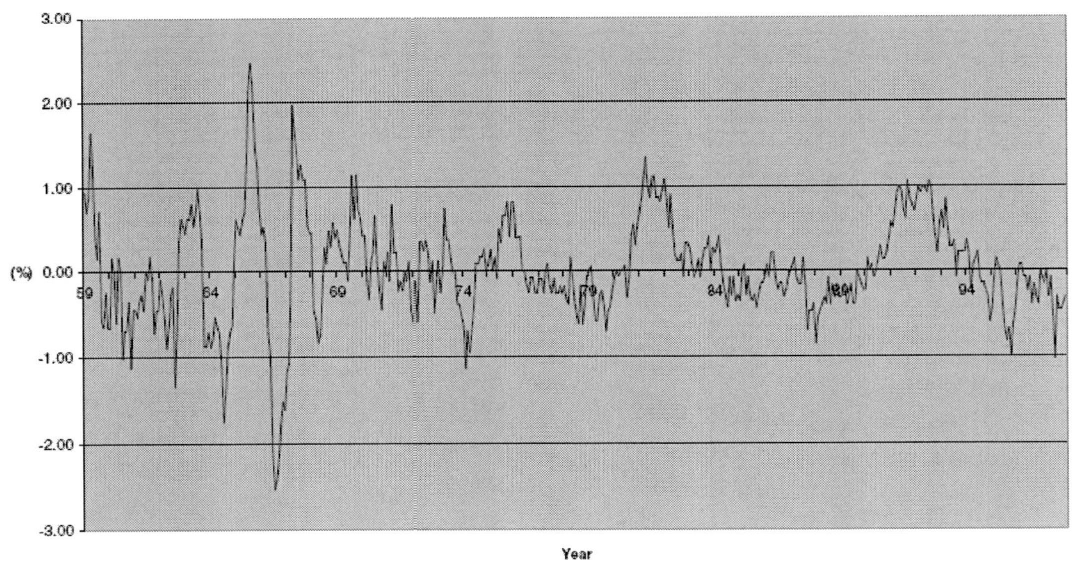

Figure 6. Net Monthly Direct Migration between High and Zero-Dividend Categories (1959-1997).

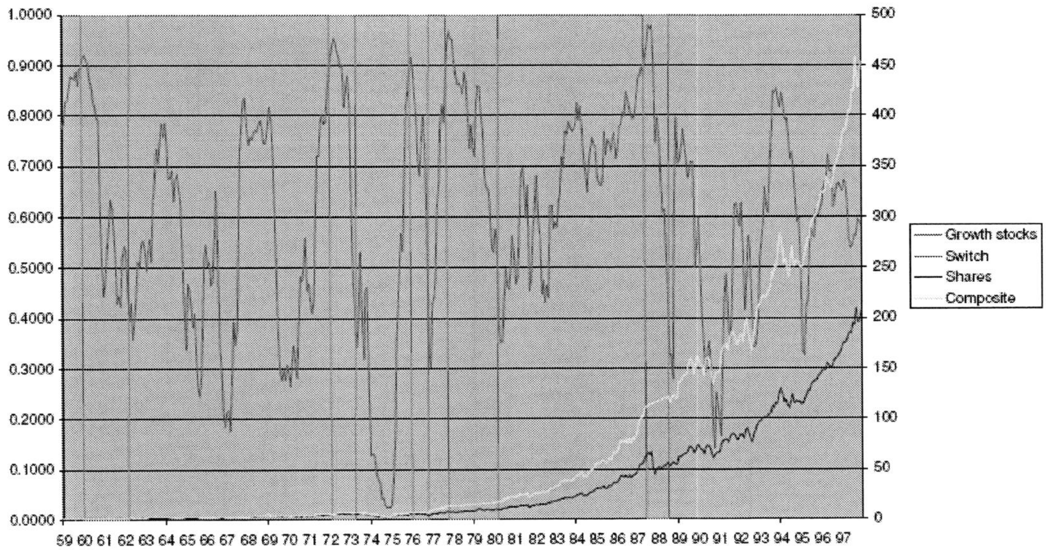

Figure 7. Ratio of Y-Y Growth stocks to all stocks (1959-1997).

The close linkage of stock characteristics to the economic cycle also manifests itself in terms of the ratio of Expanding stocks[8] to all stocks, over time (Figure 7). Clearly, this parameter is bounded (by construction) in the range $0<\eta<1$; empirically, it traverses this range almost fully, with a maximum of 0.979 (August, 1987) and minimum 0.0239 (October 1974). Figure 7 also constructs a total returns index (Dec.1958 = 1) and compares this with the index resulting from a naïve, perfect-foresight trading rule which switches between the stock index and treasury bills, as follows. If bonds are held, then factor the previous month's index by the growth (over the month) of T-bills; otherwise, factor by the growth of the stock index. The investment state (S= 0 or 1, bonds or stocks) is determined by a switching rule, as follows. If bonds are currently held, check the ratio (η) against the *lower* threshold; if above, stay in bonds, otherwise switch to stocks. If stocks are held, check the ratio (η) against the *upper* threshold; if below, stay in stocks, otherwise switch to bonds. Optimum values for the switching thresholds were determined by grid search to be (0.4, 0.9), resulting in a factor 2.19 increase in the index from 207 to 453.

CONCLUSION

Based on the full sample of data, it is possible to conclude that the concept of the 'U - shaped' relationship between returns and dividend yield may be based upon an over-simplified view of the true relationship between zero-dividend and dividend paying stocks. The migration evidence, taken together with the market capitalisation distribution evidence, would suggest that a more apposite model might be a circular, rather than a linear one. This would continue to place categories in an ordered fashion, but with categories 1 and 6 adjacent, much as the figures on a clock face place 12 and 1 adjacent.

[8] Defined in terms of stocks exhibiting strictly positive year on year increase in Market Capitalisation.

Such a model would reflect the degree of qualitative similarity between members of the two - formerly regarded as 'extreme' - categories; both in terms of their general size characteristics and in terms of the way in which changes in their evolution with time give rise to a significant proportion of direct inter-migration of their constituents (in either direction).

In the light of the evidence as presented, it is possible to conjecture as to the mechanisms which stimulate migration between these two categories, taking account of the influences also of Expansion and Contraction. Given the generally smaller size of the companies in these two groups, it would seem probable that, in the case of Expanding companies, they reach a point in their evolution whereby maturing product life cycles produce an excess of revenue over and above that required for investment. This provides the opportunity to pay dividends; payment of a relatively high dividend may attract the attention of investors in the market, and pave the way for future continued expansion.

In contrast, declining firms may elect to maintain dividends even in the face of financial distress, in order to avoid the 'stigma' associated with cutting dividends. As the share price falls, in the face of such distress, the yield will rise; thereby assuring their place, eventually, in the high yield category. There will inevitably come a time, in many instances, when this policy simply cannot be maintained, due to lack of earnings capacity. The fall into the zero-dividend category is then equally assured. Nevertheless, in some instances, the removal of the drain on resources caused by the perceived obligation to continue dividends may initiate a recovery; should this happen, and dividends be resumed, a low share price would militate toward a high yield - the cycle potentially repeats.

The analysis of the transition matrix indicates that the proportion of zero-dividend stocks among the universe of all UK quoted stocks is increasing in such a way as to gravitate toward a state in which over one in six stocks (at any one time) will pay no dividend (assuming no change in the migrating proportions within the transition matrix). This represents an increase of approximately one-quarter in that proportion. Moreover, the dynamics of this process are such that an exponential process with a time constant of approximately three years describes the speed of adjustment.

REFERENCES

Blume, M.E., (1980), "Stock Returns and Dividend Yields: Some More Evidence". *The Review of Economics and Statistics* 62, 567-577.

Christie,W.G., (1990), "Dividend Yield and Expected Returns: The Zero Dividend Puzzle". *Journal of Financial Economics* 28, 95-125.

Fama, E.F., French, K.R., (2007), "Migration", *Financial Analysts Journal*, 63 (3), 48-58.

Keim, D., (1985), "Dividend Yields and Stock Returns: Implications of Abnormal January Returns". *Journal of Financial Economics* 14, 473-489.

McManus, I.D., (2001) "Empirical Models of Asset Pricing: with particular reference to the modeling of Zero-Dividend Stocks" Unpublished PhD. Thesis, University of Southampton, U.K.

McManus, I.D., ap Gwilym, O. and Thomas, S.H., (2004), "The Role of Payout Ratio in the Relationship between Stock Returns and Dividend Yield". *Journal of Business Finance and Accounting* 31, 1355-1387.

Morgan, G., and Thomas, S.H., (1998), "Taxes, Dividend Yields and Returns in the U.K. Equity Market". *Journal of Banking and Finance* 22, 405-423.

Simon, C.P., and Blume, L. (1994) *Mathematics for Economists*. W.W. Norton and Company, New York and London.

In: Financial Asset Pricing
Editors: P. E. Schulz and B. P. Hoffmann
ISBN 978-1-61122-803-8

Chapter 3

Return Calculation for Short Time Series: Evidence from Emerging Market Mutual Funds

Péter Erdős[1] and Mihály Ormos[2*]
[1]Department of Finance, Budapest University of Technology and Economics, Budapest, Műegyetem rkp. 9., 1111, HUNGARY
[2]Department of Finance, Budapest University of Technology and Economics, Budapest, HUNGARY

Abstract

We study the methodology of return calculation in international mutual funds with investment in emerging markets particularly those with short market history. Besides daily and monthly returns we introduce a new procedure: the daily recalculated monthly returns (*DRMRs*) and investigate which is the adequate method for testing market efficiency and measuring fund performance. DRMR represents the log returns of the previous month (assuming 21 trading days in a month) and is recalculated day by day for the studied period. We show that DRMR is effective for all assets and markets for which there is no suitably long time series available.

Keywords: Return calculation; International CAPM; Mutual fund performance.

I. Introduction

We focus on return calculation when the main scope is performance measurement or testing market efficiency of debuting mutual funds in recently liberalized financial markets. Concentrating on these assets and markets, only short time series are available where annual or monthly returns cannot be used. We propose using a method for calculating the returns in

[*] Email: ormos@finance.bme.hu

empirical finance: we recalculate the monthly returns day by day assuming 21 trading days in each month which results in a daily recalculated monthly return (*DRMR*) time series. This method is widely used in the mutual fund industry for informing investors about the return of the previous month but not used in the academic literature. Using our procedure the number of observations is large enough to estimate a system of equations suitable for GRS test (Gibbons et. al, 1989) even when there is, for example, only a one-year-long time series available. The reliability of the parameters is better than that of resulting from monthly returns; while the goodness of fitting is better using DRMR comparing with simple monthly and daily returns.

Several authors apply monthly returns (e.g., Fama and MacBeth, 1973; Fama and French, 1992, 1995, 1996 a, b, 2006; Black et al., 1972; Elton et al., 1995, 1996) for testing the Capital Asset Pricing Model (CAPM) using at least five-year-long time series. Papers on mutual funds performance investigate whether portfolio managers can beat the market. The abnormal return can be determined by the alpha of the market model (Jensen, 1968). If the alpha is statistically not different from zero, the asset studied gains normal return. Several authors (e.g., Sharpe, 1966; Jensen, 1968; Kothari et al., 1995) use annual returns to measure decade-long mutual fund performance. These methods are adequate for a suitably long time series. However, if a shorter period is to be studied, the span horizon of returns is a key issue. If we use daily returns to obtain a long enough time series, the fitting of the market model deteriorates which means the standard errors of the parameters are greater. The univariate asset pricing tests are based on t-statistics which can sign no abnormal performance erroneously if the standard error of the regression is great. The GRS test is based on a multivariate t-statistics therefore if the standard errors of the regressions are great the type II error can be unacceptable.

We apply International CAPM to compare the statistical properties of the estimations using daily, monthly and daily recalculated monthly returns when time series are short. We use Morgan Stanley Capital International (MSCI) All Countries World Index as a market proxy to measure the performance of the international mutual funds listed in Bloomberg.

Generally the GRS test and the Fama-MacBeth procedure are used for testing market efficiency. But these tests have strong statistical assumptions, as normally distributed, homoskedastic, and non-autocorrelated residuals are essential for the GRS test. If we use a short time series, the normality of monthly returns cannot be rejected. However, if we use longer time series, let's say at least 80 months simple monthly returns are not normal; on the other hand, the residuals of the market model still remain homoskedastic and non-autocorrelated. Assuming normality for a short time series (e.g., less than one-year) can be misleading because the Type II error is too great. We show that monthly and DRMRs have the same distribution since we can consider monthly returns as a systematic sample of DRMRs. We show that DRMRs are highly non-normal, which means monthly returns cannot be normal, either. Autocorrelation can be eliminated with systematic sampling, but the distribution is inherited in DRMRs.

If we know that the market model residuals do not behave like white noise, we still have the possibility to test efficiency or measure performance if the time series are long enough. We can apply asymptotic chi-square asset pricing tests under general conditions (see, e.g., Cochrane, 2001). If there is only a several-month-long monthly return time series available, we cannot derive appropriate asymptotic asset pricing tests. We can use daily returns; but as Morse (1984), Brown and Warner (1985) point out the fitting of the market model is better in the case of monthly returns. Fama (1976) also states that monthly returns are better working approximations than daily returns. In our data daily returns perform worse: the average R^2 is 55%, while in the case of monthly returns it is 62%. There are three different causes why we can see differences in fitting between monthly and daily returns as Morse (1984) shows: 1, there is a measurement error in the market proxy; 2, there is a measurement error in mutual fund's returns; 3, daily returns are not stationary.

We show that all the three types of returns are stationary according to ADF (Augmented Dickey-Fuller) tests (Dickey and Fuller, 1981) so the third story is not likely which means that the different goodness of fittings are attributable to measurement error. We show that DRMRs are less sensitive to measurement error either in the dependent variable or in the independent variable which is a preferable property because there is measurement error in the variables, otherwise the R^2s would be the same for daily and monthly returns. Higher R^2s means the squared error of the estimation is smaller thus inducing more reliable parameter estimations.

If we want to measure performance of debuting assets or test market efficiency of newly traded markets we propose the use of DRMRs especially if there is measurement error either in the assets' return or in the market proxy. We prefer the DRMRs to the two rival methods. Daily returns are more sensitive to measurement error resulting in low R^2s and monthly returns are applicable when time series are too short. The latter arises if you want to measure asset performance or test market efficiency by a system of equations (see e.g., Gibbons et al., 1989) and the number of assets multiplied by the number of parameters is larger than the number of observations.

In addition, there is also practical reason to support DRMRs. Monthly returns show the gain or loss over a particular month assuming an investment exactly at the beginning of the month. Investors are rather interested in actual monthly gain/loss which can be represented more precisely by DRMRs because they compare day-on-day (assuming 21 trading days in each month) not like monthly returns. If you use monthly returns, you may compare, for example, Friday with Monday. Measuring returns between different days of the week is not adequate because there is reason to assume that returns of different days show a different pattern (see e.g., Chen, Singal, 2003). Further, in the paper we are seeking for answers to the right choice of data resolution considering the pros and cons.

In Section II. we show that DRMRs induce the best fitting of the market model and they are the least sensitive to measurement errors either in the mutual fund's return or in the market proxy. In Section III. we show the invalidity of the assumptions of standard asset pricing tests. Daily and daily recalculated monthly returns are not normally distributed, heteroskedastic and serially dependent. Monthly returns seem to be normal only in small samples but they are a systematic sample of DRMR population. In the final section of the paper we summarize our findings.

II. Goodness of Fitting

Differences between daily and monthly returns are represented by the Single World Index Model of Solnik (1974). We use *GMM* (Generalized Method of Moments, Hansen, 1982) estimation testing the returns of 26 international open-ended mutual funds incorporated in the

USA. Our data contain mutual funds listed in Bloomberg Mutual Fund Center and have at least a two-year market history; they exclude ETFs, REITs and institutional mutual funds. Analysis is carried out for the period from June 2003 to April 2008. Our mutual fund data are not free of survivorship bias (see e.g., Elton et. al,1996) but it does not affect our purpose to prove, DRMRs provide better working approximation than daily or monthly returns if the time series are short.

Solnik's model can be estimated as the CAPM with a global market portfolio,

$$R_{i,t} = \alpha_i + \beta_i(R_{m,t}) + \varepsilon_{i,t} \quad i = 1,2,...,N; \quad t = 1,2,...,T \ , \qquad (1)$$

where $R_{i,t}$ and $R_{m,t}$ are the mutual fund risk premium and the market risk premium respectively. Continuously compounded returns are calculated in US dollars.

We use Morgan Stanley Capital International (MSCI) All Countries World Index as the market proxy and the one-month US Treasury Bill returns by Ibbotson Associates as the risk-free rate. Fama and French (1998) use their own world index containing the components of MSCI EAFE (Europe, Asia and Far East) Index and the MSCI USA index additionally for international asset pricing. De Santis and Gerard (1997) use MSCI World Index for international asset pricing of developed countries. The investment focus of the mutual funds in our data is not restricted to the EAFE+US countries so we choose a broader index which includes emerging markets as well.

The regional exposure and the style of each mutual fund can be seen in Table 1.

Table 1. Regional exposures and styles

Panel A: Mutual fund number 1-13

	1	*2*	*3*	*4*	*5*	*6*	*7*	*8*	*9*	*10*	*11*	*12*	*13*
Regional	Greater	China	Greater	Greater	Greater	Russia	Russia	Korea	UK	EM	EM	Global	Global
Style	LB	LV	LB	LG	LG	N/A	N/A	LB	SB	LB	LB	MG	LB

Panel B: Mutual fund number 13-26

	14	*15*	*16*	*17*	*18*	*19*	*20*	*21*	*22*	*23*	*24*	*25*	*26*
Regional	Global	Global	Global	Global	Global	Global	Europe	Greater	Latin	Latin	Nordic	Southeast	Asia ex-
Style	LV	LG	LB	LG	MB	LG	LB	LG	LB	LG	LG	LV	LG

This table shows regional exposures and styles of mutual funds included in the data set. EM stands for Emerging Markets. L, M, S, stand for large, mid and small cap, and V, B, G indicates the investment style, value, blend and growth respectively using Morningstar's database.

As table 2 shows the goodness of fitting in the case of monthly returns measured by R^2 is seven percentage points higher than that of the daily returns (We have to note that R^2 is not suitable for direct comparisons if the dependent variables are different.We use it for illustrative purpose as Morse (1984), and Warner and Brown (1985).). The average R^2 calculated on the basis of daily returns is 55%, which is lower than the 62% statistics of monthly returns. Monthly returns have better R^2s in 21 cases out of 26. Significant improvement can be observed in some cases if monthly return is used instead of daily, particularly in mutual fund number 2, 21, 26. The deterioration is less significant in five cases. Average R^2s are relatively high compared with the results of Fama and French (1998) for country portfolios of 12 EAFE countries plus the US. Using monthly returns their average R^2 is only 39%.

Table 2. International CAPM estimated by GMM regressions using daily, monthly and daily recalculated monthly returns

$$R_{i,t} = \alpha_i + \beta_i(R_{m,t}) + \varepsilon_{i,t} \quad i = 1,2,\ldots,26; \; t = 1,2,\ldots,T$$

No.	A					B					C				
	α	$t(\alpha)$	β	$t(\beta)$	R^2	α	$t(\alpha)$	β	$t(\beta)$	R^2	α	$t(\alpha)$	β	$t(\beta)$	R^2
1	0.06	1.43	1.27	18.54	0.51	1.29	1.09	1.55	5.20	0.55	0.69	0.81	1.52	9.55	0.69
2	0.04	1.33	0.84	14.16	0.25	0.28	0.48	1.53	7.08	0.53	0.07	0.15	1.38	12.32	0.63
3	0.04	1.13	1.30	20.37	0.39	0.60	0.77	1.59	6.55	0.47	0.22	0.30	1.59	9.69	0.59
4	0.03	1.19	1.15	21.12	0.39	0.36	0.56	1.67	7.69	0.56	0.10	0.16	1.52	10.39	0.61
5	0.08	1.69	1.35	16.59	0.48	1.54	1.80	1.77	5.66	0.61	0.96	0.99	1.77	11.15	0.71
6	0.07	1.71	1.13	16.80	0.24	1.12	1.37	1.44	3.64	0.29	0.70	0.61	1.46	5.82	0.37
7	0.06	1.76	0.83	15.90	0.21	0.91	1.09	1.27	3.73	0.26	0.60	0.49	1.28	5.13	0.35
8	0.02	0.74	1.16	22.67	0.36	0.27	0.53	1.37	9.09	0.48	0.03	0.05	1.29	9.53	0.52
9	0.02	1.06	0.96	25.25	0.51	0.33	0.82	1.04	5.42	0.45	-0.02	-0.03	1.05	8.56	0.57
10	0.04	2.41	1.37	36.48	0.70	0.71	1.56	1.58	7.89	0.73	0.35	0.67	1.56	9.53	0.77
11	0.04	2.25	1.37	36.81	0.70	0.65	1.41	1.58	7.87	0.73	0.30	0.57	1.56	9.49	0.77
12	-0.02	-0.71	1.61	34.94	0.54	0.10	0.20	1.37	7.48	0.44	-0.34	-0.56	1.49	10.20	0.59
13	0.03	4.60	0.59	47.42	0.77	0.48	4.05	0.67	16.52	0.82	0.32	2.22	0.63	15.86	0.83
14	-0.01	-0.96	1.09	45.34	0.77	0.07	0.53	0.87	13.31	0.75	-0.24	-1.41	0.99	13.97	0.85
15	0.01	2.00	1.03	76.13	0.88	0.30	1.97	1.02	19.63	0.89	0.05	0.33	1.00	22.96	0.91
16	0.01	1.14	0.93	60.21	0.82	0.11	0.66	1.05	20.12	0.83	-0.11	-0.52	1.02	19.10	0.86
17	0.00	0.09	1.24	65.67	0.83	0.21	1.04	1.04	16.82	0.84	-0.18	-1.39	1.15	26.24	0.90
18	0.05	3.53	1.09	31.39	0.66	0.87	2.52	1.39	12.26	0.70	0.53	1.31	1.36	12.96	0.77
19	0.02	1.55	1.33	48.42	0.75	0.48	2.20	1.20	16.27	0.75	0.07	0.33	1.32	21.13	0.85
20	0.01	0.88	1.22	42.91	0.68	0.23	0.84	1.27	13.64	0.70	-0.06	-0.19	1.24	13.48	0.76
21	0.08	1.85	0.99	13.45	0.20	0.65	0.61	2.13	7.64	0.50	0.63	0.59	1.72	6.11	0.47
22	0.07	2.47	1.79	32.28	0.58	1.49	2.54	1.65	6.57	0.55	0.91	1.58	1.80	10.52	0.70
23	0.05	1.80	1.80	32.29	0.56	1.19	2.03	1.58	6.27	0.53	0.64	1.14	1.74	10.73	0.68
24	0.02	1.25	1.31	35.59	0.63	0.37	1.25	1.46	15.55	0.75	0.12	0.45	1.37	24.80	0.80
25	0.04	1.62	1.19	23.99	0.46	0.56	0.97	1.62	9.33	0.64	0.24	0.41	1.57	9.99	0.68
26	0.04	1.89	1.04	26.66	0.48	0.53	1.56	1.38	13.06	0.70	0.22	0.65	1.34	15.96	0.74
Ave	**0.03**		**1.19**		**0.55**	**0.60**		**1.39**		**0.62**	**0.26**		**1.37**		**0.69**

This table shows the alphas, betas and their *t-statistic*s of the market model using daily, monthly and daily recalculated monthly returns in panel A, B, C respectively. We use the Morgan Stanley Capital International (MSCI) All Countries World Index as the market proxy. *t(α)* and *t(β)* are t-statistics with Heteroskedasticity and Autocorrelation Consistent (HAC) standard errors (Andrews 1991). R^2s are not adjusted with degrees of freedom.

If conditions of asset pricing tests (normality, homoskedasticity, serial independence) are not met, we propose the use of DRMRs which are more appropriate for large sample tests if the time series is not long enough, and the fitting of the market model is even better than in the case of monthly returns.

Figure 1 shows the characteristic lines of monthly and daily returns of the same mutual fund in Panel A and Panel B respectively. Fitting is better in the case of monthly returns because they spread around the regression line randomly, on the other hand, daily returns concentrate.

Comparing Table 2 panel C with regressions on monthly returns (Table 2 panel B), we can see that the estimated betas are approximately the same. The average R^2 is significantly better than in the case of daily and monthly returns. In 20 cases out of 21 (monthly returns in 21 cases were better than daily ones) further improvement can be recognized if we use DRMRs instead of monthly returns. In four out of five cases when monthly returns fail to be better than daily ones, DRMRs do a better job than monthly returns. There is only one mutual fund in our data set which produces higher R^2 with monthly returns, although the difference is only 3 percentage points. DRMRs' fitting is significantly better than daily returns' and even better than that of the monthly returns'.

Let us assume that only a one-year-long time series is available and the performance of a specific asset is to be measured. If we use simple monthly returns only twelve data points would be available for the estimation. It does not remain without consequences: goodness of fitting decreases dramatically. As an illustration, we choose one mutual fund from our data set and compare fitting of DRMRs with monthly returns.

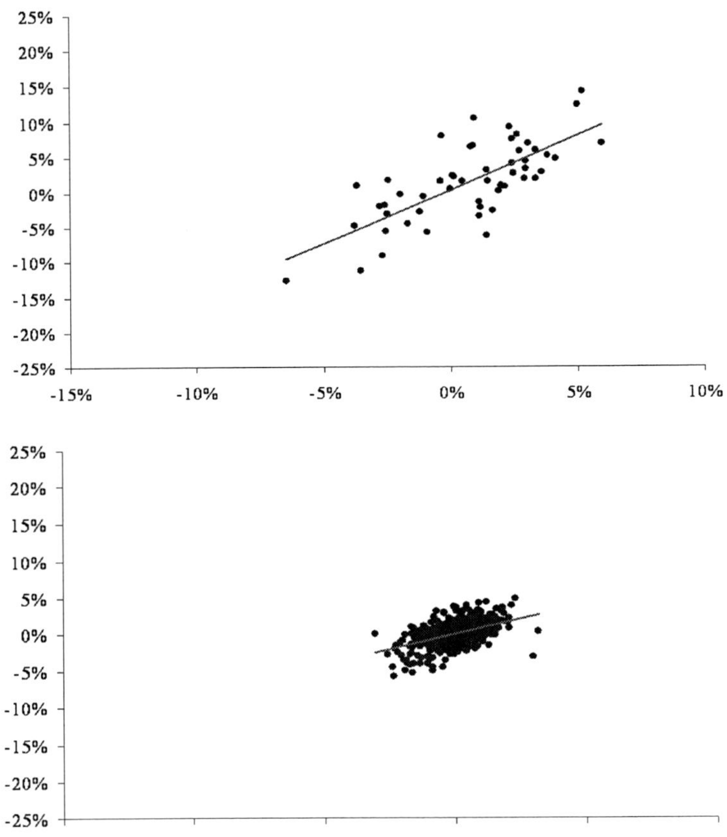

Notes: Characteristic line $(R_{2,t}=\alpha_2+\beta_2(R_{m,t})+\varepsilon_{2,t})$ of mutual fund number 2 based on monthly and daily return in Panel A and B respectively. Mutual fund number 2 is chosen for illustration because it has much better fitting when monthly returns are used instead of daily.

Figure 1. Characteristic line $(R_{2,t}=\alpha_2+\beta_2(R_{m,t})+\varepsilon_{2,t})$ of mutual fund number 2. Legend: x axis is $R_{m,t}$ (market risk premium), y axis is $R_{2,t}$ (risk premium of mutual fund number 2).

On Figure 3, Panel A the data points are spread in a well defined band around the regression line, therefore fitting is adequate. In the case of monthly returns (Panel B) the fitting is worse.

Running the CAPM regression produces similar fitting in both monthly methods which means that recalculating the monthly returns daily gives at least as good fitting as we can see in the case of simple monthly returns, however much shorter time interval is enough for an adequate analysis.

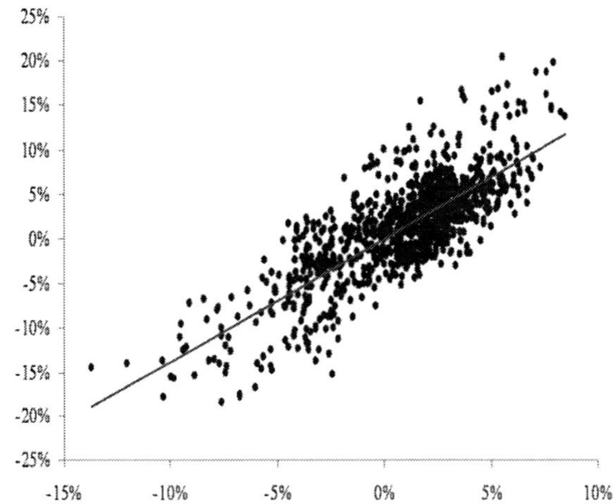

Notes: Mutual fund number 19 is chosen for illustration because its $\boldsymbol{R}^2$ is equal to the average of the 26 market model regressions included in our paper when using *DRMR*s.

Figure 2. Characteristic line $(R_{19,t}=\alpha_{19}+\beta_{19}(R_{m,t})+\varepsilon_{19,t})$ of mutual fund number 19 using daily recalculated monthly returns (*DRMR*s). *x* axis is $R_{m,t}$ (market risk premium), *y* axis is $R_{19,t}$ (risk premium of mutual fund number 19).

There can be different causes of the inequality of R^2s of monthly and daily returns. If there is no measurement error and the daily returns are stationary the R^2s would be the same independently of the method of return calculation (see Morse, 1984 for the proof).

We assume that there is measurement error at least in the market proxy because of imperfect market portfolio (see e.g., Roll, 1977). DRMRs, daily and monthly returns are stationary at any usual significance level based on ADF tests.

We test the effect of deliberately added random errors to the mutual funds' returns and to the market proxy using the Monte Carlo experiment. We find that DRMRs are the least and daily returns are the most sensitive to measurement errors.

We generate numbers from Student t-distribution with four degrees of freedom. Then we estimate the following models:

$$\begin{aligned} &a, \quad R_{i,t}=\alpha_i'+\beta_i'\left(R_{m,t}+c\tau_t\right)+\varepsilon_{i,t}' \quad i=1,2,\dots,N; \quad t=1,2,\dots,T \\ &b, \quad \left(R_{i,t}+c'\tau_t'\right)=\alpha_i''+\beta_i''R_{m,t}+\varepsilon_{i,t}'' \quad i=1,2,\dots,N; \quad t=1,2,\dots,T \end{aligned}, \qquad (2)$$

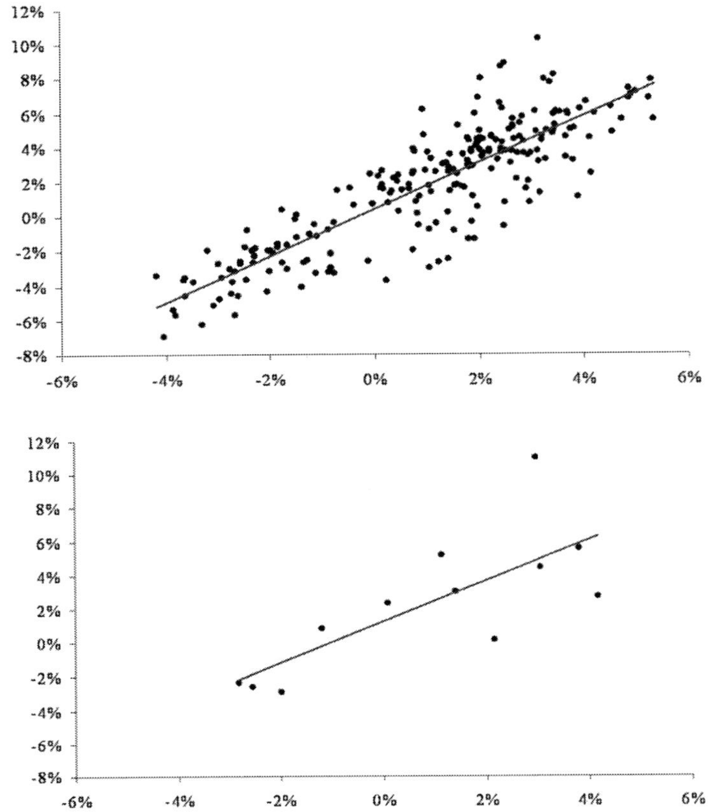

Notes: Figure shows characteristic lines $(R_{19,t}=\alpha_{19}+\beta_{19}(R_{m,t})+\varepsilon_{19,t})$ of mutual fund number 19 in the case of daily recalculated monthly returns (*DRMR*s) on Panel A, and in the case of monthly returns on Panel B for the year 2005. Mutual fund number 19 is chosen for illustration because its $\boldsymbol{R}^2$ is equal to the average of the 26 market model regressions included in our paper when using *DRMR*s.

Figure 3. Characteristic line $(R_{19,t}=\alpha_{19}+\beta_{19}(R_{m,t})+\varepsilon_{19,t})$ of mutual fund number 19. x axis is $R_{m,t}$ (market risk premium), y axis is $R_{19,t}$ (risk premium of mutual fund number 19).

where τ is the generated random error from t-distribution, and c is a constant which ensures the variance of the new variable to be (market proxy/mutual funds' returns plus the generated error) 1.2, 1.4,…,2 times more than the original variable. We use t-distribution with four degrees of freedom because it makes the distribution of the (in)dependent variable fat-tailed, which is a typical feature of asset returns. We choose four degrees of freedom to ensure to be the first four moments of the distribution finite.

Table 3 shows that DRMRs are the least sensitive to measurement error. If we use DRMRs and add random errors to the market proxy (mutual fund's returns) which makes the variance 1.2 times the original, the market model's R^2 is 45.22% (57.58%) on average. Adding random errors to daily returns the average R^2 is 37.19% (46.19%) and to monthly returns it is 39.57% (51.31%).

Table 3. The effect of random errors on the market proxy and the mutual funds' returns

	Panel A						Panel B					
	1.0	1.2	1.4	1.6	1.8	2.0	1.0	1.2	1.4	1.6	1.8	2.0
						Daily returns						
1	51.38	31.69	22.98	18.04	14.86	12.65	51.38	43.06	37.11	32.62	29.12	26.30
2	24.89	15.70	11.51	9.09	7.51	6.40	24.89	20.83	17.92	15.74	14.03	12.67
3	38.67	21.05	14.51	11.08	8.98	7.55	38.67	32.51	28.07	24.70	22.06	19.94
4	39.33	23.69	16.99	13.26	10.87	9.22	39.33	33.02	28.47	25.04	22.35	20.19
5	47.57	27.30	19.21	14.85	12.12	10.25	47.57	39.83	34.31	30.16	26.92	24.32
6	24.19	12.22	8.21	6.19	4.98	4.17	24.19	20.44	17.69	15.61	13.96	12.64
7	21.27	13.14	9.54	7.50	6.18	5.27	21.27	17.88	15.43	13.58	12.13	10.96
8	35.61	19.66	13.62	10.43	8.46	7.12	35.61	29.41	25.05	21.83	19.35	17.38
9	51.06	38.11	30.44	25.35	21.73	19.02	51.06	42.96	37.11	32.67	29.19	26.39
10	69.60	45.83	34.22	27.32	22.76	19.51	69.60	58.42	50.37	44.29	39.52	35.69
11	69.74	45.99	34.36	27.45	22.87	19.61	69.74	58.55	50.49	44.40	39.62	35.78
12	53.90	27.99	18.96	14.36	11.56	9.68	53.90	45.39	39.15	34.43	30.73	27.75
13	77.37	71.14	65.82	61.25	57.28	53.79	77.37	64.63	55.52	48.68	43.35	39.08
14	77.45	58.70	47.30	39.63	34.12	29.96	77.45	64.23	54.87	47.90	42.52	38.22
15	88.02	70.88	59.36	51.08	44.84	39.97	88.02	73.44	63.02	55.21	49.13	44.26
16	81.65	67.09	57.00	49.57	43.86	39.33	81.65	67.91	58.16	50.87	45.22	40.70
17	83.31	60.61	47.67	39.32	33.47	29.14	83.31	69.30	59.32	51.86	46.09	41.47
18	65.53	49.06	39.22	32.69	28.04	24.56	65.53	55.17	47.68	42.00	37.53	33.94
19	75.10	51.24	38.93	31.42	26.36	22.71	75.10	62.78	53.94	47.30	42.12	37.97
20	68.03	47.20	36.17	29.35	24.71	21.35	68.03	56.44	48.28	42.20	37.49	33.73
21	20.46	10.93	7.49	5.71	4.63	3.90	20.46	17.30	14.98	13.22	11.83	10.70
22	57.93	28.25	18.74	14.04	11.23	9.37	57.93	48.79	42.14	37.09	33.13	29.94
23	56.40	26.98	17.79	13.29	10.62	8.85	56.40	47.53	41.06	36.14	32.28	29.18
24	62.84	40.86	30.32	24.13	20.04	17.15	62.84	52.49	45.10	39.55	35.23	31.76
25	46.10	28.39	20.55	16.12	13.27	11.28	46.10	38.42	32.97	28.88	25.70	23.16
26	48.21	33.23	25.39	20.56	17.28	14.91	48.21	40.21	34.49	30.21	26.88	24.22
Average	55.22	37.19	28.70	23.58	20.10	17.57	55.22	46.19	39.72	34.85	31.06	28.01
						Monthly returns						
1	55.26	31.61	23.02	18.51	15.74	13.85	55.26	47.47	41.69	37.30	33.85	31.06
2	53.48	30.09	21.40	16.83	14.01	12.09	53.48	45.20	39.23	34.73	31.21	28.38
3	46.96	23.46	16.14	12.51	10.34	8.90	46.96	39.52	34.25	30.28	27.18	24.69
4	55.78	28.47	19.66	15.25	12.59	10.81	55.78	46.48	40.07	35.29	31.58	28.61
5	61.06	32.14	22.74	18.02	15.18	13.27	61.06	51.88	45.43	40.59	36.79	33.73
6	28.92	13.31	9.11	7.16	6.03	5.29	28.92	24.28	21.04	18.62	16.73	15.22
7	26.45	13.20	9.20	7.28	6.15	5.40	26.45	22.25	19.28	17.06	15.33	13.94
8	47.73	24.22	16.54	12.69	10.38	8.83	47.73	38.33	32.19	27.83	24.56	22.02
9	45.06	29.75	22.59	18.39	15.62	13.65	45.06	37.24	31.82	27.83	24.78	22.36
10	73.01	44.73	32.66	25.94	21.64	18.66	73.01	61.23	52.80	46.48	41.56	37.62
11	73.11	44.68	32.59	25.86	21.58	18.60	73.11	61.32	52.88	46.55	41.63	37.68
12	44.04	24.97	17.85	14.11	11.81	10.25	44.04	37.97	33.13	29.40	26.45	24.06
13	81.52	72.17	64.79	58.83	53.92	49.80	81.52	66.24	55.79	48.27	42.59	38.15
14	74.82	62.00	52.96	46.34	41.29	37.29	74.82	61.53	52.33	45.60	40.46	36.40
15	88.58	71.92	60.64	52.54	46.42	41.64	88.58	73.47	63.00	55.23	49.23	44.45
16	83.00	63.99	52.29	44.31	38.52	34.11	83.00	67.77	57.46	49.98	44.29	39.81
17	84.40	66.84	55.47	47.54	41.69	37.18	84.40	69.70	59.35	51.74	45.92	41.32
18	70.32	46.96	35.59	28.85	24.38	21.19	70.32	59.07	51.08	45.07	40.38	36.61
19	74.97	54.06	42.48	35.17	30.11	26.40	74.97	61.51	52.46	45.84	40.78	36.76
20	70.22	46.50	35.17	28.46	24.01	20.84	70.22	57.03	48.34	42.06	37.28	33.53
21	49.82	18.57	11.73	8.71	7.02	5.94	49.82	42.13	36.61	32.44	29.16	26.52
22	55.39	30.31	21.38	16.83	14.05	12.18	55.39	46.56	40.14	35.33	31.58	28.59
23	52.80	29.59	21.04	16.62	13.91	12.08	52.80	44.36	38.25	33.67	30.11	27.26
24	74.72	45.84	33.46	26.55	22.13	19.06	74.72	60.89	51.57	44.82	39.69	35.65
25	63.95	35.49	24.99	19.46	16.05	13.74	63.95	53.22	45.77	40.23	35.94	32.52
26	69.66	43.97	32.49	25.91	21.63	18.63	69.66	57.41	49.03	42.87	38.14	34.40
Average	61.73	39.57	30.31	24.95	21.39	18.83	61.73	51.31	44.04	38.66	34.51	31.21

Table 3 (Continued)

	Panel A						Panel B					
	1.0	1.2	1.4	1.6	1.8	2.0	1.0	1.2	1.4	1.6	1.8	2.0
	Daily recalculated monthly returns											
1	68.81	41.47	29.82	23.35	19.21	16.35	68.81	57.61	49.59	43.55	38.84	35.05
2	62.90	39.27	28.59	22.50	18.56	15.81	62.90	52.69	45.33	39.78	35.45	31.97
3	58.76	32.04	22.07	16.84	13.63	11.45	58.76	49.42	42.63	37.48	33.45	30.21
4	61.15	34.86	24.42	18.79	15.28	12.88	61.15	51.28	44.15	38.77	34.57	31.19
5	71.27	38.22	26.27	20.07	16.28	13.72	71.27	59.77	51.47	45.21	40.32	36.39
6	36.87	17.40	11.43	8.53	6.81	5.68	36.87	31.04	26.79	23.56	21.04	19.01
7	34.64	18.05	12.24	9.27	7.48	6.27	34.64	29.17	25.17	22.14	19.76	17.85
8	52.23	30.21	21.29	16.46	13.42	11.34	52.23	42.69	36.11	31.29	27.61	24.71
9	57.33	40.02	30.80	25.03	21.08	18.21	57.33	47.13	40.03	34.80	30.78	27.60
10	77.20	47.68	34.53	27.09	22.30	18.96	77.20	64.76	55.78	49.00	43.70	39.43
11	77.27	47.73	34.57	27.12	22.33	18.98	77.27	64.82	55.83	49.04	43.73	39.47
12	58.95	33.85	23.78	18.35	14.94	12.61	58.95	49.48	42.63	37.46	33.41	30.16
13	83.46	74.91	67.97	62.22	57.37	53.22	83.46	67.88	57.23	49.48	43.59	38.96
14	85.27	68.26	56.94	48.85	42.78	38.06	85.27	70.37	59.89	52.13	46.16	41.42
15	90.50	73.46	61.86	53.43	47.04	42.01	90.50	75.12	64.24	56.13	49.85	44.84
16	86.30	68.21	56.42	48.12	41.95	37.20	86.30	71.05	60.39	52.53	46.48	41.69
17	90.20	68.83	55.69	46.78	40.34	35.46	90.20	74.77	63.85	55.73	49.45	44.44
18	77.40	52.79	40.09	32.33	27.10	23.33	77.40	65.00	56.04	49.27	43.97	39.70
19	85.27	59.94	46.25	37.67	31.79	27.50	85.27	70.85	60.64	53.02	47.11	42.39
20	75.81	52.67	40.39	32.77	27.58	23.81	75.81	62.63	53.37	46.51	41.22	37.01
21	47.30	21.75	14.16	10.52	8.38	6.97	47.30	39.97	34.59	30.49	27.27	24.66
22	70.13	36.71	24.92	18.88	15.22	12.75	70.13	58.67	50.45	44.26	39.44	35.56
23	67.92	36.12	24.65	18.73	15.12	12.68	67.92	56.91	48.96	42.98	38.30	34.54
24	79.57	52.41	39.12	31.22	25.99	22.26	79.57	65.49	55.68	48.45	42.89	38.48
25	67.86	39.46	27.86	21.55	17.58	14.85	67.86	56.82	48.87	42.89	38.21	34.46
26	74.00	49.31	37.02	29.65	24.73	21.22	74.00	61.63	52.81	46.20	41.07	36.97
Average	69.17	45.22	34.35	27.93	23.63	20.52	69.17	57.58	49.33	43.16	38.37	34.55

This table shows the R^2s of the market model fitting on each mutual fund's daily, monthly and daily recalculated monthly returns. We add random errors generated from t distribution with four degrees of freedom to the market proxy in Panel A and to mutual funds's return in Panel B. We multiply the errors with a suitable scalar in each column to obtain a market/mutual fund premium which has exactly 1, 1.2,…,2 times the variance the original variable has. The R^2s are the average of 100 repeats Monte Carlo experiment.

III. Invalidity of the Assumptions of Standard Asset Pricing Tests

Small and large sample tests must be differentiated in empirical studies. Distribution of small sample test statistics can usually be derived only under strong assumptions, such as normality and other specific ones like homoscedastic, or non-autocorrelated error terms. Large sample tests are valid under less restrictive conditions but sufficiently large samples are not always available.

If we want to apply the GRS test for testing market efficiency which is usually used in the literature the following assumptions should be satisfied:

1. $\varepsilon_{i,t} \left| R_{m,s} \sim N\left(0, \Sigma = I\sigma^2(\varepsilon)\right)\right.;\ t,s = 1,2,...,T$, i.e. the conditional distribution of the residuals is normal with constant standard deviation (homoscedastic) and zero conditional expected value. $I\ (N \times N)$ is the identity matrix, $\sigma^2(\varepsilon)$ is the residual variance, $\Sigma = E(\varepsilon_t \varepsilon_t')$, where $\varepsilon_t' = (\varepsilon_{1,t}, \varepsilon_{2,t}, ..., \varepsilon_{N,t})$.
2. $E(\varepsilon_t \varepsilon_{t-l}') = 0;\ l = 1,2,...,t+1$ (non-autocorrelated).

If we use a small sample test like GRS, we have to test the validity of the above conditions. The Fama-MacBeth (1973) procedure also assumes normality in the residuals.

One of the main difficulties of testing normality of small samples by exact normality tests (e.g., D'Agostino-Pearson K^2, Jarque-Bera, 1980, etc.) is that normality of a suitably small sample can almost be rejected. If we study a one-year-long time series and calculate monthly returns, we have only 12 data points available for testing normality which can be misleading because of Type II error. We use D'Agostino-Pearson K^2 statistics for testing normality (see e.g., D'Agostino et al., 1990), which is a statistically strong test even on small samples (more than 9 elements). We apply Jarque-Bera normality test as well, the results are the same as in the case of D'Agostino-Pearson K^2 tests.

Table 4 shows that daily returns are highly nonnormal (26 time series out of 26) while monthly returns appear to be normal (25 time series out of 26) for a five-year-long period. If we use a longer period of at least 80 months (there are 23 mutual funds with such a long market history in our data) normality tests reject the normal null hypothesis at 95% significance level (see Table 5). None of the DRMR time series are normal at any usual significance level. K^2 chi-square test is a sum of squares of two separate normally distributed test statistics for skewness and kurtosis known as directional tests. We find that there are only two DRMR time series which exhibit normal distribution based on kurtosis (see Table 4). We also perform studentized range (SR) normality test based on the distribution of studentized range of standard normal random variable. It is not easy to define the distribution of range-to-deviation ratio but its quantiles can be reproduced by the Monte Carlo simulation (see Table 6, panel B). The method we use is the same as in Fama (1976). SR statistics lead to the same results as the K^2 and Jarque-Bera tests in the case of monthly returns. Table 6 panel A shows that the results are contradictory to our previous results applying SRs on daily returns and on DRMRs. Daily returns are non-normal variables, although the SRs show normality three times. DRMRs appear to be normal based on SR statistics (24 time series out of 26).

Studentized range is sensitive to deviation from the normal distribution as extreme rates have a crucial impact on the ratio but they are relatively insensitive to asymmetry causing severe type II error (see e.g., Shapiro et al, 1968). Affleck-Graves and McDonald (1989) show that directional tests based on skewness and kurtosis reject more often normality than studentized range does. SR statistics cannot capture the DRMR time series' significant negative skewness (-0.77 on average in our data). Normality of return data not necessarily induces normality in the disturbances of the market model (see e.g., Affleck-Graves and McDonald, 1989). We test the normality of the market model residuals as well. Table 7 shows that the residuals of the market model on daily returns are non-normal but DRMRs appear to be normal in five cases in our data based on K^2 test. There are more non-normal monthly residuals than return time series (6 vs. 1) in our data.

Table 4. Normality tests based on skewness and kurtosis and D'Agostino-Pearson K^2 test of return data

Panel A

	1	*2*	*3*	*4*	*5*	*6*	*7*	*8*	*9*	*10*	*11*	*12*	*13*
Z(1)	-3,73	-6,18	-4,14	-7,07	-5,90	-10,60	-10,26	-4,20	-8,12	-7,54	-7,65	-5,35	-5,74
p(Z(1))	0,00	0,00	0,00	0,00	0,00	0,00	0,00	0,00	0,00	0,00	0,00	0,00	0,00
Z(2)	3,61	9,44	9,60	8,98	4,90	12,61	11,10	6,81	9,42	8,70	8,72	3,64	6,26
p(Z(2))	0,00	0,00	0,00	0,00	0,00	0,00	0,00	0,00	0,00	0,00	0,00	0,00	0,00
K^2	26,93	127,44	109,35	130,58	58,74	271,46	228,38	64,02	154,73	132,48	134,53	41,89	72,19
p(K^2)	0,00	0,00	0,00	0,00	0,00	0,00	0,00	0,00	0,00	0,00	0,00	0,00	0,00

	14	*15*	*16*	*17*	*18*	*19*	*20*	*21*	*22*	*23*	*24*	*25*	*26*
Z(1)	-5,09	-6,13	-6,08	-1,91	-9,67	-6,76	-8,09	-9,61	-6,31	-5,80	-7,92	-8,00	-6,46
p(Z(1))	0,00	0,00	0,00	0,06	0,00	0,00	0,00	0,00	0,00	0,00	0,00	0,00	0,00
Z(2)	6,16	6,72	5,56	8,30	10,52	7,84	9,27	12,73	8,20	8,13	8,98	9,39	7,99
p(Z(2))	0,00	0,00	0,00	0,00	0,00	0,00	0,00	0,00	0,00	0,00	0,00	0,00	0,00
K^2	63,93	82,69	67,91	72,62	204,13	107,10	151,49	254,31	107,02	99,85	143,43	152,24	105,64
p(K^2)	0,00	0,00	0,00	0,00	0,00	0,00	0,00	0,00	0,00	0,00	0,00	0,00	0,00

Panel B

	1	*2*	*3*	*4*	*5*	*6*	*7*	*8*	*9*	*10*	*11*	*12*	*13*
Z(1)	-0.50	-0.80	-0.27	-0.71	-1.18	-1.61	-1.44	0.40	-1.40	-1.88	-1.89	-0.73	0.38
p(Z(1))	0.35	0.29	0.38	0.31	0.20	0.11	0.14	0.37	0.15	0.07	0.07	0.31	0.37
Z(2)	-0.10	0.67	0.13	0.81	1.01	-0.01	0.08	0.66	1.44	0.16	0.16	0.13	0.80
p(Z(2))	0.40	0.32	0.40	0.29	0.24	0.40	0.40	0.32	0.14	0.39	0.39	0.40	0.29
K^2	0.26	1.09	0.09	1.17	2.41	2.59	2.09	0.60	4.02	3.57	3.59	0.55	0.79
p(K^2)	0.88	0.58	0.96	0.56	0.30	0.27	0.35	0.74	0.13	0.17	0.17	0.76	0.67

	14	*15*	*16*	*17*	*18*	*19*	*20*	*21*	*22*	*23*	*24*	*25*	*26*
Z(1)	0.21	-1.13	-1.00	-0.15	-1.66	-0.44	-0.61	-3.02	-1.18	-1.19	-0.35	-1.08	-0.51
p(Z(1))	0.39	0.21	0.24	0.39	0.10	0.36	0.33	0.00	0.20	0.20	0.38	0.22	0.35
Z(2)	-1.63	-0.56	-0.44	-1.07	0.62	-0.09	1.36	1.75	0.88	0.83	-0.16	-0.46	0.12
p(Z(2))	0.11	0.34	0.36	0.22	0.33	0.40	0.16	0.09	0.27	0.28	0.39	0.36	0.40
K^2	2.69	1.60	1.18	1.17	3.12	0.20	2.21	12.19	2.16	2.11	0.15	1.36	0.27
p(K^2)	0.26	0.45	0.55	0.56	0.21	0.90	0.33	0.00	0.34	0.35	0.93	0.51	0.87

Panel C

	1	*2*	*3*	*4*	*5*	*6*	*7*	*8*	*9*	*10*	*11*	*12*	*13*
Z(1)	-3.26	-5.08	-5.38	-7.39	-5.64	-10.69	-9.36	-8.93	-7.18	-13.80	-13.78	-6.03	-7.39
p(Z(1))	0.00	0.00	0.00	0.00	0.00	0.00	0.00	0.00	0.00	0.00	0.00	0.00	0.00
Z(2)	1.44	5.61	6.36	5.66	2.02	2.82	2.50	3.43	2.38	8.47	8.44	1.28	4.35
p(Z(2))	0.14	0.00	0.00	0.00	0.05	0.01	0.02	0.00	0.02	0.00	0.00	0.18	0.00
K^2	12.70	57.31	69.35	86.58	35.91	122.34	93.91	91.49	57.19	262.21	261.10	38.00	73.57
p(K^2)	0.00	0.00	0.00	0.00	0.00	0.00	0.00	0.00	0.00	0.00	0.00	0.00	0.00

	14	*15*	*16*	*17*	*18*	*19*	*20*	*21*	*22*	*23*	*24*	*25*	*26*
Z(1)	-9.44	-10.85	-11.28	-10.13	-12.51	-10.78	-10.56	-15.52	-13.03	-12.23	-9.02	-11.05	-9.15
p(Z(1))	0.00	0.00	0.00	0.00	0.00	0.00	0.00	0.00	0.00	0.00	0.00	0.00	0.00
Z(2)	5.22	4.87	4.55	5.40	6.60	5.44	6.00	9.31	8.22	7.62	2.08	6.63	4.73
p(Z(2))	0.00	0.00	0.00	0.00	0.00	0.00	0.00	0.00	0.00	0.00	0.05	0.00	0.00
K^2	116.37	141.34	147.99	131.75	200.04	145.68	147.46	327.64	237.27	207.72	85.66	166.01	106.09
p(K^2)	0.00	0.00	0.00	0.00	0.00	0.00	0.00	0.00	0.00	0.00	0.00	0.00	0.00

This table shows the test statistics of normality tests and their p-values of daily, monthly and daily recalculated monthly returns in panel A, B, C respectively. Z(1) tests normality with an alternative hypothesis of non-normal distribution due to skewness. Z(2) tests normality with an alternative hypothesis of non-normal distribution due to kurtosis. D'Agostino-Pearson K^2 test statistic is the sum of squares of Z(1) and Z(2) statistics, which tests normality against non-normal distribution due to skewness and kurtosis.

Table 5. Normality tests of monthly returns based on full history

	1	*2*	*3*	*4*	*5*	*6*	*7*	*8*	*9*	*10*	*11*	*12*	*13*
Obs	28.00	54.00	129.00	102.00	28.00	137.00	91.00	140.00	177.00	143.00	143.00	269.00	190.00
Z(1)	1.05	2.82	6.51	5.03	0.80	5.18	2.19	4.21	5.90	6.12	6.10	4.69	5.03
p(Z(1))	0.23	0.01	0.00	0.00	0.29	0.00	0.04	0.00	0.00	0.00	0.00	0.00	0.00
Z(2)	-1.92	0.13	3.86	2.29	-1.67	1.19	-3.84	-0.60	1.69	2.59	2.58	0.00	-0.64
p(Z(2))	0.06	0.40	0.00	0.03	0.10	0.20	0.00	0.33	0.10	0.01	0.01	0.40	0.32
K^2	4.79	7.98	57.31	30.51	3.42	28.29	19.52	18.13	37.64	44.12	43.86	21.98	25.67
$p(K^2)$	0.09	0.02	0.00	0.00	0.18	0.00	0.00	0.00	0.00	0.00	0.00	0.00	0.00
	14	*15*	*16*	*17*	*18*	*19*	*20*	*21*	*22*	*23*	*24*	*25*	*26*
Obs	143.00	143.00	135.00	143.00	89.00	82.00	134.00	143.00	143.00	83.00	136.00	179.00	143.00
Z(1)	2.50	4.49	2.72	4.67	2.38	2.66	4.97	5.87	6.35	3.21	4.64	8.01	5.14
p(Z(1))	0.02	0.00	0.01	0.00	0.02	0.01	0.00	0.00	0.00	0.00	0.00	0.00	0.00
Z(2)	-2.14	0.54	-3.22	1.00	-4.17	-2.27	0.78	2.44	2.92	-0.84	0.82	4.87	1.53
p(Z(2))	0.04	0.35	0.00	0.24	0.00	0.03	0.29	0.02	0.01	0.28	0.29	0.00	0.12
K^2	10.84	20.47	17.77	22.80	23.05	12.20	25.27	40.45	48.85	11.00	22.22	87.85	28.77
$p(K^2)$	0.00	0.00	0.00	0.00	0.00	0.00	0.00	0.00	0.00	0.00	0.00	0.00	0.00

This table shows the test statistics of normality tests of monthly returns and their *p-values*. Full market history was used for testing normality in each case. Obs is the number of observation. *Z(1)* test of normality with alternative hypothesis of non-normal distribution due to skewness. *Z(2)* test of normality with alternative hypothesis of non-normal distribution due to kurtosis. D'Agostino-Pearson K^2 test statistic is the sum of squares of *Z(1)* and *Z(2)* statistics, which tests normality against non-normal distribution due to skewness and kurtosis.

Table 6. Studentized ratios of mutual funds

Panel A

	1	*2*	*3*	*4*	*5*	*6*	*7*	*8*	*9*	*10*	*11*	*12*	*13*
Daily	7.29	**8.82**	**9.10**	**9.93**	7.03	**11.91**	**9.65**	**9.15**	**8.78**	**8.78**	**8.78**	6.80	**8.17**
Daily recalculated monthly	6.29	6.87	7.14	**7.69**	**5.57**	6.45	6.45	6.37	6.38	6.73	6.72	6.54	6.65
Monthly	4.06	4.83	4.76	4.85	4.61	4.68	4.61	5.20	5.55	4.41	4.41	5.06	4.95
	14	*15*	*16*	*17*	*18*	*19*	*20*	*21*	*22*	*23*	*24*	*25*	*26*
Daily	**7.75**	**8.51**	**8.27**	**8.55**	**9.73**	**8.74**	**9.10**	**11.88**	**8.08**	**9.00**	**9.09**	**9.81**	**9.23**
Daily recalculated monthly	7.36	6.24	5.89	6.81	6.54	6.66	6.79	7.08	6.92	6.91	5.93	7.24	6.61
Monthly	4.14	4.34	4.55	4.06	5.01	4.92	**5.86**	4.83	4.66	4.756	4.86	4.623	4.743

Panel B

	0.05%	*0.5%*	*2.5%*	*5%*	*10%*	*90%*	*95%*	*97.5%*	*99.5%*	*99.95%*
Normal sample (1218)	5.45	5.64	5.81	5.91	6.04	7.22	7.44	7.65	8.07	8.63
Normal sample (1198)	5.44	5.61	5.79	5.90	6.02	7.22	7.44	7.66	8.10	8.63
Normal sample (58)	3.46	3.64	3.82	3.92	4.04	5.23	5.44	5.63	6.04	6.53

This table shows the empirical studentized ranges of daily recalculated monthly and monthly returns in Panel A. Our data sets contain 1218 (in the case of daily returns), 1198 (in case of daily recalculated monthly returns) and 58 (in the case of monthly returns) observations. Panel B shows the percentiles of studentized range of standard normal random sample containing 1,218, 1,198, and 58 data points. The ranges are calculated using a 50,000 repeats Monte Carlo simulation with the same sample sizes as the empirical data sets (i.e. 1,218, 1,198, and 58 data points for the daily, daily recalculated monthly and the monthly returns respectively). Bold numbers in Panel A indicate deviation from the normal distribution based on the distribution of Panel B assuming 95% significance level.

Table 7. Normality tests based on kurtosis and skewness and D'Agostino-Pearson K^2 test of residuals

Panel A

	1	*2*	*3*	*4*	*5*	*6*	*7*	*8*	*9*	*10*	*11*	*12*	*13*
Z(1)	-0.78	-3.68	-0.62	-3.28	-3.93	-8.29	-8.94	-1.15	-5.82	-3.97	-3.98	-3.46	-1.22
p(Z(1))	0.29	0.00	0.33	0.00	0.00	0.00	0.00	0.21	0.00	0.00	0.00	0.00	0.19
Z(2)	5.17	8.65	8.42	8.14	5.08	12.59	11.69	5.36	8.56	6.55	6.64	3.94	4.61
p(Z(2))	0.00	0.00	0.00	0.00	0.00	0.00	0.00	0.00	0.00	0.00	0.00	0.00	0.00
K^2	27.32	88.35	71.21	76.98	41.22	227.25	216.58	30.07	107.18	58.59	59.91	27.48	22.71
$p(K^2)$	0.00	0.00	0.00	0.00	0.00	0.00	0.00	0.00	0.00	0.00	0.00	0.00	0.00

	14	*15*	*16*	*17*	*18*	*19*	*20*	*21*	*22*	*23*	*24*	*25*	*26*
Z(1)	-0.42	0.04	-0.59	4.92	-1.70	-0.80	-6.10	-10.35	-0.37	0.69	0.96	-3.01	-2.28
p(Z(1))	0.36	0.40	0.34	0.00	0.09	0.29	0.00	0.00	0.37	0.31	0.25	0.00	0.03
Z(2)	9.46	7.80	7.11	10.96	10.18	7.57	10.21	12.55	4.77	4.94	7.57	7.21	7.19
p(Z(2))	0.00	0.00	0.00	0.00	0.00	0.00	0.00	0.00	0.00	0.00	0.00	0.00	0.00
K^2	89.68	60.85	50.85	144.32	106.44	57.93	141.53	264.71	22.89	24.92	58.22	60.98	56.88
$p(K^2)$	0.00	0.00	0.00	0.00	0.00	0.00	0.00	0.00	0.00	0.00	0.00	0.00	0.00

Panel B

	1	*2*	*3*	*4*	*5*	*6*	*7*	*8*	*9*	*10*	*11*	*12*	*13*
Z(1)	0.90	0.65	1.86	1.40	-0.87	-2.19	-0.97	2.03	-3.42	-0.95	-0.93	-0.87	-0.23
p(Z(1))	0.27	0.32	0.07	0.15	0.27	0.04	0.25	0.05	0.00	0.25	0.26	0.27	0.39
Z(2)	-0.64	-0.27	-0.10	0.36	-0.37	1.04	-0.58	1.38	2.80	0.45	0.43	1.30	-0.74
p(Z(2))	0.33	0.38	0.40	0.37	0.37	0.23	0.34	0.15	0.01	0.36	0.36	0.17	0.30
K^2	1.22	0.50	3.46	2.08	0.89	5.89	1.27	6.04	19.49	1.10	1.04	2.43	0.60
$p(K^2)$	0.54	0.78	0.18	0.35	0.64	0.05	0.53	0.05	0.00	0.58	0.59	0.30	0.74

	14	*15*	*16*	*17*	*18*	*19*	*20*	*21*	*22*	*23*	*24*	*25*	*26*
Z(1)	-1.92	1.76	0.26	1.84	0.31	2.38	0.26	-3.07	0.59	0.48	-0.03	0.93	2.09
p(Z(1))	0.06	0.08	0.39	0.07	0.38	0.02	0.39	0.00	0.34	0.36	0.40	0.26	0.04
Z(2)	2.24	0.52	-0.50	0.42	0.97	2.46	0.80	2.26	1.71	1.54	0.47	0.64	1.59
p(Z(2))	0.03	0.35	0.35	0.36	0.25	0.02	0.29	0.03	0.09	0.12	0.36	0.33	0.11
K^2	8.71	3.37	0.32	3.57	1.04	11.70	0.71	14.58	3.26	2.60	0.22	1.28	6.91
$p(K^2)$	0.01	0.19	0.85	0.17	0.59	0.00	0.70	0.00	0.20	0.27	0.90	0.53	0.03

Panel C

	1	*2*	*3*	*4*	*5*	*6*	*7*	*8*	*9*	*10*	*11*	*12*	*13*
Z(1)	3.52	4.97	5.59	2.45	-0.91	-9.57	-4.94	1.78	-10.83	-6.42	-6.41	2.94	1.78
p(Z(1))	0.00	0.00	0.00	0.02	0.26	0.00	0.00	0.08	0.00	0.00	0.00	0.01	0.08
Z(2)	-1.13	3.68	4.59	3.72	0.68	3.66	0.11	1.08	7.87	5.50	5.46	2.27	-4.49
p(Z(2))	0.21	0.00	0.00	0.00	0.32	0.00	0.40	0.22	0.00	0.00	0.00	0.03	0.00
K^2	13.69	38.28	52.35	19.85	1.30	105.05	24.44	4.35	179.22	71.51	70.82	13.80	23.30
$p(K^2)$	0.00	0.00	0.00	0.00	0.52	0.00	0.00	0.11	0.00	0.00	0.00	0.00	0.00

	14	*15*	*16*	*17*	*18*	*19*	*20*	*21*	*22*	*23*	*24*	*25*	*26*
Z(1)	7.35	2.56	-2.75	5.38	-1.10	0.35	-0.73	-11.96	-0.95	-0.37	-2.85	-4.97	1.43
p(Z(1))	0.00	0.02	0.01	0.00	0.22	0.38	0.31	0.00	0.25	0.37	0.01	0.00	0.14
Z(2)	9.58	2.55	1.19	5.07	0.71	1.32	3.23	7.97	2.78	1.78	-0.02	4.74	3.71
p(Z(2))	0.00	0.02	0.20	0.00	0.31	0.17	0.00	0.00	0.01	0.08	0.40	0.00	0.00
K^2	145.82	13.05	8.95	54.64	1.71	1.87	10.94	206.47	8.65	3.31	8.11	47.14	15.80
$p(K^2)$	0.00	0.00	0.01	0.00	0.43	0.39	0.00	0.00	0.01	0.19	0.02	0.00	0.00

This table shows the test statistics of normality tests and their p-values of market model's residuals using daily, monthly and daily recalculated monthly returns in panel A, B, C respectively. Z(1) tests normality with an alternative hypothesis of non-normal distribution due to skewness. Z(2) tests normality with an alternative hypothesis of non-normal distribution due to kurtosis. D'Agostino-Pearson K^2 test statistic is the sum of squares of Z(1) and Z(2) statistics, which tests normality against non-normal distribution due to skewness and kurtosis.

We can look at monthly returns as a sample of DRMRs. Monthly returns compare the last closing price of a given month with the last closing price of the previous month. Assuming 21 trading days a month (which is the case on average) all the monthly returns would be included in the DRMRs population so monthly returns would be a sample of DRMRs. This feature also sheds some light on non-normality of monthly returns. Monthly returns are results of systematic sampling; although, they are not fully random samples since the choice of the sampling starting point is not random.

There are numerous tests for equality of distributions, parametric and non-parametric as well. The time series in our data are not normal and we do not know the exact distribution of the returns, so only non-parametric approaches are applicable.

We use Wilcoxon rank-sum test (Wilcoxon, 1945) which is also known as Mann-Whitney U test or Mann-Whitney-Wilcoxon (henceforth *MWW*) test first introduced by Wilcoxon for equal sample sizes and then extended to arbitrary sample sizes by Mann and Whitney (1947). Hodges and Lehman (1956) argue on theoretical grounds in favor of the rank-sum test, noting that it is never much less efficient than Student's t (where less efficient means more samples are required to get the same performance) but can be infinitely more efficient. Potvin and Roff (1993) conclude that the MWW test is more powerful than the t-test for skewed distributions. MWW test is the best in our case since our data are highly skewed.

MWW test assumes that the two underlying distributions have approximately the same shape (variance) and the only difference between them is a shift in location. 58 observations of DRMRs are chosen five times randomly to obtain five independent random samples. The variances of monthly returns and of random samples from DRMRs are very close to each other indicating a powerful test. We compare the five random samples with the 58 monthly returns using MWW test which can be seen in Table 8 Panel A.

There is only one case (fund number 5) when the null hypothesis of equality in distributions can be rejected at 95% significance level.

The Kruskal-Wallis (*KW*) test (1952), the generalization of MWW test for more than two samples is also performed (Table 8 Panel B). The KW test confirms the results of MWW tests, the null hypothesis of homogenity of monthly returns and the five random samples cannot be rejected at all usual significance levels. We can conclude that monthly returns and daily recalculated monthly returns have the same distribution, some possible minor differences are only due to random sampling.

We also study the other two essential assumptions in standard asset pricing tests, homoskedasticity and serial independence. Applying the White (1980) test, the market model residuals show significant heteroskedasticity. There are only three mutual funds with heteroskedastic residuals running CAPM regressions on monthly returns. Using DRMRs, we can only accept the homoskedastic null hypothesis in five cases.

Table 9 shows the results of Breusch-Godfrey (1978) autocorrelation tests. Using daily returns, there is significant autocorrelation in the case of 23 mutual funds, while only two mutual funds show autocorrelation in the case of monthly returns at 95% significance level. The market model residuals are heteroskedastic if we use DRMRs.

Table 8. Mann-Whitney-Wilcoxon (MWW) and Kruskall-Wallis (KW) tests

Panel A

	1	*2*	*3*	*4*	*5*	*6*	*7*	*8*	*9*	*10*	*11*	*12*	*13*
1	1.85	1.50	1.73	1.48	2.00	1.03	0.95	0.12	0.51	1.25	1.25	0.96	0.69
	(0.06)	(0.13)	(0.08)	(0.13)	(0.04)	(0.30)	(0.34)	(0.90)	(0.60)	(0.21)	(0.21)	(0.33)	(0.48)
2	1.40	0.34	0.53	0.58	1.49	0.36	0.27	0.47	0.20	0.74	0.76	1.41	0.42
	(0.16)	(0.73)	(0.59)	(0.56)	(0.13)	(0.71)	(0.78)	(0.63)	(0.84)	(0.46)	(0.44)	(0.15)	(0.67)
3	0.19	0.46	0.09	0.06	0.21	0.46	0.42	0.67	0.18	0.15	0.14	0.79	0.15
	(0.84)	(0.64)	(0.92)	(0.95)	(0.83)	(0.64)	(0.67)	(0.50)	(0.85)	(0.87)	(0.89)	(0.42)	(0.87)
4	0.65	0.09	0.26	0.08	1.13	0.32	0.57	0.35	0.70	0.00	0.01	0.16	0.12
	(0.51)	(0.93)	(0.79)	(0.93)	(0.25)	(0.74)	(0.57)	(0.72)	(0.48)	(0.99)	(0.98)	(0.87)	(0.90)
5	0.91	0.89	0.91	0.85	0.52	1.36	1.50	0.63	1.11	0.74	0.70	0.21	1.00
	(0.36)	(0.37)	(0.36)	(0.39)	(0.60)	(0.17)	(0.13)	(0.52)	(0.26)	(0.46)	(0.48)	(0.83)	(0.31)

	14	*15*	*16*	*17*	*18*	*19*	*20*	*21*	*22*	*23*	*24*	*25*	*26*
1	0.76	0.80	0.88	0.10	1.14	1.13	0.52	0.64	0.88	0.76	1.02	1.45	0.91
	(0.44)	(0.42)	(0.37)	(0.91)	(0.25)	(0.25)	(0.60)	(0.52)	(0.37)	(0.44)	(0.30)	(0.14)	(0.36)
2	0.90	0.43	0.57	1.02	1.05	0.57	0.00	0.16	0.70	0.82	0.32	0.77	0.70
	(0.36)	(0.66)	(0.57)	(0.30)	(0.29)	(0.56)	(0.99)	(0.87)	(0.48)	(0.41)	(0.74)	(0.44)	(0.48)
3	0.11	0.02	0.43	0.05	0.40	0.01	0.20	0.31	0.05	0.14	0.41	0.68	0.20
	(0.90)	(0.98)	(0.66)	(0.95)	(0.68)	(0.98)	(0.84)	(0.75)	(0.96)	(0.88)	(0.68)	(0.49)	(0.84)
4	0.47	0.55	0.06	0.27	0.63	0.41	0.95	0.12	0.17	0.16	0.47	0.03	0.18
	(0.64)	(0.58)	(0.94)	(0.78)	(0.52)	(0.68)	(0.34)	(0.90)	(0.86)	(0.87)	(0.64)	(0.97)	(0.85)
5	0.78	0.67	1.06	0.22	1.05	0.95	0.82	0.81	0.26	0.23	0.57	0.66	0.64
	(0.43)	(0.50)	(0.29)	(0.82)	(0.29)	(0.34)	(0.41)	(0.41)	(0.79)	(0.81)	(0.56)	(0.50)	(0.52)

Panel B

	1	*2*	*3*	*4*	*5*	*6*	*7*	*8*	*9*	*10*	*11*	*12*	*13*
KW	6.76	6.00	4.90	4.28	6.04	4.39	4.89	2.61	1.50	2.88	2.91	3.16	1.43
	(0.24)	(0.31)	(0.43)	(0.51)	(0.3)	(0.49)	(0.43)	(0.76)	(0.91)	(0.72)	(0.71)	(0.68)	(0.92)

	14	*15*	*16*	*17*	*18*	*19*	*20*	*21*	*22*	*23*	*24*	*25*	*26*
KW	2.13	1.21	2.82	1.29	2.28	2.05	2.24	1.04	2.03	2.01	2.53	4.98	1.68
	(0.83)	(0.94)	(0.73)	(0.94)	(0.81)	(0.84)	(0.81)	(0.96)	(0.84)	(0.85)	(0.77)	(0.42)	(0.89)

This table shows the results of MWW tests comparing the monthly returns with five random samples from daily recalculated monthly returns in Panel A and the results of KW test comparing the monthly returns with the five random samples simultaneously. P-values can be seen in parenthesis.

Heteroskedasticity and autocorrelation make the standard errors of *OLS* (Ordinary Least Squares) parameter estimations inconsistent and biased so the usual *t*- and *F-tests* cannot be applied. If we use *OLS*, there are methods generating consistent covariance matrix even in the case of heteroskedasticity, such as Heteroskedasticity Consistent Covariance Matrix (*HCCM*) estimation (White, 1980). If the residuals are heteroskedastic and autocorrelated at the same time, the Heteroskedasticity and Autocorrelation Consistent (*HAC*) covariance matrix estimation (Newey and West, 1987, 1994; Andrews, 1991; Andrews and Monahan, 1992) combined with OLS parameter estimations are appropriate to make the usual F- and t-tests applicable. Therefore we calculate t-statistics with HAC covariance matrix (Andrews, 1991).

If continuously compounded daily returns are independent and identically distributed (*i.i.d.*), then on the basis of central limit theorem by increasing the number of periods to be summed, the distribution of cumulated returns is approaching the normal distribution. If the central limit theorem is valid, the distribution of monthly returns should be more normal than the daily ones. However, independence does not exist in the case of daily returns (Table 9). Furthermore, Mandelbrot (1963) proves that the central limit theorem is a special case and it is valid only if variance of the random variable is finite. Generally the distribution converges to a stable but not necessarily the normal distribution. Not normal stable symmetrical distributions have a leptokurtic feature which can be observed in daily returns (kurtosis is 5,47 on average in our data).

Table 9. Heteroskedasticity and autocorrelation tests of the market model residuals

$$R_{i,t} = \alpha_i + \beta_i (R_{m,t}) + \varepsilon_{i,t} \quad i = 1,2,...,26; \quad t = 1,2,...,T$$

Panel		1	2	3	4	5	6	7	8	9	10	11	12	13
A	p(W)	0.00	0.00	0.00	0.00	0.00	0.01	0.00	0.00	0.00	0.00	0.00	0.00	0.00
A	p(BG)	0.04	0.00	0.01	0.03	0.02	0.91	0.04	0.02	0.04	0.00	0.00	0.00	0.00
		14	15	16	17	18	19	20	21	22	23	24	25	26
A	p(W)	0.00	0.00	0.00	0.00	0.00	0.00	0.00	0.00	0.00	0.00	0.00	0.00	0.00
A	p(BG)	0.00	0.02	0.48	0.00	0.00	0.00	0.00	0.00	0.00	0.00	0.00	0.37	0.00
		1	2	3	4	5	6	7	8	9	10	11	12	13
B	p(W)	0.86	0.79	0.51	0.82	0.91	0.03	0.46	0.52	0.43	0.00	0.00	0.78	0.69
B	p(BG)	0.10	0.30	0.29	0.46	0.50	0.35	0.09	0.78	0.97	0.98	0.98	0.18	0.07
		14	15	16	17	18	19	20	21	22	23	24	25	26
B	p(W)	0.84	0.26	0.85	0.20	0.85	0.85	0.31	0.16	0.15	0.30	0.91	0.27	0.57
B	p(BG)	0.00	0.35	0.85	0.29	0.93	0.81	0.00	0.19	0.40	0.65	0.14	0.51	0.88
		1	2	3	4	5	6	7	8	9	10	11	12	13
C	p(W)	0.51	0.03	0.02	0.03	0.32	0.18	0.00	0.00	0.44	0.00	0.00	0.18	0.00
C	p(BG)	0.00	0.00	0.00	0.00	0.00	0.00	0.00	0.00	0.00	0.00	0.00	0.00	0.00
		14	15	16	17	18	19	20	21	22	23	24	25	26
C	p(W)	0.00	0.00	0.04	0.00	0.01	0.00	0.00	0.00	0.00	0.00	0.05	0.00	0.00
C	p(BG)	0.00	0.00	0.00	0.00	0.00	0.00	0.00	0.00	0.00	0.00	0.00	0.00	0.00

This table shows p-values of the White heteroskedasticity (p(W)) and Breusch-Godfrey autocorrelation tests (p(BG)) on the market model's residuals using daily, monthly, and daily recalculated monthly returns in panel A, B, C respectively. We use the Morgan Stanley Capital International (MSCI) All Countries World Index as the market proxy.

As a result of stable distribution, if daily returns are not normally distributed with infinite variance, then distribution of weekly and monthly returns will not be normal, irrespectively of the length of summation.

Fama (1976) shows empirically that the distribution of monthly returns is less leptokurtic and the frequency of extreme returns is smaller than in the case of daily returns. Unlike the theorem of stable distribution, the distribution of monthly returns approach the Gaussian distribution rather than the distribution of daily returns, but relative frequency of extreme returns and returns close to the average turn out to be a bit higher than that of normal distribution. Although our tests show that monthly returns only seem to be normal because of the too short time series and severe type II error.

Blume (1968) and Officer (1971) thoroughly study returns of single securities and portfolios and find that distribution of portfolios is of the same type as that of single securities, so it does not matter if we examine single securities or as, at present, mutual funds (portfolios).

IV. Visualizing Non-Normality

Distribution of monthly returns and DRMRs of two mutual funds can be seen in Figures 4-5. In the case of DRMRs the fat tail phenomenon can be observed on the left of the distribution, i.e. big losses are more frequent than it would be drawn from normal distribution. Small positive returns are more likely than they would be in the case of Gaussian distribution, which is well presented by the negative skewness of the distributions as the -0.87% and -0.43% in the case of mutual fund number 25 and 12 respectively. Return distribution of fund number 25 shows leptokurtosis contrary to the normal distribution (kurtosis 4.5), distribution of fund number 12 does not significantly differ from Gaussian distribution from the kurtosis point of view (3.18).

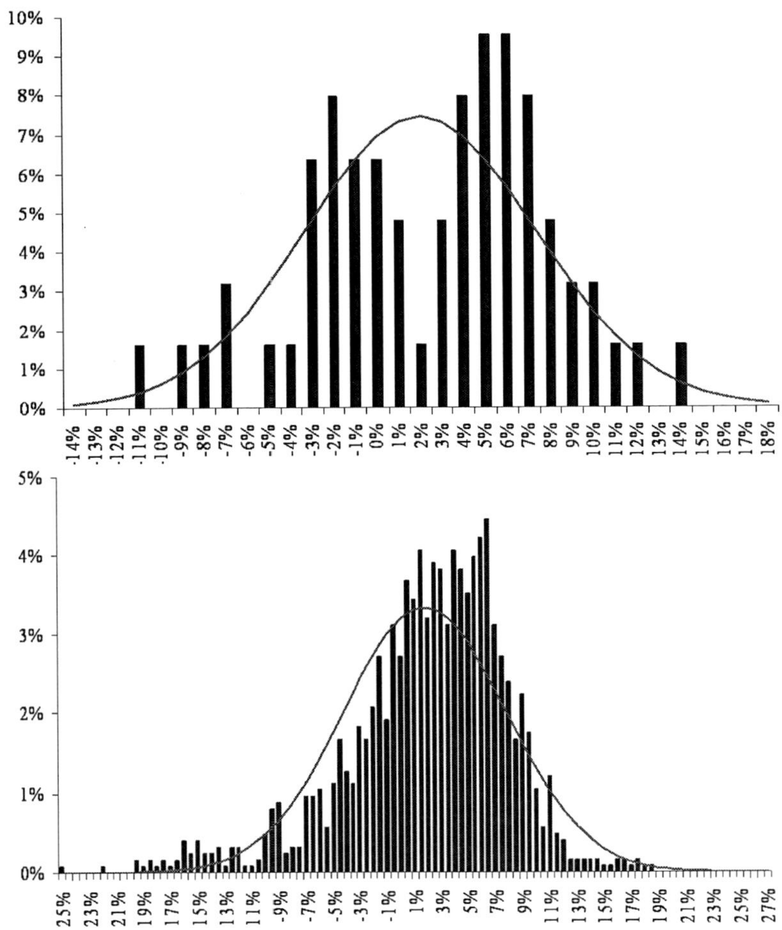

Figure 4. Histograms of monthly returns and daily recalculated monthly returns (*DRMRs*) of mutual fund number 25.

Notes: Histograms of monthly returns and *DRMRs* can be seen in Panel A and Panel B respectively. Fund number 25 is chosen for illustration because its R^2 is equal to the average of the 26 market model regressions included in our paper using when *DRMRs*. Red curves show the normal probability density functions.

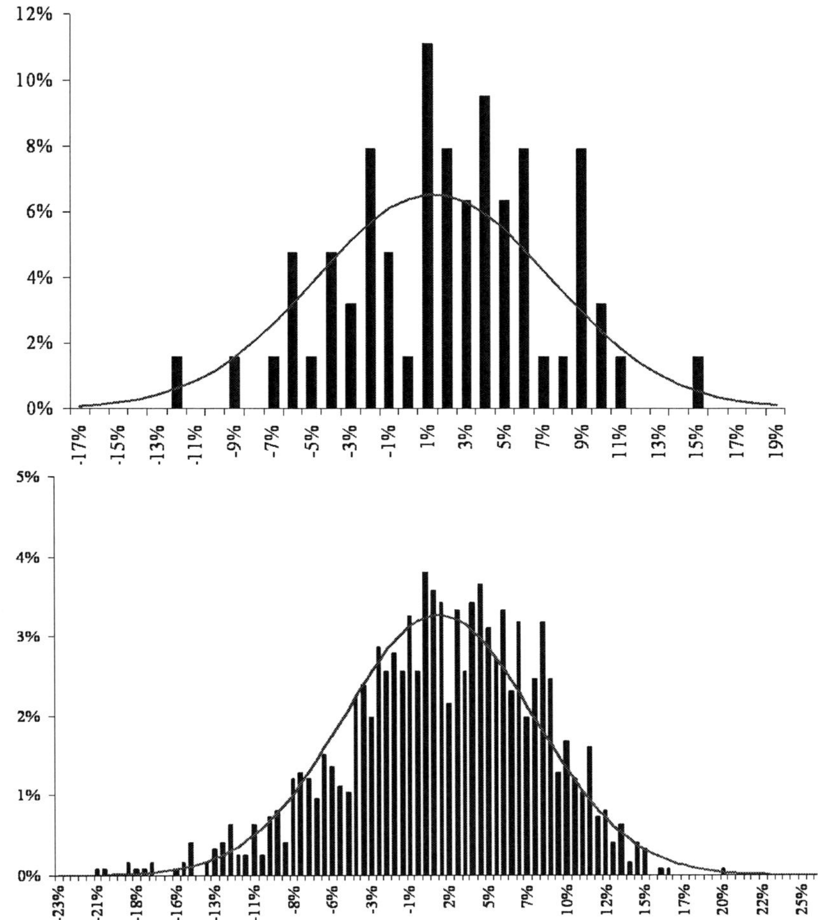

Notes: Histograms of monthly returns and *DRMR*s can be seen in Panel A and Panel B respectively. Fund number 12 is chosen for illustration because its R^2 is equal to the average of the 26 market model regressions included in our paper when using daily returns. Red curves show the normal probability density functions.

Figure 5. Histograms of monthly returns and daily recalculated monthly returns (*DRMR*s) of mutual fund number 12.

Fat tail can also be observed in the case of simple monthly returns, i.e. on the sides of empirical distribution events are more frequent than it would be drawn from normal distribution.

Looking at Figure 4-5, monthly returns are not normally distributed confirming our results in the previous section. The only reason why they seem to be normal when they are tested by D'Agostino-Pearson or other statistics is the small sample size.

If we intend to study the deviation of the empirical distribution from the normal, comparing the logarithm of the density functions can be an illustrative solution.

This procedure highlights anomalies of the empirical distribution like fat tails. The logarithm of a normal probability density function is a parabolic curve.

The use of this method is practical because the logarithm enlarges the difference between the empirical and the normal distribution most significantly in the tails.

According to Figures 6-7 daily recalculated returns fit the normal distribution better than monthly returns in the centre of the distribution. DRMRs of fund number 25 exhibit significant departures from Gauss-distribution at the tails, while in the case of fund number 12 there is no significant deviation either in the centre or at the tails.

Based on the logarithms of empirical density functions we cannot say that monthly returns are more normal than DRMRs.

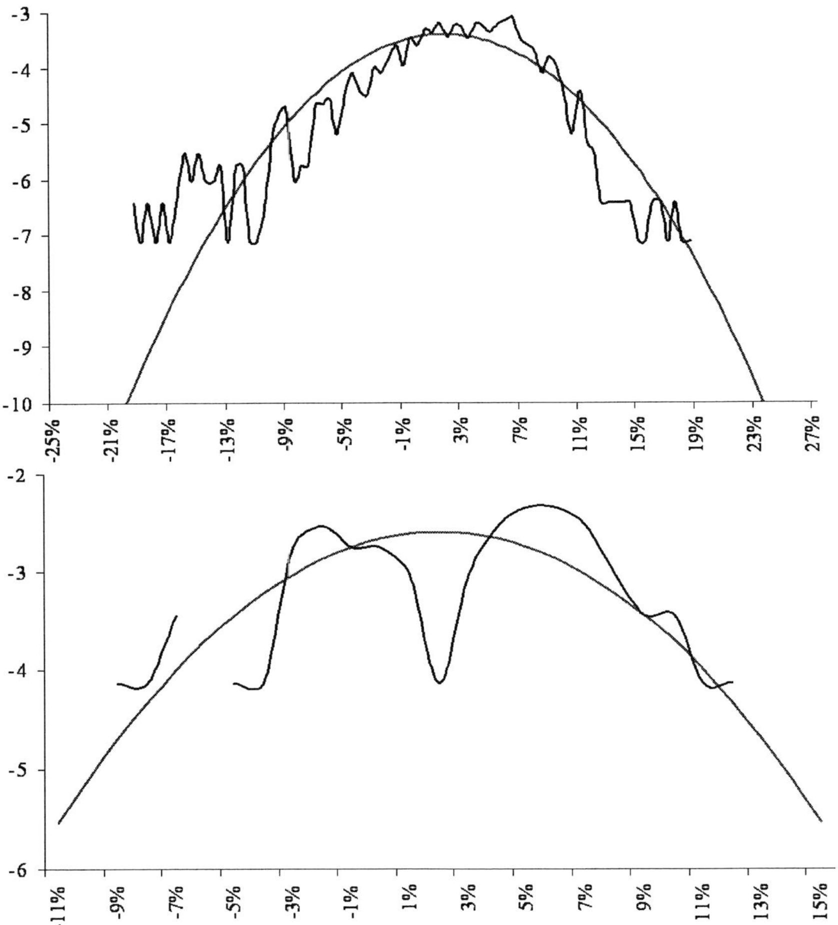

Notes: Logarithm of density function of *DRMR*s and monthly returns can be seen in Panel A and Panel B respectively. Fund number 25 is chosen for illustration because its R^2 is equal to the average of the 26 market model regressions included in our paper when using *DRMR*s. Red curves show the logarithm of normal probability density functions.

Figure 6. Logarithm of density function of daily recalculated monthly returns (*DRMR*s) and monthly returns of mutual fund number 25.

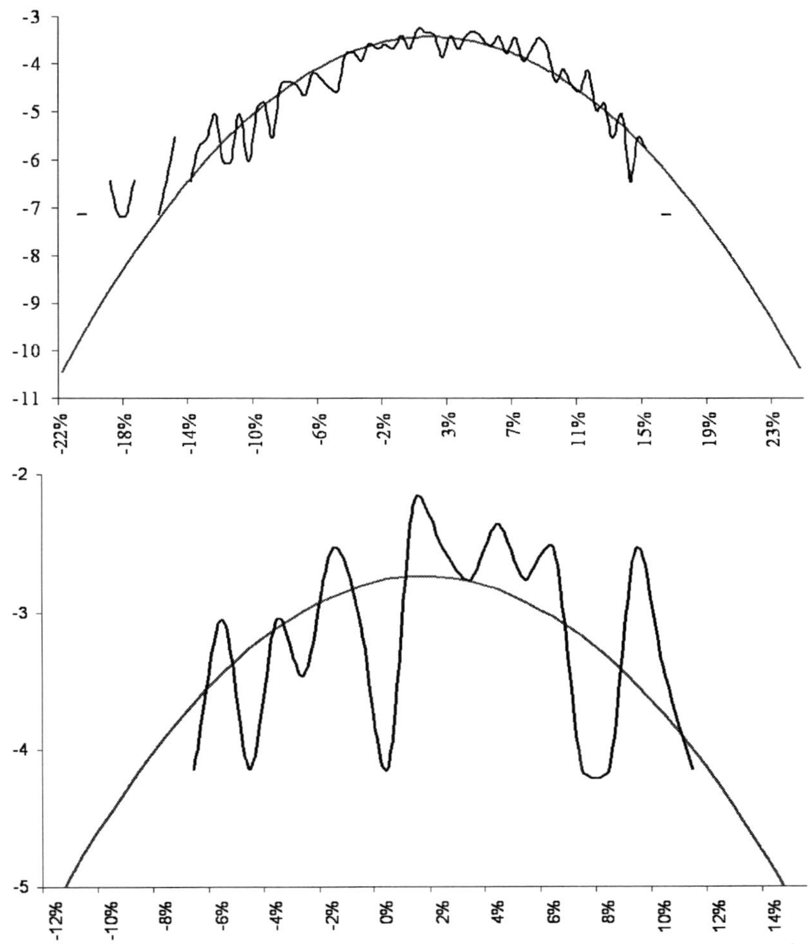

Notes: Logarithm of density function of *DRMR*s and monthly returns can be seen in Panel A and Panel B respectively. Fund number 12 is chosen for illustration because its R^2 is equal to the average of the 26 market model regressions included in our paper when using *DRMR*s. Red curves show the logarithm of normal probability density functions.

Figure 7. Logarithm of density function of *DRMR*s and monthly returns of mutual fund number 12.

CONCLUDING REMARKS

When mutual funds performance is to be evaluated, or the efficiency of capital market is to be tested, the key question is whether there is any significant abnormal return. The method used most frequently to settle the question is the calculation of Jensen alphas and their univariate or multivariate (GRS test) econometric study. From the returns calculation point of view, we face two issues. Firstly, adequate sample size is required for reliable parameter estimations. Secondly, the fewer assumptions are needed in connection with the distribution, the larger sample size is required. With large sample size, asymptotic features of the estimations can be derived, i.e. consistent standard errors of parameters which are essential for performance measurement.

In the literature most frequently daily or monthly returns are used and there is no special recipe for measuring debuting assets' performance or testing market efficiency of newly traded markets. In this paper we examine an alternative return calculation, the daily recalculated monthly returns (DRMR). Although, DRMRs are not normally distributed, serially dependent, and heteroskedastic, they can be used when no long enough time series is available. If we work on short time series, monthly returns are not applicable because the parameter estimations are not reliable and we cannot derive asymptotic asset pricing tests when, for example, normality is not valid. We show that monthly returns are not normally distributed; although, they seem to be so in small samples, but they are a systematic sample of the DRMR population.

Another possibility to solve our problem is the daily return calculation. Daily returns have all the bad properties that DRMRs do and they are the most sensitive to measurement errors in the market proxy resulting in weak fitting.

We show that DRMRs are the best working approximation when we have very limited data available. This method gives at least as good fitting of the market model as the monthly returns or even better (relatively high R^2). At the same time it does not imply dramatic decrease of data points suitable for asymptotic tests even for relatively short periods.

ACKNOWLEDGMENTS

The authors would like to thank Sunil K. Mohanty for his suggestions to this paper, and Ádám Zawadowski for his comments on an early draft. All errors are the sole responsibility of the authors.

REFERENCES

Affleck-Graves, J., and B. McDonald. "Nonnormalities and Tests of Asset Pricing Theories." *The Journal of Finance,* 44 (1989), 889-908.

Andrews, D.W.K. Heteroskedasticity and "Autocorrelation Consistent Covariance Matrix Estimation." *Econometrica,* 59 (1991), 817-858.

Andrews, D.W.K., and J.C. Monahan, "An Improved Heteroskedasticity and Autocorrelation Consistent Covariance Matrix Estimator." *Econometrica,* 60 (1992), 953-966.

Black, F.; M.C. Jensen; and M. Scholes. "The Capital Asset Pricing Model: Some Empirical Tests." In: Jensen M. C. (Eds.), Studies in the Theory of Capital Markets, Praeger, New York, (1972). 79-121.

Blume, M. E. "The Assessment of Portfolio Performance." Unpublished Ph.D. dissertation. University of Chicago (1968).

Breusch, T. "Testing for Autocorrelation in Dynamic Linear Models." *Australian Economic Papers,* 17 (1978), 334-55.

Brown, S. J., and J. B. Warner. "Using Daily Stock Returns: The Case of Event Studies." *Journal of Financial Economics,* 14 (1985), 3-31.

Chen, H., and V. Singal. "Role of Speculative Short Sales in Price Formation: The Case of the Weekend Effect". *The Journal of Finance*, 58 (2003), 685-705.

Cochrane, J. H. "Asset Pricing". Princeton University Press, Princeton (2001).

D'Agostino, R.B; A. Belanger; and R.B. D'Agostino Jr. "A Suggestion for Using Powerful and Informative Tests of Normality". *The American Statistician,* 44 (1990), 316-321.

De Santis, G., and B. Gerard. "International Asset Pricing and Portfolio Diversification with Time-varying Risk." *The Journal of Finance*, 52 (1997), 1881-1912.

Dickey, D.A., and W.A. Fuller. "Likelihood Ratio Statistics for Autoregressive Time Series with a Unit Root." *Econometrica,* 49 (1981), 1057-1072.

Elton, E.J.; M.J. Gruber; and C.R. Blake. "Fundamental Economic Variables, Expected Returns, and Bond Fund Performance." *The Journal of Finance*, 50 (1995), 1229-1256.

Elton, E.J.; M.J. Gruber; and C.R. Blake. "Survivorship Bias and Mutual Fund Performance." *The Review of Financial Studies,* 9 (1996), 1097-1120.

Fama, E.F., and J. D. MacBeth. "Risk, Return, and Equilibrium: Empirical Tests." *The Journal of Political Economy*, 81 (1973), 607-636.

Fama, E.F. Foundations of Finance, Basic Books, New York (1976).

Fama, E.F., and K.R. French. "Size and Book-to-market Factors in Earnings and Returns." *The Journal of Finance*, 50 (1995), 131-155.

Fama, E.F., and K.R. French. "Multifactor Explanations of Asset Pricing Anomalies." *The Journal of Finance,* 51 (1996a), 55-84.

Fama, E.F., and K.R. French. "The CAPM is Wanted, Dead or Alive." *The Journal of Finance*, 51 (1996b), 1947-1958.

Fama, E.F., and K.R. French. "Value Versus Growth: The International Evidence." *The Journal of Finance*, 53 (1998), 1975-1999.

Fama, E.F., and K.R. French. "The Value Premium and the CAPM." *The Journal of Finance*, 61 (2006), 2163-2185.

Gibbons, M.R.; S.A. Ross; and J. Shanken. "A Test of the Efficiency of a Given Portfolio." *Econometrica*, 57 (1989), 1121-1152.

Godfrey, L. G. "Testing for Higher Order Serial Correlation in Regression Equations when the Regressors Include Lagged Dependent Variables." *Econometrica*, 46 (1978), 1303-1310.

Jarque, C.M., and A.K. Bera. "Efficient Tests for Normality, Homoscedasticity and Serial Independence of Regression Residuals." *Economics Letters,* 6 (1980), 255–259.

Jensen, M.C. "The Performance of Mutual Funds in the Period 1945-1964." *The Journal of Finance*, 23 (1968), 389-416.

Hansen, L.P. "Large Sample Properties of Generalized Method of Moments Estimators." *Econometrica*, 50 (1982), 1029-1054.

Hodges, J.L. Jr, and E. L. Lehmann, "The Efficiency of Some Nonparametric Competitors of the "t"-test." *The Annals of Mathematical Statistics,* 27 (1956), 324-335.

Kothari, S.P.; J.Shanken; and R.G. Sloan. "Another Look at the Cross-section of Expected Stock Returns." *The Journal of Finance,* 50 (1995), 185-224.

Kruskal, W.H., and W.A. Wallis. "Use of Ranks in One-criterion Variance Analysis." *Journal of the American Statistical Association*, 47 (1952), 583-621.

Mandelbrot, B. "The Variation of Certain Speculative Prices." *The Journal of Business,* 36 (1963), 94-419.

Mann, H.B., and D.R. Whitney. "On a Test of whether One of Two Random Variables is Stochastically Larger than the Other." *The Annals of Mathematical Statistics*, 18 (1947), 50-60.

Morse, D. "An Econometric Analysis of the Choice of Daily Versus Monthly Returns in Tests of Information Content." *Journal of Accounting Research*, 22 (1984), 605-623.

Newey, W.K., and K.D. West. "A Simple, Positive Semi-definite, Heteroskedasticity and Autocorrelation Consistent Covariance Matrix." *Econometrica,* 55 (1987), 703-708.

Newey, W.K., and K.D. West. "Automatic Lag Selection in Covariance Matrix Estimation." *The Review of Economic Studies,* 61 (1994), 631-653.

Officer, R. "A Time Series Examination of the Market Factor of the New York Stock Exchange." Ph.D. dissertation, University of Chicago (1971).

Potvin, C., and D.A. Roff. "Distribution-free and Robust Statistical Methods: Viable Alternatives to Parametric Statistics." *Ecology*, 74 (1993), 1617-1628.

Roll, R. "A Critique of the Asset Pricing Theory's Tests' Part I: On Past and Potential Testability of the Theory." *Journal of Financial Economics*, 4 (1977), 129-176.

Shapiro, S.S.; M.B. Wilk; and H.J. Chen. "A Comparative Study of Various Tests for Normality." *Journal of the American Statistical Association*, 63 (1968), 1343-1372.

Sharpe, W.F. "Mutual Fund Performance." *The Journal of Business,* 39 (1966), 119-138.

Solnik, B. "The International Pricing of Risk: An Empirical Investigation of the World Capital Market Structure." *The Journal of Finance*, 29 (1974), 365-378.

White, H. "A Heteroskedasticity-consistent Covariance Matrix Estimator and a Direct Test for Heteroskedasticity." *Econometrica*, 48 (1980), 817-838.

Wilcoxon, F. "Individual Comparisons by Ranking Methods." *Biometrics Bulletin*, 1 (1945), 80-83.

In: Financial Asset Pricing
Editors: P. E. Schulz and B. P. Hoffmann
ISBN 978-1-61122-803-8

Chapter 4

RISK PREMIUM, MARKET PRICE OF RISK, AND STOCHASTIC PRICE MODELS FOR COMMODITIES

Luis M. Abadie*
Basque Centre for Climate Change (BC3)
Alameda Urquijo 4, 4º - 1ª, 48008 Bilbao (Spain)

ABSTRACT

Commodities are not financial assets, yet futures contracts on commodities are financial instruments which have been traded for over 100 years. The most relevant features in these contracts include the convenience yield, mean reversion, the risk premium, changing volatility, and seasonality, among others. The stochastic price models developed over time usually try to account for these characteristics. The choice of a particular model will depend on the specific features of the commodity and the particular purpose of the model.

The aim of this paper is twofold. First, we analyze the modelling of the market price of risk in different stochastic dynamic models. Then we derive the corresponding equation for the risk premium, and the dynamics of futures prices (both in the physical world and under the risk-neutral probability measure). We use several models with mean reversion; the standard Geometric Brownian Motion is also considered as a particular case of one of them. We explore different specifications for the market price of risk in these models. One of them allows for the possibility that the market price of risk is stochastic and correlated with the commodity price.

Second, we estimate the market price of risk for two commodities, namely coal and carbon dioxide, using the surface generated by daily futures prices for different maturities. From the stochastic models for the spot price and the equations for the futures price we obtain the stochastic dynamic models for the behaviour of futures prices in the physical world, which are used to estimate the market price of risk.

Our results allow identify the sign and size of the market price of risk for these commodities. We check whether futures prices are biased estimators of expected spot prices in both cases. We also compute the necessary correction factor to get a better estimate of the expected spot price.

---

* *E-mail:* lm.abadie@bc3research.org

Keywords: Market price of risk; risk premium; stochastic price models; commodities; futures markets.

1. Introduction

Commodities are not financial assets, yet futures contracts on commodities are financial instruments which have been traded for over 100 years. The stochastic models developed over time try to account for the main characteristics of these products, which, depending on the specific commodity in each case and on the reason why each model is used, may include the convenience yield, mean reversion, the modelling of the market price of risk, stochastic volatility, seasonality, etc. The choice of the model is therefore conditioned by the use to which it is to be put. If the purpose is to value a derivative asset with a given maturity, e.g. a European option, parameters such as stochastic volatility and the existence of jumps may be particularly relevant. But if the purpose is to evaluate flows which are or may be perceived as continuous over time, such as a megawatt-hour value perceived over a year, then some of the traits that appear in the spot price are of little significance in futures markets. For example the spot market for electricity frequently features jumps, which do not exist in the futures market for the same product because their effect is diluted in trading when sufficiently long periods (rather than a single day) are considered.

There are numerous reasons to study commodities and their associated risk premiums. As shown in Fabozzi et al. [3], many commodities have efficient, deep futures markets,[1] involving consumers, producers and financial organisations. This combination of participants that provide increased liquidity, together with the availability of many quotes, can make for better estimation of the parameters of models, including the market price of risk. The development of markets for commodities is favoured by their characteristics as products whose prices are usually correlated with inflation but uncorrelated with equities and bonds.[2] This has also favoured demand for derivatives on these products. However, these markets tend to be highly volatile, since unexpected increases in demand cannot usually be met by adjusting supply in the short term when there is no excess capacity. Such adjustments take time and the immediate consequence is a sharp change in prices.[3] The opposite happens when there is a sharp drop in demand. In the long term, if price increases are perceived as permanent new facilities can be built in principle, with a greater cost per unit produced. This will happen if demand for renewable and non renewable commodities is growing and prices exceed a certain minimum threshold so that investment in further capacity under uncertainty is justified.

This paper examines the modelling and estimation of the market price of risk (henceforth MPR) and its impact on the Risk Premium.[4] The Risk Premium (RP) is defined as the

---

[1] Basically in the case of Energy and Metals.

[2] Inflation is positively correlated with commodity prices but negatively affects equity and bond prices.

[3] When all or part of the demand can be met in the short term because excess capacity is available, more expensive facilities usually come on line, and their costs and profit margins are passed onto the cross prices.

[4] It is also frequently referred to as the ex-ante risk premium, to distinguish it from the ex-post or realised risk premium.

difference between the quoted price at time t of a futures contract with maturity T and the spot price S expected to prevail at that time T, i.e.[5]

$$RP(t,T) \equiv F(t,T) - E_t(S_T).$$

If the MPR for a commodity is positive then futures prices are downward-biased estimators of the spot prices expected in the future. This translates into a negative RP. The opposite occurs when MPR < 0, which gives rise to a positive RP, with futures prices being upward-biased estimators of future spot prices.

It is important to learn more about the MPR, as this allows one:[6]

a) to estimate the price of a commodity price at a future time more accurately;
b) to learn more about the size of the RP required by speculators in markets to cover operations by other players;
c) to improve risk management at companies (such risk management has become a necessity in the wake of market deregulation processes affecting electricity and natural gas, among others);
d) to convert spot price forecasts into equivalent futures contract prices which can be used by discounting the flows at the risk-free interest rate;
e) to compare price scenarios once the RP is adjusted for with the prices quoted on markets for the periods available, thus checking the consistency of the scenarios against actual market performance.[7]

The rest of the paper is structured as follows:

Section 2 reviews and discusses the relevant literature.

Section 3 develops and discusses the models used. The analysis is based on the use of stochastic equations, which are considered as suitable for studying the drift in the price of a specific commodity. When the MPR is included in these equations, the drift rate under the equivalent martingale measure, i.e. the performance in a risk-neutral world, is obtained; then it becomes possible to determine the futures equation compatible with the modelling of the stochastic process selected for the spot price and the form of inclusion of the MPR. On this basis, it is then possible to deduce the stochastic equation followed by a futures contract in both the risk-neutral and real (physical) worlds. This last equation can then be used to estimate the MPR, which will enable a much broader set of market data to be used than in models that study the MPR based solely on the behaviour of the spot price. Using such a large quantity of data enables the variance of the estimators to be reduced. This is useful for example when the stochastic equation for the futures price in the real world follows a geometric Brownian motion (GBM), since GBM drift estimators generally have a high asymptotic variance and the MPR usually is part of the estimated drift rate, as will be seen below.

[5] For a discussion of this definition and its implications, see Geman [4].

[6] Kolos and Ronn [6] provide a detailed analysis of these applications.

[7] This requirement for consistency with sufficiently liquid futures markets must be met for the baseline scenario, at least for those cases with the shortest time to maturity.

Section 4 develops the estimation procedures based on the use of panel data. Estimates are drawn up using the quoted prices of two commodities: coal and carbon dioxide .

Section 5 concludes.

2. REVIEW OF THE LITERATURE

Various methods have been used to estimate the underlying parameters in stochastic price models. One of them is the MPR. Cortazar and Schwartz [1] propose a least-squares error method. This method is simple and intuitive, but does not enable estimates of the volatility of estimators to be obtained, making it impossible to evaluate whether they are significant or not. Lucia and Schwartz [7] apply the nonlinear least-squares method.

Most of the journal papers that obtain the MPR as one of their results are based on the use of the Kalman filter. They include the following:

a) Schwartz [10] analyses three types of model. The first is a model with one risk factor where the spot price is assumed to show mean reversion. The second follows a GBM process, extended with an additional stochastic factor, namely the convenience yield. The third extends the second by including stochastic interest rates. In all these models there is an unobservable spot price whose behaviour is reflected in the transition equation, while the measurement equation is constructed with the quoted prices of futures contracts. In this paper estimates are drawn up from a limited number of quotes: only five prices per week using data from NYMEX and ten prices per week using Enron oil data.
b) The same data are used in a different model with a short-term component and a long-term component in Schwartz and Smith [11].
c) Manoliu and Tompaidis [8] use the Kalman filter to estimate two price models for natural gas. The first model with a stochastic factor follows an Ornstein-Uhlenbeck mean-reverting process and deterministic seasonality. The second model incorporates a second stochastic component that follows a GBM process. Daily price data are used, with 15 futures contracts per day.
d) Cortazar and Naranjo [2] develop a model that applies the Kalman Filter with a variable number of price observations per day.
e) Kolos and Ronn [6] analyse the MPR for three electricity markets (PJM, Cinergy and EEX), one natural gas market (NYMEX) and one oil market (NYMEX). Based on specific stochastic models belonging to a single family, they use the stochastic equation to estimate the MPR and the standard deviation of the estimator for each futures contract[8]. Unfortunately, most of the estimates are not significantly different from zero. These authors aggregate the estimates obtained for each contract to obtain an MPR for each market, assuming it to be the same for all futures contracts.

[8]It must be remembered that each futures contract is identified by its maturity time, begins to be quoted at a given time and ceases to be quoted on a given day prior to its settlement. Thus, each futures contract has a time series of quotes for given days which do not usually coincide perfectly with those of other contracts.

This paper presents an alternative approach for estimating both the MPR and estimates' volatility. It differs from other studies mainly in the following:

a) in the method used: if necessary a prior estimate of the spot price is obtained for each day, with a value very close to the futures contract with the shortest maturity. This calculation is not necessary if a GBM-type model is used, so in the latter case an unobservable price would not be used.
b) All available quoted prices are used, by contrast to other papers which use only a subset of them.
c) The possibility of there being no observations is admitted, and all the quotes for the longest maturity contracts are used.
d) The existence and use of very high numbers of quotes means that the volatility of the parameter estimates can be reduced.
e) Panel data are used as an estimation method, with the cross-sectional units corresponding to futures contracts, each of which is identifiable by its maturity date. This method enables a check to be made as to whether or not it is acceptable for the MPR to be the same for all the cross-sectional units.

3. Stochastic Price Models

The procedure used is as follows:

a) Choice of the stochastic model followed by the spot price. Initially a choice must be made as to whether the GBM model or a mean reversion model is valid for the commodity at hand. This section discusses how futures market quotes can help make this choice. The model chosen should be suitable for representing the commodity under study and for the specific use to which it is to be put.
b) Modelling of the MPR. There are various ways of doing this, so the most appropriate one must be selected. It is possible, for instance, to model it as a constant amount or as an amount proportional to the spot price.
c) Deduction of the compatible futures equation using the model chosen. This is done by applying Ito's lemma.
d) Finding of the stochastic equation followed by a futures contract over time in the real world. It is well known that in the risk-neutral world this equation must have no drift, but in the real world it will have a drift that is related to the MPR, which forms part of the drift along with some additional components that depend on the stochastic model chosen for the spot price.
e) Finally there is the problem of estimating the above equation, to enable parameters such as price volatility and the MPR to be deduced using all available futures prices. This is dealt with in the next section. The results and the significance levels of the parameters estimated allow a judgement to be formed as to whether futures price are unbiased estimators of expected spot prices and, as the case may be, to determine the sign and magnitude of the RP, which may vary across maturities.

The price at a time t of a futures contract for delivery at T and the expected spot price for the latter date at time t are related through the RP:

$$F(t,T) = E_t(S_T) + RP(t,T).$$

By paying in the future the sum expected plus the RP it is possible to insure oneself against adverse movements in spot prices when there is a need to purchase the commodity at time T. Similarly, a seller of the commodity can assure him/herself of a certain price at time T on the futures market, so that this price includes a RP.

3.1. The Geometric Brownian Motion (GBM) Model

Two possible MPR models within the GBM framework are considered.

3.1.1. MPR Proportional to Spot Price

This model is used very frequently for the simple case of a GBM stochastic model:

$$dS_t = \alpha S_t dt + \sigma S_t dz_t, \tag{1}$$

where S_t is the price of the commodity at time t, α is the instantaneous drift rate in the real world (assumed constant), σ denotes the instantaneous volatility of price returns, and dz_t stands for the increment to a standard Wiener process.

The risk-neutral version of this model is:

$$dS_t = (\alpha - \lambda) S_t dt + \sigma S_t dz_t, \tag{2}$$

where λS_t is the MPR[9], which as can be observed is modelled in proportion to S_t. In this case the value obtained at time t is that of a futures contract maturing at T based on the following equation:

$$F(t,T) = S_t e^{(\alpha-\lambda)(T-t)}. \tag{3}$$

Equation (3) shows that a commodity whose spot price follows a GBM should show quotes on the futures market for which the growth in absolute value increases as the time to maturity becomes longer. This behaviour can be used to identify a commodity as a good candidate for modelling with a GBM.

On the other hand, in the real world:

---

[9] An alternative specification is $\alpha - \lambda = r - \delta$, where r is the risk-free interest rate and δ is the convenience yield. Wilmott [12] includes several cases of MPR modelling.

$$E_t(S_T) = S_t e^{\alpha(T-t)}.$$

So the RP ends up looking like this:

$$RP(t,T) = F(t,T) - E_t(S_T) = S_t e^{\alpha(T-t)}[e^{-\lambda(T-t)} - 1].$$

Thus:

a) if $\lambda = 0$ then $RP(t,T) = 0$ and $F(t,T) = E_t(S_T)$. In this case the futures price is an unbiased estimator of the expected spot price.
b) if $\lambda > 0$ then $RP(t,T) < 0$. In this case the futures price is a downward-biased estimator of spot price.
c) if $\lambda < 0$ then $RP(t,T) > 0$. Here, the futures price is an un upward-biased estimator. The sign of the RP and the sign of the MPR are exactly opposite.

On the other hand, if an MPR constantly proportional to the spot price is assumed then the RP tends to zero as time t approaches maturity T. This means that the futures price is a good estimator for short maturities, because although it can be biased the magnitude of the bias may be small. The same cannot be said for long maturity periods, when the bias may be significant.

It should be further observed that the following relation between futures prices is also valid, based on two futures contracts with maturities T_1 and T_2 (with $T_1 < T_2$):

$$F(t,T_2) = F(t,T_1)_t e^{(\alpha-\lambda)(T_2-T_1)}.$$

This may in some cases enable to overcome the absence of a spot price S_t (which is sometimes unobservable).

The next step is to calculate the differential equation followed by the price of a futures contract over time. Take the following first and second partial derivatives:

$$\frac{\partial F}{\partial S} = e^{(\alpha-\lambda)(T-t)}; \quad \frac{\partial^2 F}{\partial S^2} = 0; \quad \frac{\partial F}{\partial t} = -(\alpha - \lambda) S_t e^{(\alpha-\lambda)(T-t)}.$$

Observe that the sensitivity of a futures contract with maturity T is being studied as time t increases and therefore the time remaining until maturity $\tau = T - t$ decreases.

There are two possible approaches:

a) If the objective is to work out the behaviour in the real world, e.g. to carry out estimations of parameters, then equation (1) can be used together with Ito's lemma, giving:

$$dF_t = \lambda S_t e^{(\alpha-\lambda)(T-t)} dt + \sigma S_t e^{(\alpha-\lambda)(T-t)} dz_t = \lambda F_t dt + \sigma F_t dz_t. \quad (4)$$

This equation can thus be used to estimate λ and σ from changes over time in the quoted prices of a futures contract. Equation (4) also implies that:

$$E_t(F_{t+\Delta t}) = F_t e^{\lambda \Delta t}.$$

Defining $X \equiv \ln F$, from equation (4) results:

$$dX = (\lambda - \frac{\sigma^2}{2})dt + \sigma dz_t.$$

In discrete time:

$$X_{t+\Delta t} - X_t = \ln(\frac{F_{t+\Delta t}}{F_t}) = (\lambda - \frac{\sigma^2}{2})\Delta t + \sigma\sqrt{\Delta t}\varepsilon_t, \quad (5)$$

where ε_t is a standardised Gaussian white noise.

b) If the objective is to use the differential futures price equation to undertake valuations, then equation (2) should be used. Applying Ito's lemma, this gives:

$$dF_t = \sigma S_t e^{(\alpha-\lambda)(T-t)} dz_t^* = \sigma F_t dz_t^*.$$

The asterisk indicates that we are now in a risk-neutral setting. Here the drift rate has disappeared, which may be useful for application of numerical methods such as binomial trees, as it removes any possibility of obtaining negative probabilities in calculations. In a risk-neutral world the futures price has no drift; otherwise it would be possible to obtain a positive profit with zero investment.

3.1.2. Constant MPR

Next, the same exercise is carried out with a different modelling of the MPR, which is now assumed to be constant and not to vary with the spot price. In this case the risk-neutral version of equation (1) is

$$dS_t = (\alpha S_t - \lambda)dt + \sigma S_t dz_t, \quad (6)$$

where the remaining parameters have the same meanings as in the case of the proportional MPR.

The equation that gives the value at time t of a futures contract with maturity at T is:

$$F(t,T) = \frac{\lambda}{\alpha} + [S_t - \frac{\lambda}{\alpha}]e^{\alpha(T-t)}.$$

This can easily be shown to comply with equation (6) and with the terminal condition $F(t,t) = S_t$, taking into account that $E_t^Q(S_T) = F(t,T)$, i.e. the expected value at t of S_T under the equivalent martingale measure is $F(t,T)$.

On the other hand, the expected spot price is:

$$E_t(S_T) = S_t e^{\alpha(T-t)}.$$

So in this case the RP is:

$$RP(t,T) = \frac{\lambda}{\alpha}(1 - e^{\alpha(T-t)}).$$

Observe also that the RP decreases as the maturity date of the futures contract gets nearer.

In this case the partial derivatives are: $\frac{\partial F}{\partial S} = e^{\alpha(T-t)}$; $\frac{\partial^2 F}{\partial S^2} = 0$; $\frac{\partial F}{\partial t} = -\alpha(S_t - \frac{\lambda}{\alpha})e^{\alpha(T-t)}$.

Applying Ito's lemma and using equation (1), the dynamic stochastic model of futures price in the real world is:

$$dF_t = \lambda e^{\alpha(T-t)} dt + \sigma S_t e^{\alpha(T-t)} dz_t.$$

The drift rate in this equation is very similar to equation (4): in both cases it is the MPR multiplied by $e^{\alpha(T-t)}dt$.

Similarly, under the equivalent martingale measure we have:

$$dF_t = \sigma S_t e^{\alpha(T-t)} dz_t^*.$$

3.2. Mean-Reverting Models

Two models showing mean reversion are developed below. In both cases we derive the stochastic equation of the futures price.

3.2.1. IGBM Model with MPR Proportional to Spot Price

We start from the Inhomogeneous Geometric Brownian Motion initially:

$$dS_t = k(S_m - S_t)dt + \sigma S_t dz_t,$$

where S_t is the price of the commodity at time *t*, k is the reversion speed, S_m is the expected price towards which the value of the commodity tends in the long term, σ is the instantaneous volatility and dz_t stands for the increment to a standard Wiener process.

Under the equivalent martingale measure this can be expressed as:

$$dS_t = [k(S_m - S_t) - \lambda S_t]dt + \sigma S_t dz_t^*,$$

where the MPR is proportional to S_t.

The expected price at time t can be calculated as follows:

$$\frac{E^Q(dS_t)}{dt} + (k+\lambda)E^Q(S_t) = kS_m. \tag{7}$$

This can be solved using $e^{(k+\lambda)t}$ as the integration factor, which yields:

$$E^Q(S_t) = \frac{kS_m}{k+\lambda} + C_0 e^{-(k+\lambda)t},$$

where C_0 is a constant determined according to the initial conditions. Since $E_t^Q(S_t) = S_t$ must be true, the following results:

$$C_0 = S_t - \frac{kS_m}{k+\lambda},$$

$$F(t,T) = \frac{kS_m}{k+\lambda} + (S_t - \frac{kS_m}{k+\lambda})e^{-(k+\lambda)(T-t)}. \tag{8}$$

It can easily be shown that formula (8) complies with the differential equation (7). This solution can also be shown to comply with the differential equation:

$$\frac{1}{2}\sigma^2 S^2 \frac{\partial^2 F}{\partial S^2} + [k(S_m - S_t) - \lambda S_t]\frac{\partial F}{\partial S} = \frac{\partial F}{\partial t},$$

with terminal condition $F(t,t) = S_t$.

The expected value of the future spot price for this mean- reverting model can easily be obtained via equation (8) by taking $\lambda = 0$, giving:

$$E_t(S_T) = S_m + (S_t - S_m)e^{-k(T-t)}.$$

The RP is again:

$$RP(t,T) = F(t,T) - E_t(S_T).$$

In this case a high reversion speed k reduces RP. Note that in this case $F(t,T)$ tends to S_m, while $E_t(S_T)$ approaches also S_m, thus pushing the difference toward zero.

It can also be observed that in the very long-term:

$$E(S_\infty) = S_m,$$

$$F(t,\infty) = \frac{kS_m}{k+\lambda}.$$

Therefore

$$RP(t,\infty) = \frac{-\lambda S_m}{k+\lambda}.$$

If this model is fully representative of actual behaviour in a futures market then long-term quotes will provide information on $\frac{kS_m}{k+\lambda}$, which will be related to the MPR so that when $\lambda = 0,\ F(t,\infty) = S_m$ is obtained.

Applying Ito's lemma, the following results:

$$\frac{\partial F}{\partial S} = e^{-(k+\lambda)(T-t)};\ \frac{\partial^2 F}{\partial S^2} = 0;\ \frac{\partial F}{\partial t} = (k+\lambda)[S_t - \frac{kS_m}{k+\lambda}]e^{-(k+\lambda)(T-t)}.$$

Therefore in the real world:

$$dF_t = [k(S_m - S_t)e^{-(k+\lambda)(T-t)} + [(k+\lambda)S_t - kS_m]e^{-(k+\lambda)(T-t)}]dt + \sigma e^{-(k+\lambda)(T-t)}S_t dz_t =$$

$$= \lambda S_t e^{-(k+\lambda)(T-t)}dt + \sigma S_t e^{-(k+\lambda)(T-t)}dz_t \tag{9}$$

The model contains a term structure of volatility (TSOV) consistent with the Samuelson [9] effect, which implies that volatility $\sigma_S \equiv \sigma e^{-(k+\lambda)(T-t)}$ increases as the futures contract approaches its maturity. Since risk is linked to volatility, $\lambda_S \equiv \lambda e^{-(k+\lambda)(T-t)}$ is smaller for higher values of $T-t$. If k is high, the drift rateof the above equation is small.

If one considers two futures contracts with maturities T_1 and T_2 (with $T_1 < T_2$), the following results:

$$F(t,T_1) = \frac{kS_m}{k+\lambda} + [S_t - \frac{kS_m}{k+\lambda}]e^{-(k+\lambda)(T_1-t)},$$

$$F(t,T_2) = \frac{kS_m}{k+\lambda} + [S_t - \frac{kS_m}{k+\lambda}]e^{-(k+\lambda)(T_2-t)}.$$

From this pair the following can be deduced:

$$F(t,T_2) = \frac{kS_m}{k+\lambda} + [F(t,T_1) - \frac{kS_m}{k+\lambda}]e^{-(k+\lambda)(T_2-T_1)}.$$

The GBM model is a particular case of this IGBM model when $S_m = 0$ and $\alpha = -k$. In this case:

$$F(t,T)_{GBM} = S_t e^{(\alpha-\lambda)(T-t)},$$

which is the same result obtained above.

3.2.2. IGBM Model with Constant MPR

Under the equivalent martingale measure this can be expressed as:

$$dS_t = [k(S_m - S_t) - \lambda]dt + \sigma S_t dz_t^*,$$

where the MPR is a constant amount and not a proportion of S_t.

The expected price at a time T can be found as follows:

$$\frac{E(dS_t)}{dt} + kE(S_t) = kS_m - \lambda, \tag{10}$$

which can be solved using e^{kt} as an integration factor, resulting in:

$$E(S_t) = \frac{kS_m - \lambda}{k} + C_0.$$

C_0 is a constant which is determined according to the initial conditions. Since $E_t^Q(S_t) = S_t$ must hold, the following results:

$$F(t,T) = (S_m - \frac{\lambda}{k}) + [S_t - (S_m - \frac{\lambda}{k})]e^{-k(T-t)}. \tag{11}$$

It can easily be shown that formula (11) complies with differential equation (10). This solution complies with the differential equation:

$$\frac{1}{2}\sigma^2 S^2 \frac{\partial^2 F}{\partial S^2} + [k(S_m - S_t) - \lambda]\frac{\partial F}{\partial S} = \frac{\partial F}{\partial t},$$

with terminal condition: $F(t,t) = S_t$.

It can also be observed that in the very long term:

$$E(S_\infty) = (S_m - \frac{\lambda}{k}).$$

If this model is fully representative of actual behaviour in a futures market then long-term quotes will provide information on this value, which is the long-term equilibrium price minus an MPR λ divided by k. Thus, if the reversion speed k is very high then the price will be more predictable and the risk will be smaller.

The expected value of the future spot price for this mean- reverting model can be obtained easily from equation (11) by making $\lambda = 0$, which gives:

$$E_t(S_T) = S_m + (S_t - S_m)e^{-k(T-t)}.$$

The RP in this case is:

$$RP(t,T) = F(t,T) - E_t(S_T) = \frac{\lambda}{k}(e^{-k(T-t)} - 1).$$

In this case a high reversion speed k reduces the RP.

Differentiating $F(t,T)$ in (11) with respect to S_t and t and applying Ito's lemma, the following results:

$$\frac{\partial F}{\partial S} = e^{-k(T-t)}; \quad \frac{\partial^2 F}{\partial S^2} = 0; \quad \frac{\partial F}{\partial t} = k[S_t - (S_m - \frac{\lambda}{k})]e^{-k(T-t)}.$$

Therefore:

$$dF = [k(S_m - S_t)e^{-k(T-t)} + k[S_t - (S_m - \frac{\lambda}{k})]e^{-k(T-t)}]dt + \sigma e^{-k(T-t)} S_t dz_t =$$

$$= \lambda e^{-k(T-t)} dt + \sigma e^{-k(T-t)} S_t dz_t.$$

As can be observed, now the drift rate does not include S_t.

Considering two futures contracts maturing at T_1 and T_2 (with $T_1 < T_2$), we have:

$$F(t,T_1) = (S_m - \frac{\lambda}{k}) + [S_t - (S_m - \frac{\lambda}{k})]e^{-k(T_1 - t)},$$

$$F(t,T_2) = (S_m - \frac{\lambda}{k}) + [S_t - (S_m - \frac{\lambda}{k})]e^{-k(T_2 - t)}.$$

From this pair we can deduce:

$$F(t,T_2) = (S_m - \frac{\lambda}{k}) + [F(t,T_1) - (S_m - \frac{\lambda}{k})]e^{-k(T_2 - T_1)}.$$

In the GBM case (i.e. $S_m = 0$ and $\alpha = -k$) with the modelling of the MPR chosen we have:

$$F(t,T)_{GBM} = \frac{\lambda}{\alpha} + [S_t - \frac{\lambda}{\alpha}]e^{\alpha(T-t)};$$

This is the same result obtained above.

3.2.3. Schwartz's Model

Next, Schwartz's [10] model is developed, but with a different specification of the MPR as λS_t in the differential equation for the spot price under the equivalent martingale measure.[10] The starting point is the following stochastic process:

$$dS_t = k(\mu - \ln S_t)S_t dt + \sigma S_t dz_t. \tag{12}$$

The risk-neutral version of this process with the modelling of the MPR chosen is:

$$dS_t = [k(\mu - \ln S_t)S_t - \lambda S_t]dt + \sigma S_t dz_t^*. \tag{13}$$

In this case, defining $X_t \equiv \ln S_t$ the model takes this form:

$$dX_t = [k(\mu - X) - \lambda - \frac{\sigma^2}{2}]dt + \sigma dz_t^*,$$
$$dX_t = k(X_m^* - X_t)dt + \sigma dz_t^*,$$

[10] In Schwartz's [10] original model this appears as a MPR for the log price.

with $X_m^* \equiv \mu - \frac{\sigma^2}{2k} - \frac{\lambda}{k}$. Using the properties of the log-normal distribution, hence the futures price equation is obtained as:

$$F(t,T) = e^{[e^{-k(T-t)}\ln S_t + (1-e^{-k(T-t)})X_m^* + \frac{\sigma^2}{4k}(1-e^{-2k(T-t)})]} = e^{[\bullet]}.$$

As can be checked, $F(t,t) = S_t$.

In this case,

$$\frac{\partial F}{\partial S} = \frac{e^{-k(T-t)}}{S} e^{[\bullet]}; \quad \frac{\partial^2 F}{\partial S^2} = -\frac{e^{-k(T-t)}}{S^2} e^{[\bullet]} + \frac{e^{-2k(T-t)}}{S^2} e^{[\bullet]};$$

$$\frac{\partial F}{\partial t} = (ke^{-k(T-t)} \ln S_t - kX_m^* e^{-k(T-t)} - \frac{\sigma^2}{2} e^{-2k(T-t)}) e^{[\bullet]}.$$

Using equation (12) and applying Ito's lemma the dynamics of the futures price is:

$$dF = e^{[\bullet]}(k\mu e^{-k(T-t)} - \frac{\sigma^2}{2} e^{-k(T-t)} - kX_m^* e^{-k(T-t)})dt + \sigma e^{-k(T-t)} e^{[\bullet]} dz_t.$$

Since $X_m^* \equiv \mu - \frac{\sigma^2}{2k} - \frac{\lambda}{k}$, the following is obtained:

$$dF = (\lambda e^{-k(T-t)}) e^{[\bullet]} dt + \sigma e^{-k(T-t)} e^{[\bullet]} dz_t.$$

So in the physical world:

$$dF = \lambda e^{-k(T-t)} F_t dt + \sigma e^{-k(T-t)} F_t dz_t. \tag{14}$$

This equation also includes the term structure of the volatility (TSOV) $\sigma_S \equiv \sigma e^{-k(T-t)}$.

Under the equivalent martingale measure the behaviour of futures price simplifies to:

$$\frac{dF}{F} = \sigma e^{-k(T-t)} dz_t^*.$$

Defining $Y \equiv \ln F$ in equation (14) the following results: $\frac{\partial Y}{\partial F} = \frac{1}{F}$; $\frac{\partial^2 Y}{\partial F^2} = -\frac{1}{F^2}$; $\frac{\partial Y}{\partial t} = 0$. So applying Ito's lemma and taking $\sigma_S \equiv \sigma e^{-k(T-t)}$ and $\lambda_S \equiv \lambda e^{-k(T-t)}$ we get:

$$dY = (\lambda e^{-k(T-t)} - \frac{\sigma_S^2}{2})dt + \sigma_S dz_t^*.$$

3.3. Two-Factor Model: IGBM with Stochastic MPR

An additional case is developed below with an extension of the model, where the MPR is stochastic. To prevent analysis from becoming too complicated, the MPR here is not multiplied by S_t.

The starting point is a spot price equation which has the following form under the equivalent martingale measure:

$$dS_t = [k(S_m - S_t) - \lambda_t]dt + \sigma S_t dz_t^{1*}.$$

The stochastic MPR is modelled as follows:

$$d\lambda_t = \sigma_\lambda dz_t^2,$$

with $dz_t^1 dz_t^2 = \rho dt$ so that $E(\lambda_T) = \lambda_t$.

Taking expected values, the following is obtained:

$$F(t,T) = (S_m - \frac{\lambda_t}{k}) + [S_t - (S_m - \frac{\lambda_t}{k})]e^{-k(T-t)}. \tag{15}$$

In this case the futures price must satisfy:

$$\frac{1}{2}\sigma^2 S^2 \frac{\partial^2 F}{\partial S^2} + \sigma\sigma_\lambda \rho S \frac{\partial^2 F}{\partial S \partial \lambda} + \frac{1}{2}\sigma_\lambda^2 \frac{\partial^2 F}{\partial \lambda^2} + [k(S_m - S_t) - \lambda_t]\frac{\partial F}{\partial S} = \frac{\partial F}{\partial t},$$

where $\frac{\partial^2 F}{\partial S^2} = 0$; $\frac{\partial^2 F}{\partial S \partial \lambda} = 0$; $\frac{\partial^2 F}{\partial \lambda^2} = 0$; $\frac{\partial F}{\partial S} = e^{-k(T-t)}$; $\frac{\partial F}{\partial \lambda} = \frac{e^{-k(T-t)} - 1}{k}$; and $\frac{\partial F}{\partial t} = -k[S_t - (S_m - \frac{\lambda_t}{k})]e^{-k(T-t)}$.

It can be shown to comply with these requirements. It also complies with the terminal condition $F(t,t) = S_t$.

In this case, applying Ito's lemma:

$$dF = \lambda_t e^{-k(T-t)} dt + \sigma e^{-k(T-t)} S_t dz_t^1 + \sigma_\lambda \frac{e^{-k(T-t)} - 1}{k} dz_t^2.$$

3.4. Summary of Stochastic Models

Table 1 below summarises the stochastic models described and their corresponding futures price equations according to the MPR specified.

Table 2 shows the stochastic dynamics of the futures contracts depending on the spot model and the MPR. As can be seen, in all cases except the GBM with proportional MPR the dynamics depends on the maturity T of the futures contract.

As can be seen, the expected value of dF_t obtained in futures markets determines the sign of the MPR. If the price of a specific futures contract *i* with maturity T_i tends to increase when t increases, this is symptomatic of the existence of a positive MPR.

In this case the futures prices may possibly be downward-biased estimators of expected spot prices. The opposite is true if the prices in general for futures contracts with maturity T_i tend to decrease when t increases.

Table 1. Spot Models and Futures Prices

Spot Model (dS_t)	MPR	Futures price ($F(T,t)$)
$\alpha S_t dt + \sigma S_t dz_t$	λS_t	$S_t e^{(\alpha-\lambda)(T-t)}$
$k(S_m - S_t)dt + \sigma S_t dz_t$	λS_t	$\frac{kS_m}{k+\lambda} + (S_t - \frac{kS_m}{k+\lambda})e^{-(k+\lambda)(T-t)}$
$k(\mu - \ln S_t)S_t dt + \sigma S_t dz_t$	λS_t	$e^{[e^{-k(T-t)}\ln S_t + (1-e^{-k(T-t)})X_m^* + \frac{\sigma^2}{4k}(1-e^{-2k(T-t)})]}$
$\alpha S_t dt + \sigma S_t dz_t$	λ	$\frac{\lambda}{\alpha} + [S_t - \frac{\lambda}{\alpha}]e^{\alpha(T-t)}$
$k(S_m - S_t)dt + \sigma S_t dz_t$	λ	$(S_m - \frac{\lambda}{k}) + [S_t - (S_m - \frac{\lambda}{k})]e^{-k(T-t)}$
$k(S_m - S_t)dt + \sigma S_t dz_t^1$ $d\lambda_t = \sigma_\lambda dz_t^2$	λ_t	$(S_m - \frac{\lambda_t}{k}) + [S_t - (S_m - \frac{\lambda_t}{k})]e^{-k(T-t)}$

Table 2. Spot Models and Futures Price Dynamics

Spot Model (dS_t)	MPR	Futures Dynamics (dF_t)
$\alpha S_t dt + \sigma S_t dz_t$	λS_t	$\lambda F_t dt + \sigma F_t dz_t$
$k(S_m - S_t)dt + \sigma S_t dz_t$	λS_t	$\lambda S_t e^{-(k+\lambda)(T-t)} dt + \sigma S_t e^{-(k+\lambda)(T-t)} dz_t$
$k(\mu - \ln S_t)S_t dt + \sigma S_t dz$	λS_t	$\lambda e^{-k(T-t)} F_t dt + \sigma e^{-k(T-t)} F_t dz_t$
$\alpha S_t dt + \sigma S_t dz_t$	λ	$\lambda e^{\alpha(T-t)} dt + \sigma S_t e^{\alpha(T-t)} dz_t$
$k(S_m - S_t)dt + \sigma S_t dz_t$	λ	$\lambda e^{-k(T-t)} dt + \sigma e^{-k(T-t)} S_t dz_t$
$k(S_m - S_t)dt + \sigma S_t dz_t^1$ $d\lambda_t = \sigma_\lambda dz_t^2$	λ_t	$\lambda_t e^{-k(T-t)} dt + \sigma e^{-k(T-t)} S_t dz_t^1 + \sigma_\lambda \frac{e^{-k(T-t)} - 1}{k} dz_t^2$

4. Estimation

The estimation is drawn up considering the quotes available as a panel dataset, where each cross-sectional unit is a particular futures contract maturing on a specific date, whose quoted price over time is known. These futures contracts, of course, begin to be quoted on a specific day and disappear just before their settlement date[11] , which means that some data are omitted from the panel dataset. Estimations for GBM with a proportional MPR, IGBM and MPR proportional to spot price are drawn up.

4.1. Sample Description

Two datasets are used: futures quotes for CO_2 emission allowances and futures quotes for coal. The EU allowance futures prices are for the EUA ETS (Emissions Trading Scheme). They are taken from the European Climate Exchange (ECX) for the period from 04/22/2005 to 06/11/2010. In that period there are five contracts with maturities in December within the Kyoto Protocol commitment period (2008-12), and two contracts beyond Kyoto with maturities in December-2013 and December-2014. Figure 1 shows the time paths of emission allowance prices. The figure 2 shows the same information as a surface.

In the case of coal, the futures prices for Central Appalachian Coal (from NYMEX) are used. The sample runs from 1/4/2007 to 6/16/2010. The quotes are for futures contracts with monthly maturities. A maximum of 41 monthly quotes per day are used. Figure 3 shows their

[11]This settlement can be based on price differences or on actual delivery of the commodity in return for the settlement price.

time profile. F01 denotes the futures contract with the shortest maturity time, F12 the contract with the twelfth shortest, and so on.

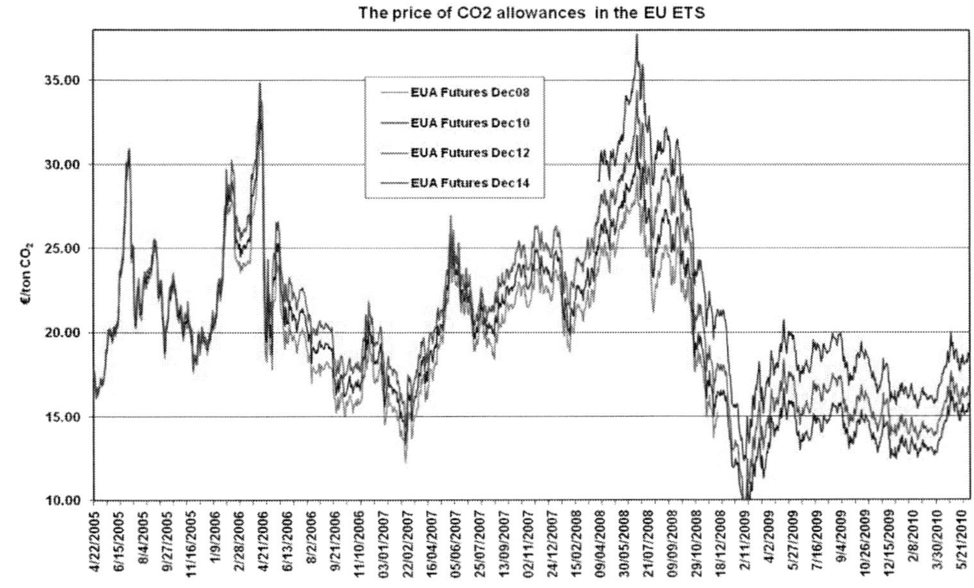

Figure 1. EUA Futures Prices (from ECX).

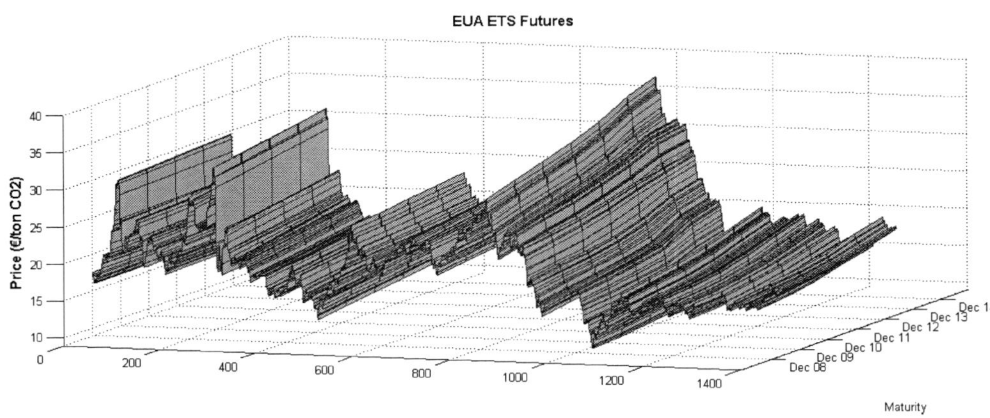

Figure 2. EUA Futures Price Surface.

Figure 4 shows the quotes on 06/16/2010, the last day of the sample period. The graph includes an estimated futures curve obtained by minimising the square errors between the curve and the actual prices.

Figure 5 shows the trend in coal quotes. It is slightly different in form because the data for 5/21/2009 to 6/16/2010 are structured as panel data. It can be seen that certain contracts disappear when their settlement date is reached and others are quoted for the first time.

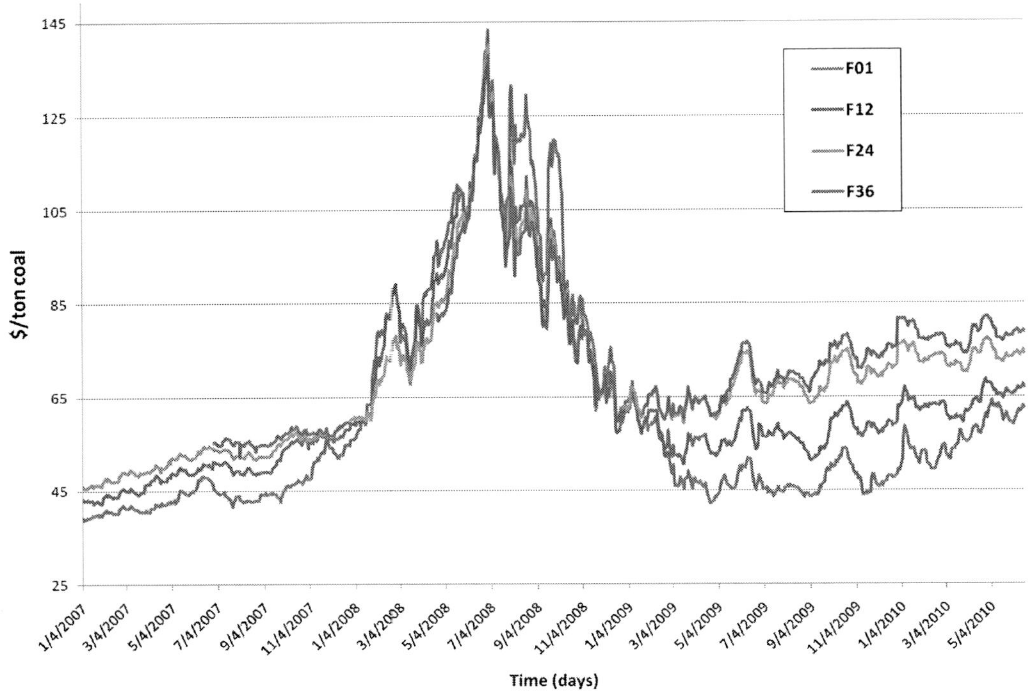

Figure 3. Central Appalachian Coal Futures prices (from NYMEX).

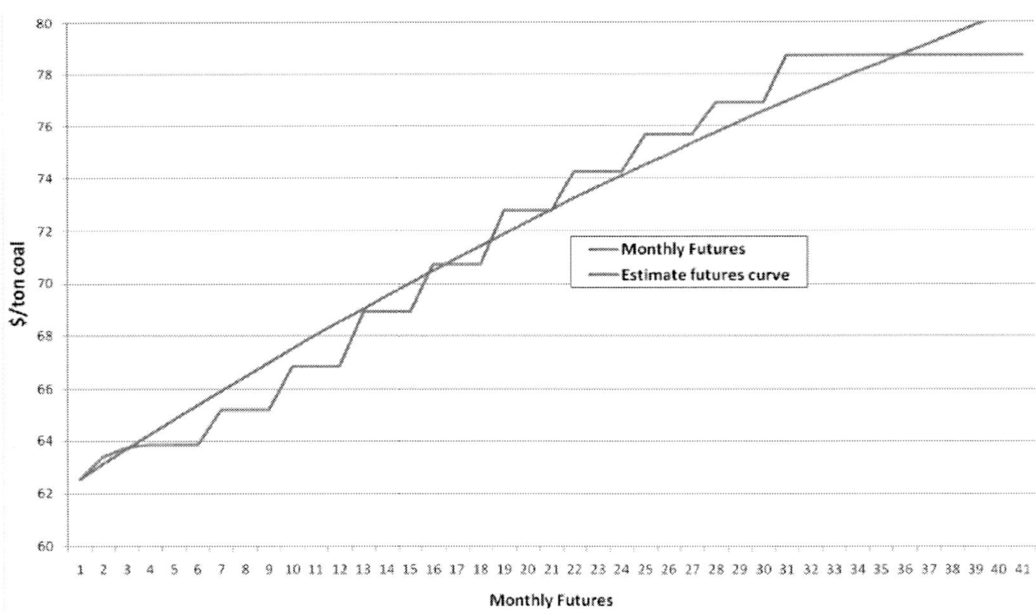

Figure 4. Central Appalachian Coal futures prices on 06/16/2010.

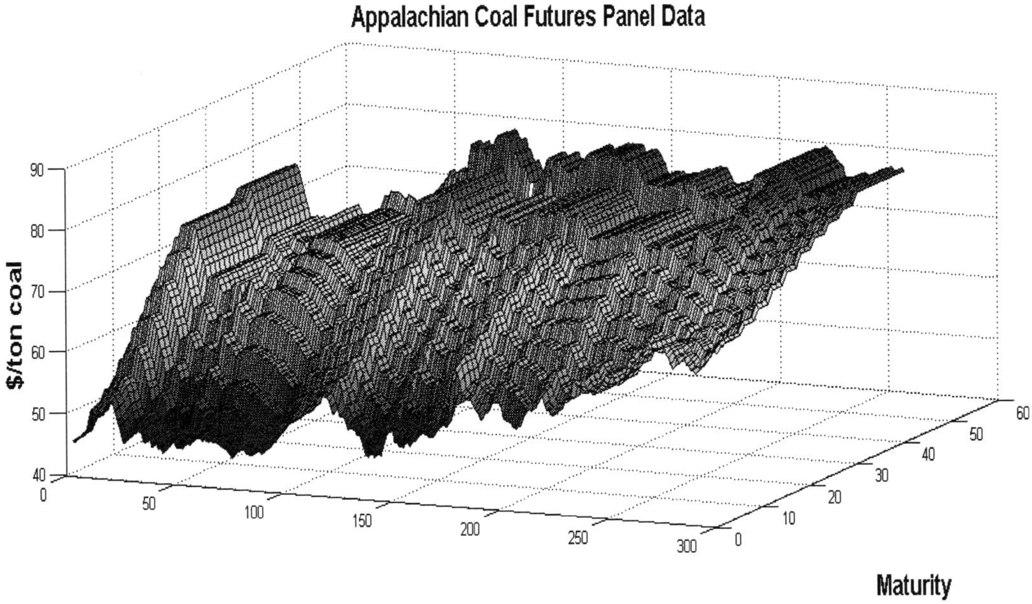

Figure 5. Central Appalachian Coal Futures Panel Data.

4.2. The GBM Case with Proportional MPR

Taking the natural logarithm $X_t \equiv \ln F$, equation (5) establishes that in discrete time:

$$\Delta X = X_{t+\Delta t} - X_t = (\lambda - \frac{\sigma^2}{2})\Delta t + \sigma\sqrt{\Delta t}\varepsilon_t.$$

The analysis of panel data can be represented as:

$$\Delta X_{it} = \beta_0 + u_{it}$$

where β_0 stands for the common intercept, and u_{it} is the error term. The model is estimated by pooled OLS with 7,160 observations corresponding to 7 cross-sectional units, giving:

As can be observed, in spite of the large number of futures prices the drift rate cannot be estimated accurately, because it is not significantly different from zero (the absolute value of *t*-ratio is small and the *p*-value is high). This problem is analysed in detail in Gourieroux and Jasiak [5].

Table 3. Estimation of the GBM model

	Estimate	Std. error	*t*-ratio	*p*-value
$\hat{\beta}_0$	-0.000192709	0.000322	-0.5984	0.5496

It is, however, possible to obtain an accurate estimate for volatility, given that the asymptotic variance of the estimator is $\frac{\sigma^4}{N}$, where $N =$ 7,160 is the number of observations. With the standard deviation of the dependent variable obtained in the estimation of 0.027249, the following is obtained:

$$\hat{\sigma} = 0.027249\sqrt{252} = 0.432564.$$

If the estimate $\hat{\beta}_0$ is used, taking into account an average of 252 trading days per year, the estimate for MPR is:

$$\frac{\Delta \hat{X}}{\Delta t} = \hat{\lambda} - \frac{\hat{\sigma}^2}{2} \Rightarrow \hat{\lambda} = 252\,\hat{\beta}_0 + \frac{\hat{\sigma}^2}{2} = 0.0450.$$

The MPR is positive but not significant.

Panel data estimations with fixed and random effects give the same results. Using these results, we can reject the hypothesis that the cross-sectional units have a different intercept. In other words, the data are consistent with the hypothesis of a common β_0 for all futures contracts.

4.3. The IGBM Case with Proportional MPR

This model is now applied to the data for coal. Mean reversion is assumed since Figure (5) shows that on all trading days prices on the futures market tend to reach an equilibrium value for long maturities. This is consistent with a stochastic mean-reverting model for the spot price.

The futures contracts in general tend to be quoted over time at higher than initial prices; see Figure 6.

Figure 7 shows the difference between the last and first quotes available for each futures contract used. These differences are very often positive.

The starting point for the estimation is equation (9):

$$dF = \lambda S_t e^{-(k+\lambda)(T-t)} dt + \sigma S_t e^{-(k+\lambda)/T-t)} dz_t,$$

which can be rewritten as:

$$\frac{dF}{S_t e^{-(k+\lambda)(T-t)}} = \lambda dt + \sigma dz_t.$$

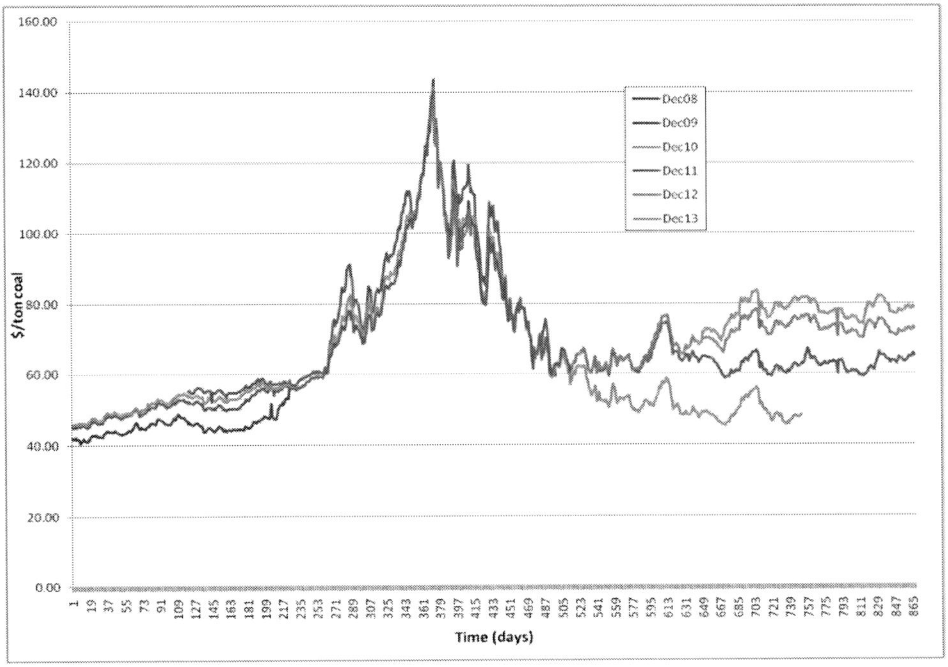

Figure 6. Time series of prices of coal futures contracts.

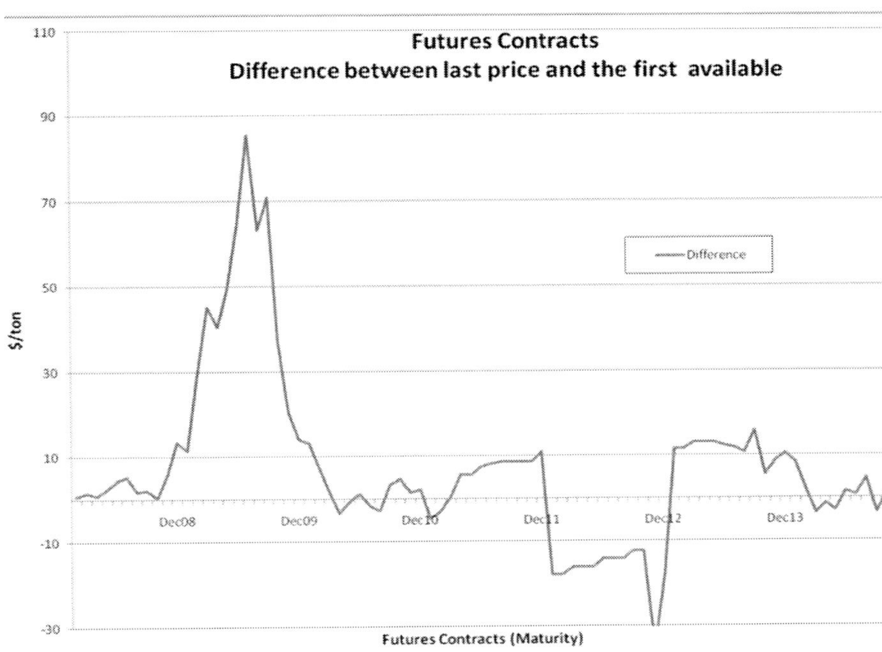

Figure 7. Difference between the last and the first price available.

If the value of $k+\lambda$ for the dataset and the value of S_t for each day t in the series are known, the same model of panel data can be used as in the previous case. It must be pointed out that $k+\lambda$ forms part of the futures equation and can be calculated relatively easily together with the value $\frac{kS_m}{k+\lambda}$, which also appears in the formula. The starting point for this is:

$$F(t,T_i)=\frac{kS_m}{k+\lambda}+[F(t,T_1)-\frac{kS_m}{k+\lambda}]e^{-(k+\lambda)(T_i-T_1)},$$

where T_1 corresponds to the futures contract with the nearest maturity date (F01) and T_i is the maturity of the *i*-th's futures contract. Note that using this formula forces the estimated futures curve to pass through the futures price with the nearest maturity, which is useful for subsequently estimating the spot price on each day, S_t.

Once the values of $k+\lambda$ and $\frac{kS_m}{k+\lambda}$ that best fit the quotes available are obtained , the estimated value $\hat{S}_t$ for each day can be calculated using $F(t,T_1)$ as follows:

$$\hat{S}_t=\frac{kS_m}{k+\lambda}+[F(t,T_1)-\frac{kS_m}{k+\lambda}]e^{+(k+\lambda)(T_1-t)}.$$

Here it can be seen that as T_1-t becomes smaller, the estimated value $\hat{S}_t$ approaches $F(t,T_1)$.

Given the behaviour of the series in Figure (3), which reflects a period of strong growth and subsequent decline in prices, two datasets are used:

a) All the 33,115 observations with 81 cross-sectional units.
b) Only the information from 01/01/2009 onwards, i.e. 14,827 observations distributed in 58 cross-sectional units.

Non linear least squares estimation yields:

Table 4. Estimation of the IGBM model

Parameter	Full Sample	Restr. sample 2009-10	$t^*_{1/2}$ (years)
$k+\lambda$	0.2303	0.407628	3.0095
$\frac{kS_m}{k+\lambda}$	83.5952	81.7089	1.7004

The estimate for $k+\lambda$ implies that the time required for the expected price on the futures market to reach a point halfway between the current price and the long-term equilibrium price is:

$$t^*_{1/2} = \frac{\ln 2}{k+\lambda} \text{ years.}$$

This is consistent with the Figure 5.

In discrete time we have:

$$\frac{F(t+\Delta t, T) - F(t,T)}{S_t e^{-(k+\lambda)(T-t)}} = \lambda \Delta t + \sigma \sqrt{\Delta t} \varepsilon_t,$$

where ε_t is a standardised Gaussian white noise. The sign of the MPR is determined by $F_{t+\Delta t} - F_t$: if the price of a futures contract tends to rise as maturity gets closer, the MPR is positive and the RP is negative.

Panel data estimation with fixed effects yields:

Table 5. Estimation of parameter β_0 and MPR.

Sample	Estimate	Std. error	*t*-ratio	MPR
Full sample	0.000891613	0.000159886	5.577	0.2247
Restr. sample 2009-10	0.000833999	0.000316764	2.633	0.2102

With both samples the estimates of β_0 are significantly different from zero. The estimate for the MPR in this case is computed as:

$$\hat{\lambda} = 252 \hat{\beta}_0 .$$

The results show that there is a positive, significant MPR for the coal quotes (higher than 20 %). Note, though, that the MPR has less influence on the upward trend of prices in a futures contract when the contract is far from maturity, since it is multiplied by $e^{-(k+\lambda)(T-t)}$. As a result, it must be concluded that, for this particular commodity, futures prices are downward-biased estimators of expected spot prices and the RP is negative.

CONCLUSIONS

Better knowledge of the market price of risk (MPR) is important for valuation and hedging activities on the markets involved. It is reflected in the risk premium (RP) demanded by market participants. However, in some cases the MPR cannot be estimated with absolute precision. A case in point is when the spot price follows a GBM model: in this case a broader sample may help improve estimations by reducing the asymptotic volatility of the estimator.

For the case of CO_2 emission allowances a positive but non significant MPR is obtained. Although its value is not conclusive, estimating it increases knowledge of the workings of these markets. As a result, knowledge of market prices alone is not sufficient to reliably obtain and use an expected price for emission permits in the real world for a future time T.

In the case of the dataset for coal, the result is a positive and significant MPR, which is an indicator of an expected future spot price higher than the corresponding futures market price. The availability of more information and a larger number of contracts traded each day combine with the use of a mean-reverting model to help make these results significant.

Further development is advisable to implement and estimate models with MPRs which are variable over time. Yet more information may be needed to estimate the parameters in such a way that they are significant.

REFERENCES

[1] Cortazar, G. and Schwartz, E. S. (2003) Implementing a stochastic model for oil futures prices. *Energy Economics* Vol. 25 pp 215-238.

[2] Cortazar, G. and Naranjo, L. (2006) An N-factor Gaussian model of oil futures prices. *Journal of Futures Markets* 26(3) 243-268.

[3] Fabozzi, F.J., Füss, R. and Kaiser, D.G. (Eds.)(2008) The Handbook of Commodity Investing. John Wiley and Sons, Hoboken, New Jersey, US.

[4] Geman, H. (2005) Commodities and commodity derivatives. Wiley, West Sussex, UK.

[5] Gourieroux, C. and Jasiak, J.(2001) Financial Econometrics. Princeton University Press, Princeton, New Jersey, US.

[6] Kolos, S.P and Ronn, E.I.(2008) Estimating the commodity price of risk for energy prices. *Energy Economics*. Vol. 30 pp 621-641.

[7] Lucia, J. and Schwartz, E.S. (2002) Electricity prices and power derivatives: evidence from the nordic power exchange. *Review of Derivatives Research* 5(1),5-50.

[8] Manoliu, M. and Tompaidis, S. (2002) Energy futures prices: term structure models with Kalman filter estimation. *Applied Mathematical Finance* 9, 21-43.

[9] Samuelson, P.A. (1965) Proof that properly anticipated prices fluctuate randomly. *Industrial Management Review* 6, 41-49.

[10] Schwartz, E.S. (1997) The stochastic behavior of commodity prices: Implications for valuation and hedging. *Journal of Finance* 52(3), 923-973.

[11] Schwartz, E, and Smith, J.E. (2000) Short-Term Variations and Long-Term Dynamics in Commodity Prices. *Management Science*, Vol. 46. No 7, pp. 893-911.

[12] Wilmott, P. (2006) Paul Wilmott on Quantitative Finance. John Wiley and Sons, West Sussex, UK.

Reviewed by José M. Chamorro (Dpt. Financial Economics II, University of the Basque Country, Spain).

In: Financial Asset Pricing
Editors: P. E. Schulz and B. P. Hoffmann
ISBN 978-1-61122-803-8

Chapter 5

AUSTRALIAN HOUSE PRICES AFFORDABILITY: AN INTERNATIONAL COMPARISON OF THE DETERMINANTS OF HOUSE PRICE'S PERFORMANCE 1980 – 2009

Yiyang Liu* and Kevin Daly
University of Western Sydney, Mararthur

ABSTRACT

A recent study comparing international housing affordability finds Australia has three of the five most unaffordable housing markets in the world. One reason for Australia's ranking is that the house price bubble in Australia unlike elsewhere has not yet burst. Demographia believes it will burst eventually, but this is a controversial view in Australia. Many analysts claim Australia did not build as many houses during the boom as were built in other markets, and therefore we will not see the massive price declines that other countries have experienced. In this research we forward several reasons why Australia's house prices are unlikely to succumb to the price falls experienced in the US, UK and Europe generally. Based on historical and current data the paper provides a comparative analysis of the determinants of house prices in Australia and the US, including an analysis of housing affordability. From the evidence presented, the factors, which played the most significant roles in creating the conditions for the US house bubble, were not evident for the Australian housing market. In fact, the growing demand push factors combined with the constrained supply factors in providing new housing stock in particular for the major cities of Melbourne and Sydney appear to have anything but abated.

* Email: K.Liu@uws.edu.au

INTRODUCTION

In the housing affordability literature, three concepts of affordability are used; purchase affordability, repayment affordability and income affordability. Purchase affordability considers whether a household is able to borrow enough funds to purchase a house, repayment affordability considers the burden imposed on a household repaying the mortgage while income affordability simply measures the ratio of house prices to income. In this paper income, affordability provides the basis for comparing the relative prices of both US and Australian housing while purchase and repayment affordability compares the financial costs and regulations across both markets.

Several factors drive housing affordability; from the demand side demographic influences, changes in finance costs and immigration exert varying degrees of influences on house prices, while on the supply side the main drivers are land availability, infrastructure costs, government taxes and transfers. The paper is formatted as follows firstly we compare house prices in Australia and the US using a number of alternative measurements, we next examine the main drivers of house prices across both markets within a demand and supply framework, we next investigate the differences between the US and Australian regulations regards the provision of housing finance, finally the conclusion contrasts some policy implications drawn from the study for both markets.

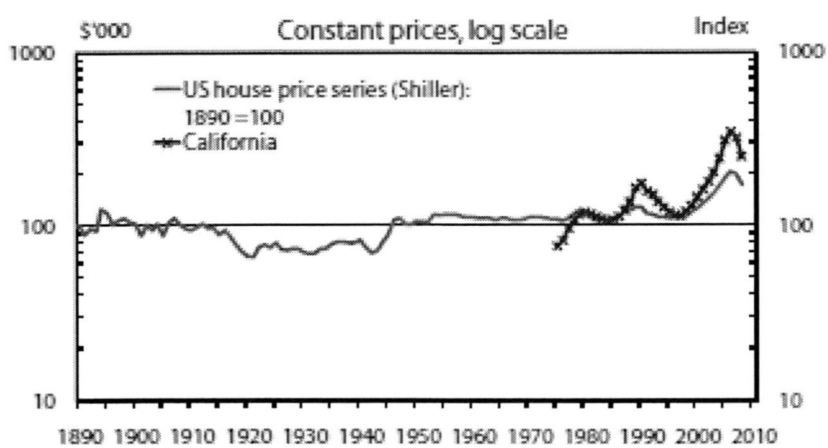

Note: U.S. house price series is deflated by the US CPI and indexed at 1890=100, and is from Schiller (2009); the California series is OFHEO series, deflated by the US CPI. The series has been indexed to the US price series at 1980 when price levels for US and California were at the same level.

Figure 1. US House Price Series 1890-2008 and California 1975-2008.

Australia's house prices rose 87 per cent in real terms between1996 – 2007, this rise is more significant than that experienced in past cycles and is according to Stapledon an acceleration from the trend rate since 1975 (2.9 %) and further back to the 1950's (Figure 2). The U.S is different in so many ways to Australia's housing market; these variations will be discussed later in the paper. In historical terms US house prices rose in real terms by 60 per cent (4.8 per cent per annum) between 1960 and their peak in the Sept quarter 2006. The long term trend growth in the US is about 1.6 per cent (Figure 1), however in the aftermath of the

2007/08 recession the US experienced significant falls ranging from 9 per cent and 30 per cent according to Case and Shiller respectively between the Sept peak 2006 and the December quarter 2008.

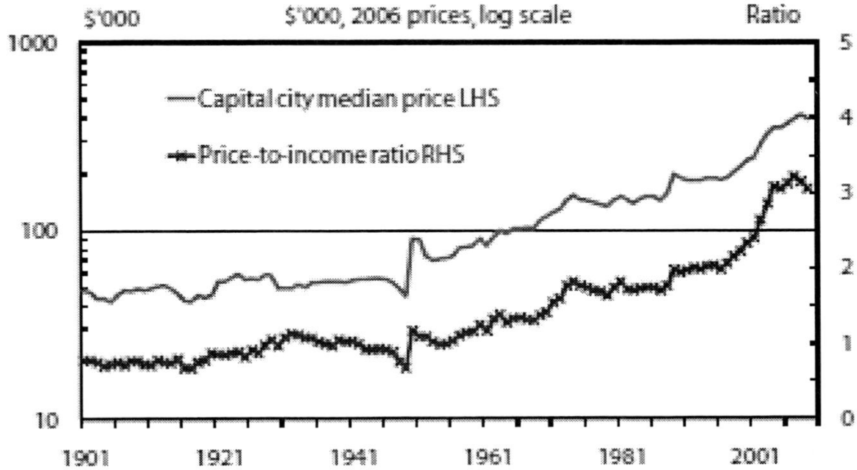

Note: The capital cities median house price series and price-to-income ratios for Australia are from Stapledon (2007), updated for 2008. The price to income series is an estimate of the value of all housing to nominal GDP, the latter being the only consistent income series for the period from 1901.

Figure 2. Australian Median House Price Series and Price-to-Income Ratio, 1901-2008.

Income affordability (i.e., the ratio of house prices to income) takes a more long-term picture of affordability; as a median measure, it compares the ratio of mortgage repayments on an average household loan to average household earnings. Banks and real estate institutes and government agencies typically employ the measure.

Demographia International uses income affordability to derive the following index, house prices are considered to be 'severely unaffordable' if the price-to-income ratio exceeds a median multiple of 5.1, seriously unaffordable (4.1 – 5), moderately unaffordable (3.1 – 4), affordable (3 or <). Accordingly in the 3rd quarter of 2008, 24 Australian towns and cities (out of 64 markets globally) were deemed severely unaffordable. Of the 272 markets surveyed in 2009, there were 103 affordable markets, (98 in the US) this is an improvement from 87 in 2008. Among the major markets, Vancouver is the least affordable (9.3), followed by Sydney (9.1), Melbourne (8.0), Adelaide (7.4), London (7.1), New York (7.0) and San Francisco (7.0).

Confirming the above income affordability data, a 2007 OECD study claims the price of housing relative to incomes is 50 per cent higher in Australia than in other countries as a group. Over the peaks of the recent global financial crisis house prices in Australia did experience a decrease but nothing compared to the decrease in prices reported in US UK or Ireland. The OECD found the estimated over-valuation of Australian homes in 2004 was 51.8 per cent. The next highest over-valuation was in Britain at 32.8 per cent. The OECD concludes that Australian house prices are higher due to a lack of housing stock, higher migration levels, low interest rates and more competition from lenders. Another factor with special importance to Australia is the growth in people investing in property specifically to rent. Buy-to-let mortgages have grown in most nations. Around seven per cent of loans in Britain are for investment, while in the US 15 per cent of home sales were for investment, the comparative figure for Australia is around 30 per cent (by late 2003). In New South Wales, the rate was 42 per cent of all mortgages, and in Victoria it was 35 per cent.

The Reserve Bank of Australia has shown that the price to income ratio was at or below 3.0 in Australia, Canada, Ireland, New Zealand, the United Kingdom and the United States until the late 1980s or late 1990s. Figure 3 shows that the trend for Australia's house price ratio doubled by 2003 falling slightly over 2005/06 and then increasing again over 2007/08 falling slightly again in 2009.

Source RBA.

Figure 3. Australia's House Price to Income.

Comparing the affordability for first homebuyers and house prices, Figure 4 shows that for over a decade affordability declined to 2008. Potential first home purchasers were unable to become homebuyers because rising house prices had increased the deposit gap and repayment requirements.

Many young adults were remaining for longer periods in the parental home or sharing housing instead of forming independent households. First homebuyer affordability improved by 36 per cent in the year to September 2009, due to the reduction in interest rates and measures such as the First Home Grant scheme, although this has since been partially reversed.

The Drivers of Australian House Prices - Bubble or Fundamentals!

In Australia, there is consensus amongst government and the private sector that there is a severe housing crisis, with rampant un-affordability and a housing shortage. Today, the median income household would be required to pay more than 50 percent of its income to service a new mortgage on the median priced house in Sydney or Melbourne. In Dallas-Fort Worth or Atlanta with similar populations, the household would pay under 20 percent.

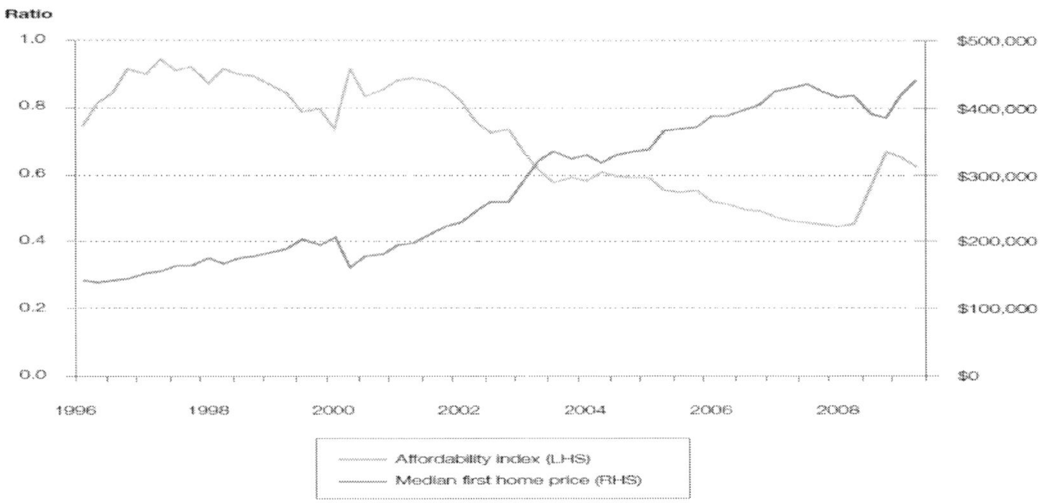

Note: The affordability index is based on the ratio of average weekly ordinary-time earnings to the income required to service the mortgage requires to buy a median-priced dwelling with a ten per cent deposit and a maximum debt service ratio of 30 percent (assuming a 25-year loan at standard variable bank housing interest rates).

Source: Hosing Industry Association – Commonwealth Bank, unpublished data on median first home prices, HIA-CG, 2010; Reserve Bank of Australia, Indicator lending rates. 'Standard variable bank housing loans". Statistical Table F5, RBA, Canberra, 2010; Reservce Bank of Australia, Labour Costs. 'Full time adult average weekly ordinary time earning'. Statistical Table G6, RBA, Canberra, 2010.

Figure 4. House Price Affordability and Median First Home Price.

The loss of housing affordability in Sydney and Melbourne is partly due to land use regulation at both the state and local level, which has virtually eliminated affordable land for building. On average, it takes from 6.25 to 14.5 years to convert urban fringe land into new houses.

In August 2009, Statement of Monetary Policy the RBA states, "The number of housing starts is likely to remain at levels well below most estimates of underlying demand. Lifting home-building in the longer-run will require further progress on the supply side, including addressing factors that are increasing the cost of development of new housing, both on the edges of cities and closer to the city centres." The gap between dwelling supply and underlying demand has led to pressures on house prices and rent levels, and thus to housing affordability problems concentrated among low-income households.

Figure 5 shows the gap between population growth and housing commencements is increasing, as the latter appears to be going in the opposite direction to population growth.

The National Housing Supply Council estimate that over the five years to 2013, the overall gap between total underlying demand and total supply is projected to grow to 203,000 dwellings (based on assumptions of medium growth in supply and underlying demand).

Australia's third largest home loan mortgage provider the ANZ bank housing forecasts suggest that if housing supply remains on its current trajectory "by mid-2010 Australia will have an unprecedented underlying housing shortage of 250,000 dwellings!". The blue bars in Figure 6 below show ANZ Bank's estimates of housing demand less housing supply.

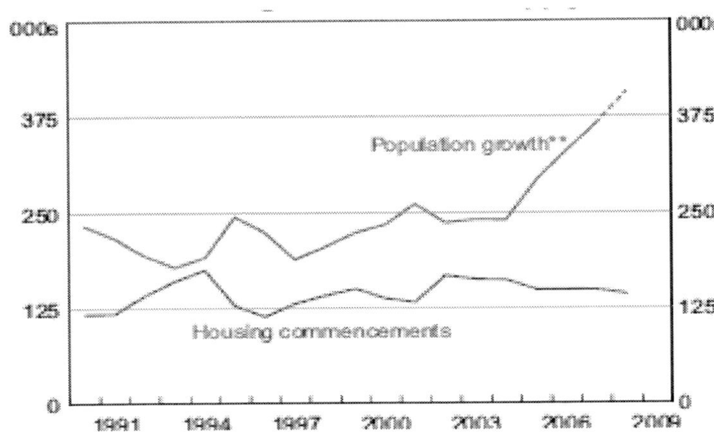

Figure 5. Housing Demand and Supply.

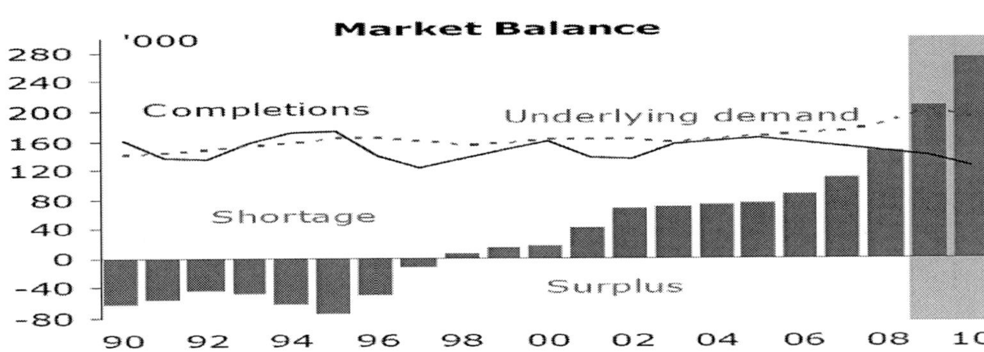

Figure 6. Housing Demand – Housing Supply.

The Housing Bubble in the US

The housing bubble in the United States grew up alongside the stock bubble in the mid-90s, for detailed analysis of the events leading to the bubble's peak and eventual bust refer to Shiller (2006) (Shiller, R. 2006. *Irrational Exuberance* (2nd edition). Princeton, NJ: Princeton University Press). Essentially consumers who had increased their wealth substantially with the extraordinary run-up of stock prices were spending with the savings rate out of disposable income falling from close to 5.0 percent in the middle of the decade to just over 2 percent by 2000. The stock wealth induced consumption boom encouraged consumers to spend some of their new stock wealth on housing. This increase in demand had the effect of triggering a housing bubble because in the short-run the supply of housing is relatively fixed. The expectation that prices would continue to rise led homebuyers to pay far more for homes than they would have otherwise, making the expectations self-fulfilling.

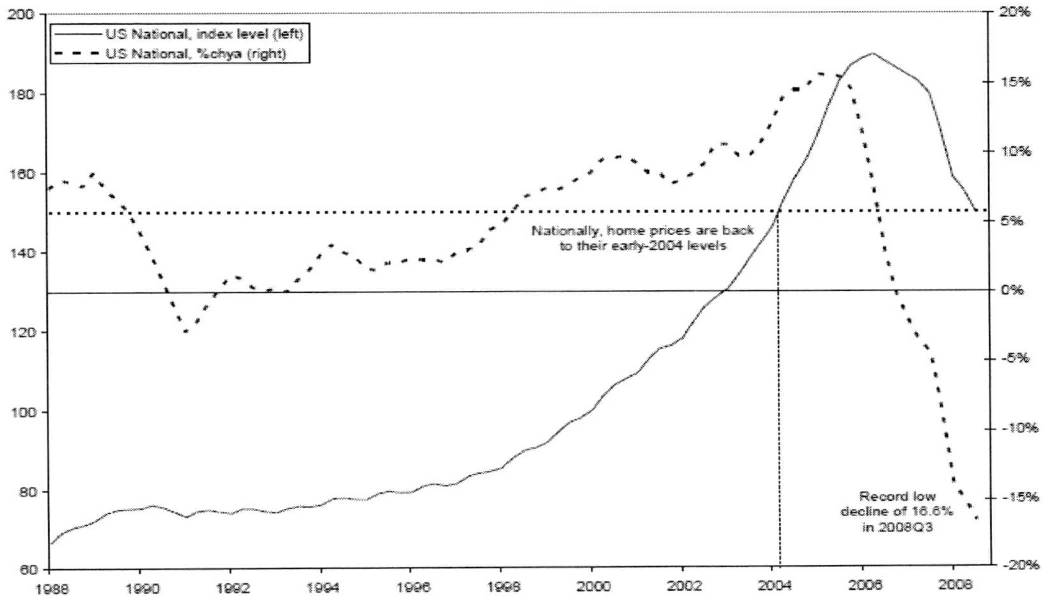

Figure 7. S&P/Case-Shiller U.S. National Home Price Index.

Source: Standard & Poor's and Fiserv. Data through 2008 Q3.

By 2002, (Figure 7) house prices had risen by nearly 30 percent after adjusting for inflation. Given the long history of stable house prices shown in the government data, and the even longer history in the data series constructed by Shiller, it should have been evident that house prices, were being driven by a speculative bubble rather than the fundamentals of the housing market.

The run-up in prices in both the ownership and rental markets was having a substantial supply-side effect, as housing starts rose substantially from the mid-90s through the late 90s. By 2002, Figure 8 housing starts were almost 25 percent above the average rate over the three years immediately preceding the start of the bubble (1993-95). The increase in building showed up first as an over-supply of rental housing, with the vacancy rate rising to near record levels above 9.0 percent in 2002, compared to a rate of 7.5 percent in the mid-90s.

The extraordinarily low interest rates accelerated the run-up in house prices. From the fourth quarter of 2002 to the fourth quarter of 2006, real house prices rose by an additional 31.6 percent, an annual rate of 7.1 percent. This fuelled even more construction, with housing starts eventually peaking at 2,070,000 in 2005, more than 50 percent above the rate in the pre-bubble years.

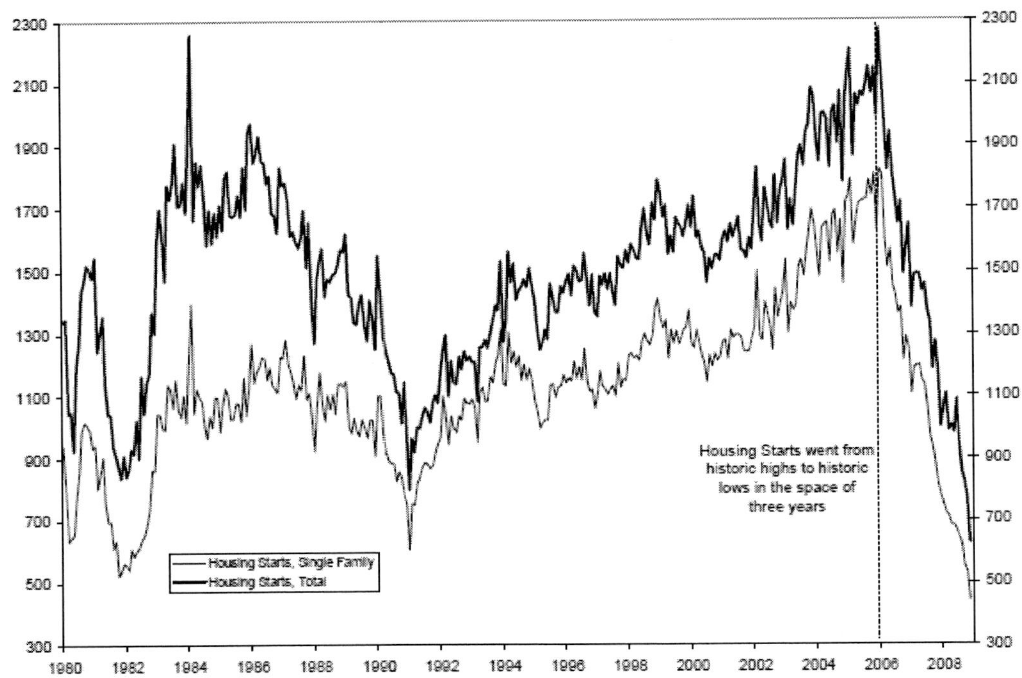

Figure 8. Housing Starts.

Source: U.S. Census Bureau, SAAR. Data through November 2008.

The bubble did begin in burst in 2007, as the building boom led to over-supply where prices could no longer be supported as Figure 7 shows by the middle of 2007, prices nationwide had peaked and began to head downward. This process accelerated through the fall of 2007 and into 2008.

The story from the demand side brought into place the makings for a 'perfect storm'. The lead up to the bubble witnessed a relaxation in lending standards, default rates began to soar in 2006 and 2007, and banks began to tighten their standards and to require larger down payments. The most severe tightening took place in the markets (20 to 25 percent down payment) with the most rapidly falling prices, which in turn excluded many potential homebuyers from the market.

By the end of 2007, real house prices had fallen by more than 15 percent from peak. House prices in many of the most over-valued markets, primarily along the two coasts, had fallen by more than 20 percent. The rate of price decline in the Shiller indexes imply that real house prices will be down by more than 30 percent from their 2007 peaks by the end of 2008. This would mean a loss of more than $7 trillion in housing bubble wealth (approximately $100,000 per homeowner). The lost wealth is almost equal to 50 percent of GDP.

HOUSING FINANCE - AUSTRALIA VS. US

The Reserve Bank of Australia tightened monetary policy in the lead up to the global financial crisis over the period May 2002–March 2005 and then more aggressively till September 2008.

However, in the US interest rates went in the opposing direction where the Fed used stimulatory monetary policy to boost activity in 2003–2006, fuelling the over-building.

The 'housing finance system 'which operates in the US differs significantly compared to that operating in Australia in several respects. In Australia, there is one supervisor for all banks (Australian Prudential Regulatory Authority) and non-bank deposit-taking institutions, but there are multiple regulators in the US. The single regulator now appears to be a factor explaining the better performance of the Australian banking system.

In the US, the widespread use of non-recourse loans allow a mortgagee, if the value of the property is less than the mortgage, to walk away and the mortgagor has no recourse to the mortgagee for the shortfall. In Australia, the mortgagee would have a liability for any shortfall.

To help facilitate non-recourse loans the US Fannie-Mae provided a public subsidy to the housing market by providing free mortgage insurance (guarantee on mortgage payments). This allowed US banks and other loan originators to shift mortgages off their balance sheets. By contrast, most mortgages in Australia are included in banks' balance sheets.

The rate of defaults and foreclosures, jumped sharply in the US in 2008 (Figure 9). By contrast, Australia has experienced historically lower default rates *visà-vis* those in the US. Higher default rates will increase supply and place downward pressure on house prices. In the US the result of high-risk lending was the build up in non-performing loans from 1 percent to 5 percent over 2007-09.

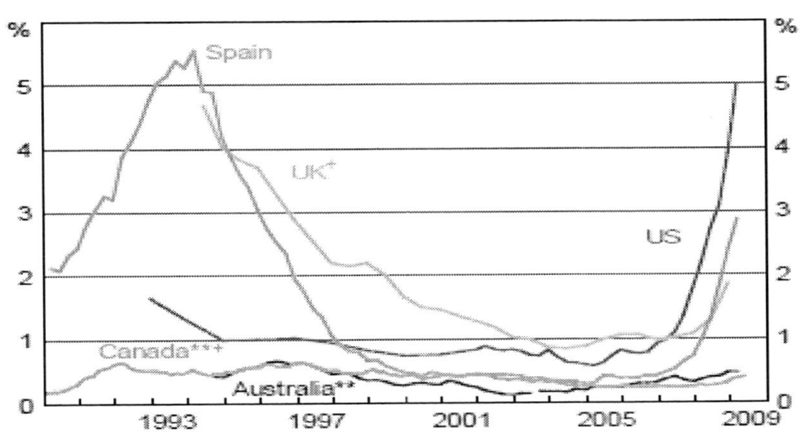

Figure 9. Non-performing Housing Loans. (Percent of loans.)

Due to running on a different housing cycle in Australia the problems of overbuilding that occurred in the US in the run up to the crisis was not an issue in Australia.

The US subprime market exploded during this period, rising from less than 9 percent of the market in 2002 to 25 percent of the market by 2005. Also, many of the Alt-A mortgages issues in the years from 2005-2007 were interest only loans or option-ARMs, which required borrowers to just meet interest payments on their mortgage. The subprime and Alt-A categories together comprised more than 40 percent of the loans issued at the peak of the bubble. By contrast, there was a very small subprime market in Australia, which at its height would have amounted to approximately 10 per cent of housing loans. The fact that these loans in Australia are non-recourse prevented even the most stressed mortgage holder's form walking away from their liabilities, in the end when default was the only option the percentage of defaults on house mortgagees relative to total house mortgages was approximately 1 – 2 percent.

Gan and Hill (2009) show that deregulation of the Australian mortgage market resulted in an increase of the average mortgage length and per period mortgage-payment-to-income ratio. In this new environment, it appears that purchase affordability has improved without any impact on repayment affordability. That is, a household with a given initial level of wealth and expected future income stream can now buy a more expensive house than it could previously (i.e., purchase affordability has improved), but the burden of repayment for any particular mortgage (i.e., repayment affordability) has indebted the households with longer repayments. This outcome is exacerbated in an environment of rising house prices.

SUMMARY AND CONCLUSION

As data in this paper indicates, Australia has the most unaffordable housing among developed economies. A recent release by the Australian Bureau of Statistics indicates that home ownership fell from 72 percent of households to 68 percent between 1994-5 and 2007-8. Over the same period, the United States, with similar demographics and demographic trends, experienced an increase from 65 percent to 68 percent.

Land use regulation policies have severely reduced housing affordability in many Australian markets. By contrast markets in the US with more traditional, more responsive planning will continue to supply housing for the next generation for approximately the same share of household income as in previous generations.

The housing gap between total underlying demand and total supply in Australia is estimated to have increased by approximately 78,800 dwellings in the year to June 2009 to a cumulative shortfall of 178,400 dwellings.

In the US, the most severe house price declines occurred in the bubble markets of California, Florida, Phoenix and Las Vegas. Virtually all of these markets experienced house price declines of 50 percent or more from the peak of the housing bubble. By contrast the explosion in Sydney and Melbourne housing prices continues after the financial crisis.

If the supply of additional housing does not keep up with increased underlying demand, the outcomes may include higher prices (which should stimulate additional supply, but might further reduce effective demand for privately produced housing), homelessness, more people living in caravans or sharing accommodation, larger household sizes and adult children staying longer in the parental home. Low-income households would be particularly disadvantaged.

Higher immigration rates into Australia have a significant influence on the demand for housing, especially given the large proportion of young adults among the immigrant population. Continued high migration alongside the fall in dwelling production levels in

2009–10 is likely to put more pressure on the housing market, especially for lower income households. The planning system is critical for delivering an adequate supply of dwellings and land to meet future demand.

In conclusion we have surveyed a broad range of factors which directly impinged on house prices in the US and Australian markets, examined the data both historically and in the lead up to the housing bubble and then bust in the US. From the evidence, the factors, which played the most significant roles in creating the conditions for the US house bubble, were not evident for the Australian housing market. In fact, the growing demand push factors combined with the constrained supply factors in providing new housing stock in particular for the major cities of Melbourne and Sydney appear to have anything but abated. These conditions can only lead to continuing rise in house prices for these markets or a levelling of prices given that further price increase is unsustainable.

REFERENCES

ABS (Australian Bureau of Statistics) (various) Statistician's Census Reports, Canberra.

ABS (Australian Bureau of Statistics) (2010) *Building Activity, Australia, March 2010.*

Demographia International (2010), 6th Annual Demographia International Housing Affordability Survey, downloadable at _http://www.demographia.com/dhi-ix2010 q3.pdf_.

OECD (2005) 'Recent house price development', Appendix 3, *OECD Economic Outlook*, 78, OECD, Paris, pp. 193–228.

Quan, G. and Hill, R.J. (2009), Measuring housing affordability: Looking beyond the median Journal of Housing Economics 18 (2009) 115–125.

RBA (Reserve Bank of Australia) (2009) Statistical table F2: Capital market yields — Government bonds, available: http://www.rba.gov.au/Statistics/AlphaListing/alpha _listing_i.html [accessed 24 April 2009].

Shiller, R. J. (2009) Home page, available: http://www.econ.yale.edu/~shiller/.

Stapledon, N. (2009). "Symposium: The Global Financial Crisis Housing and the Global Financial Crisis: US versus Australia" *The Economic and Labour Relations Review Vol. 19 No. 2, pp. 1–16.*

In: Financial Asset Pricing
Editors: P. E. Schulz and B. P. Hoffmann
ISBN: 978-1-61122-803-8

Chapter 6

COMPUTATIONAL FINANCE FOR STOCHASTIC VOLATILITY AND CORRELATION

Jun Ma*
NIE, Nanyang Technological University,
1, Nanyang Walk, 637616, Singapore

Abstract

Risk inhomogeneously changes through time, which gives rise to important impact on derivative securities pricing theory. In past two decades, in either industry or academics, it is gradually realized that the factor, i.e., the volatility, stochastically changes over time. Consequently, a lot of models have been developed to explain the empirically observed deviations from Black-Scholes formula. In this book chapter, to figure out another unnoticed stochastic factor, we check the historical correlation in several exchange rates, and find that the correlations vary more violently than their volatilities. On the other hand, based on the market price of index option, its implied correlation is investigated, which can not coincide with the realized one at all. This fact means the pricing of options in market is not based on same measure. Therefore, we introduce a more sophisticated scenario, namely, stochastic correlation, to describe such a phenomenon. As a stochastic process with two bounds is highlighted to describe the time-varying correlation, we can build up the partial differential equation for pricing multi-asset option. Meanwhile, we also incorporate the random correlation in the stochastic volatility model, and give its solution. Finally, the correlation risk in interest rate product is analyzed. This work is helpful for hedging risk better.

1. Overview

Since a lot of factors affect the stock market, nobody in the market is able to ensure the price goes up or down. In other words, there is no simple way to predict the future price of stock. Instead of accurately forecasting the stock price, we have to adopt the uncertainty in the stock market, i.e., the variation in today's stock price can not determine its change in tomorrow's market, which means they are almost irrelevant, or, at least, weakly

*E-mail address: jun-ma@mail.goo.ne.jp

linked. This is to say the independence of conditional probabilities $P(S(t_1 > t)|S(t))$ on prices $S(t_2 < t)$, where S, P and t stand for price of underlying asset, its probability and time respectively. This property, i.e., Markov property, exactly fulfils the definition of steps taken by the drunkard, namely, random walk. In the beginning of 20th century, Bachelier analyzed the stock price movement and found that the price presents the absence of memory property and evolves as a continuous Markov process (see Bachelier, 1900). Furthermore, he realized the stock price can be simulated by continuous time random walk, i.e., $S_t = S_0(1 + W_t)$, where W_t is a standard Brownian motion. However, the evident drawback of this model is that the stock price can present negative value. To eliminate the impossibly negative value, Black and Scholes proposed geometric Brownian motion to describe the movement of stock price, i.e., $S_t = S_0 \exp((r - \frac{\sigma^2}{2})t + \sigma W_t)$, where r and σ are risk-free interest rate and volatility of stock price respectively, and simultaneously, derived their pricing formula for European style option (see Black and Scholes, 1972). Figure 1 displays price of SP 100 index from May 2009 to May 2010. In untrained eyes, this might be a standard path of geometric Brownian motion since the price goes up with random fluctuation. But in place 1, the prices goes up faster than normal one, and in places 2 and 3, the stock declines more sharply, which means the magnitude of variation per unit time is not constant. Since the parameter, volatility, in the preceding model is chosen as constant, we must confront a question, i.e., does the Black-Scholes formula give a correct price? On the other hand, in vanilla call options of European style, strike price can be set as value less or more than contemporary price, i.e., in or out of the money. If using Black-Scholes to determine the volatility, i.e., implied volatility embedded in the market price, we can find the price of call option in the money gives larger implied volatility than the one embedded in the option at the money, where the strike price in call option is exactly set as contemporary asset price. Sometimes, the implied volatility for out of the money is larger than the one for at the money, which we call volatility smile. But at the volatility skew, the implied volatility for out the money is almost same magnitude as the one from at the money. This means if using Black-Scholes formula to price the option, we actually use various measures. This phenomenon attributes to the fact that the true distribution of asset price is different from the Black-Scholes assumption, i.e., lognormal distribution. Compared to lognormal one, generally, the true distribution of stock shows thicker tail at low asset price but comparatively thinner tail at high price region. But the distribution of currency might present extremes at both tails.

To develop a reliable risk-neutral measure for pricing vanilla and exotic options simultaneously, a lot of efforts have been committed. Derman and Kani introduced the concepts of local volatility, which means volatility is locally dependent on asset price (see Derman and Kani, 1994). They also proposed a numerical algorism to compute the local volatility function at each time node and consequently determined the instantaneous volatility. Therefore, their approach can reproduce market option price for both of strike and the time to maturity. To solve the problem of fat-tail in distribution and volatility smile, Variance Gamma process is defined to naturally describe the volatility, kurtosis and skewness based on its three parameters (see Madan, Carr, and Chang, 1998). Another approach to highlight the factor for the above mentioned difference may lies in the historical data. From historical stock price or exchange rate, using generalized autoregressive conditional heteroskedasticity method or maximum likelihood method, we can extract their volatility. Taking the exchange rates

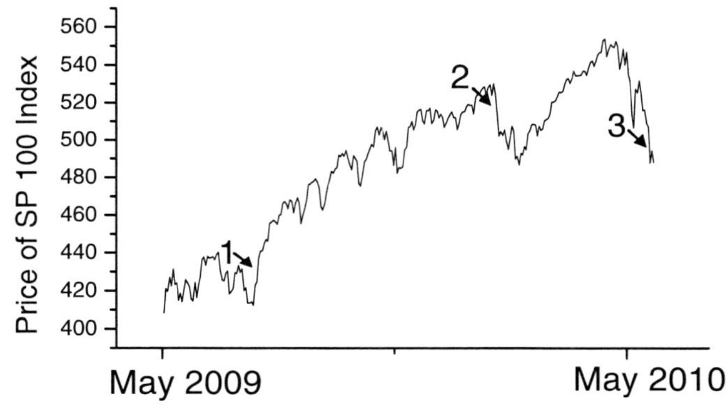

Figure 1. The price of SP 100 index from May 2009 to May 2010.

i.e., US Dollar/Euro and US Dollar/Jpy Yen as two examples, we estimate their volatilities and plot them in figure 2(a) and (b). We can see the volatilities fluctuate between 0.2% and 0.7% per day, and sometimes, they are below 0.2% and sometimes, above 1.0%. From figure 2, we conclude the dramatic fluctuation itself constructs a path of stochastic process. To give a solution, in 1987, Hull and White suggested instantaneous volatility follows an independent stochastic process with mean-reversion, i.e., $dV = \alpha(\beta - V)dt + \sigma_V V^\epsilon dW_V$, where V determines the motion of underlying asset by $\frac{dS}{S} = rdt + \sqrt{V}dW_S$, and ϵ is a positive constant less than one. Subsequently, based on the stochastic volatility, some analytical approaches are introduced (see Stein and Stein, 1991), and furthermore, in 1993, Heston introduced a square root process for stochastic volatility, i.e., $\epsilon = \frac{1}{2}$ in preceding volatility process, which however can be correlated to some other uncertainty sources, and it is used to derive a semi-closed form pricing formula for European style option, which can reproduce the volatility smile. The implied volatility decreases with the strike level, but on the other hand, increases with the time to expiration of the option, i.e., Samuelson effect (see Samuelson, 1965). To quantitatively capture this feature of volatility smile, a closed-form implied volatility formula is necessary as well. To fulfil such a requirement, two processes, i.e., $dS = \sigma S^\beta dW_S$ and $d\sigma = \alpha\sigma dW_\sigma$, where $dW_S dW_\sigma = \rho dt$, are constructed to describe the movements of forward price or underlying price, and its volatility (see Hagan, Kumar, Lesniewski and Woodward, 2002). This model called as stochastic Alpha, Beta, Rho model (SABR), which gives rise to closed-form approximation formula to extract correct implied volatility, and certainly yields good pricing formulas for vallina options. Then using the market price of vallina option, the calibration of parameters can be performed, which can be used to safely price some other options, e.g., exotic ones.

On the other hand, in vast literatures (see Kwok, 2008), less attention has be paid to correlation, in general, which is simply taken as constant. We prepare the correlation between two exchange rates, i.e., US Dollar/Euro and US Dollar/Jpy Yen, in figure 3, where the correlation presents violent fluctuations. Within one year, the correlation changes from positive to negative many times, and even reaches -0.3 or -0.5 numerous times. From this figure, we can conclude that the average correlation might be 0.3 or 0.4, but its value can change from 0.9 to -0.9, and therefore, it is totally wrong to take a constant correlation. The correlation between the two exchange rates from 1999 to 2010 can be treated as a stochastic

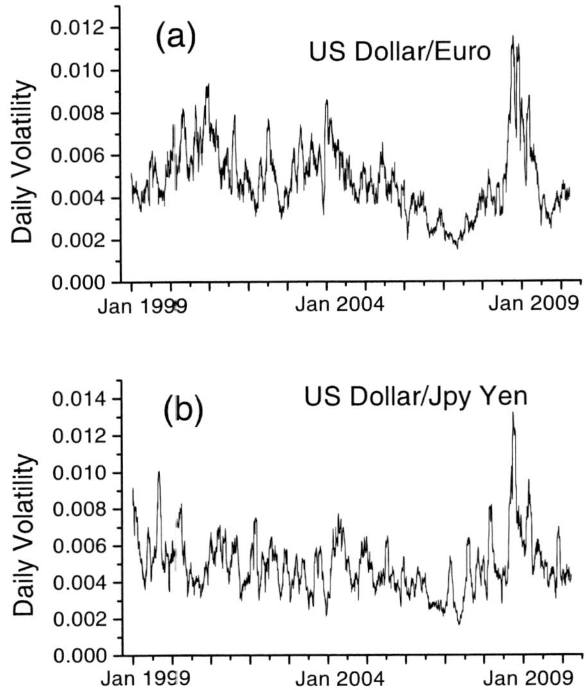

Figure 2. (a) and (b) are for the volatilities of exchange rate of US Dollar/Euro, and US Dollar/Jpy Yen, respectively.

process with a mean reversion close to 0.4, whose range is however almost from -1 to 1.

2. The Model

Based on the fact that the extremes are often induced by investment expectation, we can know the option price releases such information on what will happens in the future. In currency market, the speculated government interventions or policy make the rate tend to deviate from the parity, which causes fluctuation, and gives rise to stochastic volatility. In stock market, as long as the price goes down, generally, it leads to increasing leverage of the firm, which subsequently increases the uncertainty. Another factor is that the components of the firm, e.g., debt or capital, and so on, generally have different volatility. Under different economic circumstances, each component behaves uniquely. That is why we never expect the volatility is a constant. But this reason is also true for correlation. Consider the components of two firms. The total correlation consists of sub-correlation between the components from two firm, but those sub-correlations must be different and undergo unique performance under different economic circumstances. As a conclusion, we can not expect that the total correlation is a constant.

On the other hand, if pricing a muti-asset option, we always confront the implied correlation. Then a question arise: does the realized correlation well match the implied correlation extracted from the market price of derivative securities? If they are different, it

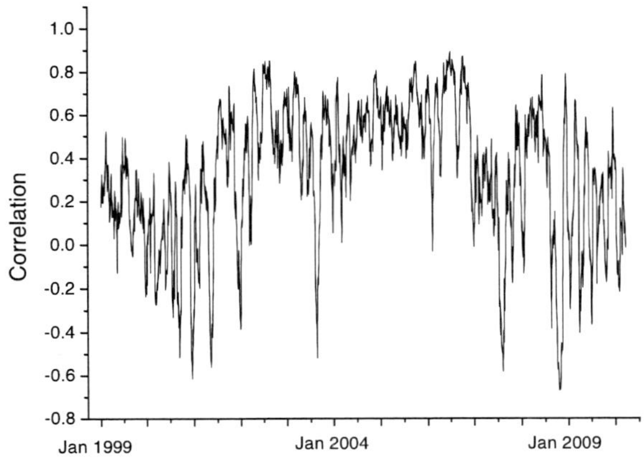

Figure 3. The correlation between two exchange rates, i.e., US Dollar/Euro and US Dollar/Jpy Yen.

may imply arbitrage opportunity. To investigate this problem, we utilize the most liquid index options, i.e., SP 100 index option. It is known this index price I consists of the 100 blue-chip stocks, S_i,

$$I = \sum_{i=1}^{100} w_i S_i \tag{1}$$

where w_i is the weight of ith stock in the index. Therefore, the volatility of the index price, σ_I, consists of 4950 correlations in the index as follows

$$\sigma_I^2 = \sum_{i=1}^{100} w_i^2 \sigma_{S_i}^2 + 2 \sum_{1 \le i < j \le 100} w_i w_j \sigma_{S_i} \sigma_{S_j} \rho_{ij}, \tag{2}$$

where σ_{S_i} is volatility of S_i and ρ_{ij} is the correlation between S_i and S_j. But the vast amount of correlation causes a tedious comparison of realized correlations to implied ones. To figure out the essential information, an alternative way is introduced to define an aggregate correlation. Then, a single quantity is sufficient to describe the average correlation, which can be denoted by $\hat{\rho}$ in the following equation,

$$\sigma_I^2 = \sum_{i=1}^{100} w_i^2 \sigma_{S_i}^2 + 2 \sum_{1 \le i < j \le 100} w_i w_j \sigma_{S_i} \sigma_{S_j} \hat{\rho}. \tag{3}$$

So $\hat{\rho}$ can be determined by

$$\hat{\rho} = \frac{\sigma_I^2 - \sum_{i=1}^{100} w_i^2 \sigma_{S_i}^2}{2 \sum_{1 \le i < j \le 100} w_i w_j \sigma_{S_i} \sigma_{S_j}}. \tag{4}$$

Based on the option prices, implied volatilities in above equation can be easily estimated, and subsequently, using the price of European style option on SP 100 index, the implied correlation can be calculated. On the other hand, the realized volatility can be extracted from historical stock price data, and could be substituted in the above equation to calculate the realized correlation. Then comparing the implied correlation to the realized one, we can know whether they match well or not, which is plotted in figure 4. During past months, the market performed substantial movements, which is particularly helpful to understand the correlation risk. Based on the option with expiration on May 10 and July 10, we calibrated the correlation in SP 100 index option from the end of April to July, 2010. We know that at the end of April, its implied volatility was comparatively small, but shortly it grew at double or triple in May, but from June to July, it declined slowly. On the other hand, the implied volatility of most of individual stock options does not have such a feature, namely, they are seldom synchronized. As a result, the implied correlation is non-flat, which exhibits the structure in figure 4. Unlike the implied correlation, the realized correlation always shows randomness, and just get close to implied one initially but departs from it soon with big fluctuations even after the time average is imposed as well. In figure 4, it is evident that it is impossible to unify the implied correlation and realized one at all, which justifies our preceding conclusion. Besides the option on SP 100 index, there are many other muti-asset options, and some implied correlations have structure as well, i.e., non-flat parameter. Some others do not have evident structure due to less liquidity, but their price sensitivity to correlation means the hedging strategies is of particular importance from the perspective of eliminating risk, which jointly affirms that the variation of correlation must still be investigated.

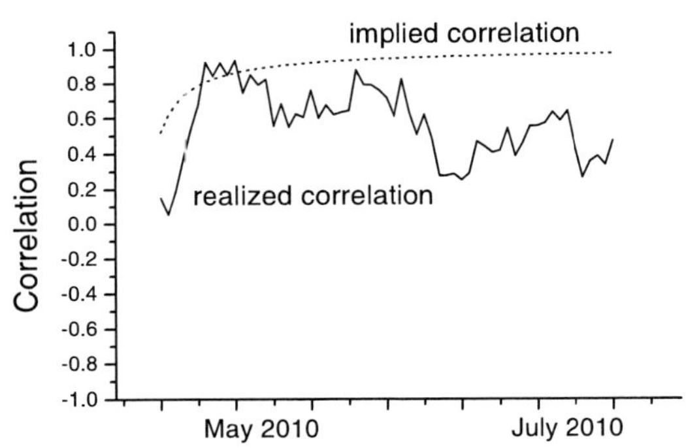

Figure 4. The dot and solid lines respectively stand for the implied and realized correlation from April to July, 2010.

Since some options might share same parameters, this fact reminds us that the important target of pricing model is to unify the parameters for all options, otherwise it means arbitrage opportunity exists. Based on the above analysis and empirical study, we extract the substantial difference between the correlation implied from the market price and realized one, which means that we need to promote our marginal distribution model to close the loophole. A simple viewpoint is that in case of distribution with fat tails, correlation may not be a suitable measure of dependence. But, the fact is if selecting the variables correctly, we still can use the correlation to reflect the varying dependence (see Nelsen, 1999). Another possible solution might be inspired from the concept of local volatility. As above stated, the local volatility algorithm leads to implied volatility surface matches the local one easily, which reminds us the local correlation is possible way to solve this problem, i.e., jointly using two local volatilities and one price-dependent correlation, one still can unify the parameters in the measure. On the other hand, the violent fluctuations in figure 3 exhibit that the correlation is unstable at all, or definitely shows Markov property, which gives a clue of another answer, i.e., using a stochastic process to describe the random walk of correlation. Certainly, the stochastic correlation can be merged with the stochastic volatilities to form a time-varying covariance, which can be highlighted in the Wishart process (see Fonseca, Grasselliac, Tebaldi, 2008). But conventionally, we decompose the risk kinds into price levels such as delta hedge, volatility such as vega and gamma hedges, and the rest, which is correlation risk. Thus, it is convenient to figure out the risk hedging approach using the stochastic correlation directly. In figure 3, the feature of the graph is the correlation concentrates on 0.4, and wander around -1 to 1, which reminds us that a mean-reverting stochastic process with two bounds is appropriate candidate. To fulfil so many requirements for the stochastic correlation, we select the Jacobi process to study computational finance for stochastic volatility and correlation (see Ma, 2004, 2009a, 2009b, 2010), which reads,

$$d\rho = (\dot{\rho} - g\rho)dt + \sigma_\rho \sqrt{(a-\rho)(\rho-b)}dW_\rho, \tag{5}$$

where a and b are upper and lower bounds respectively, $1 \geq a \geq b \geq -1$ and $a \geq \dot{\rho} \geq b$, $\dot{\rho}/g$ is the equilibrium value of correlation coefficient, and g is a positive parameter. Generally, at initial time point t, the value of correlation is deterministic, which means its distribution is a delta function, and the distribution at time $T > t$ must follow the Kolmogorov forward equation. To solve the partial differential equation for the evolution of stochastic process, the variable separation method is popularly used, which gives the easiest way to derive the probability kernel. Now, the first thing is to figure out the eigenvalue λ_k and eigenfunction $\varphi_k(\rho)$ of the Markov generator of the Jacobi process, which is

$$L = \frac{\sigma_\rho^2}{2}(a-\rho)(\rho-b)\frac{d^2}{d\rho^2} + (\dot{\rho} - g\rho)\frac{d}{d\rho}. \tag{6}$$

Then the variable separation method imposes the following equation for eigenvalue and eigenfunction of operator L, which yeilds

$$L\varphi_k(\rho) = -\lambda_k \varphi_k(\rho). \tag{7}$$

Subsequently, the part of ordinary differential equation versus ρ in variable separation method must be

$$\frac{\sigma_\rho^2}{2}(a-\rho)(\rho-b)\frac{d^2\varphi_k(\rho)}{d\rho^2} + (\dot{\rho} - g\rho)\frac{d\varphi_k(\rho)}{d\rho} + \lambda_k\varphi_k(\rho) = 0. \tag{8}$$

Introducing a transformation like $\rho = \frac{a-b}{2}\rho' + \frac{a+b}{2}$, the above equation becomes

$$\frac{\sigma_\rho^2}{2}(1-\rho'^2)\frac{d^2\varphi_k(\rho')}{d\rho'^2} + (\frac{2\dot{\rho}}{a-b} - g\frac{a+b}{a-b} - g\rho')\frac{d\varphi_k(\rho')}{d\rho'} + \lambda_k\psi_k(\rho') = 0. \tag{9}$$

To transform this equation to the standard Jacobi differential equation (see Szego, 1975), we can use coefficient $\frac{2}{\sigma_\rho^2}$ to multiply left and right sides of above equation simultaneously, which yields

$$(1-\rho'^2)\frac{d^2\varphi_k(\rho')}{d\rho'^2} + [\frac{2}{\sigma_\rho^2}(\frac{2\dot{\rho} - ag - bg}{a-b}) - \frac{2}{\sigma_\rho^2}g\rho']\frac{d\varphi_k(\rho')}{d\rho'} + \frac{2}{\sigma_\rho^2}\lambda_k\varphi_k(\rho') = 0, \tag{10}$$

whose eigenvalue and eigenfunction are

$$\lambda_k = -\frac{\sigma_\rho^2}{2}k(k + \frac{2g}{\sigma_\rho^2} - 1) \tag{11}$$

and

$$\varphi_k(\rho') = [\frac{(2k + \frac{2g}{\sigma_\rho^2} - 1)\Gamma(k + \frac{2g}{\sigma_\rho^2} - 1)k!}{2^{\frac{2g}{\sigma_\rho^2}-1}\Gamma(k + \frac{2ga-2\dot{\rho}}{\sigma_\rho^2(a-b)})\Gamma(k + \frac{2\dot{\rho}-2gb}{\sigma_\rho^2(a-b)})}]^{1/2} P_k^{(\frac{2ga-2\dot{\rho}}{\sigma_\rho^2(a-b)}-1, \frac{2\dot{\rho}-2gb}{\sigma_\rho^2(a-b)}-1)}(\rho'). \tag{12}$$

The Jacobi polynomials read

$$\begin{aligned} & P_k^{(\frac{2ga-2\dot{\rho}}{\sigma_\rho^2(a-b)}-1, \frac{2\dot{\rho}-2gb}{\sigma_\rho^2(a-b)}-1)}(\rho') \\ = & \frac{(\frac{2ga-2\dot{\rho}}{\sigma_\rho^2(a-b)})_k}{k!} {}_2F_1(-k, k + \frac{2g}{\sigma_\rho^2} - 1; \frac{2ga-2\dot{\rho}}{\sigma_\rho^2(a-b)}; \frac{1-\frac{2\rho}{a-b}+\frac{a+b}{a-b}}{2}), \end{aligned} \tag{13}$$

where $(\frac{2ga-2\dot{\rho}}{\sigma_\rho^2(a-b)})_k = (\frac{2ga-2\dot{\rho}}{\sigma_\rho^2(a-b)})(\frac{2ga-2\dot{\rho}}{\sigma_\rho^2(a-b)} + 1)(\frac{2ga-2\dot{\rho}}{\sigma_\rho^2(a-b)} + 2)\cdots(\frac{2ga-2\dot{\rho}}{\sigma_\rho^2(a-b)} + k)$ and ${}_2F_1$ is the hypergeometric polynomials. It should be noted that to guarantee $a \geq \rho \geq b$, the inequalities $(ga-\dot{\rho}) \geq \sigma_\rho^2(a-b)/2$ and $(\dot{\rho}-gb) \geq \sigma_\rho^2(a-b)/2$ must be fulfilled. Generally, the temporal part in variable separation method gives rise to decay factors, which wipes off most of eigenfunction contributions in the following probability kernel for the Jacobi process, i.e.,

$$\begin{aligned} P(\rho_0, \rho; 0, \tau) = & \sum_{k=0}^{\infty} e^{\lambda_k \tau}(1 + \frac{a+b}{a-b} - \frac{2\rho}{a-b})^{\frac{2ga-2\dot{\rho}}{\sigma_\rho^2(a-b)}-1} \\ & (1 - \frac{a+b}{a-b} + \frac{2\rho}{a-b})^{\frac{2\dot{\rho}-2gb}{\sigma_\rho^2(a-b)}-1} \varphi_k(\rho_0)\varphi_k(\rho), \end{aligned} \tag{14}$$

as $\tau \to \infty$, where $\tau = T - t$, and ρ_0 is the correlation at the initail moment $t = 0$.

In figure 5, taking $a = 0.9, b = -0.8, \dot{\rho} = 0.2, \sigma_\rho = 1.0$ and $g = 1.7$, we depict respectively $\tau = 0.05, 0.12, 0.5$ for initial correlation $\rho_0 = 0.3$. One can see at $\tau = 0.05$, the correlation concentrates its density around the initial value like a delta function, but diffuses at $\tau = 0.12$, and almost reaches its saturation distribution at $\tau = 0.5$ due to the big value of $\sigma_\rho = 1.0$. This means at $\tau = 0.5$, except the first one or two eigenfunctions, the big eigenvalues suppress the contribution from the corresponding eigenfunction, whose spatial distribution is consequently close to the asymptotic one.

3. The Pricing Equation

Evidently, the correlation must involve several random variables, and our model inevitably involves muti-asset options. In current market, the multi-asset options are frequently traded, and its payoff is determined by the terminal prices of a couple of possibly correlated underlying assets. The typical products are exchange, quanto, spread, maximum or minimum option on several assets. Now, we introduce how to incorporate the stochastic correlation

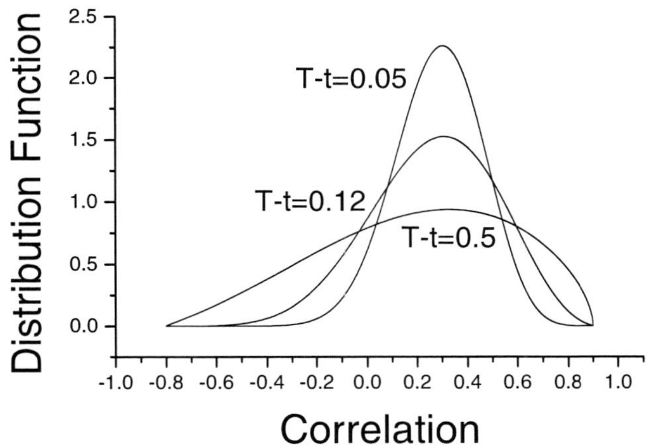

Figure 5. The time evoltion of correlation distribution function at $T - t = 0.05, 0.12, 0.5$, whose parameters for the Jacobi process are $a = 0.9$, $b = -0.8$, $\dot{\rho} = 0.2$, $\sigma_\rho = 1$ and $g = 1.7$.

in the high-dimensional Ito's Lemma and derive its pricing dynamics of partial differential equation. In this section, the exchange and quanto option are selected as examples since they are actively traded.

Take European style two-asset option as example, whose payoff at T, the time of expiration, denoted by $PF(S_1, S_2, T)$, is determined by the terminal prices of two underlying asset, S_1 and S_2. The Balck-Scholes algorithm can be extended to high-dimensional scenario, and we can assume that in the real world, two underlying assets undergo geometric Brownian motions, which read

$$\begin{aligned} dS_1 &= \mu_1 S_1 dt + \sigma_1 S_1 dW_1, \\ dS_2 &= \mu_2 S_2 dt + \sigma_2 S_2 dW_2, \end{aligned} \tag{15}$$

where σ_1, σ_2 are price volatility of first and second underlying asset respectively, dW_1 and dW_2 are two correlated standard Weiner processes, whose correlation coefficient follows $dW_1 dW_2 = \rho dt$. To simplify the problem, in above equations, we treat the volatilities, σ_1 and σ_2, as constants in this section. As pointed out before, taking constant correlation or just using the cumulative correlation might be misleading or result in disaster. This means that as the investors make operational decision, particularly with significant leverage using the cumulative or constant correlation, they need to be correct about the bet every day, and not only at the terminal date. Consequently, we think it is safe to undertake a stochastic correlation, which takes a random walk following the square root process in the true world, which yields

$$d\rho = (\dot{\rho} - \alpha\rho)dt + \sigma_\rho \sqrt{(a - \rho)(\rho - b)} dW_\rho, \tag{16}$$

where, $\dot{\rho} - \alpha\rho$ is the mean-reversion in the real world. Certainly, the above process is not independent, and might be linked to some uncertainty sources such as S_1 and S_2, which can be written as

$$\begin{aligned} dW_1 dW_\rho &= \rho_1 dt, \\ dW_2 dW_\rho &= \rho_2 dt, \end{aligned} \tag{17}$$

where ρ_1, ρ_2 are two constants. It is obvious that ρ, ρ_1, ρ_2 give rise to the following correlation matrix

$$\begin{pmatrix} 1 & \rho & \rho_1 \\ \rho & 1 & \rho_2 \\ \rho_1 & \rho_2 & 1 \end{pmatrix}, \tag{18}$$

which must be semi-definite positive. Then we know

$$(1 - \rho_2^2 - \rho_1^2 + 2\rho\rho_1\rho_2 - \rho^2) \geq 0, \tag{19}$$

can guarantee the determinant for equation (18) is positive or zero, whose solution reads

$$\rho_1\rho_2 + \sqrt{(1-\rho_1^2)(1-\rho_2^2)} \geq a \geq \rho \geq b \geq \rho_1\rho_2 - \sqrt{(1-\rho_1^2)(1-\rho_2^2)}. \tag{20}$$

In the market, an option position is sensitive to the volatility change, which exists in any position with an asset with uncertain payoff. Hence, the investor can be short or long volatility by selling or buying an option and delta hedging. Since option involving several underlying assets is more sensitive to correlation, similarly, this reminds how to construct the portfolio for a multi-asset option is an important problem. Let $\bar{C}(S_1, S_2, t)$ be the price of a two-asset option under stochastic correlation. Then a portfolio $\bar{C}_1 + \Delta_\rho \bar{C}_2$ can allow us to maintain risk-neutral with respect to stochastic correlation, where $\bar{C}_1, \bar{C}_2$ could be two options with different maturity or striking price. On the other hand, to hedge the risk from uncertainty of underlying asset prices, we need to compensate two amounts of underlying assets, which give rise to whole portfolio

$$\Pi = \bar{C}_1 + \Delta_\rho \bar{C}_2 + \Delta_1 S_1 + \Delta_2 S_2. \tag{21}$$

Using the high-dimensional Ito's lemma, we can write the variation of the a two-asset option price $\bar{C}$ as stochastic differential equation, which is

$$\begin{aligned} d\bar{C} &= [\frac{\partial \bar{C}}{\partial t} + \frac{1}{2}\sigma_1^2 S_1^2 \frac{\partial^2 \bar{C}}{\partial S_1^2} + \frac{1}{2}\sigma_2^2 S_2^2 \frac{\partial^2 \bar{C}}{\partial S_2^2} + \rho\sigma_1\sigma_2 S_1 S_2 \frac{\partial^2 C}{\partial S_1 \partial S_2} \\ &+ \sigma_1\sigma_\rho\rho_1 S_1 \sqrt{(a-\rho)(\rho-b)} \frac{\partial^2 \bar{C}}{\partial\rho\partial S_1} \\ &+ \sigma_2\sigma_\rho\rho_2 S_2 \sqrt{(a-\rho)(\rho-b)} \frac{\partial^2 \bar{C}}{\partial\rho\partial S_2} + \frac{1}{2}\sigma_\rho^2 (a-\rho)(\rho-b) \frac{\partial^2 \bar{C}}{\partial\rho^2}]dt \\ &+ \frac{\partial \bar{C}}{\partial S_1} dS_1 + \frac{\partial \bar{C}}{\partial S_2} dS_2 + \frac{\partial \bar{C}}{\partial \rho} d\rho. \end{aligned} \tag{22}$$

To keep the whole portfolio risk-neutral, the following equality

$$d\Pi = r\Pi dt \tag{23}$$

must be fulfilled, where r is still the risk-free rate. Then substituting $d\bar{C}_1, d\bar{C}_2, dS_1, dS_2$ in above equation, we can deduce the amounts $\Delta_1, \Delta_2, \Delta_\rho$ as follows

$$\begin{aligned}
\Delta_1 &= \frac{\partial \bar{C}_1/\partial \rho}{\partial \bar{C}_2/\partial \rho} \times \frac{\partial \bar{C}_2}{\partial S_1} - \frac{\partial \bar{C}_1}{\partial S_1}, \\
\Delta_2 &= \frac{\partial \bar{C}_1/\partial \rho}{\partial \bar{C}_2/\partial \rho} \times \frac{\partial \bar{C}_2}{\partial S_2} - \frac{\partial \bar{C}_1}{\partial S_2}, \\
\Delta_\rho &= -\frac{\partial \bar{C}_1/\partial \rho}{\partial \bar{C}_2/\partial \rho}.
\end{aligned} \tag{24}$$

The drift term in equation (15) must become rdt to form the risk-neutral process for underlying assets. On the other hand, the risk premium $\Lambda(\rho, t)$ can be absorbed in the drift term of the Jacobi process in the real world, which can be supposed to be linearly proportional to the random correlation. Then the drift term can be rewritten as $(\dot{\rho} - \alpha\rho + \Lambda(\rho, t))dt = (\dot{\rho} - g\rho)dt$, and consequently, the risk-neutral process for correlation returns to equation (5). Certainly equation (20) is still fulfilled to maintain the relationship $a \geq \rho \geq b$. Based on equation (5), we can substitute $d\rho$ in the relevant terms in equations (22,23), i.e., in $d\bar{C}_1$ and $d\bar{C}_2$ and find the stochastic correlation term dW_ρ disappears. Then, using the portfolio coefficients in equation (24), the uncertainty terms related to S_1 and S_2 in equation (22,23) are eliminated, and subsequently, by the comparison of its rest deterministic terms in left side to the ones in right side, we arrive at the pricing equation for two-asset option

$$\begin{aligned}
&\frac{\partial \bar{C}}{\partial t} + rS_1\frac{\partial \bar{C}}{\partial S_1} + rS_2\frac{\partial \bar{C}}{\partial S_2} + (\bar{\rho} - g\rho)\frac{\partial \bar{C}}{\partial \rho} + \frac{1}{2}\sigma_1^2 S_1^2\frac{\partial^2 \bar{C}}{\partial S_1^2} + \frac{1}{2}\sigma_2^2 S_2^2\frac{\partial^2 \bar{C}}{\partial S_2^2} \\
+ &\ \rho\sigma_1\sigma_2 S_1 S_2\frac{\partial^2 \bar{C}}{\partial S_1 \partial S_2} + \sigma_1\sigma_\rho\rho_1 S_1\sqrt{(a-\rho)(\rho-b)}\frac{\partial^2 \bar{C}}{\partial \rho \partial S_1} \\
+ &\ \sigma_2\sigma_\rho\rho_2 S_2\sqrt{(a-\rho)(\rho-b)}\frac{\partial^2 \bar{C}}{\partial \rho \partial S_2} \\
+ &\ \frac{1}{2}\sigma_\rho^2(a-\rho)(\rho-b)\frac{\partial^2 \bar{C}}{\partial \rho^2} - r\bar{C} = 0.
\end{aligned} \tag{25}$$

Except the quanto option, the above partial differential equation is the general tool to price the two-asset option. But this equation can be simplified furthermore for one kind of option such as exchange, the better-of and worst-of two asset rainbow options, and so on. If treating correlation between dS_1 and dS_2 as constant, we can define a new random quantity $\chi = \frac{S_1}{S_2}$, whose distribution is still lognormal and its variance is $\sigma_1^2 + \sigma_2^2 - 2\rho\sigma_1\sigma_2$ by Ito's lemma, which reminds us their pricing equation can be reduced to two-dimension if we take S_2 as numeraire. Since the individual stock price undergoes geometric Brownian motion, we can conclude pricing dynamics must be a linear homogeneous equation versus S_1 and S_2. Therefore, a linear homogeneous payoff function versus χ allows us to simplify the pricing equation. Of a pile of options, many contingent claims, such as, the exchange, better-of and worst-of two assets rainbow option, yield a linear payoff in $\frac{S_1}{S_2}$. Take exchange option as example, which supplies the holder the right to exchange underlying asset one for asset two. It is evident that this option can be treat as a call option on S_1 with strike S_2

or a put option on S_2 with strike S_1, whose payoff function at expiry $PF(S_1, S_2, T) = Max(S_1 - S_2, 0)$ must be linear homogeneous. Taking S_2 as numeraire, the new price can be defined as $c(\chi, \rho, t) = \frac{\bar{C}(S_1, S_2, t)}{S_2}$, and similarly, the boundary condition at expiration time T becomes $Max(\chi - 1, 0)$. Then substituting the following transformations,

$$\frac{\partial \bar{C}}{\partial S_1} = \frac{\partial c}{\partial \chi}, \qquad \frac{\partial \bar{C}}{\partial S_2} = c - \chi \frac{\partial c}{\partial \chi}$$
$$\frac{\partial^2 \bar{C}}{\partial S_1^2} = \frac{1}{S_2}\frac{\partial^2 c}{\partial \chi^2}, \frac{\partial^2 \bar{C}}{\partial S_2^2} = \frac{\chi^2}{S_2}\frac{\partial^2 c}{\partial \chi^2}, \qquad \frac{\partial^2 \bar{C}}{\partial S_2 \partial S_1} = -\frac{S_1}{S_2^2}\frac{\partial^2 c}{\partial \chi^2}, \tag{26}$$

we arrive at the two-dimensional pricing equation

$$\begin{aligned}
&\frac{\partial c}{\partial t} + (\dot{\rho} - g\rho)\frac{\partial c}{\partial \rho} + \frac{1}{2}\dot{\sigma}^2\chi^2\frac{\partial^2 c}{\partial \chi^2} + \frac{1}{2}\sigma_\rho^2(a-\rho)(\rho-b)\frac{\partial^2 c}{\partial \rho^2} \\
&+\sigma_\rho(\sigma_1\rho_1 - \sigma_2\rho_2)\sqrt{(a-\rho)(\rho-b)}\chi\frac{\partial^2 c}{\partial \rho \partial \chi} \\
&+\sigma_2\sigma_\rho\rho_2\sqrt{(a-\rho)(\rho-b)}\frac{\partial c}{\partial \rho} = 0,
\end{aligned} \tag{27}$$

whose boundary conditions are

$$\begin{aligned}
c(0, \rho, t) &= 1, \\
\lim_{\chi \to \infty} \frac{c(\chi, \rho, t)}{\chi} &= 1, \\
c(\chi, \rho, T) &= Max(\chi - 1, 0).
\end{aligned} \tag{28}$$

In equation (27), $\dot{\sigma} = \sqrt{\sigma_1^2 - 2\rho\sigma_1\sigma_2 + \sigma_2^2}$. The pricing equation (27) remains valid for all options whose payoff is linear homogeneous in S_1 and S_1. For example, rewriting the payoff function of the worst-of two asset option, $PF(S_1, S_2, T) = Min(S_1, S_2)$ as $c(\chi, \rho, T) = Min(\chi, 1)$, and using it as boundary condition, we still can use equation (27) to price the option paying minimum value of underlying assets.

As mentioned before, the pricing equation (25) is not applicable for quanto options, which is exposed to two uncertainty sources, i.e., the price of an underlying asset and currency exchange rate. There are some actively traded quanto options such as equity-linked foreign exchange call, fixed exchange rate foreign equity call, foreign equity call struck in foreign currency or in domestic currency, and so on. In this section, we only introduce the fixed exchange rate foreign equity call and analyze the rest in next section. The fixed exchange rate foreign equity option is a right to buy or sell a future contract on an asset or index which is in foreign country, but the contract is settled in domestic currency. For example, the Nikkei stock index option is traded in Singapore, which means its payoff is determined by the terminal price of the foreign index or asset in Japanese yen and is subsequently converted to domestic currency, i.e., Singapore dollar. This indicates the final price is equal to the terminal index price in yen times the amount of Singapore dollars per yen. Based on this case, we realize that besides the uncertainty of underlying asset price, the holder inevitably confronts another uncertainty from the exchange rate which fluctuates more frequently.

The quanto option is defined based on a foreign asset, which can be mathematically given by geometric Brownian motion in a real world

$$dS_F = \mu_F S_F dt + \sigma_F S_F dW_F, \tag{29}$$

where S_F, σ_F are the price of foreign underlying asset and its constant volatility, respectively, and, dW_F is a standard Weiner process. Although the spread between domestic and foreign interest rates imposes a forward rate, we still use the following geometric Brownian motion in the real world to describe the exchange rate, which reads

$$dS_D = \mu_D S_D dt + \sigma_D S_D dW_D, \tag{30}$$

where S_D, σ_D are the value of exchange rate and its constant volatility, and dW_D is a standard Weiner process as well. The instantaneous correlation between dW_F and dW_D can be defined as

$$dW_F dW_D = \rho_t dt, \tag{31}$$

and we assume ρ_t in the real world follows equation (16) as well. Certainly, all constraints for this process must be maintained. Without loss of generality, we treat another two relationships between the processes as nonzero value, namely,

$$\begin{aligned} dW_F dW_\rho &= \rho_F dt, \\ dW_D dW_\rho &= \rho_D dt, \end{aligned} \tag{32}$$

which still impose all inequalities like equations (19,20).

We use $\bar{C}(S_F, S_D, t)$, $C(S_F, S_D, t)$ to denote the price of option with stochastic and constant correlation, respectively. As in preceding option, to guarantee the whole cash flow is risk-neutral, we need two sub-portfolios, and each consists of a quanto option, an open interest of foreign currency to hedge the corresponding risk, and a quantity of foreign underlying asset. Same as in the preceding options, the two quanto options could have different expiration or striking price. So the total portfolio is denoted by $\bar{\Pi} = \Pi_1 + \Delta_\rho \Pi_2$, which must follow the risk-neutral equation, namely,

$$d\bar{\Pi} = r_D \bar{\Pi} dt, \tag{33}$$

where r_D is domestic rate. To solve the above equation, first, we have to write a value of the first single sub-portfolio as

$$\Pi = C - \Delta_D S_D - \Delta_F S_F S_D, \tag{34}$$

where the minus means that as long as buy a quanto option, we have to simultaneously take short position for foreign currency and foreign underlying asset. In other words, except the correlation risk, $-\Delta_D S_D$, the amount of foreign currency short valued in domestic one, and $-\Delta_F S_F S_D$, underlying foreign asset short valued in domestic currency, can neutralize the risk from the quanto option.

The equations (29, 30) allow us to calculate dS_F and dS_D, but to calculate $d\Pi$, the last factor we need is $d\bar{C}$. Hence, based on Ito's lemma, we write the value variation of quanto option

$$
\begin{aligned}
d\bar{C} &= [\frac{\partial \bar{C}}{\partial t} + \frac{1}{2}\sigma_D^2 S_D^2 \frac{\partial^2 \bar{C}}{\partial S_D^2} + \frac{1}{2}\sigma_F^2 S_F^2 \frac{\partial^2 \bar{C}}{\partial S_F^2} + \rho\sigma_D\sigma_F S_D S_F \frac{\partial^2 \bar{C}}{\partial S_D \partial S_F} \\
&+ \sigma_D \sigma_\rho \rho_D S_D \sqrt{(a-\rho)(\rho-b)} \frac{\partial^2 \bar{C}}{\partial \rho \partial S_D} \\
&+ \sigma_F \sigma_\rho \rho_F S_F \sqrt{(a-\rho)(\rho-b)} \frac{\partial^2 \bar{C}}{\partial \rho \partial S_F} + \frac{1}{2}\sigma_\rho^2 (a-\rho)(\rho-b) \frac{\partial^2 \bar{C}}{\partial \rho^2}]dt \\
&+ \frac{\partial \bar{C}}{\partial S_D} dS_D + \frac{\partial \bar{C}}{\partial S_F} dS_F + \frac{\partial \bar{C}}{\partial \rho} d\rho. \qquad (35)
\end{aligned}
$$

Notice that to maintain risk-neutral, during time space dt, $-\Delta_D$ of foreign currency must give extra value $-\Delta_D S_D r_F dt$, where r_F is the foreign interest rate, and on the other hand, the value of $-\Delta_F$ shares of foreign asset measured in domestic currency, i.e., $-\Delta_F S_F S_D$ must supply the first order variation, $-\rho\sigma_D\sigma_F\Delta_F S_F S_D dt$. Substituting each piece of total cash flow, and equation (29,30) for dS_D and dS_F in $d\bar{\Pi}$, we can get the amount of individual portfolio to make equation (33) valid, which are the following

$$
\begin{aligned}
\Delta_F &= \frac{1}{S_D}\frac{\partial \bar{C}}{\partial S_F}, \\
\Delta_D &= \frac{\partial \bar{C}}{\partial S_D} - \frac{S_F}{S_D}\frac{\partial \bar{C}}{\partial S_F}, \\
\Gamma_\rho &= -\frac{\partial \bar{C}_1/\partial \rho}{\partial \bar{C}_2/\partial \rho}. \qquad (36)
\end{aligned}
$$

Equation (35) holds for any kind of quanto option, but for fixed exchange rate foreign equity option, we only need the amount Δ_D of foreign currency to hedge, which reminds us that S_D is non-relevant for $\bar{C}$. Then substituting equation (35, 36) in equations (33, 34), using the same approach as in the preceding options, we get the pricing formula for fixed exchange rate foreign equity option as follows

$$
\begin{aligned}
&\frac{\partial \bar{C}}{\partial t} + (r_F - \rho\sigma_F\sigma_D)S_F \frac{\partial \bar{C}}{\partial S_F} + (\dot{\rho} - g\rho)\frac{\partial \bar{C}}{\partial \rho} + \frac{1}{2}\sigma_F^2 S_F^2 \frac{\partial^2 \bar{C}}{\partial S_F^2} \\
&+ \sigma_F \sigma_\rho \rho_F S_F \sqrt{(a-\rho)(\rho-b)} \frac{\partial^2 \bar{C}}{\partial \rho \partial S_F} \\
&+ \frac{1}{2}\sigma_\rho^2 (a-\rho)(\rho-b)\frac{\partial^2 \bar{C}}{\partial \rho^2} - r_D \bar{C} = 0. \qquad (37)
\end{aligned}
$$

Like in preceding option, in risk-neutral world, the stochastic process of correlation coefficient must be equation (5) as well after manipulating the premium of correlation risk. On the other hand, if rewriting $r_F - \rho\sigma_F\sigma_D$ as $r_D - (r_D - r_F + \rho\sigma_F\sigma_D)$, by comparison, we immediately know the drift term in risk-neutral dS_D must be $(r_D - r_F)dt$, and the drift term in risk-neutral dS_F must be $(r_F - \rho\sigma_F\sigma_D)dt$.

Then, using the terminal price at expiration $C(S_F, T) = \dot{S}_D Max[S_F(T) - E_F, 0]$ where E_F and $\dot{S}_D$ are the strike price and a fixed exchange rate respectively. After we simplified a high-dimensional stochastic differential equation to a two dimensional partial differential equation, the price of quanto option could be stably solved as well as its Greeks are accurately accessible. To compare the price with constant correlation, we solve equation (37) by finite difference method in this section. The Crank-Nicolson finite difference algorithm is widely popular for numerically computing partial differential equation, whose main merits are its second order accuracy and stability. Discretizing equation (37), the central difference is chosen in the Crank-Nicolson method to increase its stability and accuracy, and, jointly using the boundary condition, i.e., $\dot{S}_D Max[S_F(T) - E_F, 0]$, we solve the price of the quanto option under stochastic correlation and compare it with the one with constant correlation, whose closed form solution reads

$$C = \dot{S}_D S_F e^{(r_F - r_D - \rho\sigma_F\sigma_D)\tau} N(d_1) - \dot{S}_D E_F e^{-r_D\tau} N(d_2), \tag{38}$$

where N is cumulative function, $\tau = T - t$, and

$$d_1 = \frac{\ln \frac{S_F}{E_F} + (r_F - \rho\sigma_F\sigma_D + \frac{\sigma_F^2}{2})\tau}{\sigma_F\sqrt{\tau}}, d_2 = d_1 - \sigma_F\sqrt{\tau}. \tag{39}$$

The difference $(\bar{C}(\rho_0) - C(\rho_0))/E_F$ is plotted in figure 6 (a) where $\dot{S}_D = 1, r_D = 0.1, r_F = 0.05, \sigma_D = 1.0, \sigma_F = 1.1$ $\sigma_\rho = 0.9, T - t = 0.12, \dot{\rho} = 0.02, \rho_F = -\rho_D = 0.02, g = 2.2$, and $a = 0.85, b = -0.85$. Initial correlation at time $t = 0$ is denoted by ρ_0. Since the diffusion at $T - t = 0.12$ only causes a small deviation of ρ_T from the initial value ρ_0, the price difference between two models is tiny. Taking parameters same as in figure 6(a) except $T - t = 0.35$, and comparing the numerical output to the one with constant correlation in figure 6 (b), we could find larger price difference than in $T - t = 0.12$. But we should note that $(\bar{C}(\rho_0) - C(\rho_0))/E_F$ for this option is large around $\rho \sim \pm 0.85$ in figure 6(b). The fact, i.e., the larger $S_F(t = 0)$, the bigger difference between $\bar{C}(\rho_0) - C(\rho_0)$, is practically important, which exactly why we select fixed exchange rate foreign equity call to illustrate the importance of correlation risk. If the price difference deduced by correlation risk is almost zero in any region of ρ_0 as $S_F(t) >> E_F$ or $S_F(t) << E_F$, the stochastic correlation must be less important. Actually, in other kinds of foreign equity option such as foreign equity call struck in foreign currency, and foreign call in domestic currency, the correlation risk is important only for option at the money, and turns to be almost zero for deep in or out-of the money.

4. An Analytical Pricing Formula

In general, it is difficult to derive a closed-form expression within a multi-factor model. In particular, it seems probability kernel of the whole system might be impossibly available, and consequently, the its absence prevents rigorously deriving any closed-form pricing formula under stochastic correlation. However, figure (3) reminds us that the fluctuations in the varying correlation hit the maximum and minimum possible values, namely, 1 and -1, many times, which can solve the inequalities i.e., equations (19, 20), $\rho_1 = \rho_2 = 0$. Especially, from equation (20), we can conclude the small absolute value of ρ_1, ρ_2 solely gives rise to the big magnitude of correlation variation, e.g., from -1 to 1, and must raise the upper bound of stochastic correlation to 1, and simultaneously reduces its lower bound to -1. So

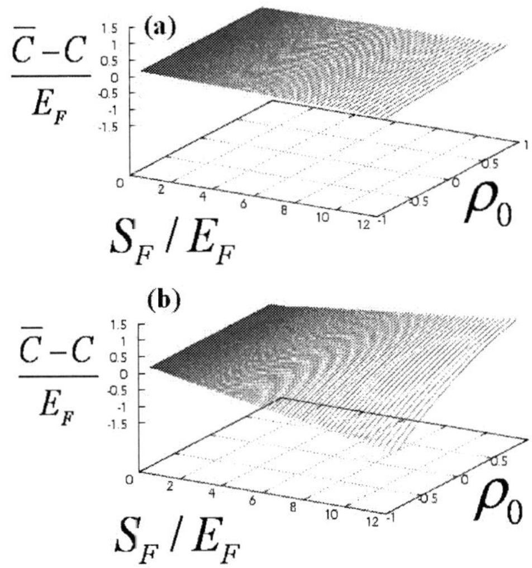

Figure 6. The price difference $\frac{\bar{C}(\rho_0)-C(\rho_0)}{E_F}$ for $T-t=0.12$ and 0.35. $\bar{C}(\rho_0)$ stands for the price of quanto option with the stochastic correlation coefficient, and $C(\rho_0)$ is the one with constant correlation coefficient, and E_F is the strike price. In plot (a), the parameters for $\bar{C}$ are taken as $\dot{S}_D=1, r_D=0.1, r_F=0.05, \sigma_D=1.0, \sigma_F=1.1, T-t=0.12, \dot{\rho}=0.02, \rho_F=-\rho_D=0.02, g=2.2, \sigma_\rho=0.9$, and $a=0.85, b=-0.85$. (b) is for $T-t=0.35$. All parameters are same except the constant correlation is taken as ρ_0 for C where ρ_0 is the correlation at the initial time.

the knowledge we can learn from equation (20) is that if the range of varying correlation is from -1 to 1, the Jacobi process must be independent of other processes.

We know the price of the option with two assets S_1 and S_2 at maturity T is determined by the terminal distribution of its payoff, which is denoted as $PF[S_1(T), S_2(T)]$. Although as pointed before, the joint distribution of $S_1(T)$ and $S_2(T)$ might be impossibly accessible, based on the independence of the Jacobi process, we still try to decompose the whole probability kernel into several components. Therefore, we investigate, anyway, what is the correlation between $S_1(T)$ and $S_2(T)$ under a stochastic correlation path. Equally dividing the ρ path into n pieces from $t=0$ to $t=T$, it can be defined that S_1^i and S_2^i are the asset prices at the end of ith period. To describe the two time series $\ln(\frac{S_1^i}{S_1^{i-1}}), \ln(\frac{S_2^i}{S_2^{i-1}})$, we use two sequences: $\sigma_1\Delta W_1^1, \sigma_1\Delta W_2^1, \sigma_1\Delta W_3^1, \cdots, \sigma_1\Delta W_n^1$ and $\sigma_2(\rho_1\Delta W_1^1+\sqrt{1-\rho_1^2}W_1^2), \sigma_2(\rho_2\Delta W_2^1+\sqrt{1-\rho_2^2}W_2^2), \sigma_2(\rho_3\Delta W_3^1+\sqrt{1-\rho_3^2}W_3^2), \cdots, \sigma_2(\rho_n\Delta W_n^1+\sqrt{1-\rho_n^2}W_n^2)$, where ΔW_i^1 and ΔW_i^2 are two independent Weiner processes, namely, $E[\Delta W_i^1\Delta W_i^1]=E[\Delta W_i^2\Delta W_i^2]=\Delta t$, $E[\Delta W_i^1\Delta W_i^2]=0$, where Δt is time step. Then covariance between the paths of time series $\ln(\frac{S_1^i}{S_1^{i-1}}), \ln(\frac{S_2^i}{S_2^{i-1}})$ can be calculated as

$$\begin{aligned}
&\sigma_1\sigma_2 E[(\Delta W_1^1+\Delta W_2^1+\Delta W_3^1\cdots+\Delta W_n^1)\\
&\times(\rho_1\Delta W_1^1+\sqrt{1-\rho_1^2})W_1^2+\rho_2\Delta W_2^1+\sqrt{1-\rho_2^2}W_2^2+\rho_3\Delta W_3^1+\sqrt{1-\rho_3^2}W_3^2\\
&+\cdots+\rho_n\Delta W_n^1+\sqrt{1-\rho_n^2}W_n^2)]\\
&=\sigma_1\sigma_2\Delta t[\rho_1+\rho_2+\rho_3+\cdots+\rho_n]. \qquad (40)
\end{aligned}$$

Furthermore, we can derive the standard deviation for path of asset one and two respectively, which yield

$$\sigma_1\sqrt{E[(\Delta W_1^1+\Delta W_2^1+\cdots+\Delta W_n^1)^2]}=\sigma_1\sqrt{n\Delta t},$$
$$\sigma_2\sqrt{E[(\rho_1\Delta W_1^1+\sqrt{1-\rho_1^2}W_1^2+\rho_2\Delta W_2^1+\sqrt{1-\rho_2^2}W_2^2+\cdots+\rho_n\Delta W_n^1+\sqrt{1-\rho_n^2}W_n^2)^2]}$$
$$=\sigma_2\sqrt{n\Delta t}. \tag{41}$$

It should be emphasized that the above calculation is based on the independence of ρ_t process. It means our forthcoming conclusion i.e., the correlation between two paths of S_1 and S_2 is its average value of the path of ρ_t, does not hold for any stochastic correlation linked to S_1 or S_2 since its connection to S_1 or S_2 gives rise to some extra terms in equations (40, 41) which distort the following new definition of equation (42). Based on the covariance and two standard deviations, the final correlation between two paths under stochastic correlation is nothing but its average exactly, which reads

$$\frac{\sigma_1\sigma_2\Delta t[\rho_1+\rho_2+\rho_3+\cdots+\rho_n]}{\sigma_1\sigma_2\sqrt{n\Delta t}\sqrt{n\Delta t}}=\frac{\rho_1+\rho_2+\rho_3+\cdots+\rho_n}{n}, \tag{42}$$

where the average actually gives a new definition

$$\tilde{\rho}=\frac{1}{\tau}\int_0^{\tau}\rho_t dt. \tag{43}$$

Now, it is easy to know based on two geometric Brownian motions, $\ln\frac{S_1(T)}{S_1(0)}$ and $\ln\frac{S_2(T)}{S_2(0)}$ still present normal distribution, but conditioned on a correlation coefficient of $\tilde{\rho}$.

Generally option price at t is determined by the final price distribution, $\theta[S_1(T),S_2(T)|S_1(t),S_2(t),\rho_t]$, which yields

$$\bar{C}(S_1(t),S_2(t),\rho_t,t)$$
$$=e^{-r(T-t)}\int_0^\infty\int_0^\infty PF[S_1(T),S_2(T)]\theta[S_1(T),S_2(T)|S_1(t),S_2(t),\rho_t]dS_1(T)dS_2(T). \tag{44}$$

Although as pointed before, the final price distribution is impossibly accessible, it still can be decomposed into two parts, i.e., one is the lognormal distribution conditioned on $\tilde{\rho}$, and the other is the distribution of $\tilde{\rho}$. Thus, we rewrite the final price distribution as

$$\theta[S_1(T),S_2(T)|S_1(t),S_2(t),\rho_t)]$$
$$=\int_b^a n[S_1(T),S_2(T)|S_1(t),S_2(t),\tilde{\rho}]\Omega[\tilde{\rho}|S_1(t),S_2(t),\rho_t]d\tilde{\rho}, \tag{45}$$

where $n[S_1(T),S_2(T)|S_1(t),S_2(t),\tilde{\rho}]$ depicts the distribution for a class of path of S_1,S_2 conditional upon $\tilde{\rho}$, and $\Omega[\tilde{\rho}|S_1(t),S_2(t),\rho_t]$ is the distribution function of $\tilde{\rho}$. Substituting the above equation into equation (44), the option prices can be rewritten as

$$\begin{aligned}
&\bar{C}(S_1(t),S_2(t),\rho_t,t)\\
=\;& e^{-r(T-t)}\int_0^\infty\int_0^\infty\int_b^a PF[S_1(T),S_2(T)]n[S_1(T),S_2(T)|S_1(t),S_2(t),\tilde{\rho}]\\
\times\;& \Omega[\tilde{\rho}|S_1(t),S_2(t),\rho_t]d\tilde{\rho}dS_1(T)dS_2(T)\\
=\;& \int_b^a\{e^{-r(T-t)}\int_0^\infty\int_0^\infty PF[S_1(T),S_2(T)]n(S_1(T),S_2(T)|S_1(t),S_2(t),\tilde{\rho})\\
\times\;& dS_1(T)dS_2(T)\}\Omega[\tilde{\rho}|S_1(t),S_2(t),\rho_t]d\tilde{\rho}.
\end{aligned} \tag{46}$$

$n[S_1(T), S_2(T)|S_1(t), S_2(t), \tilde{\rho}]$, means the the bunch of the price paths in the geometric Brownian motions conditional upon $\tilde{\rho}$ must produce a standard lognormal distribution, which reminds that those paths are still in Black-Scholes framework measured in $\tilde{\rho}$ distribution. Consequently, in above equation, the inner integral generates nothing but the Black-Scholes formula with the average correlation coefficient and $\tilde{\rho}$ must be used to substitute the constant correlation coefficient. Now, we get closer to the pricing formula for the option, which reads

$$\bar{C}(S_1, S_2, \rho_t) = \int_b^a C_{BS}(\tilde{\rho})\Omega(\tilde{\rho})d\tilde{\rho}, \tag{47}$$

where C_{BS} is the Black-Scholes pricing formula conditioned on correlation $\tilde{\rho}$. It seems that $\Omega(\tilde{\rho})$ is impossibly available, but remembering the kernel of the Jacobi process is accessible, therefore, the moments of $\tilde{\rho}$ can be figured out, and we can substitute them to expand the above formula. Then, based on the Taylor series expansion, we arrive at the following option pricing formula as follows

$$\begin{aligned}
&\bar{C}(S_1(t), S_2(t), \rho_t) \\
&= \bar{C}_{BS}(\bar{\tilde{\rho}}) + \frac{1}{2}\frac{\partial^2 \bar{C}_{BS}}{\partial \rho^2}|_{\bar{\tilde{\rho}}}\mathrm{Var}(\tilde{\rho}) + \frac{1}{6}\frac{\partial^3 \bar{C}_{BS}}{\partial \rho^3}|_{\bar{\tilde{\rho}}}\mathrm{Skew}(\tilde{\rho}) + \cdots \\
&= \bar{C}_{BS}(\bar{\tilde{\rho}}) + \frac{1}{2}\frac{\partial^2 \bar{C}_{BS}}{\partial \rho^2}|_{\bar{\tilde{\rho}}}(\overline{\tilde{\rho}^2} - (\bar{\tilde{\rho}})^2) \\
&+ \frac{1}{6}\frac{\partial^3 C_{BS}}{\partial \rho^3}|_{\bar{\tilde{\rho}}}(\overline{\tilde{\rho}^3} - 3\overline{\tilde{\rho}^2} \cdot \bar{\tilde{\rho}} + 2(\bar{\tilde{\rho}})^3) + \cdots.
\end{aligned} \tag{48}$$

Now, the last assignment is to evaluate the mean, variance and skew of $\tilde{\rho}$. Since absolute value of ρ_t is less than one, the kurtosis of $\tilde{\rho}$ is extremely small, and the the fourth term in equation (48) is basically much less than the procession requirement in market. So, we need not to derive $\overline{\tilde{\rho}^4}$ and even higher order terms. The evolution kernel of the risk-neutral Jacobi process in section 2 is the key tool to derive $\bar{\tilde{\rho}}$, $\overline{\tilde{\rho}^2}$, $\overline{\tilde{\rho}^3}$. $P(\rho_0, \rho; 0, t)$ can be used to directly derive the expectation of $\tilde{\rho}$ under the risk-neutral measure, i.e., $E^Q(\frac{1}{\tau}\int_0^\tau \rho_t dt)$, which yields

$$\begin{aligned}
\bar{\tilde{\rho}} &= \frac{1}{\tau}\int_b^a \int_0^\tau \rho P(\rho_0, \rho; 0, t)dtd\rho \\
&= \frac{1}{\tau}\int_b^a \int_0^\tau [\rho \sum_{k=0}^{\infty} e^{-\frac{\sigma_\rho^2}{2}k(k+\frac{2g}{\sigma_\rho^2}-1)\tau}(1 + \frac{a+b}{a-b} - \frac{2\rho}{a-b})^{\frac{2ga-2\dot{\rho}}{\sigma_\rho^2(a-b)}-1} \\
&(1 - \frac{a+b}{a-b} + \frac{2\rho}{a-b})^{\frac{2\dot{\rho}-2gb}{\sigma_3^2(a-b)}-1} \times \varphi_k(\rho_0)\varphi_k(\rho)]dtd\rho \\
&= \sum_{k=0}^{\infty} \frac{1 - e^{-\frac{\sigma_\rho^2}{2}k(k+\frac{2g}{\sigma_\rho^2}-1)\tau}}{\frac{\sigma_\rho^2}{2}k(k+\frac{2g}{\sigma_\rho^2}-1)\tau}\varphi_k(\rho_0)\int_b^a d\rho[\rho(1 + \frac{a+b}{a-b} - \frac{2\rho}{a-b})^{\frac{2ga-2\dot{\rho}}{\sigma_\rho^2(a-b)}-1} \\
&\times (1 - \frac{a+b}{a-b} + \frac{2\rho}{a-b})^{\frac{2\dot{\rho}-2gb}{\sigma_\rho^2(a-b)}-1}\varphi_k(\rho)].
\end{aligned} \tag{49}$$

We need to spend a little more space to deduce $\overline{\tilde{\rho}^2}$. The expectation of $\tilde{\rho}^2$ can be transformed as $\frac{1}{\tau^2}E^Q[(\int_0^\tau \rho_{t_1}dt_1)(\int_0^\tau \rho_{t_2}dt_2)] = \frac{1}{\tau^2}E^Q[\int_0^\tau \int_0^\tau \rho_{t_1}\rho_{t_2}dt_1dt_2]$. Then the integrating domain can be specified as two parts i.e., part $t_1 > t_2$ and the other $t_2 > t_1$, whose contributions to the whole value are identical. Then, substituting the probability kernel in one part, we get

$$
\begin{aligned}
E^Q[\int_0^\tau \int_0^\tau \rho_{t_1}\rho_{t_2}dt_1dt_2] &= \frac{2}{\tau^2}\int_0^\tau dt_1 \int_f^h d\rho_x\rho_x P(\rho_0,\rho_x;0,t_1)\int_0^{\tau-t_1} dt_2 \\
&\quad \int_f^h d\rho_y\rho_y P(\rho_x,\rho_y;0,t_2),
\end{aligned} \tag{50}
$$

furthermore, performing the integrations results in

$$
\begin{aligned}
\overline{\tilde{\rho}^2} &= \frac{2}{\tau^2}\int_b^a\{\int_0^\tau [\rho_x P(\rho_0,\rho_x;0,t_1)\int_b^a \rho_y \int_0^{\tau-t_1} P(\rho_x,\rho_y;0,t_2)dt_2 d\rho_y]dt_1\}d\rho_x \\
&= \frac{2}{\tau^2}\sum_{k,h=0}^{\infty}[\frac{1-e^{-\frac{\sigma_\rho^2}{2}k(k+\frac{2g}{\sigma_\rho^2}-1)\tau}}{\frac{\sigma_\rho^4}{4}h(h+\frac{2g}{\sigma_\rho^2}-1)k(k+\frac{2g}{\sigma_\rho^2}-1)}
\end{aligned} \tag{51}
$$

$$
\begin{aligned}
&- \frac{e^{-\frac{\sigma_\rho^2}{2}h(h+\frac{2g}{\sigma_\rho^2}-1)\tau} - e^{-\frac{\sigma_\rho^2}{2}k(k+\frac{2g}{\sigma_\rho^2}-1)\tau}}{\frac{\sigma_\rho^4}{4}h(h+\frac{2g}{\sigma_\rho^2}-1)(k(k+\frac{2g}{\sigma_\rho^2}-1)-h(h+\frac{2g}{\sigma_\rho^2}-1))}] \\
&\times \varphi_k(\rho_0)\int_b^a\int_b^a d\rho_x d\rho_y[\rho_x(1+\frac{a+b}{a-b}-\frac{2\rho_x}{a-b})^{\frac{2ga-2\dot{\rho}}{\sigma_\rho^2(a-b)}-1} \\
&(1-\frac{a+b}{a-b}+\frac{2\rho_x}{a-b})^{\frac{2\dot{\rho}-2gb}{\sigma_\rho^2(a-b)}-1} \\
&\times \varphi_k(\rho_x)\varphi_h(\rho_x)\rho_y(1+\frac{a+b}{a-b}-\frac{2\rho_y}{a-b})^{\frac{2ga-2\dot{\rho}}{\sigma_\rho^2(a-b)}-1} \\
&(1-\frac{a+b}{a-b}+\frac{2\rho_y}{a-b})^{\frac{2\dot{\rho}-2gb}{\sigma_\rho^2(a-b)}-1}\varphi_h(\rho_y)].
\end{aligned} \tag{52}
$$

Finally, using the same skill, we define expectation of $\tilde{\rho}^3$ to be $\frac{1}{\tau^3}E^Q[\int_0^\tau \int_0^\tau \int_0^\tau \rho_{t_1}\rho_{t_2}\rho_{t_3}dt_1dt_2dt_3]$ and specify the integrating domain as six parts. We select one part of the domain and integrate over it, which yields

$$
\begin{aligned}
&E^Q[\int_0^\tau\int_0^\tau\int_0^\tau \rho_{t_1}\rho_{t_2}\rho_{t_3}dt_1dt_2dt_3] \\
&= \frac{6}{\tau^3}\int_b^a d\rho_x \int_0^\tau dt_1\rho_x P(\rho_0,\rho_x;0,t_1)\int_b^a d\rho_y\int_0^{\tau-t_1} dt_2\rho_y P(\rho_x,\rho_y;0,t_2) \\
&\times \int_b^a d\rho_z \int_0^{\tau-t_2-t_1} dt_3\rho_z P(\rho_y,\rho_z,0;t_3).
\end{aligned} \tag{53}
$$

Again, substituting the kernel in the above equation, we arrive at

$$
\begin{aligned}
\overline{\rho^3} &= \frac{6}{\tau^3}\sum_{k=0,h=0,f=0}^{\infty}\Bigg[\frac{e^{-\frac{\sigma_\rho^2}{2}h(h+\frac{2g}{\sigma_\rho^2}-1)\tau}-e^{-\frac{\sigma_\rho^2}{2}k(k+\frac{2g}{\sigma_\rho^2}-1)\tau}}{\frac{\sigma_\rho^6}{8}f(f+\frac{2g}{\sigma_\rho^2}-1)(h(h+\frac{2g}{\sigma_\rho^2}-1)-f(f+\frac{2g}{\sigma_\rho^2}-1))(k(k+\frac{2g}{\sigma_\rho^2}-1)-h(h+\frac{2g}{\sigma_\rho^2}-1))}\\
&- \frac{e^{-\frac{\sigma_\rho^2}{2}f(f-\frac{2g}{\sigma_\rho^2}-1)\tau}-e^{-\frac{\sigma_\rho^2}{2}k(k+\frac{2g}{\sigma_\rho^2}-1)\tau}}{\frac{\sigma_\rho^6}{8}f(f+\frac{2g}{\sigma_\rho^2}-1)(h(h+\frac{2g}{\sigma_\rho^2}-1)-f(f+\frac{2g}{\sigma_\rho^2}-1))(k(k+\frac{2g}{\sigma_\rho^2}-1)-f(f+\frac{2g}{\sigma_\rho^2}-1))}\\
&- \frac{e^{-\frac{\sigma_\rho^2}{2}h(h+\frac{2g}{\sigma_\rho^2}-1)\tau}-e^{-\frac{\sigma_\rho^2}{2}k(k+\frac{2g}{\sigma_\rho^2}-1)\tau}}{\frac{\sigma_\rho^6}{8}f(f+\frac{2g}{\sigma_\rho^2}-1)h(h+\frac{2g}{\sigma_\rho^2}-1)(k(k+\frac{2g}{\sigma_\rho^2}-1)-h(h+\frac{2g}{\sigma_\rho^2}-1))}
\end{aligned} \tag{54}
$$

$$
\begin{aligned}
&+ \frac{1-e^{-\frac{\sigma_\rho^2}{2}k(k+\frac{2g}{\sigma_\rho^2}-1)\tau}}{\frac{\sigma_\rho^6}{8}f(f+\frac{2g}{\sigma_\rho^2}-1)h(h+\frac{2g}{\sigma_\rho^2}-1)k(k+\frac{2g}{\sigma_\rho^2}-1)}\Bigg]\varphi_k(\rho_0)\\
&\times \int_b^a\int_b^a\int_b^a d\rho_x d\rho_y d\rho_z\Big[\rho_x(1+\frac{a+b}{a-b}-\frac{2\rho_x}{a-b})^{\frac{2ga-2\rho}{\sigma_\rho^2(a-b)}-1}(1-\frac{a+b}{a-b}+\frac{2\rho_x}{a-b})^{\frac{2\rho-2gb}{\sigma_\rho^2(a-b)}-1}\\
&\varphi_k(\rho_x)\varphi_h(\rho_x)\\
&\times \rho_y(1+\frac{a+b}{a-b}-\frac{2\rho_y}{a-b})^{\frac{2ga-2\rho}{\sigma_\rho^2(a-b)}-1}(1-\frac{a+b}{a-b}+\frac{2\rho_y}{a-b})^{\frac{2\rho-2gb}{\sigma_\rho^2(a-b)}-1}\varphi_h(\rho_y)\varphi_f(\rho_y)\\
&\times \rho_z(1+\frac{a+b}{a-b}-\frac{2\rho_z}{a-b})^{\frac{2ga-2\rho}{\sigma_\rho^2(a-b)}-1}(1-\frac{a+b}{a-b}+\frac{2\rho_z}{a-b})^{\frac{2\rho-2gb}{\sigma_\rho^2(a-b)}-1}\varphi_f(\rho_z)\Big].
\end{aligned} \tag{55}
$$

In the next figure, we test the above formulas for computing the option price and find that the first couple of eigenvalue and eigenfunctions generally could guarantee very good accuracy since the eigenvalue $\lambda_k \sim -k^2$ and the exponentially decaying factor $e^{\lambda_n\tau}$ wipes off most of terms in equations (49-53).

As mentioned before, an important topic is to observe the analytical properties of option price within the framework of equation (48). Besides fixed exchange rate foreign equity call, there are four kinds of actively traded quanto option, i.e., equity-linked foreign exchange call, foreign equity call struck in domestic currency, and foreign equity call struck in foreign currency, whose terminal payoff functions read

$$
\begin{aligned}
PF_1(T) &= S_F(T)Max[S_D(T)-E,0], && (56)\\
PF_2(T) &= Max[S_D(T)S_F(T)-E_D,0], && (57)\\
PF_3(T) &= S_D(T)Max[S_F(T)-E_F,0]. && (58)
\end{aligned}
$$

The last one in above equation means the call is struck in foreign currency, whose payment is directly converted to domestic currency following the spot exchange rate at expiry, so, its price in domestic currency is the product of the call in foreign currency with contemporary exchange rate, which means it does not have any correlation sensitivity at all. In foreign equity call struck in domestic currency, E_D is E_D units of domestic currency for one unit of strike price of the underlying asset measured by exchange rate, and evidently, the correlation must be associated with its price, which can be read off from the following formulas,

$$
\begin{aligned}
C_1 &= S_FS_DN(d_1^1)-S_FEe^{-(r_D-r_F+\rho\sigma_S\sigma_F)\tau}N(d_2^1), && (59)\\
C_2 &= S_DS_FN(d_1^2)-E_De^{-r_D\tau}N(d_2^2), && (60)\\
C_3 &= S_DS_FN(d_1^3)-S_DE_Fe^{-r_F\tau}N(d_2^3)], && (61)
\end{aligned}
$$

where

$$d_1^1 = \frac{\ln\frac{S_D}{E} + (r_D - r_F + \rho\sigma_D\sigma_F + \frac{\sigma_D^2}{2})\tau}{\sigma_D\sqrt{\tau}}, d_2^1 = d_1^1 - \sigma_D\sqrt{\tau}, \tag{62}$$

$$d_1^2 = \frac{\ln\frac{S_F S_D}{E_D} + (-r_D + \frac{\sigma_F^2+\sigma_D^2-2\rho\sigma_F\sigma_D}{2})\tau}{\sqrt{(\sigma_F^2+\sigma_D^2-2\rho\sigma_F\sigma_D)\tau}},$$

$$d_2^2 = d_1^2 - \sqrt{(\sigma_F^2+\sigma_D^2-2\rho\sigma_F\sigma_D)\tau}, \tag{63}$$

$$d_1^3 = \frac{\ln\frac{S_F}{E_F} + (r_F + \frac{\sigma_F^2}{2})\tau}{\sigma_F\sqrt{\tau}}, d_2^3 = d_1^3 - \sigma_F\sqrt{\tau}. \tag{64}$$

It is clear what happens as the stochastic correlation is take into account for pricing the foreign equity option. The absence of correlation coefficient in equation (59) implies the varying correlation never affects the price of foreign equity call struck in foreign currency, which justifies our preceding conclusion. Equation (58) is the pricing formula for foreign equity call struck in domestic currency, which highlights the correlation only in d_1^2, d_2^2. So, in this option at the money, i.e., $E_D \approx S_F S_D$, the stochastic correlation affects the option price evidently, but for deep in or out of the money, the variation of correlation in d_1^2, d_2^2 does not give any corresponding change of $N(d_1^2)$ or $N(d_2^2)$, and obviously, the effect of correlation risk can be ignored. Now, we can compare the price of fixed exchange rate foreign equity call with other options. In Black-Scholes pricing formula for fixed exchange rate foreign equity call, i.e., equation (38), there is a independent factor $e^{(r_F-r_D-\rho\sigma_1\sigma_2)\tau}$, whose corresponding term, i.e., $\overline{\rho}$ in equation (48) greatly affect the price through the variation of correlation. This term is helpful for understanding what happens in figure 6(a) and 6(b). Since based on the small equilibrium value of correlation, we conclude that at $\rho_0 \sim -0.85$, $\overline{\rho}$ is greater than the initial correlation coefficient, and at $\rho_0 \sim 0.85$, $\overline{\rho}$ must be less than the initial one. In equation (48), the factor $e^{(r_F-r_D-\overline{\rho}\sigma_F\sigma_D)\tau}$ in the zeroth order term dominates the price under stochastic correlation which results in a conclusion, i.e., the value under stochastic correlation must be larger than the price with constant one at $\rho_0 \sim 0.85$ or vice versus at $\rho_0 \sim -0.85$. Therefore, what we can learn is that $S_F e^{(r_F-r_D-\overline{\rho}\sigma_F\sigma_D)\tau}N(d_1)$ in equation (48) still affect the price even for deep in or out of the money, and the price difference never vanishes and should be linearly proportional to the initial price of foreign underlying asset, as seen in figure (6). Based on equation (57), a similar conclusion, i.e., the correlation risk is always important for equity-linked foreign exchange call, can be made.

The volatility smile or skew plays important role in pricing single-asset option, and they must exist in multi-asset option pricing. Note in the preceding models, no stochastic volatility has been highlighted. So, realizing that the absence of stochastic volatility in any model is misleading, we try to incorporate the varying volatility and correlation in a model simultaneously. Certainly, the stochastic volatility gives rise to more obstacles for an explicit pricing formula. To simplify the problem, we impose only one uncertainty source to the volatilities of two underlying assets. On the other hand, we still use equation (5) to describe the independent random walk of correlation. To demonstrate the impact of stochastic correlation on the price easily, we choose the correlation option. In a vallina call on a single asset, the positive spread between the terminal price of asset and the strike determines the payoff for option. Besides the product option, i.e., a contract to grant a future right to buy or sell the product of two underlying assets for the strike, one still can create another option to capture an opportunity to trade two spreads in assets jointly, whose payoff is $Max[S_1(T) - E_1, 0] \times Max[S_2(T) - E_2, 0]$, where E_1 and E_2 are two striking prices. Although the volatilities are set as stochastic, we only arrange one random source, and subsequently, in risk-neutral world, the dynamics for stochastic volatilities can be set as the following (see Bakshi and Madan, 2000)

$$\begin{aligned}\frac{dS_1}{S_1} &= rdt + \sigma_1\sqrt{V}dW_1,\\ \frac{dS_2}{S_2} &= rdt + \sigma_2\sqrt{V}dW_2,\\ dV &= (\Phi_V - \kappa_V V)dt + \sigma_V\sqrt{V}dW_V,\end{aligned} \tag{65}$$

where V stands for the stochastic variance factor, and the relationships are given by $dW_1dW_2 = \rho$, $dW_1dW_V = \rho_{1V}$, and $dW_2dW_V = \rho_{2V}$. This ρ-constant model prices the correlation option $C(S_1, S_2, V_0, \tau)$ by the following formula

$$C(S_1, S_2, V_0, \tau) = \frac{e^{-\eta_1 \ln E_1 - \eta_2 \ln E_2}}{(2\pi)^2}$$
$$\int_{-\infty}^{\infty}\int_{-\infty}^{\infty} Re[\frac{e^{-i(\psi_1 \ln E_1 + \psi_2 \ln E_2) - r\tau} H(\tau; \Xi_1, \Xi_2)}{(\eta_1 + i\psi_1)(\eta_1 + 1 + i\psi_1)(\eta_2 + i\psi_2)(\eta_2 + 1 + i\psi_2)}] d\psi_2 d\psi_1, \tag{66}$$

where V_0 is initial volatility, η_1 and η_2 are chosen as two real numbers to define $\Xi_1 = \psi_1 - (1 + \eta_1)i$, $\Xi_2 = \psi_2 - (1 + \eta_2)i$, and the characteristic function is

$$\begin{aligned}H(\tau; \Xi_1, \Xi_2) &= \exp[i\Xi_1 \ln S_1(0)\\ &+ i\Xi_2 \ln S_2(0) + i(\Xi_1 + \Xi_2)r\tau + \frac{2\zeta(1 - e^{-\phi\tau})}{2\phi - (\phi - \nu)(1 - e^{-\phi\tau})}V_0\\ &- \frac{2\Phi_V}{\sigma_V^2}\ln(1 - \frac{(\phi - \nu)(1 - e^{-\phi\tau})}{2\phi}) - \frac{\Phi_V}{\sigma_V^2}(\phi - \nu)\tau],\end{aligned} \tag{67}$$

with

$$\begin{aligned}\nu &= \kappa_V - i(\rho_{1V}\sigma_1\Xi_1 + \rho_{2V}\sigma_2\Xi_2)\sigma_V,\\ \phi &= \sqrt{\nu^2 - 2\sigma_V^2\zeta},\\ \zeta &= -0.5(\sigma_1^2\Xi_1^2 + \sigma_2^2\Xi_2^2 + 2\rho\sigma_1\sigma_2\Xi_1\Xi_2) - 0.5i(\sigma_1^2\Xi_1 + \sigma_2^2\Xi_2).\end{aligned} \tag{68}$$

Having defined an independent Jacobi process to incorporate the stochastic correlation ρ, we still could use a Taylor series expansion to derive the price of the option under stochastic volatility and correlation. To derive an explicit pricing equation for this multi-factor model, the sensitivities of option price versus the correlation in first several order, i.e., $\frac{\partial H}{\partial \rho}$, $\frac{\partial^2 H}{\partial \rho^2}$ and $\frac{\partial^3 H}{\partial \rho^3}$ have been deduced in appendix.

Substituting $\frac{\partial H}{\partial \rho}$, $\frac{\partial^2 H}{\partial \rho^2}$, and $\frac{\partial^3 H}{\partial \rho^3}$, the pricing formula for the option with stochastic volatility and correlation can be expanded as

$$
\begin{aligned}
& \bar{C}(S_1, S_2, V_0, \rho_0) \\
= \; & \frac{e^{-\eta_1 \ln E_1 - \eta_2 \ln E_2}}{(2\pi)^2} \int_{-\infty}^{\infty}\int_{-\infty}^{\infty} Re[\frac{e^{-i(\psi_1 \ln E_1 + \psi_2 \ln E_2 - ir\tau)} H(\tau; \Xi_1, \Xi_2)}{(\eta_1 + i\psi_1)(\eta_1 + 1 + i\psi_1)(\eta_2 + i\psi_2)(\eta_2 + 1 + i\psi_2)}] d\psi_2 d\psi_1 \\
+ \; & \frac{1}{2}\frac{e^{-\eta_1 \ln E_1 - \eta_2 \ln E_2}}{(2\pi)^2} \int_{-\infty}^{\infty}\int_{-\infty}^{\infty} Re[\frac{e^{-i(\psi_1 \ln E_1 + \psi_2 \ln E_2 - ir\tau)} \frac{\partial^2 H(\tau;\Xi_1,\Xi_2)}{\partial \rho^2}|_{\overline{\rho}}}{(\eta_1 + i\psi_1)(\eta_1 + 1 + i\psi_1)(\eta_2 + i\psi_2)(\eta_2 + 1 + i\psi_2)}] d\psi_2 d\psi_1 \\
\times \; & (\overline{\rho^2} - (\overline{\rho})^2) \\
+ \; & \frac{1}{6}\frac{e^{-\eta_1 \ln E_1 - \eta_2 \ln E_2}}{(2\pi)^2} \int_{-\infty}^{\infty}\int_{-\infty}^{\infty} Re[\frac{e^{-i(\psi_1 \ln E_1 + \psi_2 \ln E_2 - ir\tau)} \frac{\partial^3 H(\tau;\Xi_1,\Xi_2)}{\partial \rho^3}|_{\overline{\rho}}}{(\eta_1 + i\psi_1)(\eta_1 + 1 + i\psi_1)(\eta_2 + i\psi_2)(\eta_2 + 1 + i\psi_2)}] d\psi_2 d\psi_1 \\
\times \; & (\overline{\rho^3} - 3\overline{\rho^2} \cdot \overline{\rho} + 2(\overline{\rho})^3) + \cdots, \qquad (69)
\end{aligned}
$$

whose coefficients, namely, $\overline{\rho}$, $\overline{\rho^2}$, $\overline{\rho^3}$, are still given by equations (49-53).

We use Monte Carlo method to compute the price of equation (63) model with constant ρ, whose results are compared to the one from equation (67) in figure (7). In dot and thin lines of figure (7), taking $E_1 = E_2 = 1$, $S_1(0) = 1.1$, $S_2(0) = 1.2$, $\tau = 5$, $r = 0.1$, $\rho = 0.6$, $\rho_{1V} = -\rho_{2V} = 0.12$, $V_0 = 0.9$ $\sigma_1 = 0.6$, $\sigma_2 = 0.7$, $\Phi_V = 0.55$, $\kappa_V = 1.1$, and $\sigma_V = 0.6$, the semi-closed form solution, equation (64) for constant correlation gives rise to the price 2.87, but the saturation price for constant $\rho = 0.6$ from the Monte Carlo method is above 2.90, about 2.93. Therefore, the error from Monte Carlo is not so tiny. On the other hand, we calculate the option price with stochastic correlation. The price from the first three terms of equation (67) for $\rho_0 = 0.6$, $\dot{\rho} = 0.5$ plotted by dash line is 1.75, but the saturation value from the Monte Carlo method plotted by thick line is 1.78. In the stochastic correlation cases, it seems that the average error of the Monte Carlo method presents almost same magnitude as constant correlation case. Note the path numbers in Monte Carlo is 300000. If wanting to get a stable value or reliable precision, actually, in Monte Carlo method, we need to check more paths and spend much longer time than the one needed in equation (67). Moreover, this figure reminds us that if using the initial correlation as the constant correlation, one may get totally wrong price.

5. Correlation Risk for the Interest-Rate Contingent Claim

In the previous sections, we select the constant risk-free interest rate. It is sufficiently good since the maturity of option is comparatively short. Certainly, the interest rate is not constant and many interest rate products have been consequently created and used to hedge the rate variation. In the market, we can observe several kinds of interest-rate contingent claim, which are the kind involving single interest rate such as caplet or floor, path-dependent kind such as Bermudan swaption, and the kind involving several interest rates such as option on a maximum or minimum value of two yield, and the spread option. The last kind is obviously correlation-dependent, and in this section, we want to briefly describe how to manipulate the correlation-dependent interest-rate contingent claim and eliminate its correlation risk. In current studies, academicians and financial industry specified the necessary element from observed market, and developed many stochastic processes for underlying rate, which can

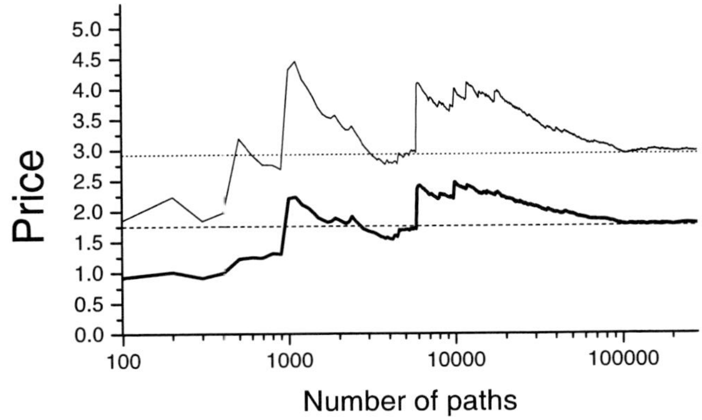

Figure 7. Dot and thin lines give a comparison of correlation option price of equation (63) model from the Monte Carlo method to the one from equation (64) with constant correlation. Dot and thin solid lines share common parameters, $K_1 = K_2 = 1$, $S_1(0) = 1.1$, $S_2(0) = 1.2$ $\tau = 5$, $r = 0.1$, , $\rho = 0.6$, $\rho_{1V} = -\rho_{2V} = 0.12$, $V_0 = 0.9$ $\sigma_1 = 0.6$, $\sigma_2 = 0.7$, $\Phi_V = 0.55$, $\kappa_V = 1.1$, and $\sigma_V = 0.6$. Dash and thick solid lines are from equation (67) with stochastic correlation and the Monte Carlo method, which share common parameters as in dash and thin lines except $\dot{\rho} = 0.5$, $\rho_0 = 0.6$, $a = -b = 0.8$, $g = 1.7$, $\sigma_\rho = 1.0$.

be consistent with the market(See Vasicek, 1977; Cox, Ingersoll, Ross, 1985; Ho, lee, 1986; Black, Derman, Toy, 1990; Hull, White, 1990; Health, Jarrow, Morton, 1992; Longstaff, Schwartz, 1992; Brace, Gatarek, Musiela, 1997; Mougeot, 2000). The above models handle the single rate contingent claim quite well. But, on the other hand, the multi-interest-rate products have been quickly developed and are frequently traded in interest-rate risk management. Actually, using the relationship between two rates or yields, we can create many derivative instruments. Therefore, how to handle the correlation risk steadily is an urgent challenging. In this section, we try to give a solution.

In the preceding sections, we always use the geometric Brownian motion to describe behaviour of stock price, which is much different from the one of interest rate. The interest rate always presents the mean-reversion feature due to economic logic. Adoption of geometric Brownian model presented before means the interest rate always goes up, which is impossible in real world since the high interest rates eventually suppress or destroy economics. Therefore, the Ornstein-Uhlenbeck process is wildly selected for instantaneous risk-free interest rate, which reads in risk-neutral world

$$dr = a_r(b_r - r)dt + \sigma_r dW_r, \tag{70}$$

where a_r, b_r are mean reverting speed and equilibrium rate, respectively. Based on the above process, the bond conditioned on the initial rate r_0 at $t = 0$ and maturity T can be discounted

$$B(r_0, T) = \exp[(b_r - \frac{\sigma_r^2}{2a_r^2})(\frac{1 - e^{-a_r T}}{a_r} - T) - \frac{\sigma_r^2}{4a_r^3}(1 - e^{-a_r T})^2 - \frac{r_0}{a_r}(1 - e^{-a_r T})], \tag{71}$$

which is Vasicek pricing formula exactly and can be used to price other kind of interest-rate contingent claim. As emphasized before, the daily variation in several rates can be used to design many interest-rate products, e.g., the better-of rainbow option, whose payoff is based on the maximum value of two interest rates. Consider two interest rates, whose dynamics in risk-neutral world still yield Ornstein-Uhlenbeck process as follows

$$
\begin{aligned}
dX &= a_X[b_X - \rho_{rX}\sigma_r\sigma_X(1-e^{-a_r(T-t)})/a_r^2 - X]dt + \sigma_X dW_X, && (72)\\
dY &= a_Y[b_Y - \rho_{rY}\sigma_r\sigma_Y(1-e^{-a_r(T-t)})/a_r^2 - Y]dt + \sigma_Y dW_Y, && (73)
\end{aligned}
$$

where the coefficients follow $\rho_{rX} = dW_r dW_X/dt$, $\rho_{rY} = dW_r dW_Y/dt$, and the relationship between two Weiner processes follows $dW_X dW_Y = \rho_{XY}dt$. If treating all correlation as constant, based on the payoff function for the better-of rainbow option, i.e., $PF(T) = Max(X, Y)$, the pricing formula can be deduced as the following

$$
C(X_0, Y_0; \rho_{AB}, T) = B(r_0, T)[\bar{Y}_T N(-d_{XY}) + \bar{X}_T N(d_{XY}) + \frac{\Upsilon_{XY}}{\sqrt{2\pi}}e^{-d_{XY}^2/2}], \quad (74)
$$

where X_0, Y_0 are value of two interest rates at $t = 0$,

$$
\begin{aligned}
d_{XY} &= \frac{\bar{A}_T - \bar{B}_T}{\Upsilon_{AB}}, && (75)\\
\bar{X}_T &= e^{-a_X T}[X_0 + a_X\int_0^T e^{a_X t}[b_X - \frac{\rho_{rX}\sigma_r\sigma_X}{a_r^2}((1-e^{-a_r(T-t)})]dt && (76)\\
&= e^{-a_X T}X_0 + (b_X - \frac{\rho_{rX}\sigma_r\sigma_X}{a_r^2})(1-e^{-a_X T})\\
&+ \frac{a_X\rho_{rX}\sigma_r\sigma_X}{a_r^2(a_X+a_r)}(1-e^{-(a_X+a_r)T}), && (77)\\
\bar{Y}_T &= e^{-a_Y T}[Y_0 + a_Y\int_0^T e^{a_Y t}[b_Y - \frac{\rho_{rY}\sigma_r\sigma_Y}{a_r^2}((1-e^{-a_r(T-t)})]dt && (78)\\
&= e^{-a_Y T}Y_0 + (b_Y - \frac{\rho_{rY}\sigma_r\sigma_Y}{a_r^2})(1-e^{-a_Y T})\\
&+ \frac{a_Y\rho_{rY}\sigma_r\sigma_Y}{a_r^2(a_Y+a_r)}(1-e^{-(a_Y+a_r)T}), && (79)\\
\Upsilon_{XY} &= \sqrt{\Upsilon_X^2 + \Upsilon_Y^2 - 2\sigma_X\sigma_Y\int_0^T \rho_{XY}e^{-(a_X+a_Y)(T-t)}dt} && (80)\\
&= \sqrt{\Upsilon_X^2 + \Upsilon_Y^2 - \frac{2\rho_{XY}\sigma_X\sigma_Y}{a_X+a_Y}(1-e^{-(a_X+a_Y)T})}, && (81)\\
\Upsilon_X &= \sqrt{\frac{\sigma_X^2}{2a_X}(1-e^{-2a_X T})e^{-a_X T}}, && (82)\\
\Upsilon_Y &= \sqrt{\frac{\sigma_Y^2}{2a_Y}(1-e^{-2a_Y T})e^{-a_Y T}}. && (83)
\end{aligned}
$$

The above equation is for constant correlations. To price the correlation risk, we can define the variations of $\rho_{XY}, \rho_{rX}, \rho_{rY}$ as three independent Jacobi processes. Similarly, based on

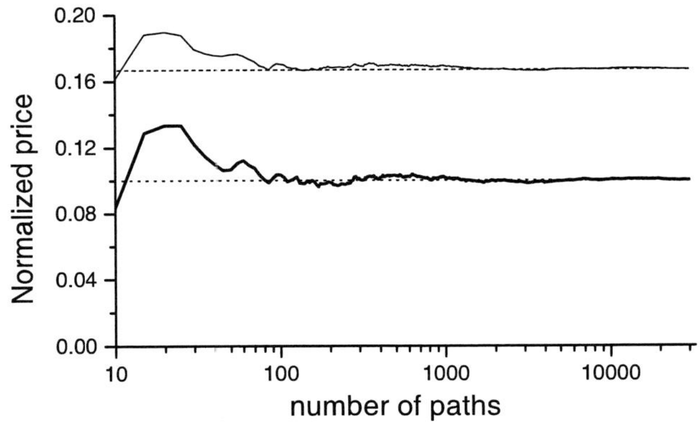

Figure 8. Normalized price of better-of rainbow option on two yields. The horizontal axis is number of paths, and vertical axis is normalized price, i.e., $C(X_0, Y_0; \rho_{XY}(0), \rho_{rX}(0), \rho_{rY}(0))/B(r_0, T)$. The dot line from equation (85) and the thicker solid one from Monte Carlo are for stocahstic ρ_{XY},ρ_{rX}, and ρ_{rY}, whose parameters are $\rho_{XY}(t = 0) = -0.03$, $\dot{\rho} = 0.05$, $g = 2.1$, $\sigma_\rho = 0.7746$, $a = -b = 0.1$ in $d\rho_{XY}$; $\rho_{rX}(t = 0) = -0.87$, $\dot{\rho} = 0.7$, $g = 2.0$, $\sigma_\rho = 0.7071$, $a = -b = 0.88$ in $d\rho_{rX}$; $\rho_{rY}(t = 0) = 0$, $\dot{\rho} = 0.002$, $g = 1.1$, $\sigma_\rho = 0.01$, $a = -b = 0.008$ in $d\rho_{rY}$. In this figure, $X_0 = 0.05$, $\sigma_X = 0.02$, $a_X = 0.3$, $b_X = 0.05$, $Y_0 = 0.07$, $\sigma_Y = 0.09$, $a_Y = 0.35$, $b_Y = 0.08$, $a_r = 0.02$, and time to maturity is 5. The dash from equation (72) and thin solid line from Monte Carlo are for constant correlation, whose paramters are same except $\rho_{XY} = -0.03$, $\rho_{rX} = -0.87$ and $\rho_{rY} = 0$.

equations (74, 76, 78), we define three random variables

$$\tilde{\rho}_{XY} = \int_0^T \rho_{XY}(t) e^{-(a_X + a_Y)(T-t)} dt, \tag{84}$$

$$\tilde{\rho}_{rX} = \int_0^T \rho_{rX}(t)(e^{a_X t} - e^{-a_r T} e^{(a_r + a_X)t}) dt, \tag{85}$$

$$\tilde{\rho}_{rY} = \int_0^T \rho_{rY}(t)(e^{a_Y t} - e^{-a_r T} e^{(a_r + a_Y)t}) dt, \tag{86}$$

which can be substitued to the equation below to price the coorelation risk, namely,

$$\begin{aligned}\bar{C}(X(t), Y(t); \rho_{XY}(t), \rho_{rX}(t), \rho_{rY}(t)) &= \sum_{j=0}^{\infty} \{ \frac{1}{j!} E^Q[(\tilde{\rho}_{XY} - \bar{\tilde{\rho}}_{XY}) \frac{\partial}{\partial \rho_{XY}} \\ &+ (\tilde{\rho}_{rX} - \bar{\tilde{\rho}}_{rX}) \frac{\partial}{\partial \rho_{rX}} + (\tilde{\rho}_{rY} - \bar{\tilde{\rho}}_{rY}) \frac{\partial}{\partial \rho_{rY}}]^j \\ &\times C_{BS}(X(t), Y(t); \rho_{XY}(t), \rho_{rX}(t), \rho_{rY}(t))|_{\rho_{XY} = \bar{\tilde{\rho}}_{XY}, \rho_{rX} = \bar{\tilde{\rho}}_{rX}, \rho_{rY} = \bar{\tilde{\rho}}_{rY}} \}. \end{aligned} \tag{87}$$

This formula could be easily compared to Monte-Carlo method, and their results are depicted in figure 8, where the Monte Carlo and equations (85) match well. In figure 8. $C(X_0, Y_0; K, T)/B(r_0, T)$ is the normalized price of the better of rainbow option on two yields. The dot line from equation (85) is consistent with the thicker solid line from the Monte Carlo, which are for stochastic correlation. The dash line from equation (72) and thin solid one from Monte Carlo are for constant correlation, which match well. This figure justifies that the initial correlation can not be treated as the constant correlation as well.

6. Conclusion

Based on our investigations, the correlation risk is as important as the volatility risk. Generally, implied correlation extracted from market information is different from the realized one for a given maturity. In general sense, correlation risk is defined as the difference between them. There are many ways to define the risk-neutral correlation processes, such as, $d\rho = [\bar{\rho} + g\ln[(a-\rho)(\rho-b)]dt + \sigma[(a-\rho)(\rho-b)]^{\epsilon}dW$, which could guarantee the correlation coefficient never hits the bounds. To derive the pricing formula analytically, we propose $\epsilon = \frac{1}{2}$ and correlation risk premium is linearly proportional to spot value of correlation, which results in the Jacobi process, i.e., $d\rho = (\bar{\rho} - g\rho)dt + \sigma\sqrt{(a-\rho)(\rho-b)}dW$. In this theory , the correlation coefficient undergoes the random motion around the mean-reversion value but is within the region from the upper bound $a \leq 1$ to the lower one $b \geq -1$. Based on the Jacobi process, the partial differential equation for option pricing under stochastic correlation is deduced, which can be numerically solved and the solution justifies that as long as the maturity of option is long or the correlation variation is obvious, the price with constant correlation might be misleading. This is to say that we have to use this model to eliminate correlation risk based on the pricing formula and portfolio strategy. On the other hand, a series expansion formula for pricing the stochastic volatility and correlation is derived. Conventionally, the cumulative correlation coefficient is selected in the market, which might be treated as the average correlation at most. This means, the conventional pricing mechanism might be able to capture the first term in our series expansion pricing formula, but definitely, misses second and third terms which occupy five percents of total value. The second and third terms are important as well since they could be used to catch the structure of implied correlation. Certainly, the trading strategy can be designed to hedge the correlation risk. For example, we can judge the current implied correlation leads to a cheap index option price, then, immediately, the index option can be bought and the option on the component can be sold based on the appropriate portfolio. If the implied correlation leads to an expensive index option price, then, the index option can be sold and the option on the component can be bought. Another way is that trading an index option results in a correlation risk, but it can be hedged by applying a basket option highlighting the component of the basket option. In the currency market, if the correlation risk results from an option on the basket consisting of Japanese Yen, and British pounds, U.S. dollar, then, a best-of call allows the owner to buy any of the currencies that increases the most at the expiation of the option, which must be used to eliminate the risk.

Appendix

$$\frac{\partial H}{\partial \rho} = (-2\frac{\Phi_V A_2}{\sigma_V^2 A_1} + \frac{\Phi_V \tau A_0}{\phi} + V_0 \frac{A_4}{A_3^2})H$$

with

$$\begin{aligned}
A_0 &= -\sigma_1\sigma_2\Xi_1\Xi_2,\\
B_0 &= -\sigma_V^2 A_0(1-e^{-\phi\tau})/\phi-(\phi-\nu)\tau\sigma_V^2 A_0 e^{-\phi\tau}/\phi,\\
A_1 &= 1-\frac{(\phi-\nu)(1-e^{-\phi\tau})}{2\phi},\\
A_2 &= -0.5\frac{\sigma_V^2 A_0(\phi-\nu)(1-e^{-\phi\tau})}{\phi^3}-0.5\frac{B_0}{\phi},\\
A_3 &= 2\phi-(\phi-\nu)(1-e^{-\phi\tau}),\\
A_4 &= 2A_0(1-e^{-\phi\tau})A_3-2\zeta\tau\sigma_V^2 A_0A_3e^{-\phi\tau}/\phi\\
&\quad +2\zeta(1-e^{-\phi\tau})(2\sigma_V^2X_0/\phi+B_0).
\end{aligned}$$

The second order is

$$\begin{aligned}
\frac{\partial^2 H}{\partial\rho^2} &= [-2\Phi_V(A_5A_1-A_2^2)/(\sigma_V^2A_1^2)+\Phi_V\sigma_V^2\tau A_0^2/\phi^3\\
&\quad +A_6V_0/A_3^2+4\sigma_V^2A_0A_4V_0/(A_3^3\phi)\\
&\quad +2A_4B_0V_0/A_3^3]H+(-2\Phi_VA_2/(\sigma_V^2A_1)\\
&\quad +\Phi_V\tau A_0/\phi+A_4V_0/A_3^2)\frac{\partial H}{\partial\rho}
\end{aligned}$$

with

$$\begin{aligned}
A_5 &= -\sigma_V^2A_0B_0/\phi^3-0.5B_1/\phi-\frac{3}{2}\sigma_V^4A_0^2(\phi-\nu)(1-e^{-\phi\tau})/\phi^5,\\
A_6 &= -2A_0^2A_3\tau\sigma_V^2e^{-\phi\tau}/\phi-2A_0(1-e^{-\phi\tau})(2\sigma_V^2A_0/\phi+B_0)\\
&\quad -2\tau\sigma_V^2A_0^2A_3e^{-\phi\tau}/\phi+2\zeta\tau\sigma_V^2A_0e^{-\phi\tau}(2\sigma_V^2A_0/\phi+B_0)/\phi\\
&\quad -2\zeta\tau^2\sigma_V^4A_0^2A_3e^{-\phi\tau}/\phi^2-2\zeta\tau\sigma_V^4A_0^2A_3e^{-\phi\tau}/\phi^3\\
&\quad +2A_0(1-e^{-\phi\tau})(2\sigma_V^2A_0/\phi+B_0)+2\zeta A_7,\\
A_7 &= -2\tau\sigma_V^4A_0^2e^{-\phi\tau}/\phi^2-\tau\sigma_V^2A_0B_0e^{-\phi\tau}/\phi\\
&\quad +(1-e^{-\phi\tau})(2\sigma_V^4A_0^2/\phi^3+B_1),
\end{aligned} \tag{88}$$

$$\begin{aligned}
B_1 &= \tau\sigma_V^4A_0^2e^{-\phi\tau}/\phi^2-\sigma_V^4A_0^2(1-e^{-\phi\tau})/\phi^3\\
&\quad +\tau\sigma_V^4A_0^2e^{-\phi\tau}/\phi^2-(\phi-\nu)\tau^2\sigma_V^4A_0^2e^{-\phi\tau}/\phi^2\\
&\quad -(\phi-\nu)\tau\sigma_V^4A_0^2e^{-\phi\tau}/\phi^3.
\end{aligned}$$

The third order is

$$\begin{aligned}
\frac{\partial^3 H}{\partial\rho^3} &= [-2\Phi_VA_8/(\sigma_V^2A_1)+2\Phi_VA_5A_2/(\sigma_V^2A_1^2)\\
&\quad +4\Phi_VA_2A_5/(\sigma_V^2A_1^2)-4\Phi_VA_2^3/(\sigma_V^2A_1^3)+3\Phi_V\tau\sigma_V^4A_0^3/\phi^5\\
&\quad +A_9V_0/A_3^2+2A_6(2\sigma_V^2A_0/\phi+B_0)V_0/A_3^3+4\sigma_V^2A_0A_6V_0/(A_3^2\phi)\\
&\quad +12\sigma_V^2A_0A_4(2\sigma_V^2A_0/\phi+B_0)V_0/(A_3^4\phi)+4\sigma_V^4A_0^2A_4V_0/(A_3^3\phi^3)\\
&\quad +2A_6B_0V_0/A_3^3+2A_4B_1V_0/A_3^3+6A_4B_0(2\sigma_V^2A_0/\phi+B_0)V_0/A_3^4]H\\
&\quad +2[-2\Phi_VA_5/(\sigma_V^2A_1)+2\Phi_VA_2^2/(\sigma_V^2A_1^2)+\Phi_V\tau\sigma_V^2A_0^2/\phi^3\\
&\quad +A_6V_0/A_3^2+4\sigma_V^2A_0A_4V_0/(A_3^3\phi)+2A_4B_0V_0/A_3^3]\frac{\partial H}{\partial\rho}\\
&\quad +[-2\Phi_VA_2/(\sigma_V^2A_1)+\Phi_V\tau A_0/\phi+A_4V_0/A_3^2]\frac{\partial^2 H}{\partial\rho^2}
\end{aligned}$$

with

$$
\begin{aligned}
A_8 &= -B_1\sigma_V^2 A_0/\phi^3 - \frac{9}{2}B_0\sigma_V^4 A_0^2/\phi^5 - \frac{1}{2}B_2/\phi - \frac{1}{2}\sigma_V^2 A_0 B_1/\phi^3 \\
&\quad -\frac{15}{2}\sigma_V^6 A_0^3(\phi-\nu)(1-e^{-\phi\tau})/\phi^7, \\
A_9 &= 6\tau\sigma_V^2 A_0^2(2\sigma_A^2 A_0/\phi + B_0)e^{-\phi\tau}/\phi - 6\tau^2\sigma_V^4 A_0^3 A_3 e^{-\phi\tau}/\phi^2 \\
&\quad -6\tau\sigma_V^4 A_0^3 A_3 e^{-\phi\tau}/\phi^3 + 4\zeta\tau^2\sigma_V^4 A_0^2 e^{-\phi\tau}(2\sigma_V^2 A_0/\phi + B_0)/\phi^2 \\
&\quad +2\zeta\tau\sigma_V^2 A_0 e^{-\phi\tau}(2\sigma_V^4 A_0^2/\phi^3 + B_1)/\phi \\
&\quad +4\zeta\tau\sigma_V^4 A_0^2 e^{-\phi\tau}(2\sigma_V^2 A_0/\phi + B_0)/\phi^3 \\
&\quad -2\zeta\tau^3\sigma_V^6 A_0^3 e^{-\phi\tau}/\phi^3 - 6\zeta\tau^2\sigma_V^6 X_0^3 e^{-\phi\tau}A_3/\phi^4 \\
&\quad -6\zeta\tau\sigma_V^6 A_0^3 e^{-\phi\tau}A_3/\phi^5 + 2A_0A_7 + 2\zeta A_{10}, \\
A_{10} &= -2\tau^2\sigma_V^6 A_0^3 e^{-\phi\tau}/\phi^3 - 4\tau\sigma_V^6 A_0^3 e^{-\phi\tau}/\phi^4 - \tau\sigma_V^2 A_0 B_1 e^{-\phi\tau}/\phi \\
&\quad -\tau^2\sigma_V^4 A_0^2 B_0 e^{-\phi\tau}/\phi^2 - \tau\sigma_V^4 A_0^2 B_0 e^{-\phi\tau}/\phi^3 \\
&\quad -\tau\sigma_V^2 A_0(2\sigma_V^4 A_0^2/\phi^3 + B_1)e^{-\phi\tau}/\phi \\
&\quad +(1-e^{-\phi\tau})(6\sigma_V^6 A_0^3/\phi^5 + B_2), \\
B_2 &= 3\tau^2\sigma_V^6 A_0^3 e^{-\phi\tau}/\phi^3 + 6\tau\sigma_V^6 A_0^3 e^{-\phi\tau}/\phi^4 - 3\sigma_V^6 A_0^3(1-e^{-\phi\tau})/\phi^5 \\
&\quad -(\phi-\nu)\tau^3\sigma_V^6 A_0^3 e^{-\phi\tau}/\phi^3 \\
&\quad -3(\phi-\nu)\tau^2\sigma_V^6 A_0^3 e^{-\phi\tau}/\phi^4 - 3(\phi-\nu)\tau\sigma_V^6 A_0^3 e^{-\phi\tau}/\phi^5.
\end{aligned}
$$

References

Bachelier, L. (1900). Thorie de la spculation, Gauthier-Villars.

Bakshi, G., and Madan, D. (2000). "Spanning and derivative-security valuation", *Journal of Financial Economics*, **55**, 205-238.

Black, F., and Scholes M. (1973). "The pricing of options and corporate liabilities", *Journal of Political Economy* **81(3)** 637-654.

Black, F., Derman, E., and Toy, W. (1990). "A one-factor model of interest rates and its application to treasury bond options", *Financial Analysts Journal* 33-39.

Brace, A.D., D. Gatarek, and Musiela, M. (1997). "The market model of interest rate dynamics", *Mathematical Finance,* **7**, 127-155.

Cox, J.C., Ingersoll, J. E., and Ross, S. A. (1985). "A theory of term structure of interest rate", *Econometrica,* **53** 385-407.

Derman, E. and Kani, I. (1994). "Riding on smile", *Risk* **7(2)** 32-39.

Fonseca, J. D., Grasselliac, M., and Tebaldi, C. (2008). "A Multifactor Volatility Heston Model", *Quantitative Finance,* **8(6)** 591-604.

Hagan, P. S., Kumar, D., Lesniewski, A. S., and Woodward, D. E. (2002). "Managing Smile Risk", September, *Wilmott,* 84-108.

Health, D., Jarrow, R., and Morton, A. (1992). "Bond pricing and the term structure of interest rates: A new methodology for contingent claims valuation", *Econometrica,* **60**, 77-105.

Heston, S. L. (1993). "A Closed-Form Solution for Options with Stochastic Volatility with Application to Bond and Currency Options", *The Review of Financial Studies*, **6(2)**, 327-343.

Ho, T. S., and Lee, S. (1986). "Term structure movements and pricing interest rate contingent claims", *Journal of Finance*, **41** 1011-1028.

Hull, J. C. and White, A. (1987). "The Pricing of Options on Asset with Stochastic Volatilities", Journal of Finance, **42**, 281-300.

Hull, J. C. and White, A. (1990). "Pricing interest-rate derivative securities", *Review of Financial Studies*, **3**, 573-592.

Kwok, Y. K. (2008). *Mathematical Models of Financial Derivatives"*, 2nd ed. (Springer-Verlag Press).

Longstaff, F. A., Schwartz, E. S. (1992). "Interest Rate and Term Structure: A Two-factor General Equilibrium Model", *Journal of Finance*, **47(4)** 1259-1282.

Ma, J. (2004). "A Stochastic Correlation Model with Mean Reversion for Pricing Maximum Options", Working paper, National University of Singapore.

Ma, J. (2009a). A Stochastic Correlation Model "with Mean Reversion for Pricing Multi-asset Options", *Asia Pacific Financial Markets* **16**, 97-109.

Ma, J. (2009b). "Pricing Foreign Equity with Stochastic Correlation and Volatility", *Annals of Economics and Finance*, **10** 303-327.

Ma, J. (2010) "Multi-factor Models for Pricing Correlation-dependent Interest-rate Contingent Claim", *International Review of Applied Financial Issues and Economics* , forthcoming issue.

Madan, D. B., Carr, P. P. and Chang, E. C. (1998). "The Variance Gamma Process and Option Pricing" *European Finance Review* , **2(1)**, 79-105.

Mougeot, N. (2000). "Credit Spread and Specification and the Pricing of Spread OPtions", Working Paper, University of Lausanne.

Nelsen, R. B. (1999). "An Introduction to Copula", Lectures Notes in Statistics 139, (Springer-Verlag press).

Samuelson, P. A. (1965). "Proof that Properly Anticipated Fluctuate Randomly", *Industrial Management Review*, **6** 41-49.

Stein, E. M., and Stein, J. C. (1991). "Stock Price Distribution with Stocahstic Volatility: an Analytic Approach", *Review of Financial Studies*, **4** 727-752.

Szego G. (1975) Jacobi Polynomials Ch.4 in *Orthogonal Polynomials*, 4th ed. (Providence, RI: American Mathematical Society).

Vasecik, O. A. (1977). "An Equilibrium Model of Bond Pricing and a Test of Market Efficiency", *Journal of Financial Economics*, **5** 177-188.

In: Financial Asset Pricing
Editors: P. E. Schulz and B. P. Hoffmann

ISBN 978-1-61122-803-8

Chapter 7

AN EMPIRICAL TEST OF THE CONSUMPTION-BASED ASSET PRICING MODEL (CCAPM) IN LATIN AMERICA

Guilherme Kirch[1]*, Paulo Renato Soares Terra[2] and Tiago Wickstrom Alves[3]

[1]FEEVALE University College, Institute of Applied Social Sciences
RS239 #2755, Novo Hamburgo RS 93352-000, Brazil
[2]UFRGS University, Universidade Federal do Rio Grande do Sul,
School of Management, Rua Washington Luís 855, Office 321,
Porto Alegre RS 90010-460, Brazil
[3]UNISINOS University, Universidade do Vale do Rio dos Sinos,
Graduate Program in Economics, Avenida Unisinos 950,
São Leopoldo RS 93022-000, Brazil

ABSTRACT

This study investigates whether the Consumption-based Capital Asset Pricing Model (CCAPM) is consistent with the data from four Latin-American countries: Brazil, Chile, Colombia, and Mexico. Empirical results showed that there is a statistically significant relationship between mean excess returns and consumption betas in the countries cited above, with the exception of Mexico. Such results are, in part, similar to the results reported in previous studies for the United States of America.

Keywords: Capital Markets; Assets Pricing Models; CCAPM; Latin America; Two-Stage Cross-Sectional Regressions.

* Tel: +55 51 99 59 37 55, guilherme.kirch@terra.com.br

1. INTRODUCTION

According to Mehra and Prescott (1985), historically, the average return on stock market shares in the United States has exceeded the average return on the short-term virtually default-free bond. Analyzing the period from 1889 to 1978, they found that the real average annual return of the Standard and Poor's 500 Index is 6.98%, while that of the United States Government risk-free debt bond is 0.8%, resulting in an equity premium of 6.18% per year.

In principle, according to asset pricing theory, an equity premium of this magnitude could only be explained by the risk inherent in the stock market, that is, the stocks, as they carry a higher risk than near-risk-free bonds, would need to compensate investors with higher average rates of return, which, in equilibrium, would be sufficient to balance the demand and the supply of these bonds. According to Abel (1991), this basic principle underpins the Capital Asset Pricing Model (CAPM), initially developed in the 1960s and enhanced since then.

However, as demonstrated by Mehra and Prescott (1985), the equity premium observed in the North American financial market, in the period from 1889 to 1978, can not be explained by an intertemporal equilibrium model, more specifically the Consumption-Based Capital Asset Pricing Model (CCAPM), which, according to Abel (1991), is perhaps one of the most important advances of the CAPM. This empirical inconsistency of the model proposed by the modern neoclassical theory of asset pricing has been denominated by Mehra and Prescott (1985) the equity premium puzzle.

According to Kocherlakota (1996), in order to better understand why the equity premium seen in the North American economy constitutes a puzzle, it is useful to review the bases of modern neoclassic theory of asset pricing. According to this theory, the differences between the average returns of the various financial securities are attributed to the level at which the return of these securities would covary with the consumption of the typical investor.

Kocherlakota (1996) asserts that, for the CAPM, the consumption flow of the typical investor is perfectly correlated with the return of the stock market and, thus, the risk of a given asset can be measured by the covariance of its returns with the return of the stock market. In the CCAPM, an intertemporal equilibrium model based on the 'representative agent', the consumption flow of the typical investor is perfectly correlated with the per capita consumption and, consequently, the risk of an asset can be measured by the covariance of its returns with the rate of growth of per capita consumption.

Based on these considerations, it is possible to clearly specify what Mehra and Prescott (1985) define as the equity premium puzzle: within a reasonable interval of risk aversion on the part of the representative agent, the covariance of the real average return of the stock market and of the real average rate of the risk-free asset with the real rate of growth of consumption are not sufficiently different to explain the average equity premium of 6.18% per annum seen in the North American data for the period 1889 to 1978. In other words, stocks do not display high enough risk in comparison to the short-term U.S. T-Bill to justify such the higher excess returns.

Prior to Mehra and Prescott (1985) identifying this empirical inconsistency, Grossman and Shiller (1981) and Hansen and Singleton (1983) had already empirically tested the representative agent model and, in both cases, the estimated parameters led to the rejection of the CCAPM for the data from the North American economy. Other empirical studies based on the North American economy have also demonstrated that the CCAPM is inconsistent, particularly the studies of Mankiw and Shapiro (1986) and Grossman, Melino and Shiller (1987). The only evidence found to be favorable to the CCAPM in the North American setting is presented by Breeden, Gibbons and Litzenberger (1989), which reported the existence of a statistically significant relationship between expected returns and the consumption beta, although the expected linear relationship between the variables had been rejected.

In the international economy, Campbell (1996) tested the CCAPM in several developing countries and his results revealed the existence of the equity premium puzzle in almost all the countries – of the twelve countries tested only one failed to present the phenomenon – showing that the puzzle is an internationally robust phenomenon.

In Latin America, especially in those countries included in the present study, the findings are mixed. In Brazil, the studies of Issler and Piqueira (2000), Sampaio (2002), Bonomo and Domingues (2002) among others, point to the inexistence of the puzzle, hence corroborating with the CCAPM. However, evidence recently presented by Cysne (2005) indicates that the equity premium puzzle is to be found in Brazil. Opazo (1998) and Bravo and Oyarzún (2001) tested the existence of the puzzle in the Chilean economy and confirmed the phenomenon there. In Colombia, Osorio and Puerta (2004) estimate the relative risk aversion coefficient close to zero, corroborating with the CCAPM.

The equity premium puzzle and all the studies that have demonstrated empirical inconsistencies when testing the CCAPM imply serious restrictions to the representative agent models. Therefore, testing the model in other countries, mainly among the emerging economies, becomes of great importance for the modern neoclassical theory of asset pricing, as favorable evidence for the model, in emerging countries, could shed new light on this theory and could provide the better understanding of the causes of its rejection in other countries; while the rejection of the model in these countries could lead academics to reformulate the theoretical bases supporting the model, incorporating new characteristics, in a way that the model becomes more compatible with the observed behavior of the individuals.

Given this situation, the aim of the present study is to empirically test whether the Consumption-Based Capital Assets Pricing Model (CCAPM) is consistent with the economic data from four Latin American countries: Brazil, Chile, Colombia and Mexico. More specifically, it intends to: 1) verify whether the theoretical implications associated with the CCAPM are confirmed by the empirical test proposed in this study; 2) demonstrate whether the CCAPM is capable of adequately explaining the differences between the returns on financial assets (stocks) in each country analyzed; and 3) compare the empirical results of the tests in this study of Latin American countries with previous studies in the literature.

According to Cochrane (2005, p.41), "the consumption-based model is, in principle, the complete answer to all asset pricing questions, but works poorly in practice", that is, despite being insightful from the theoretical point of view, in practice, there are difficulties with the CCAPM that are made evident by the large number of studies that reject the model at the international level. In spite of the empirical rejections, the author emphasizes that instead of inventing, testing and rejecting new models, studies such as those of Mehra and Prescott (1985) and Hansen and Jagannathan (1991), for example, have offered new insights into the characteristics of the model, thus, opening the door to improvements of the model that may allow it to adjust to economic data more easily.

The present study can further the understanding of the CCAPM by testing it in the emerging countries of Latin America, contributing towards the theoretical enhancement of the model and advancing the understanding of the factors that lead to its rejection at an international level.

Furthermore, it should be pointed out that, to the best knowledge of the authors, empirical tests of the nature intended in the present study have not yet been carried out in relation to the CCAPM in Latin American countries. To date, the studies performed in these countries have focused on the estimation of some parameters of the model, such as the risk aversion coefficient and the stochastic discount factor, but have not carried out cross-sectional regressions in order to verify the capacity of the CCAPM to explain the differences between the returns obtained from a certain class of financial assets, as the present study aims to do. Therefore, the findings obtained from the research can be considered original and it is hoped that they will contribute towards improving the understanding of the behavior of the model in these countries.

This study is structured as follows: in section 2, the CCAPM is presented; the research method is detailed in section 3, where the econometric model, the hypotheses, the data collection and treatment are all dealt with; in section 4, the results of the empirical test are shown for each country analyzed and finally, in the last section, the conclusions drawn in relation to the study are put forward.

2. The Intertemporal Model of Capital Asset Pricing CCAPM[1]

According to Varian (1992), the study of asset markets requires the general equilibrium approach, given that the value of a particular risky asset depends on the presence or absence of other risky assets that might serve as complements to, or substitute for that asset; and, as will be seen, the equilibrium price of a given asset, in an environment of uncertainty and intertemporal optimization of utility, will depend on its covariance with aggregated consumption.

For Duffie (2001), there are three pillars underpinning the theory of asset pricing: arbitrage, optimization and equilibrium. Arbitrage, according to this author, can be represented by a portfolio with a non-positive market value that offers a positive payment at some future date, that is, arbitrage is a portfolio that offers 'something for nothing'. In a competitive market, the opportunity for arbitrage should naturally be eliminated and, consequently, asset pricing should be based on the 'absence of arbitrage'. Optimization

[1] Intertemporal asset pricing models originated in the work of Merton (1973). He developed an equilibrium model consistent with the maximization of the expected utility, in an economy where individuals can trade continually in time and the investment opportunities are stochastic. According to Breeden (1979), in Merton's model the excess return of any asset is given by a 'multi-beta' version of the CAPM, the number of betas being defined by one plus the number of state variables necessary to describe the modifications in the set of investment opportunities. With the aim of making Merton's model more empirically treatable, Breeden (1979) demonstrated that the multiple betas could be concentrated in a single beta: the consumption beta. In this case, the expected return of any asset should be determined by its covariance with aggregate consumption, since the latter is perfect and negatively correlated to the marginal utility of an additional monetary unit of wealth. Grossman and Shiller (1982) show that the Breeden's results are obtained even after some assumptions are relaxed.

requires that individuals have well-behaved preferences and, thus, maximize their expected utility. Lastly, the condition of equilibrium determines that the prices of diverse assets should lead to an equilibrium allocation, that is, an allocation that satisfies the budgetary restrictions of individuals and that maximizes their utility given their endowments, so achieving a Pareto-efficient distribution.

In the paragraphs below, the intertemporal model of consumption-based capital asset pricing model is formally presented, beginning with the problem of intertemporal maximization of utility by the representative agent and the first order condition for the optimal consumption decision and portfolio formation.

Assuming that there is a representative agent in the economy, it is possible to model this typical investor, according to Cochrane (2005, p. 4), by the utility function defined on the current and future values of consumption:

$$U(c_t, c_{t+1}) = u(c_t) + \delta E_t[u(c_{t+1})], \tag{1}$$

where:

u is the utility function defined on the consumption in each period;

c_t denotes the consumption in the period t;

c_{t+1} denotes the consumption in the period $t+1$, a random variable, since the investor does not know her/his wealth in the following period and, therefore, does not know how much he will decide to consume in the period in question;

δ is the subjective discount factor and its theoretical limits are: $0 < \delta < 1$;

E_t is the expectations operator conditioned by the information available in the period t.

The utility function is restricted to the class of Constant Relative Risk Aversion (CRRA), a convenient and frequent form employed in real business cycle theory (MEHRA and PRESCOTT, 2003):

$$u(c_t) = \frac{c_t^{1-\gamma}}{1-\gamma}, \tag{2}$$

where:

γ is the Arrow-Pratt relative risk aversion coefficient.

This utility function (2), according to Cochrane (2005), is increasing, reflecting the desire for greater consumption in each period, and concave, denoting the decreasing marginal utility, that is, each additional monetary unit of consumption produces less satisfaction than the previous monetary unit of consumption.

By means of this modeling, given by (1) and (2), the impatience as well as the aversion to risk of the typical investor is captured. The subjective discount factor, δ, is the value by which the future utility is discounted and represents the impatience of the investor. The lower its value, the greater the impatience, that is, the greater is the preference for present consumption in relation to future consumption. The relative risk aversion coefficient, γ, measures the concavity of the utility function and the greater its value, the greater the aversion to risk on the part of the investor. Moreover, the form of the utility function (2) restricts the elasticity of the intertemporal substitution from being the inverse of the relative risk aversion coefficient, hence, the greater the aversion to risk the lesser the desire for intertemporal substitution of consumption. Therefore, the risk averse investor prefers a flow of consumption that is stable throughout states of nature and over time (Mehra and Prescott, 2003; Cochrane, 2005).

Denoting the price of an asset by p_t and its expected future payoff by x_{t+1}, it is possible, using the above defined framework, to determine the present value (p_t) of the future cash flow (x_{t+1}), that is, how much the investor will be willing to pay today for an asset that provides an expected future payoff of the order of x_{t+1}. In the case of a share of stock, the expected future payoff is the price of the stock plus the dividend to be received in the following period, that is, $x_{t+1} = p_{t+1} + d_{t+1}$. According to Cochrane (2005), x_{t+1} is a random variable, given that the investor does not know exactly what she/he will receive in the future for the investment made in the present, but she/he can assess the probability of several possible outcomes and determine the expected value of the investment.

Assuming that the investor can freely buy or sell any quantity of the future expected payoff x_{t+1} at the price p_t, denoting the original level of consumption (prior to making any investment) by e and denoting by ω the amount of a given stock that the investor wishes to buy, her/his intertemporal choice problem is given by (COCHRANE, 2005, p. 5):

$$\max_{\omega} u(c_t) + E_t\left[\delta u(c_{t+1})\right], \text{ subject to:}$$

$$c_t = e_t - p_t\omega,$$

$$c_{t+1} = e_{t+1} + x_{t+1}\omega$$

The first-order condition for the optimal consumption decision and portfolio formation is obtained by substituting the restrictions above in the objective function and setting the derivative with respect to ω to zero (COCHRANE, 2005, p. 5):

$$p_t u'(c_t) = E_t\left[\delta u'(c_{t+1})x_{t+1}\right], \tag{3}$$

This equation, according to Mehra and Prescott (2003), expresses the condition for intertemporal optimization of consumption: the loss in the present utility ($p_t u'(c_t)$), due to the reduction in consumption in favor of the purchase of an additional unit of a determined asset at the price p_t, should be equal to the expected gain in the discounted future utility ($E_t\left[\delta u'(c_{t+1})x_{t+1}\right]$), resulting from the expected increase in the future consumption due to the sale of the asset for p_{t+1} and the receipt of dividends at the value d_{t+1} (in the case that the asset is a stock). According to Cochrane (2005), the investor will buy more or less of a determined asset until the equation (3) is satisfied, that is, until the loss in the present utility equals the expected gains in the future utility.

Rearranging (3) the central asset pricing formula is obtained (COCHRANE, 2005, p. 6):

$$p_t = E_t\left[\delta \frac{u'(c_{t+1})}{u'(c_t)} x_{t+1}\right] \tag{4}$$

According to Cochrane (2005), the expression $\delta \frac{u'(c_{t+1})}{u'(c_t)}$ is known as the stochastic discount factor, that is, the random value by which the expected future payoff of each asset is discounted in order to determine its present value (p_t). This factor is also denominated the marginal rate of substitution, that is, the rate at which the investor would be willing to substitute future consumption for present consumption.

Asset pricing theory requires that the expected future payoff of an asset be discounted by a factor adjusted to the specific systematic risk. Although the stochastic discount factor is unique for all assets, equation (4) incorporates a correction for the specific systematic risk of each stock, as demonstrated below.

By denoting the stochastic discount factor as m_{t+1}, the basic asset pricing equation (4) can be expressed in the following form:

$$p_t = E_t(m_{t+1}x_{t+1}) \tag{5}$$

When both sides of (5) are divided by p_t the basic pricing equation in terms of expected returns is obtained instead of that of expected future payoffs:

$$1 = E_t(m_{t+1}R_{t+1}), \tag{6}$$

where:

$R_{t+1} = \frac{x_{t+1}}{p_t}$ is the gross expected return.

According to Cochrane (2005), the gross return can be thought as a payoff with a price equal to 1 (one), as demonstrated by equation (6).

Given that the expectation of the product of two variables is equal to the product of its expectations plus the covariance between them, it is possible to rewrite (5) as:

$$p_t = E_t(m_{t+1})E_t(x_{t+1}) + Cov(m_{t+1}, x_{t+1}), \tag{7}$$

In general, this equation (7), shows that the price of any asset is a function of three factors:

1) The stochastic discount factor: the greater this value the greater the desire of the investor to transfer present consumption to the future, as in this case the discounted marginal utility of the future consumption is high in relation to the marginal utility of the present consumption, and, consequently, the greater the price of any asset that permits the transference of income intertemporally;
2) Expected future payoff: maintaining the discount rate constant, the greater the future payoff of an asset the greater its present value will be; and,
3) Covariance between the stochastic discount factor and the expected future payoff: assets whose payoffs covary positively with the stochastic discount factor tend to pay more when the marginal utility of consumption is high and less when the marginal utility of consumption is low. Therefore, assets so characterized should be sold at the highest price, as they smooth the investor's flow of consumption.

From equation (6), it can be seen that the gross return of a risk-free asset is equal to the inverse of the stochastic discount factor:

$$R_{f,t+1} = \frac{1}{E_t(m_{t+1})}, \tag{8}$$

where:

$R_{f,t+1}$ is the gross return of the risk-free asset in the next period, definitely known in the period t and, therefore, expectations-free, as shown below:

$$1 = E_t(m_{t+1}R_{f,t+1}) = E_t(m_{t+1})R_{f,t+1}$$

Substituting the stochastic discount factor in (7) by (8) leaves:

$$p_t = \frac{E_t(x_{t+1})}{R_{f,t+1}} + Cov(m_{t+1}, x_{t+1}) \tag{9}$$

According to Cochrane (2005, p. 13), the first term on the right side of (9) is the standard formula of the discounted present value and represents the price of an asset when the investors are risk neutral. The second term is an adjustment for the specific systematic risk of the asset in question, given by the covariance of its payoffs with the stochastic discount factor.

In order to better understand this risk adjustment, substitute m_{t+1} in (9) by $\delta\frac{u'(c_{t+1})}{u'(c_t)}$ to obtain:

$$p_t = \frac{E_t(x_{t+1})}{R_{f,t+1}} + \frac{\mathrm{cov}[\delta u'(c_{t+1}), x_{t+1}]}{u'(c_t)} \tag{10}$$

Assets whose payoffs covary negatively with consumption (positively with marginal utility) smooth the investor's consumption flow, while those assets whose payoffs covary positively with consumption (negatively with marginal utility) make the investor's consumption flow more volatile. As previously defined, risk averse investors prefer a stable consumption flow over time and throughout the states of nature, therefore such investors attribute greater value to those assets that offer stability in the consumption flow, as shown in equation (10). Assets whose payoffs covary positively with consumption (negatively with marginal utility) are considered risky assets, as they increase the consumption volatility, and, consequently, *ceteris-paribus*, in equilibrium would have to be traded at lower prices.

In the vast majority of studies about asset pricing models, returns are used instead of prices in order to test the implications of such models, since returns are typically stationary over time, which is a characteristic required in studies based on time series (Gujarati, 2003). Accordingly, it is considered opportune to derive the pricing formulas in terms of expected gross returns.

Based on equation (6) and applying the definition of the expectation of the product of two variables, the following is obtained:

$$1 = E_t(m_{t+1})E_t(R_{t+1}) + Cov(m_{t+1}, R_{t+1}) \tag{11}$$

Following Cochrane (2005), knowing that the gross return of the risk-free asset is given in (8), it is possible to rewrite (11) as:

$$E_t(R_{t+1}) - R_{f,t+1} = -R_{f,t+1}Cov(m_{t+1}, R_{t+1}), \tag{12}$$

or

$$E_t(R_{t+1}) - R_{f,t+1} = -\frac{Cov[u'(c_{t+1}), R_{t+1}]}{E_t[u'(c_{t+1})]} \tag{13}$$

Equations (12) and (13) show that the risk premium of any asset is a function of the covariance of its returns with the stochastic discount factor (marginal utility). Assets whose returns covary positively with the stochastic discount factor (marginal utility) will have a negative risk premium, while assets whose returns covary negatively with the stochastic discount factor (marginal utility) will have a positive risk premium.

According to Cochrane (2005), it is convenient to express equation (12), for the purposes of the empirical tests, in the following form:

$$E_t(R_{i,t+1}) = R_{f,t+1} + \left(\frac{Cov(m_{t+1}, R_{i,t+1})}{Var(m_{t+1})}\right)\left(-\frac{Var(m_{t+1})}{E_t(m_{t+1})}\right) \tag{14}$$

or

$$E_t\left(R_{i,t+1}\right) = R_{f,t+1} + \beta_{i,m}\lambda_m, \tag{15}$$

where:

$E_t\left(R_{i,t+1}\right)$ is the expected return of the asset i, $i = 1, ..., N$;

$\beta_{i,m}$ is the slope coefficient of the regression of returns of the asset i on the stochastic discount factor and, hence, is a measure of the sensibility of the returns of the asset i to changes to the stochastic discount factor;

λ_m is the premium for exposure to the risk factor or simply the risk premium.

Equations (14) and (15) show that there is a linear relationship between the expected return and the slope coefficient (beta) of the assets. The risk premium, λ_m, is strictly negative, is unique for all assets and its value depends on the volatility of the stochastic discount factor. The slope coefficient (beta), a measure of the systematic risk, varies throughout the assets in accordance with the exposure of each to the risk factor. In general, the betas will be negative, since most assets are characterized by returns that covary negatively with the stochastic discount factor (marginal utility – COCHRANE, 2005; JAGANNATHAN and WANG, 2005).

According to Cochrane (2005), given that $u'(c) = c^{-\gamma}$ and, hence, $m_{t+1} = \delta\left(c_{t+1}/c_t\right)^{-\gamma}$, it is possible to perform a Taylor approximation of equation (14) in order to express the betas in terms of the growth rate of consumption instead of the stochastic discount factor. Jagannathan and Wang (2005) show that this approximation reduces the effects of the measurement errors in the aggregate consumption and, therefore, there are advantages in their use in empirical tests. The result of this approximation is illustrated below:

$$E_t\left(R_{i,t+1}\right) = R_{f,t+1} + \beta_{i,\Delta c}\lambda_{\Delta c}, \tag{16}$$

where:

$\beta_{i,\Delta c}$ is the slope coefficient of the regression of returns on asset i on the consumption growth rate, which is commonly referred to as the 'consumption beta';

$\lambda_{\Delta c} = \gamma\,\mathrm{var}(\Delta c)$ is the premium for exposure to the risk factor 'consumption growth rate'.

Equation (16) implies a linear relationship between the expected return and the consumption beta of an asset and is known as the Consumption-Based Capital Asset Pricing Model (CCAPM). The consumption beta is an individual measure of exposure to the risk factor 'consumption growth rate' and, for the vast majority of assets, its value is strictly positive. The premium for exposure to risk is strictly positive and, according to Cochrane (2005), it is determined by (absolute) aversion to risk and by the volatility of consumption, that is, the more averse individuals are to risk, or the greater the environmental risk, the greater the risk premium demanded.

Lastly, it is important to point out that the CCAPM, according to Jagannathan and Wang (2005, p. 4), "has the advantage that its validity can be evaluated using sample analogues of means, variances and covariances of returns and per capita consumption growth rates without the need for specifying how these moments change over time in some systematic stochastic fashion". It should also be highlighted that, according to Cochrane (2005, p. 41), the use of the pricing equation (16) "do not require us to take any stand on exogeneity or endogeneity, or general equilibrium. This is the condition that must hold for any asset, for any production technology".

3. METHOD, HYPOTHESES, SAMPLING, DATA COLLECTION AND TREATMENT

3.1. Estimation Process

According to the CCAPM, given by equation (16), there is a positive relationship between the expected return and the consumption beta of the assets. In the present study, we test this relationship by using cross-sectional regression of the risk premiums on the consumption betas of a given set of assets (shares traded on the stock exchange). In the following paragraphs more details are given regarding to the process of estimating the parameters of the model.

The theoretical model given by equation (16) is based on expected returns (*ex-ante*), nevertheless, such values are not observable and, thus, make estimation of the model unfeasible. To get round this problem, Huang and Litzenberger (1988, p. 304) suggest adopting the assumption of *rational expectations*,[2] as "under rational expectations, the realized rates of return on assets in the given time period are drawings from the *ex ante* probability distributions of returns on those assets". Therefore, based on this assumption, the use of realized returns (*ex-post*) in the estimation of the empirical model can be justified.

Besides using realized returns, it is convenient to set model (16) in terms of risk premium of the assets over the risk-free asset, which gives the following cross-sectional regression model:

$$R_i^e = \lambda_0 + \lambda_1 \beta_{i,\Delta c} + u_i,\ i = 1, ..., \text{N}, \tag{17}$$

where:

$R_i^e = R_{i,t} - R_{f,t}$ is the risk premium of asset *i*, $i = 1, ..., \text{N}$;

$\beta_{i,\Delta c}$ is the consumption beta of asset *i*, $i = 1, ..., \text{N}$;

λ_0 and λ_1 are parameters to be freely estimated by the regression model (17). The theoretical expectation is that the parameter λ_0, the regression constant, equals zero, as the risk premium of an asset whose covariance with the growth rate of per capita consumption is

[2] For more details on the assumption of rational expectations, see Muth (1961), Lucas (1978, p. 1431), and Huang and Litzenberger (1988, p. 304), among others.

null, theoretically, should be equal to zero. With regard the parameter λ_1, the slope coefficient, the expectation is that it will be positive and statistically significant, given that it should represent the premium for exposure to the risk factor 'consumption growth rate'.

u_i is the stochastic error term of the asset i, $i = 1, ..., N$, and it is expected to present the usual properties of white noise.[3]

In the econometric model (17) the explanatory variable is the consumption beta of asset i, a variable that can not be directly observed, but can be estimated from time series regressions. This way, the two-stage cross-sectional regression method proposed by Black, Jensen and Scholes (1972) and Fama and MacBeth (1973) is employed. In short, this method consists in estimating, in the first stage, the consumption beta for each asset by means of time series regressions and, in the second stage, performing cross-sectional regression of the econometric model (17) using the consumption betas obtained in the previous stage as the explanatory variable.

The choice of this method of regression is made, primarily, because of its extensive use in tests of capital asset pricing models, such as the CAPM and the CCAPM.[4] According to Jagannathan and Wang (1998, p. 1285), although there are more sophisticated methods for testing linear beta-pricing models, the method proposed by Black, Jensen and Scholes (1972) and Fama and MacBeth (1973) has been preferred in many empirical studies. Furthermore, according to the same authors, this method allows a clear interpretation of the results in economic terms, while with more sophisticated methods there is greater difficulty in interpreting the results obtained.

Another relevant aspect in the choice of this method, according to Lettau and Ludvigson (2001, p.1254), concerns the advantages in applying the cross-sectional regression method from Fama and MacBeth (1973) in samples characterized by a small number of time series observations and by a reasonable number of cross-sectional observations, as is the case with the sample studied in the present study. According to these authors, in samples where the number of time series observations is small relative to the number of cross-sectional observations, the use of the Generalized Method of Moments (GMM) with estimation of the weighted matrix is not appropriate, since, in small samples, this form of estimation will result in a poor estimation of that matrix.

This argument can naturally be extended to the maximum likelihood estimation (MLE), since, according to Gujarati (2003, p. 91), the maximum likelihood estimator of the variance of the error terms (σ^2) can only be considered unbiased in the case that the sample size (n) increase indefinitely, that is, the maximum likelihood estimator of σ^2 is asymptotically unbiased. Corroborating with this limitation, Maddala (2001, p. 64) asserts that "the MLE method is an estimation method for large samples". Therefore, considering the limited size of our sample, it is understood that the MLE method is not the most appropriate method for the empirical tests to be carried out in the present study.

---

[3] For more details on such properties, see Gujarati (2003) and Maddala (2001).

[4] Of particular interest among the empirical studies that adopt the two-stage cross-sectional regression method for testing CCAPM are: Mankiw and Shapiro (1986), Elyasiani and Nasseh (2000), Lettau and Ludvigson (2001) and Jagannathan and Wang (2005). With regard the tests of the CAPM model, the following empirical studies can be highlighted: Black, Jensen and Scholes (1972), Fama and MacBeth (1973), Blume and Friend (1973), Mankiw and Shapiro (1986), Fama and French (1992), Jagannathan and Wang (1996), Elyasiani and Nasseh (2000), Lettau and Ludvigson (2001) and Jagannathan and Wang (2005).

Given these considerations, the estimation of the parameters in (17) by the two-stage cross-sectional regression method is convenient and suitable, and, therefore, will be the method adopted in the empirical tests in the present study.

3.1.1. Details of the Two-stage Cross-sectional Regression Method

As previously mentioned, the first stage consists in estimating the consumption beta of each asset *i* by means of a time series regression for each asset in the sample. According to the CCAPM, estimation of this parameter can be performed by employing the following econometric model, which relates the risk premium of a given asset with the growth rate of per capita consumption:

$$R^e_{i,t} = \alpha_i + \beta_{i,\Delta c}\Delta c_t + \varepsilon_{i,t}\text{ , } t = 1, \ldots, \text{T for each } i,\ i = 1, \ldots, \text{N}, \tag{18}$$

where:

$R^e_{i,t}$ is the risk premium of the asset *i* in the period *t*.

Δc_t is the growth rate of per capita consumption in the period *t*.

α_i is the intercept of the asset *i* to be estimated by the regression model (18). According to Cochrane (2005), these intercepts are equal to the pricing errors of the model and the theoretical expectation is that they be equal to zero.

$\beta_{i,\Delta c}$ is the slope coefficient to be estimated by the time series regression of $R^e_{i,t}$ on Δc_t and corresponds to the consumption beta of the asset *i*. This estimated parameter will be the explanatory variable in the cross-sectional regressions in the second stage of the method.

$\varepsilon_{i,t}$ is the stochastic error term of the asset *i* in the period *t*.

To conclude the first stage, the average risk premiums of each asset *i* are computed throughout the sample and these will be the dependent variables in the cross-sectional regressions in the second stage. Therefore, at the end of the first stage, an N x 1 vector of the average risk premiums, whose typical element is $\bar{R}^e_i$, and an N x 1 vector of the consumption betas, whose typical element is $\hat{B}_{i,\Delta c}$, are obtained.

The second stage of the method consists in estimating the λ_0 and λ_1 parameters of the econometric model (17). As this model is not expressed in terms of estimated average risk premiums and consumption betas, it is modified in order to meet the necessities of the study, as follows:

$$\bar{R}^e_i = \lambda_0 + \lambda_1 \hat{\beta}_{i,\Delta c} + u_i\text{ , } i = 1, \ldots, \text{N}, \tag{19}$$

where:

$\bar{R}^e_i$ is the average risk premium of the asset *i*, *i* = 1, ..., N, obtained in the first stage.

$\hat{\beta}_{i,\Delta c}$ is the consumption beta of the asset i, $i = 1, ..., N$, estimated in the first stage.

Also, it is intended to extend the econometric model (19) in order to test another implication suggested by the CCAPM. According to this pricing model, the consumption beta is the only measure of the systematic risk of an asset and, therefore, no other variable could explain the risk premium of the assets. In order to test this implication, in the same way that Lintner (1965) and Levy (1978), it is verified whether the residual variances present a statistically significant risk premium in the cross-sectional regression. This variable is formed by the variances of the residuals of the time series regressions for estimation of the consumption betas of each asset. Therefore, when the intention is to test this latter implication, the econometric model (19) is extended as shown below:

$$\bar{R}_i^e = \lambda_0 + \lambda_1 \hat{\beta}_{i,\Delta c} + \lambda_2 VR_i + u_i \text{ , } i = 1, ..., N, \tag{20}$$

where:

VR_i is the variance of the residuals of the time series regression for estimation of the consumption beta of the asset i.

3.1.2. Limitations of the Two-Stage Cross-sectional Regression Method

As previously stated, the 'true' consumption betas are not directly measurable and, hence, are estimated by time series regressions. Nevertheless, the use of estimated betas instead of the 'true' consumption betas represents a measurement error in the explanatory variable, a problem known as the *errors-in-variables problem* or *EIV problem.*

According to Gujarati (2003), measurement errors in the explanatory variable cause the violation of a crucial hypothesis of the classical linear regression model: the hypothesis that there is no correlation between the explanatory variable and the stochastic error term. If this hypothesis is violated the estimators by ordinary least squares (OLS) will be biased and inconsistent, even asymptotically.

According to Gujarati (2003) and Maddala (2001), when there are measurement errors in the explanatory variable the estimation of the parameters of the model behave in the following manner: I) the slope coefficient will not converge to its true value and, admitting that its true value is positive, will be underestimated, that is, biased towards zero; and, II) the intercept, given the underestimation of the slope coefficient, will be overestimated, that is, will be biased away from zero. Therefore, in the case that the problem of the errors in variables is not corrected the consequences for the estimation of the linear model derived from the CCAPM will be the following:

- underestimation of the risk premium, which could lead to the rejection of the relationship implied by the model; and,
- overestimation of the intercept, which could lead to the conclusion that this parameter is greater than zero when in fact it is not.

One of the most frequently used approaches for correcting the problem of errors in variables, when testing capital asset pricing models, is the formation of portfolios (HUANG and LITZENBERGER, 1988).[5] According to these authors, if the measurement errors are not correlated with the criterion used to group the assets, the variance of the measurement errors associated to the portfolio betas approximates zero, the closer the number of assets in each portfolio tends towards infinite, eliminating the bias in the estimations of the parameters.

Besides the possibility of eliminating the problem of errors in variables, Cochrane (2005, p. 436) suggests some other motives from the formation of portfolios:

- Individual stock betas vary over time as the size, leverage, and risk of the business change. Portfolio betas may be more stable over time, and hence easier to measure accurately.
- Individual stock returns are so volatile that you cannot reject the hypothesis that all average returns are the same… By grouping stocks into portfolios based on some characteristic (other than firm name) related to average returns, you reduce the portfolio variance and thus make it possible to see average return deferences (sic).

Therefore, the formation of portfolios allows part of the excessive volatility that characterizes individual returns to be eliminated and gives plausibility to the assumption that the betas are stationary (when such assumption is made).

Despite these positive aspects, the formation of portfolios has not been recommended in the specialized literature on econometrics (COCHRANE, 2005). Thus, in the following paragraphs some of the negative aspects related to this procedure will be discussed and assessed in order to arrive at a decision regarding its adoption or otherwise.

According to Roll (1977, p. 131), in his critique of asset pricing theory tests, the formation of portfolios can lend support to the theory even when it is false. This would occur because individual assets deviations from exact linearity can cancel out in the formation of portfolios. That is, as the number of assets in each portfolio tends to infinity, the individual assets deviations from exact linearity tend to be cancelled out. It leads the expected deviation of the portfolio to be equal to zero, and, as a consequence, to support the model even though it may be false. This criticism naturally extends to the CCAPM, since it establishes a linear relationship between the returns of the assets and their respective consumption betas.

For Kim (1995, p. 1609), the construction of a finite set of well-diversified portfolios is difficult in practice and, accordingly, the grouping of assets within portfolios does not fulfill its initial purpose of eliminate, asymptotically, the bias in the estimations of the parameters.

Kim (1997, p. 464) points to three advantages arising from the use of individual assets instead of portfolios in the cross-sectional regressions: I) it ensures the full use of the information about the cross-sectional behavior of the individual stocks, which can be lost with the formation of portfolios; II) it avoids bias arising from *data-snooping*;[6] and, III) it avoids

---

[5] For instance, such procedure has been adopted in the following empirical tests of the CCAPM and/or CAPM: Black, Jensen and Scholes (1972), Fama and MacBeth (1973), Blume and Friend (1973), Fama and French (1992), Jagannathan and Wang (1996), Elyasiani and Nasseh (2000), Lettau and Ludvigson (2001), Jagannathan and Wang (2005), among others.

[6] According to Lo and MacKinlay (1990), the data-snooping bias, regarding portfolio formation in tests of asset pricing models, derives from the clustering of assets in portfolios according to a criteria that is not theoretically related to the return of the assets but that presents an empirical relation derived from the same data set used to implement the tests. These authors show that such bias may lead to the rejection of the model with unit probability even when it is true.

arbitrary formation of portfolios, as the allocation criteria and/or the number of portfolios can influence the estimations of the parameters.[7]

Given these arguments concerning the formation of portfolios, it becomes apparent that there are some disadvantages[8] that should be weighed against the possible benefits arising from the use of this procedure. Only then can the decision be made on whether to use the procedure or otherwise. It is important to note that the benefits of the formation of portfolios depend, to a great extent, on the characteristics of the sample used in the study and, therefore, in the following paragraphs, it will be discussed whether or not such benefits can be obtained with the sample that we used.

The sample used in the present study is characterized by a relatively small number of assets, in each analyzed country, when compared with samples used in other countries, such as the United States of America, for example. There are on average around 80 assets in each of the four countries included in the study, varying from 27 assets in the case of Colombia to 141 assets in the case of Brazil, while in empirical tests of CAPM and/or CCAPM carried out in the United States this number frequently exceeds 2,000 assets.

As previously stated, the bias arising from the problem of errors in variables can only be eliminated by the formation of portfolios if the number of assets in each portfolio tends towards infinity, this presupposes a sample, in terms of number of assets, large enough to form a reasonable number of well-diversified portfolios. The sample obtained in the present study does not appear to fulfill this presupposition and, thus, may make the formation of portfolios unfeasible in terms of the number and size desired.

According to Kim (1995), there is a trade-off between bias and efficiency of the estimates that depends on the number of portfolios. As the number of portfolios increases and, consequently, the number of assets in each portfolio diminishes, the magnitude of the bias resulting from the errors in variables increases while the variance in the estimations decreases (enhancing their efficiency), and vice-versa. Given the aforementioned characteristics of the sample in the present study, it is understood that the number of assets available is not sufficiently large to produce unbiased estimates together with efficient parameters.

With regard the difficulties on the formation of well-diversified portfolios, pointed out by Kim (1995) in a reality where the number of assets is relatively large, it is believed that this difficulties are even greater in countries characterized by a relatively small number of assets, as is the case of the Latin American countries. This being the case, it is believed that the benefits arising from the grouping of assets into portfolios can not be obtained from the sample used in the present study.

A possible method of enlarging the number and size of the portfolios to the desired levels would be the random formation of portfolios, based on a resampling method such as *bootstrapping*. According to this method, from the sample, n portfolios, composed of m *assets*, would be randomly withdrawn, so that each asset could be part of several portfolios. However, according to Huang and Litzenberger (1988), the random formation of portfolios can maximize the variance of the estimates and, as a consequence of this, lead to inefficient estimation of the parameters.

---

[7] For evidence on the sensibility of parameter estimates to the portfolio formation criteria see, for instance, Kothari, Shanken and Sloan (1995) and Lo (2004), among others.

[8] Other implications of the portfolio formation procedure, not directly related to the research method used, can be found in Berk (2000) and Grauer and Janmmat (2004).

It can, therefore, be concluded that in the present study the formation of portfolios will not achieve its main purpose: the elimination of the bias resulting from the problem of errors in variables. Given this situation and the fact that the procedure is subject to arbitrariness, biases, and other limitations, it is decided that an alternative approach is needed to correct the problem. In the following paragraphs, the approach adopted in the present study, together with its limitations will be discussed.

According to Huang and Litzenberger (1988), the problem of errors in variables can be corrected through estimators that incorporate the impact of the measurement errors in the explanatory variable. According to Campbell, Lo and MacKinlay (1997), this approach to the problem of errors in variables is first developed by Litzenberger and Ramaswamy (1979) and refined by Shanken (1992).

Shanken (1992) notices that even though the measurement errors decline in the proportion that the time series size increases and, thus, lead to T-consistent estimators of the second-stage parameters, the effects on the inference can not be ignored, not even in large samples. In order to solve this problem, the aforementioned author derives the corrected asymptotic variances.

Cochrane (2005, p. 240) suggests that Shanken's (1992) corrected asymptotic variances can be derived by assuming that the stochastic errors (ε_{it}) of the time series regressions, used in the estimation of the consumption betas, are independent and identically distributed (i.i.d.) over time and independent of the factors. Based on these suppositions, the following corrected formula for the calculation of the variance–covariance matrix of the parameters of the *cross-sectional* regression is obtained:

$$\sigma^2\left(\hat{\lambda}\right) = \frac{1}{T}\left[(X'X)^{-1}X'\Sigma X(X'X)^{-1}\left(1+\Gamma'\Sigma_f^{-1}\Gamma\right)+\begin{bmatrix}0 & 0\\ 0 & \Sigma_f\end{bmatrix}\right], \tag{21}$$

where:

$\sigma^2\left(\hat{\lambda}\right)$ is the 2 x 2 variance–covariance matrix of the estimated coefficients in the *cross-sectional* regression;

T is the size of time series used for the estimation of the consumption betas, that is, number of years, quarters or months in the sample;

X is a matrix N x 2 of data, N being the number of assets used in the *cross-sectional* regression. The first column of this matrix is formed by 1s (a vector N x 1 of ones), representing the intercept term, and the second column contains the consumption betas of the assets;

Σ is the N x N matrix of variance-covariance of the residues from the time series regressions used for the estimation of the consumption betas;

Γ is a vector of the estimated slope coefficients in the *cross-sectional* regression; and

Σ_f is the population variance of the growth rate of per capita consumption.

Note that this formula requires that the model presents the intercept term and that this is only applicable to the variances of the intercept and of the slope coefficient of the consumption beta variable. In this way, the correction given by (21) is only applied to the *cross-sectional* regressions of the average risk premiums on the consumption betas (19). Regarding the regression of the average risk premiums on the consumption betas and the residual variances (20) traditional statistical inferences are used, emphasizing that in this case, when the two explanatory variables are measured with error, both are biased[9] and, therefore, caution should be adopted when interpreting the results.

It should also be pointed out that the correction proposed in the present study has some limitations, which are: it makes suppositions concerning the distribution of the residues that may not be confirmed by the data; and it is an asymptotic correction, that is, it is only valid in large samples. The latter limitation is of particular concern and demands that caution should be used in interpreting the results. Nonetheless, there is a need for a correction from the econometric perspective and, it should be applied with the aim of obtaining tests of hypotheses more reliable.

Another possible econometric problem related to the method adopted in the present study, according to Shanken (1992), arises from the fact that the cross-sectional regressions employ average risk premiums and betas estimated throughout the entire period of the sample. According to the author, this could have an undesired spurious cross-sectional relation as a result of the statistical dependence between such risk premiums and betas, since both are estimated with data from the same period.

According to Shanken (1992, p.9), under assumptions typically made in the literature, average returns (or risk premiums) and betas estimated throughout the entire period of the sample are not correlated and, assuming joint normality of the asset returns and factors, such variables are statistically independent. So, the spurious cross-sectional relation is avoided. The assumptions necessary in order to obtain such results are formally described in Shanken (1992, p.7) and, put briefly, consist in:

- The stochastic error terms of the time series regressions should be independently and identically distributed (i.i.d.) over time;
- The factors should be generated by a stationary process such that the first and second sample moments converge in probability, as $T \rightarrow \infty$, to the true moments;
- The factors are asymptotically normally distributed.

Additionally, it is important to note that, according to Shanken (1992), the estimation of a single beta for each asset throughout the entire time period of the sample can reduce the measurement errors of the consumption betas, since the errors decline in proportion to the increase in the extension of the estimation period. However, it should be pointed out that this approach assumes that the consumption betas are stationary, thus ignoring the findings of Cornell (1981) regarding their non-stationarity. It should also be noted that this approach, besides being used in the present study has also been adopted in the studies of Mankiw and Shapiro (1986) and Lettau and Ludvigson (2001).

---

[9] See Maddala (2001).

3.2. Formulation of Hypotheses

In order to ascertain the adherence of the CCAPM to the data from four Latin American countries (Brazil, Chile, Colombia and Mexico), it is examined whether the theoretical implications derived from the model can be confirmed by the empirical test proposed in this study. In this section, the theoretical implications of the model are defined, and those implications give rise to the research hypotheses.

According to the CCAPM, the differences between assets returns are determined by the differences between their consumption betas, the latter being a measure of exposure of the returns from an asset to the risk factor 'growth rate of per capita consumption'. The greater the consumption beta of an asset, the greater its risk and, consequently, the greater its expected return should be. Therefore, the CCAPM implies a positive linear relation between the average returns (or average risk premiums) and the consumption betas. This implication is central to the CCAPM and gives rise to the primary hypothesis:

Primary Null Hypothesis (H_0)*:* There is not a positive and statistically significant relation between the average risk premiums and the consumption betas of the assets, that is:

$$H_0 : \lambda_1 = 0,$$

where:

λ_1 is the slope coefficient of the cross-sectional regression of the average risk premiums on the consumption betas.

Primary Alternative Hypothesis (H_1): There is a positive and statistically significant relation between the average risk premiums and the consumption betas of the assets, that is:

$$H_1 : \lambda_1 > 0$$

In the CCAPM, the consumption beta appears as the only measure of systematic risk of the asset, that is, nothing apart from exposure to the risk factor 'growth rate of per capita consumption' should systematically affect the expected returns of the assets. Thus, the consumption beta is a complete measure of the risk of any asset. This implication results in the following secondary hypothesis to be tested:

Secondary Null Hypothesis (H_0')*:* the consumption beta of an asset is a complete measure of its systematic risk. Thus, it is that:

$$H_0' : \lambda_2 = 0,$$

where:

λ_2 is the slope coefficient of the residual variances variable in the cross-sectional regression determined by the econometric model (20).

Secondary Alternative Hypothesis (H_1')*:* the consumption beta of an asset is not a complete measure of its systematic risk, that is:

$$H_1': \lambda_2 > 0.$$

Lastly, a specification test of the econometric model (19) is carried out. According to the CCAPM, if all individuals are able to invest or borrow at the risk-free interest rate, the intercept of the regression of the average risk premiums on the consumption betas should be equal to zero (Sharpe-Lintner's hypothesis). However, if this interest rate does not exist, it can be assumed that an asset exists in the economy whose covariance with the growth rate of per capita consumption is equal to zero (zero-beta) and, hence, the intercept need not necessarily be equal to zero (Black's hypothesis). It is important to note that the rejection of the Sharpe-Lintner's hypothesis favors the specification given by Black (1972), while the acceptance of that hypothesis does not imply the rejection of the latter. Thus, the third pair of hypotheses to be tested is:

Third Null Hypothesis (H_0''): There is a risk-free interest rate in the economy at which all individuals are able to invest and borrow, that is:

$$H_0'': \lambda_0 = 0,$$

where:

λ_0 is the intercept of the cross-sectional regression of the average risk premiums on the consumption betas – econometric model (19).

Third Alternative Hypothesis (H_1''): There is not a risk-free interest rate in the economy in which all individuals are able to invest and borrow, that is:

$$H_1'': \lambda_0 \neq 0.$$

3.3. Description of the Sample

The frequency of the data used in the present study is quarterly and this choice is based, fundamentally, on three important aspects related to empirical tests of the CCAPM: i) According to Breeden, Gibbons and Litzenberger (1989), the longer the time interval in which the consumption is reported, the less affected the data are by temporary fluctuations and measurement errors in this variable; ii) Furthermore, according to these authors, in the proportion that the time interval decreases, non-durable consumer goods become "more durable"; and iii) According to Jagannathan and Wang (2005, p.2), "working with a longer horizon attenuates the errors that may arise due to ignoring the effect of habit formation on preferences".

As can be seen, the use of longer time intervals is preferable when performing tests of the CCAPM. Annual series would be the most recommended. However, in the present study, characterized by a consumption series whose publication only began in the 1990s, the use of a series at such a frequency would result in a very small number of observations.

The period covered by the research in each of the countries (Brazil, Chile, Colombia and Mexico) is determined by the availability of the series of growth in aggregated consumption.

Thus, Table 1 shows the period in which these series are available, as well as the number of quarters covered in each country in the present study.

The initial sample of firms, in each country, refers to all the traded stocks whose quotes are available in the database of Economática®. The criteria for firm selection, in the present study, must fulfill two purposes: i) generate a sample of the most traded stocks in each country; and, ii) generate samples with a considerable number of stocks, in such a way as to obtain significant and representative results for each economy in the study.

Table 1. Period of Study for Each Country

Country	Initial Quarter	Final Quarter	Number of Quarters
Brazil	1991:Q2	2004:Q4	55
Chile	1996:Q2	2005:Q2	37
Colombia	1994:Q2	2005:Q2	45
Mexico	1993:Q2	2005:Q3	50

It should be noted that only the primary and secondary hypotheses can lead to the rejection of the CCAPM, given that they both test the theoretical implications of the model, while the third hypothesis is merely a test of the specification and, therefore, does not have the power to reject the pricing model subjected to the empirical tests.

In the present study, quarterly returns of the financial assets are computed by aggregating the monthly returns into quarters by means of capitalization of these returns. Given that returns are necessary at a monthly frequency, the selection criteria basically refer to the quantity of months, within a determined period, in which the stocks have been quoted. Hence, in order to be included in the sample of their respective country, the stocks must obey the following selection criteria: present one (1) quotes in at least "X" months and "Y" quotes in at least "Z" months, in which "X", "Y" and "Z" are numbers to be defined for each country according to the number of months available and observing the objective of including a significant number of stocks in the sample. This method of selection is also used by Mellone Junior (1999) when testing the CAPM in Brazil.

Table 2 shows the "X", "Y" and "Z" values for each country in the study. The period shown in Table 2, includes, besides the monthly frequency, an extra quarter at the beginning of the period in relation to the previous table (Table 1). This occurs because it is necessary to have quotes lagged in one period to calculate the returns of financial assets. Considering the information contained in Table 2 as a whole, it should be clear that the criteria are more restrictive in the cases of Brazil and Chile, requiring one (1) quote in 67% of the months and 11 quotes in 50% of the months, while in Colombia and Mexico these criteria are less restrictive, so that the two aforementioned objectives are fulfilled satisfactorily.

Applying the above defined selection criteria, we get the set of stocks that makes up the sample of each of the countries under analysis. Table 3 shows the number of stocks initially collected from the Economática® database, the number of stocks that are selected according to the previously described criteria, the number of stocks excluded, the number of stocks that constitutes the final sample and the percentage of the final sample in relation to the initial one, for each country in the study.

Table 2. "X", "Y" And "Z" Values of the Selection Criteria for Each Country

Country	Period	Total Months	Number of Months ≥ 1 Quote ("X")	% of Total	Number of Quotes ("Y")	Number of Months ≥ "Y" Quotes ("Z")	% Total
Brazil	1991:M1-2004:M12	168	112	67%	11	84	50%
Chile	1996:M1-2005:M6	114	76	67%	11	57	50%
Colombia	1994:M1-2005:M6	138	69	50%	5	46	33%
Mexico	1993:M1-2005:M9	153	77	50%	8	51	33%

Table 3. Initial and Final Sample for Each Country

Country	Initial Sample	Firms Selected	Exclusions	Final Sample	% Total
Brazil	860	142	1	141	16%
Chile	259	75	1	74	29%
Colombia	77	28	1	27	35%
Mexico	185	80	1	79	43%

Observing Table 3, it can be noticed that the selection criteria significantly reduced the number of stocks in comparison with the initial sample. This is necessary because the objective is to obtain a sample with the most traded stocks from each country. It is important to bear in mind that liquidity is an important factor when testing pricing models, as Ribenboim (2002) states when testing the CAPM with Brazilian data. However, as Rodrigues (2000) notes, upon selecting the most traded firms some degree of bias in terms of survival could be imputed. Nonetheless, it is believed that this bias should not influence the results, as *a priori*, in an efficient market, there should be no difference in the pricing of "winning" and "losing" assets.

Regarding the exclusions shown in Table 3, these refer to the stocks that underwent extraordinary alterations in their prices overnight (possibly a recording mistake in the Economática® database). It is understood that these exclusions are necessary, given that the average returns of these stocks are clearly influenced by the return on a single day.

It is noteworthy that the final Brazilian sample is the one that has the largest number of stocks, although it is the least representative in relation to the initial sample. Despite this, the sample is composed of the largest Brazilian firms and in terms of market value can be considered representative.

3.4. Data Collection

In order to carry out the empirical tests on the CCAPM the following data are necessary: a) returns on stocks; b) aggregate consumption of non-durable goods and services; c) rates of return on risk-free assets; d) consumer price index; e) resident population.

The series of daily stock quotes, adjusted for inflation and dividends, from each of the countries are collected from the Economática® database. The deflator used to adjust the prices in real terms is the Consumer Price Index (CPI) of each country.

With regard the quarterly consumption of non-durable goods and services,[10] in Brazil, this series, is provided by Pessoa (2006). This series is available for the period 1991:Q1 to 2004:Q4. For the remaining Latin American countries, the series of quarterly consumption of non-durable goods and services is collected as shown in Table 4.

As proxy for the returns on risk-free assets, the interest rates from each country in the analysis are used. In Brazil, the Selic (*Sistema Especial de Liquidação e Custódia*) rate is used, which is the basic rate of interest of the economy, serves as a reference for other rates of interest in the country. The nominal monthly series of this rate is collected from the website of the Instituto de Pesquisa Econômica Aplicada (IPEADATA).

Table 4. Sources for the Series Consumption of Non-Durable Goods and Services: Chile, Colombia and Mexico

Country	Source	Availability
Chile	Banco Central de Chile	1996:Q1-2005:Q2
Colombia	Departamento Administrativo Nacional de Estadística (DANE)	1994:Q1-2005:Q2
Mexico	Instituto Nacional de Estadística Geografia e Informática (INEGI)	1993:Q1-2005:Q3

In the case of Chile[11] and Colombia,[12] the interest rates available from the International Financial Statistics (IFS) database of the International Monetary Fund (IMF) are used. Of those available, the '*Lending Rate*' is chosen, as it presents the lowest volatility in relation to the other rates of interest. The nominal annualized series of this interest rate is collected on a monthly basis.

---

[10] In the CCAPM model, the risk factor is the rate of growth of per capita consumption. Nevertheless, there is no effective direct measure of individual consumption, but only a measure of the expenditures with consumption. According to Breeden, Gibbons and Litzenberger (1989) this difference between consumption in theory and its measurement in the real world leads to the following problem: goods and services are not necessarily consumed at the same time that they are purchased. In order to minimize this problem, the empirical test involving CCAPM make use of the expenditures with non-durable goods and services of individuals, excluding the expenditures with durable goods, since the consumption flow of this kind of good is much more difficult to estimate. As only a fraction of the effective consumption is used in empirical tests of the CCAPM, it becomes subject to the same problem reported by Roll (1977) in testing of the CAPM model: the non-observable true market portfolio. However, like Breeden (1979, p. 292), it is believed that the consumption of non-durable goods and services represents a much larger fraction of the true consumption flow of individuals when compared with the fraction that the stock market occupies in the true market portfolio.

[11] In Chile a number of different interest rates could be used as proxies for risk-free asset, for example: the interest rate of the 90-day securities offered by the Chilean Central Bank – PRBC (*Tasas de interés de los pagarés y bonos licitados por el Banco Central de Chile*), the interest rate of the 90-day bonds and certificates offered by the Chilean Central Bank – PDBC, and the monetary policy rate. However, it was not possible to use these in the present study, due to the unavailability of data covering the entire research period as well as the various structural breaks.

[12] The interest rate series of the 90-day term deposits (*Tasa de Interés de los Certificados de Depósito a Término a 90 días*), which would represent a good proxy for the risk-free asset in Colombia, underwent a change in its methodology in July 1993. As this change occurred during the period covered by the research in Colombia we decided not to use this series.

In Mexico, the 91-day Cetes (*Certificados de la Tesorería de la Federación*) are used as proxy for the returns on the risk-free assets. According to Castellanos and Oviedo (2004), these certificates are credit bonds issued by the Mexican Federal Government and liquidated on their maturity. According to the same authors, the yield from these public debt bonds serve as a base for determining the other rates of interest in the Mexican economy, which warrants the use of this bond as a proxy for risk-free asset. The series of nominal monthly yields of the 91-day Cetes are collected from the website of the Banco Central do Mexico.

Table 5. Sources for the Series Consumer Price Index for Each Country

Country	Source	Unit
Brazil	Instituto de Pesquisa Econômica Aplicada (IPEADATA)	Monthly Percent
Chile	IMF's International Financial Statistics (IFS)	Index
Colombia	IMF's International Financial Statistics (IFS)	Index
Mexico	Banco Central de Mexico	Index

As the interest rates in Latin American countries are expressed in nominal terms, including those collected from the IMF database, it is necessary to deflate them in order to obtain real series. To ensure coherence regarding the deflator used to adjust the series of stock prices in real terms, the Broad Consumer Price Index (IPCA) for the Brazilian series and the Consumer Price Index (CPI) for the other Latin American countries are used. These price indexes are collected on a monthly basis, as shown in Table 5.

Data regarding the resident population in each quarter is necessary to compute the per capita consumption series. In Brazil the consumption series obtained is already expressed in per capita terms, therefore data is not collected regarding the resident population for this country. In the other Latin American countries the annual estimated population series are collected from the following databases: Chile – Instituto Nacional de Estadísticas (INE); Colombia – Departamento Administrativo Nacional de Estadística (DANE); and Mexico – Comissão Econômica para America Latina and Caribe (CEPAL).

In order to make a comparison with the Latin American countries in the study, data is also collected from the United States. A series of real monthly returns on 25 weight-valued portfolios of Fama and French and the interest rate of the one-month U.S. Treasury Bill are obtained from Kenneth R. French's website.[13]

The series necessary for the formation of the growth rate of per capita consumption of non-durable goods and services are collected from the website of the Bureau of Economic Analysis, Division: National Income and Product Accounts (NIPA).[14]

3.5. Data Treatment

The data collected is the base for the construction of the time series necessary for application of the empirical test proposed in the present study. The series used in the

[13] http://mba.tuck.dartmouth.edu/pages/faculty/ken.french/data_library.html

[14] http://www.bea.gov/national/index.htm

regressions detailed below, are multiplied by 100 in order to obtain their percentage values. The remaining aspects related to the construction of the series are described below.

Beginning with the daily stock quotes traded on the stock exchange in each of the countries, the simple mean of the prices of each of the stocks in each of the months is obtained. These series of average monthly prices are then used in calculating the monthly return of each stock. This process of calculating the monthly returns is used by Mellone Junior (1999) and Ribenboin (2002) when testing the CAPM in Brazil. This is believed to be the most suitable procedure of all those available, as it takes into consideration all the quotes of a determined month in order to calculate the monthly return, instead of being based on only an initial and final quote, for example. The real quarterly series of stock returns are computed by capitalizing the monthly stock returns.

By the capitalization of the monthly interest rates within each quarter, the nominal quarterly series of interest rates from each one of the countries is obtained. For Chile and Colombia, where the interest rates are annualized, the rates are converted to a monthly base from which the capitalization within each quarter is obtained. The interest rate series from each one of the countries are then deflated by their respective Consumer Price Index, which resulted in quarterly series of real interest rates.

The quarterly risk premiums are formed from the difference between the series of real quarterly returns on stocks and the series of real quarterly returns on the risk-free asset of each country. The risk premiums are the dependent variables in the time series regressions for estimation of the consumption betas of each asset (1st stage of the regression method).

The average risk premium of each stock is calculated from these time series, based on the simple arithmetic average of the quarterly risk premiums. These average values are the dependent variables in the cross-sectional regressions carried out in the present study (2nd stage of the regression method).

Given that not all the stocks presented returns in all the quarters of the sample,[15] for the purposes of statistical inference and estimation, the missing observations are substituted by estimates. These estimates are obtained in the following manner:

1) Using the available information for each stock, the intercepts and consumption betas are estimated by means of the econometric model (18);
2) Based on these coefficients and in the growth rate of consumption series, whose observations are available for the entire sample, the missing risk premiums are calculated using the following equation:

$$R^e_{i,t} = \alpha_i + \beta_{i,\Delta c} \Delta c_t$$

According to Greene (1997, p. 430), this method of estimating the missing data is widely known as first-order regression. For this author, the method maintains the non-tendentious property of the estimators and apparently produces a gain in efficiency, given that the errors of the model in the formerly missing observations equal to zero. However, the author

[15] In Brazil, a total of 7,755 (55 x 141) observations, 439 (5.66% of the total) are estimated. In Chile, a total of 2,738 (37 x 74) observations, 66 (2.41% of the total) are estimated. In Colombia, of a total of 1,215 (45 x 27) observations, 239 (19.67% of the total) are estimated. In Mexico, of a total of 3,950 (50 x 79) observations, 585 (14.81% of the total) are estimated.

emphasizes "the gain in efficiency from using these fitted values may be illusory" and that "the overall conclusion seems to be that in the single-equation regression context, filling in missing values of *y* is not a good idea".

Despite these warnings, estimates are made of the missing values, as the corrected variance estimates require complete time series of the returns. It should be pointed out that the results do not appear to be sensitive to the use of these estimates.

In order to maintain the comparability of the CCAPM, as suggested in the literature, the series of consumption of non-durable goods and services are adjusted for seasonality.

The method chosen for this is the 'ratio to moving average' of the E-views statistical software. The Brazilian, Colombian and North-American series are already adjusted for seasonality. The per capita series[16] are constructed based on the series adjusted for seasonality, by dividing them by the quarterly population of each country. The quarterly population series are obtained from the geometric interpolation of the annual series. Lastly, the growth rate of per capita consumption is obtained by dividing the per capita consumption of one quarter by the per capita consumption of the previous quarter and subtracting one.

For the purposes of analyzing the stock market behavior in each country over time, an equally weighted portfolio is formed of all the stocks contained in the final sample. Hence, time series are obtained with the real quarterly returns of the stock portfolio of each one of the countries in the study, including the United States. For the same purposes, a series of the excess returns (risk premium) of the stock portfolio is constructed by the difference between the series of real quarterly returns on the stock portfolio and the series of real quarterly returns on the risk-free asset of each country.

4. Analysis of the Results

Table 6 shows some statistical descriptions of the main time series used in carrying out the empirical tests. For the benefit of comparison, the statistics from the North-American series for the period 1991:Q1-2005:Q2 have also been included. The analysis of this data shows that the average risk premium (equity premium) is positive for all the countries with the exception of Colombia. Brazil has the highest average risk premium, with a value of 4.78% per quarter, followed by the United States, Mexico, and Chile, where the risk premiums are respectively 3.16%, 1.51% and 0.60% per quarter. According to the theory outlined above, the higher the risk premium, the greater the risk aversion of the individuals and/or the greater the risk of the environment (variability of consumption). With regard to Colombia, the existence of a negative risk premium (-2.37% per quarter) suggests that the stock portfolio is less risky than the asset considered to be risk free, an assumption that will be confirmed in the following analysis.

It can be seen that Brazil, Mexico, and the United States have very similar average growth rates of per capita consumption, varying from 0.39% per quarter for Brazil to 0.47% per quarter for the United States. At the extremes is Colombia, with an average growth rate of per capita consumption of 0.05% per quarter, and Chile, whose average growth rate of per capita consumption is 0.72% per quarter.

---

[16] This procedure is not necessary in the case of Brazil, since the Brazilian series obtained is already expressed in per capita terms.

Table 6. Time Series Descriptive Statistics

Country	Risk Premium	ΔC	Market Volatility	ΔC Volatility	Cov (Market, ΔC)	Cov (RF, ΔC)	Covariance Difference
Brazil	4.78%	0.39%	2.48	3.46	7.8147	-1.1685	8.9832
Chile	0.60%	0.72%	4.15	1.65	-1.1179	-0.3253	-0.7926
Colombia	-2.37%	0.05%	13.00	15.60	0.7165	-0.3258	1.0423
Mexico	1.51%	0.42%	4.76	5.10	2.5491	1.1280	1.4211
E.U.A.	3.16%	0.47%	2.20	0.74	0.2265	-0.0162	0.2427

Risk Premium = mean sample risk premium; ΔC = average rate of growth of per capita consumption; Market Volatility = Coefficient of variation (ratio between the standard deviation and the sample mean) of the return on the stock portfolio; Volatility ΔC = Coefficient of variation (ratio between the standard deviation and the sample mean) of the rate of growth of per capita consumption; Cov(Market, ΔC) = Covariance of returns on stock portfolio and the rate of growth of per capita consumption; Cov(RF, ΔC) = Covariance of the return on risk-free asset and the rate of growth of per capita consumption; Covariance Difference = Difference between Cov(Market, ΔC) and Cov(RF, ΔC). The mean values are expressed in percentage points per quarter; The covariances are obtained from the data expressed in this measurement unit.

Looking at the volatility of the stock portfolio and the growth rate of per capita consumption, it can be seen that there are great differences in these figures between Chile and the United States, the stock portfolios being much more volatile than the growth rate of per capita consumption.[17] The greater this difference, the greater the level of risk aversion necessary to explain the variations in the prices in stock market given a variation in the per capita consumption. In the other countries, Brazil, Colombia, and Mexico, the growth rate of per capita consumption is seen to be slightly more volatile than the stocks portfolio, suggesting that the level of risk aversion on the part of individuals is lower in these countries, *ceteris paribus*. Colombia can be seen to have the greatest volatility in the per capita consumption series (15.60) among the countries in the sample, followed by Mexico (5.10), Brazil (3.46), Chile (1.65), and the United States (0.74). It is important to point out that, according to the theory, the greater the volatility in this series the greater the risk in the environment.

When analyzing the covariance between the return and consumption series, it can be seen that in all the countries, with the exception of Chile, the covariance of the returns of the stock portfolio with the growth rate of consumption is greater than the covariance of the returns of the risk-free asset with the growth rate of consumption. In these countries, therefore, the returns of the stock portfolio are shown to be of greater risk than the returns of the asset that is considered risk-free, suggesting that there is a positive risk premium among these assets. In Brazil, Mexico, and the United States there is a positive risk premium (equity premium), corroborating the theory. In Colombia, as highlighted previously, the stock portfolio had a negative risk premium,[18] in contrast to the prediction of the theory which suggests that the greater exposure of this portfolio to risk should lead to a positive risk premium in relation to

[17] This corroborates the evidence reported in previous studies regarding the excessive variability in the North American share market. See, for example, Grossman and Shiller (1981) and the review made at an international level by Campbell (1996).

[18] It is important to note that this negative risk premium is highly influenced by the frequent negative returns presented by this portfolio at the start of the period covered by the sample. By limiting the sample to the period 2000:Q1 to 2005:Q2 a positive risk premium in the range of 3.51% per quarter is obtained.

the risk-free asset. With regard to Chile, in the period under analysis, the opposite behavior to that seen in the other countries is found, that is, the returns of the stock portfolio present less risk than the returns of the asset considered risk-free. This fact is really quite intriguing and leads to the following question: how can be explained the positive risk premiums of these assets in the Chilean economy?

Another important aspect to be noted is the magnitude of the differences between these covariances. According to the CCAPM, the greater this difference, the greater the risk of the stock portfolio in relation to the risk-free asset and, so, the lower the level of risk aversion necessary to explain the risk premium among these assets. This relationship between the risk premium, the covariance, and the relative risk aversion coefficient is demonstrated by the equation of the determination of the risk premium of the stocks given by Grossman, Melino and Shiller (1987, p. 316):

$$E_t\left(R_i^e\right) = \gamma \operatorname{cov}\left(R_i^e, \Delta c\right),$$

where: $\operatorname{cov}(R_i^e, \Delta c) = \operatorname{cov}(R_i, \Delta c) - \operatorname{cov}(R_f, \Delta c)$.

Analysis of these differences, shown in Table 6, reveals that Brazil has the greatest difference between the risk levels of the stock portfolio and the risk-free asset, while among the other countries this distinction is relatively small.

Before proceeding with the analysis of the cross-sectional regressions it is important to verify the stationarity of the series of growth rates of per capita consumption of each country, since this is a property required in the time series regressions necessary for the estimation of the consumption betas. To this end, the Augmented Dickey-Fuller Unit Root Test is performed, in which the null hypothesis is that the time series has a unit root, that is, it is non-stationary. The results reject the null hypothesis at the 1% significance level for the consumption series of Brazil, Chile, and Colombia, and at a significance level of 5.31% for the consumption series of Mexico.

Similarly, it is important to investigate whether or not the model satisfies the main classical hypotheses of the linear regression model, since the desirable properties of the estimators (absence of bias and minimal variance) and the validity of the significance tests depend on their confirmation.[19]

Regarding the homoskedasticity of the residuals, the White test shows that the null hypothesis that the residuals are homoskedastic in the regressions carried out for Brazil and Chile cannot be rejected. In the regressions carried out in Colombia and Mexico, the White test points to the rejection of the null hypothesis at a significance level of 5% and 10%, respectively. The presence of heteroskedasticity, according to Gujarati (2003), does not destroy the properties of non-tendentiousness and of consistency of the OLS estimators, but they do lose efficiency, even in large samples. Therefore, in such cases, caution should be used when interpreting the results obtained.

The Durbin-Watson test points to the absence of first-order serial correlation of the residuals and the Breusch-Godfrey test suggests that the null hypothesis of absence of second-

[19] The quantitative results of the tests for heteroskedasticity, autocorrelation of higher order, and non-normality of the residues are not reported here. However, such results can be requested from the authors.

order serial correlation cannot be rejected. These findings are present in all regressions performed.

The normality of the residuals is not rejected in the regressions carried out for Brazil, Chile, and Colombia.[20] In the regression for Mexico, this hypothesis is rejected at the level of significance of 5% for all the applied tests. According to Gujarati (2003), the hypothesis of normality is not essential if the aim is only to obtain an estimate, as the estimators of ordinary least squared are the best linear unbiased estimators (BLUE) whether the residuals are normally distributed or otherwise. However, according to the same author, the usual *t*-statistics may not follow the Student-*t* distributions, that is, such statistics may not be valid in small samples, affecting the tests of the hypotheses. In this case, therefore, greater caution should be applied to the results obtained with the cross-sectional regression carried out on the Mexican financial assets.

Table 7. Results of the Cross-sectional Regressions of the Average Risk Premiums on the Consumption Betas

Country	Constant		Consumption Betas		R^2	Adj. R^2	F-Stat	Durbin-Watson
Brazil	2.7176		0.3522		0.1183	0.112	18.6513	1.88145
	0.98848		1.35215	*				
Chile	0.8861		0.43499		0.141	0.129	11.8141	2.09442
	0.47923		1.4942	*				
Colombia	-3.1677		0.3312		0.2048	0.173	6.4389	1.71532
	-2.02802	*	1.92362	**				
Mexico	0.7059		0.0738		0.002	-0.011	0.1547	2.12198
	0.46705		0.17122					

These results refer to the cross-sectional regression of model (19). Coefficient estimates (first line) and Shanken (1992) corrected t-statistics (second line) are reported for each country, alongside the coefficients of determination, F-statistic, and Durbin-Watson statistic for the regressions.

* Significant at the 10% level; ** Significant at the 5% level.

Table 7 shows the results of the cross-sectional regression of the average risk premiums on the consumption betas in each country analyzed: Brazil, Chile, Colombia, and Mexico. The main purpose of the regression is to verify whether the central implication of the pricing model in question can be confirmed, that is, whether there is a statistically significant relationship between the average risk premiums and the consumption betas.

Based on the corrected *t*-statistics, it can be seen that the constant is statistically different from zero only in Colombia, with a significance level of 10%, thus rejecting the third null hypothesis and suggesting that the specification zero-beta, proposed by Black (1972), is more suitable in the Colombian case. In the other countries, this hypothesis cannot be rejected at the usual levels of significance. Therefore, the hypothesis of Sharpe-Lintner, that there is a risk-free asset being freely traded in the economies of Brazil, Chile, and Mexico cannot be rejected.

---

[20] The normality tests applied are: Jarque-Bera (assimptotic), Lilliefors (D), Cramer-von Mises (W2), Watson (U2), and Anderson-Darling (A2).

The slope coefficient of the variable 'consumption beta' is shown to be positive and statistically significant in the cross-sectional regressions carried out in Brazil, Chile, and Colombia, rejecting the primary null hypothesis and showing that there is a statistically significant relationship between the average risk premiums and the consumption betas in these countries. These findings corroborate the CCAPM in the above mentioned countries, since the principal implication derived from the model is confirmed by the empirical test. It is of particular note that the level of significance necessary for the rejection of the primary null hypothesis is 10% in Brazil and Chile and 5% in Colombia. In Mexico the value of the slope coefficient is at 0.0738, although statistically insignificant at the usual levels of significance, failing to reject the primary null hypothesis. The non-rejection of this hypothesis implies the rejection of the CCAPM in Mexico, as there is no positive and statistically significant relationship between the average risk premiums and the consumption betas in that country. It is important to point out that the Shanken (1992) adjusted t-statistics would be based on an asymptotic correction and, therefore, should be analyzed with caution.

By assessing the adjusted R^2 and R^2, it is possible to get some idea of how well the CCAPM explains the differences between the average risk premiums of the assets in the countries under study. The adjusted R^2 values vary from a minimum of -0.011 (Mexico) to a maximum of 0.173 (Colombia), indicating that, taking into account the degrees of freedom, only a small fraction (-1.1% in Mexico and 17.3% in Colombia, for example) of the cross-sectional variations of the average risk premiums are explained by the CCAPM. Coefficients of determination of this magnitude indicate that the model explains poorly the differences between the returns of the diverse financial assets (stocks). Therefore, this finding restricts the practical use of the model in most actual financial decisions, such as: cost of capital, determining expected returns, resource allocation, etc.

Table 8. Results of the Cross-Sectional Regressions of the Average Risk Premiums on the Consumption Betas and Residual Variances

Country	Constant		Consumption Betas		Residual Variances	
Brazil	0.4641		0.2336	***	0.0020	***
	0.78221		3.16688		6.54439	
Chile	0.5069		0.4144	***	0.0011	
	1.08739		3.23547		1.03306	
Colombia	-4.1689	**	0.3147	**	0.0031	
	-2.67914		2.36084		0.77365	
Mexico	0.2537		-0.0177		0.0009	
	0.52486		-0.08976		1.39997	*

These results refer to the cross-sectional regression of model (20). Coefficient estimates (first line) and usual t-statistics (second line) are reported for each country.

* Significant at the 10% level; ** Significant at the 5% level; and *** Significant at the 1% level.

The results of the regression of the average risk premiums on the consumption betas and the residual variance, the purpose of which is to test the secondary null hypothesis that the consumption beta is a complete measure of the risk of an asset, are presented in Table 8. In Brazil and Mexico the slope coefficient of the variable 'residual variance' is shown to be positive and statistically significant at the levels of 1% and 10%, respectively, rejecting the secondary null hypothesis. These findings show that the consumption beta may not be a complete measure of asset risk and imply the rejection of the CCAPM in these countries. In the other countries, Chile and Colombia, the slope coefficient of this variable is not significantly different from zero at the usual levels of significance, corroborating the secondary null hypothesis and suggesting that the consumption beta could be used as a complete measure of asset risk in these countries. Lastly, it is appropriate to point out that these regressions are susceptible to the problem of measurement errors in variables and, therefore, their results should be interpreted with caution.

Table 9 presents a summary of the results of the hypotheses tests performed in the four Latin American countries, as well as the benchmark, i.e. the United States. For the United States, the results obtained by Lettau and Ludvigson (2001) based on quarterly data covering the period 1963:3 to 1998:3 are used, which can be found in Table 8 of their paper. In that study, the authors run a cross-sectional regression of the returns of the 25 Fama and French portfolios on the consumption betas of these portfolios.

The primary null hypothesis states that the slope coefficient of the consumption betas is equal to zero. This hypothesis is considered the most important as it refers to the central idea of the model, that is, the existence of positive and statistically significant relationship between the average risk premiums and the consumption betas, consequently its non-rejection would imply the empirical inconsistency of the CCAPM. Analysis of Table 9 shows that the hypothesis is rejected in Brazil, Chile, and Colombia. The rejection of the CCAPM, according to this hypothesis, is verified only for Mexico and the United States (benchmark).

Table 9. Summary of the Tests of the Hypotheses in Each Country

Country	Primary H_0	Secondary H_0'	Tertiary H_0''	R^2
Brazil	Reject	Reject	Cannot Reject	0.11196
Chile	Reject	Cannot Reject	Cannot Reject	0.12903
Colombia	Reject	Cannot Reject	Reject	0.17300
Mexico	Cannot Reject	Reject	Cannot Reject	-0.01096
USA[#]	Cannot Reject	*	*	0.13000

[#] Source: Lettau and Ludvigson (2001); * Hypothesis not tested explicitly.

The secondary null hypothesis states that the consumption beta is a complete measure of the risk of an asset, that is, there is no other risk factor, apart from the covariance of the returns with the growth rate of per capita consumption, that systematically affects the returns of the assets. This hypothesis, like the first, can lead to the rejection of the CCAPM. In observing Table 9 it can be seen that this hypothesis is rejected in Brazil and Mexico, suggesting the rejection of the model in these countries. In contrast, in Chile and Colombia there is no such rejection of this hypothesis, thus demonstrating that these countries are the only ones that corroborate all the theoretical implications derived from the model.

The coefficients of determination, represented by the adjusted R^2 of the cross-sectional regressions in each country, demonstrate that the explanatory power of the CCAPM is very small in the countries under study and also in the North-American benchmark. Even in those countries where there appears to be a positive and statistically significant relationship between the average risk premiums and the consumption betas, the explanatory power of the model is at best 17.3% of the cross-sectional variation of the returns of the assets in the financial market (Colombia).

These combined results suggest that the adherence of the CCAPM to the data from Latin American economies is very weak. Although the data from Chile and Colombia do not reject the CCAPM outright, the explanatory power of the model in relation to these countries, as in the remaining countries, is unsatisfactory. In the cases of Brazil and México, the findings are even more unfavorable to the CCAPM. In the former, though there is a statistically significant relationship between the average risk premiums and the consumption betas, the residual variance is shown to be statistically significant in the cross-sectional regressions, in contrast to the theoretical prediction of the model. In the latter, besides the variable residual variances being statistically significant, there appears to be no statistically significant relationship between the average risk premiums and the consumption betas, thus leading to the rejection of the CCAPM. Given these restrictions to the model and considering the fact that several studies indicate the rejection of the model at an international level,[21] we conclude that this is a worldwide phenomenon, affecting both developed and developing countries.

As mentioned before, the third null hypothesis is more a specification test than a test of the implications of the CCAPM. It requires a statistically insignificant intercept in the cross-sectional regression. This hypothesis does not have the power to reject the model and its only purpose is to verify which of the alternate specifications is correct (Sharpe-Lintner's risk-free asset or Black's zero-beta asset). Based on the results in Table 9, it can be seen that the third null hypothesis is rejected only in Colombia, suggesting that Black's zero-beta specification (1972) is the most suitable in that country, while Sharpe-Lintner's more restrictive specification appears to be more consistent with the data from the other Latin American economies.

In summary, the weak performance of the CCAPM in the Latin American countries analyzed in the present study is quite evident. The model is not capable of satisfactorily explaining the realized returns of the assets in these countries and the theoretical implications of the model are only fully confirmed in Chile and Colombia. Considering the evidence from other studies at an international level, it is understood that some assumptions that form the base of the model need to be modified, which represents the main implication of the present study, as well as those of other studies that highlight the inconsistencies of the CCAPM, for the modern neoclassic theory of asset pricing.

At this point, it is pertinent to reflect on the statement made by Mankiw and Shapiro (1986, p. 458) that "the apparent rejection of the consumption CAPM is potentially attributable to failure of one of the many auxiliary assumptions". According to these authors, the weak explanatory power of the CCAPM could be explained by, among other aspects, non-stable preferences, costs of adjustment in consumption, durability of non-durable goods, and so on.

Nonetheless, it should be borne in mind that, as Cochrane (2005, p. 455) emphasizes, the point of departure for understanding which risks affect the prices and expected returns of assets is: the individual's first order conditions for saving and portfolio formation, that is, the consumption-based model. Accordingly, models with more restrictive assumptions regarding

---

[21] See, for instance, the results from Campbell (1996) and Carmichael and Samson (2005).

the investor behavior and the stochastic discount factor could be of help in better understanding the demand for financial assets.

Following this line of thought, it is worth highlighting three studies carried out in the United States that offer encouraging results regarding the CCAPM: the study from Lettau and Ludvigson (2001) that uses a conditional model of CCAPM to explain the differences between asset returns; the study by Parker and Julliard (2005) that defines the risk of an asset as the covariance of its returns with the accumulated growth in consumption over various quarters following the occurrence of returns; and Jagannathan and Wang (2005) study in which they begin with the assumption that the investors revise their consumption and portfolio decisions in the fourth quarter of each year.

Besides proposing modifications to the original model, these three studies also offer evidence that the CCAPM can explain a significant part of the variations in the average returns of the financial assets. In our opinion, the test of these models in the countries of Latin America is the next step to be taken in attempting to increase the understanding of the factors that affect asset risk in financial markets.

CONCLUSION

The objective of this study is to verify whether the Consumption-Based Capital Asset Pricing Model (CCAPM) is consistent with the economic data from the following Latin American countries: Brazil, Chile, Colombia, and Mexico. To this end, the theoretical implications of the model in question are checked against the data from those countries and, moreover, the capacity of the model to explain the differences between the returns of assets (stocks) in the financial markets of each country is assessed.

In summary, the tests of the hypotheses and the explanatory capacity of the CCAPM suggest the rejection of the model in Brazil and Mexico, while in Chile and Colombia the model only offered unsatisfactory power of explanation of the average risk premiums of the assets. In the United States, the rejection of the model is demonstrated by the study by Lettau and Ludvigson (2001), whose results are reproduced in Table 9.

However, in the same way as Faff (1998), these results need to be seen in the context of several empirical problems and assumptions made in order to make the testing of the CCAPM viable. Thus, it is important to question up to what point the results are influenced by: non-stable betas, durability of the non-durable goods, failure to observe the true flow of individual consumption, asymptotic correction for the problem of errors in variables, etc.

With regard to the objectives of the present study, it is believed that they have been fully achieved, since it is shown to be possible to assess the explanatory capacity of the model and test the implications derived from it. Furthermore, comparisons are made with data previously obtained relating to the United States, whose results are very similar to those found in this study.

The present study has contributed towards increasing the understanding of the behavior of the CCAPM in the Latin American countries under study. The empirical evidence of this study corroborates with the evidence reported for other countries, such as the United States, and suggests that modifications to the original model, such as those proposed by Lettau and Ludvigson (2001), Parker and Julliard (2005), and Jagannathan and Wang (2005), might be implemented in the future in order to allow a better understanding of the CCAPM and of the factors determining risk in Latin American financial markets.

This study has also contributed to the empirical literature in proposing tests with individual assets, instead of the formation of portfolios, in countries characterized by a relatively small number of assets. The use of portfolios is very common in tests of asset pricing models, and they are constructed with the objective of mitigating the problem of errors in variables and reducing the volatility of individual assets. However, as underscored previously, there are some inconveniences associated with the formation of portfolios, mainly in countries characterized by a small number of financial assets, as is the case of the Latin American countries. Hence, the use of individual assets with a correction for the problem of errors in variables is recommended in the tests.

As a potential theme for future studies in Latin American countries, the application of the conditional CCAPM as proposed by Lettau and Ludvigson (2001) is suggested. With regard to the studies of Parker and Julliard (2005) and Jagannathan and Wang (2005), it is of particular interest that they both require extended time series in order to achieve more reliable results. The execution of studies of such a nature is also recommended with the purpose of correcting the problem of errors in variables aimed at finite samples.

ACKNOWLEDGMENTS

This research is largely based on the M.Sc. thesis of Guilherme Kirch, who is grateful to CAPES for financial support. A substantial part of this research is developed while Paulo R. S. Terra was affiliated with Universidade do Vale do Rio dos Sinos. The authors are thankful to Marcelo de Sales Pessoa for providing part of the data for this study, and to the overall help of Felipe Kirch, Magda M. B. L. Donia and Tim Donovan. The authors are indebted to Ricardo P. C. Leal, Roberto C. Moraes, and Rodrigo O. Soares for their comments and suggestions on an earlier draft. The authors are also thankful to referees, discussants, and participants of the VI Brazilian Finance Meeting (Vitória, 2006) for their input on an earlier version of this paper. All remaining errors are the authors' sole responsibility.

REFERENCES

Abel, Andrew B., 1991, The equity premium puzzle, *Business Review* Sept/Oct, 3-14.

Araújo, Eurilton, 2004, Avaliando três especificações para o fator de desconto estocástico através da fronteira de volatilidade de Hansen and Jagannathan: Um estudo empírico para o Brasil, *Working Paper*, Ibmec Business School.

Araújo, Eurilton, Josis Fajardo Barbachan, and Leonardo C. di Tavani, 2004, CAPM usando uma carteira sintética do PIB brasileiro, In: IV Encontro Brasileiro de Finanças, *Annals...*, Rio de Janeiro.

Berk, Jonathan B., 2000, Sorting out sorts, *The Journal of Finance* 55, 407-427.

Black, Fischer, 1972, Capital market equilibrium with restricted borrowing, *The Journal of Business* 45, 444-455.

Black, Fischer, Michael C. Jensen, and Myron S. Scholes, 1972, The capital asset pricing model: Some empirical tests, In: Michael C. Jensen, Org., *Studies in the Theory of Capital Markets* (Praeger, New York, 79-121).

Blume, Marshall E., and Irwin Friend, 1973, A new look at the capital asset pricing model, *The Journal of Finance* 28, 19-33.

Bonomo, Marco, and Gabriela Bertol Domingues, 2002, Os puzzles invertidos no mercado brasileiro de ativos, In: Marco Bonomo, Org., *Finanças Aplicadas ao Brasil* (FGV, São Paulo, 105-120).

Bravo, Karin, and Carlos Oyarzún, 2001, Consumption and asset return dynamics in the Chilean economy. In: Encuentro de Economistas, *Banco de Papers*, Punta de Tralca, Universidad de Chile, Faculdad de Ciências Económicas y Administrativas, available at: http://econ.facea.uchile.cl/encuentro/Consumption%20and%20Assets%20Return%20Dynamics%20EE.pdf.

Breeden, Douglas T., 1979, An intertemporal asset pricing model with stochastic consumption and investment opportunities, *Journal of Financial Economics* 7, 265-296.

Breeden, Douglas T., Michael R. Gibbons, and Robert H. Litzenberger, 1989, Empirical tests of the consumption-oriented CAPM, *The Journal of Finance* 46, 231-262.

Campbell, John Y., 1996, Consumption and the stock market: Interpreting international experience, *Working Paper*, NBER 5610.

Campbell, John Y., Andrew W. Lo, and A. Craig MacKinlay, 1997, *The Econometrics of Financial Markets* (Princeton University Press, New Jersey).

Campbell, John Y., and John H. Cochrane, 1999, By force of habit: the consumption-based explanation of aggregate stock market behavior, *Journal of Political Economy* 107, 205-251.

Campbell, John Y., and John H. Cochrane, 2000, Explaining the poor performance of consumption-based asset pricing models, *The Journal of Finance* 55, 2863-2878.

Carmichael, Benoît, and Lucie Samson, 2005, Consumption growth as the risk factor? Evidence from Canadian financial markets, *Journal of International Money and Finance* 24, 83-101.

Castellanos, Sara G., and Marco A. Oviedo, 2004, Análisis de las posturas óptimas en las subastas primarias de títulos gubernamentales: Resultados de un enfoque econométrico estructural, *Documento de Investigación nº 2004-7*, Dirección General de Investigación Económica, Banco de Mexico.

Cochrane, John H., 2005, *Asset Pricing: Revised Edition* (Princeton University Press, New Jersey).

Constantinides, George M., 1982, Intertemporal asset pricing with heterogeneous consumers and without demand aggregation, *Journal of Business* 55, 253-267.

Cornell, Bradford, 1981, The consumption based asset pricing model: A note on potential tests and applications, *Journal of Financial Economics* 9, 103-108.

Cysne, Rubens Penha, 2005, Equity premium puzzle: Evidence from Brazilian data, *Ensaios Econômicos EPGE* nº 586, Fundação Getúlio Vargas.

Duffie, Darrell, 2001, *Dynamic Asset Pricing Theory* (Princeton University Press, New Jersey).

Elyasiani, Elyas, and Alireza Nasseh, 2000, Non nested procedures in econometric tests of asset pricing theories, *The Journal of Financial Research* 23, 103-128.

Faff, Robert W., 1998, The empirical relationship between aggregate consumption and security prices in Australia. *Pacific-Basin Finance Journal* 6, 213-224.

Fama, Eugene F., and James D. Macbeth, 1973, Risk, return, and equilibrium: Empirical tests, *Journal of Political Economy* 71, 607-636.

Fama, Eugene F., and Kenneth R. French, 1992, The cross-section of expected stock returns, *The Journal of Finance* 47, 427-465.

Ferson, Wayne E., and John J. Merrick Jr., 1987, Non-stationarity and stage-of-the-business-cycle effects in consumption-based asset pricing relations, *Journal of Financial Economics* 18, 127-146.

Grauer, Robert R., and Johannus A. Janmaat, 2004, The unintended consequences of grouping in tests of asset pricing models, *Journal of Banking and Finance* 28, 2889-2914.

Greene, William H., 1997, *Econometric Analysis* (Prentice Hall, New Jersey).

Grossman, Sanford J., and Robert J. Shiller, 1981, The determinants of the variability of stock market prices, *The American Economic Review* 71, 222-227.

Grossman, Sanford J., Ângelo Melino, and Robert J. Shiller, 1987, Estimating the continuous-time consumption-based asset-pricing model, *Journal of Business and Economic Statistics* 5, 315-327.

Gujarati, Damodar N., 2003, *Basic Econometrics* (McGraw-Hill, New York).

Hansen, Lars Peter, and Kenneth J. Singleton, 1983, Stochastic consumption, risk aversion, and the temporal behavior of asset returns, *Journal of Political Economy* 91, 249-265.

Hansen, Lars Peter, and Ravi Jagannathan, 1991, Implications of security market data for models of dynamic economies, *Journal of Political Economy* 99, 225-262.

Huang, Chi-fu, and Robert H. Litzenberger, 1988, *Foundations for Financial Economics* (Prentice Hall, New Jersey).

Issler, João Victor, and Natalia Scotto Piqueira, 2001, Estimando a aversão ao risco, a taxa de desconto intertemporal, e a substutibilidade intertemporal do consumo no Brasil usando três tipos de função utilidade, *Ensaios Econômicos EPGE* nº 424, Fundação Getúlio Vargas.

Jagannathan, Ravi, and Zhenyu Wang, 1996, The conditional CAPM and the cross-sectional of expected returns, *The Journal of Finance* 51, 3-53.

Jagannathan, Ravi, and Zhenyu Wang, 1998, An asymptotic theory for estimating beta-pricing models using cross-sectional regression, *The Journal of Finance* 53, 1285-1309.

Jagannathan, Ravi, and Yong Wang, 2005, Consumption risk and the cost of equity capital, *Working Paper*, NBER 11026.

Kim, Dongcheol, 1995, The errors in the variables problem in the cross-section of expected stock returns, *The Journal of Finance* 50, 1605-1634.

Kim, Dongcheol, 1997, A reexamination of firm size, book-to-market, and earnings price in the cross-section of expected stock returns, *Journal of Financial and Quantitative Analysis* 32, 463-489.

Kocherlakota, Narayana R., 1996, The equity premium: It's still the puzzle, *Journal of Economic Literature* 34, 42-71.

Kothari, S. P., Jay Shanken, and Richard G. Sloan, 1995, Another look at the cross-section of expected stock returns, *The Journal of Finance* 50, 185-224.

Lettau, Martin, and Sydney Ludvigson, 2001, Resurrecting the (C)CAPM: the cross-sectional test when risk premia are time-varying, *Journal of Political Economy* 109, 1238-1287.

Levy, Haim, 1978, Equilibrium in an imperfect market: a constraint on the number of securities in the portfolio, *The American Economic Review* 68, 643-658.

Liang, Bing, 2000, Portfolio formation, measurement errors, and beta shifts: a random sampling approach, *The Journal of Financial Research* 23, 261-284.

Lintner, John, 1965, Security prices, risk, and maximal gains from diversification, *The Journal of Finance* 20, 587-615.

Litzenberger, Robert H., and Krishna Ramaswamy, 1979, The effect of personal taxes and dividends on capital asset prices: Theory and empirical evidence, *Journal of Financial Economics* 7, 163-195.

Lo, Andrew W., and A. Craig MacKinlay, 1990, Data-snooping biases in tests of financial asset pricing models, *Review of Financial Studies* 3, 431-467.

Lo, Ingrid, 2004, Portfolio formation can affect asset pricing tests, *Journal of Asset Management* 5, 203-216.

Lucas, Robert E., 1978, Asset prices in an exchange economy, *Econometrica* 46, 1429-1445.

Maddala, G. S., 2001, *Introduction to Econometrics* (Wiley, Chichester).

Mankiw, N. Gregory, and Matthew D. Shapiro, 1986, Risk and return: consumption beta versus market beta, *Review of Economics and Statistics* 68, 452-459.

Mehra, Rajnish, and Edward C. Prescott, 1985, The equity premium: the puzzle, *Journal of Monetary Economics* 15, 145-161.

Mehra, Rajnish, and Edward C. Prescott, 2003, The equity premium in retrospect, *Working Paper*, NBER 9525.

Mellone Junior, Geraldo, 1999, Evidência empírica da relação cross-section entre retornos e earnings to price ratio e book to market ratio no Mercado de Ações do Brasil no Período de 1995 a 1998, In: XXIII Encontro Nacional de Programas de Pós-Graduação em Administração, *Annals...* , Foz do Iguaçu.

Merton, Robert C., 1973, An intertemporal capital asset pricing model, *Econometrica* 41, 867-887.

Muth, John F., 1961, Rational expectations and the theory of price movements, *Econometrica* 29, 315-335.

Opazo R., Luis A., 1998, Evaluación comparada de modelos de valoración de activos: el caso del premio accionario en Chile, *Revista de Análisis Econômico* 13, 53-80.

Osorio, Isabel Cristina Montoya, and Juan Manuel Restrepo Puerta, 2004, Existe el enigma de la prima de riesgo en el mercado bursátil colombiano? 1993-2002. *Ecos de Economía*, No. 19, 31-58.

Parker, Jonathan A., and Christian Julliard, 2005, Consumption risk and the cross section of expected returns, *Journal of Political Economy* 113, 185-222.

Pessoa, Marcelo de Sales, 2006, *Reproduzindo os momentos dos retornos dos ativos Brasileiros com aversão a desapontamento generalizada*, Doctoral dissertation, Escola de Pós-Graduação em Economia (EPGE), Fundação Getúlio Vargas, Rio de Janeiro.

Ribenboim, Guilherme, 2002, Testes de versões do modelo CAPM no Brasil, In: Marco Bonomo, Org., *Finanças Aplicadas ao Brasil* (FGV, São Paulo, 17-40).

Rodrigues, Murilo Ramos Alambert, 2000, O efeito valor, o efeito tamanho e o modelo multifatorial: Evidências do caso brasileiro, In: XXIV Encontro Nacional de Programas de Pós-Graduação em Administração, *Annals...* , Florianópolis.

Roll, Richard, 1977, The critique of the asset pricing theory's tests part I: On past and potential testability of the theory, *Journal of Financial Economics* 4, 129-176.

Sampaio, Frederico Santana, 2002, Existe equity premium puzzle no Brazil?, In: Marco Bonomo, Org., *Finanças Aplicadas ao Brasil* (FGV, São Paulo, 87-104).

Shanken, Jay, 1992, On the estimation of beta-pricing models. *The Review of Financial Studies* 5, 1-33.

Sharpe, William F., 1964, Capital asset prices: the theory of market equilibrium under conditions of risk. *The Journal of Finance* 19, 425-442.

Varian, Hal R., 1992, *Microeconomic Analysis* (Norton and Company, New York).

In: Financial Asset Pricing
Editors: P. E. Schulz and B. P. Hoffmann
ISBN: 978-1-61122-803-8

Chapter 8

Intricate Asset Price Dynamics and One-Dimensional Discontinuous Maps

F. Tramontana*, L. Gardini† and F. Westerhoff‡
Department of Economics and Quantitative Methods,
University of Urbino, Via Saffi 42, 61029 Urbino, Italy
Department of Economics, University of Bamberg,
Feldkirchenstrasse 21, 96045 Bamberg, Germany

Abstract

In this chapter we consider a simple financial market model following the pioneering works by R. Day, described by one-dimensional piecewise linear maps, either being continuous or discontinuous. We shall see how rich the related dynamics are, with sequences of stable cycles and chaotic intervals. Our results explain, among other things, the emergence of intricate bull and bear markets dynamics, as observed in many actual financial markets. Due to its simplicity, the model allows both a useful analytical study and a qualitative interpretation of the dynamic outcomes. We describe bifurcation sequences with both period increment by one and by two, and we illustrate the wide regions of chaotic behavior.

1. Introduction

In this chapter we are interested in a piecewise linear model, in the case of both continuous and discontinuous maps, which comes from the study of financial markets where heterogeneous speculators follow simple technical and fundamental trading rules to determine their orders. As we will see, our model is able to generate complex dynamics. For instance, asset prices can be highly volatile and display irregular switches between bull and bear markets, as also studied recently in [1] and [2]. Inspired by the seminal papers by R. Day ([3, 4]), such simple deterministic models are still sufficiently up-to-date to interpret the current financial crises.

*E-mail address: f.tramontana@univpm.it
†E-mail address: laura.gardini@uniurb.it
‡E-mail address: frank.westerhoff@uni-bamberg.de

The financial market model we discuss in this chapter goes back to [5]. However, there are so many possible scenarios associated with that particular piecewise linear model that it is impossible to investigate all of the results in one contribution. In [5], we focused on cases in which the two linear pieces of the map have either positive or negative slopes. Now we focus on the case in which the right branch of the map has a negative slope while left has a positive slope. However, both branches have positive offsets. Due to the assumptions about the shape of the map, there is only one equilibrium, located on the right part of the map. It always exists, and can be stable or unstable. If it is unstable, however, the global dynamics are nevertheless bounded: we observe cyclical or chaotic motion, and the trajectory flips back and forth between the left and the right side of the map.

The main point in the analysis of non-smooth systems (continuous and discontinuous) is the occurrence of *border collision bifurcations* (BCB), due to the merging (or collapse) of some invariant set (a fixed point, a periodic point of a cycle, or the boundary of any invariant set) with the kink point at which the function changes its definition. This may lead to a drastic change, unexpected (i.e. impossible) in the framework of smooth systems. Such border collision bifurcations (the term was coined by Nusse and Yorke in 1992 [6], (see also [7]) are responsible, for example, for the direct transition from a regular regime to chaotic dynamics, or even to divergence ([8, 9, 10, 11]). It is not an easy task to analyze the effect of a collision of an invariant set with a kink point, a boundary for the map definition. It is, in effect, a global bifurcation that depends on the shape of the map on "the other side" of the collision, and may lead to several different dynamic effects. For example, the dynamics can suddenly change from an attracting fixed point to an attracting cycle of any period, or to chaotic dynamics, and true chaos or strict chaos in the sense of [12], and especially robust chaos [13], since it is persistent as a function of the parameters.

The chapter is organized as follows. The model is introduced in Section 2. In Section 3 we describe some of the model's properties, including the degeneracy of all the flip bifurcations of any cycle occurring in the model under our assumptions. In Section 4 we determine the BCB curves associated with the periodicity regions of cycles with the symbol sequence L^kR and the related curves at which their degenerate flip bifurcation occurs. In Section 5 we determine the BCB curves associated with the periodicity regions of cycles with the symbol sequence LR^k, which are paired with overlapping portions. Section 6 concludes the chapter.

2. A Simple Piecewise Linear Financial Model

In this section, we briefly recall the financial market model proposed in [5] and clarify the economic meaning of our underlying parameter setting. We refer the reader to [5] for more empirical evidence and theoretical justification for our behavioral model as well as for related literature on agent-based models and general properties of asset price dynamics, the so-called stylized facts.

Let us start with the derivation of the model, which contains five types of agents: a market maker, two types of chartists and two types of fundamentalists. The market maker adjusts prices with respect to excess demand in the usual way. The log of price P for period $t+1$ is

$$P_{t+1} = P_t + a(D_t^{C,1} + D_t^{C,2} + D_t^{F,1} + D_t^{F,2}), \tag{1}$$

where a is a positive price adjustment parameter, $D_t^{C,1}$ and $D_t^{C,2}$ are the orders of the two types of chartists, and $D_t^{F,1}$ and $D_t^{F,2}$ are the orders of the two types of fundamentalists, respectively. Any positive (negative) excess demand, given by the four terms in brackets, leads to a price increase (decrease). Without loss of generality, we assume $a = 1$.

Chartists believe in the persistence of bull and bear markets. The orders of type 1 chartists are formalized as

$$D_t^{C,1} = \begin{cases} +c^{1,a}(P_t - F) & if \;\; P_t - F > 0 \\ +c^{1,b}(P_t - F) & if \;\; P_t - F < 0 \end{cases}, \tag{2}$$

where $c^{1,a}$ and $c^{1,b}$ are positive reaction parameters and F is the log of the fundamental value. Accordingly, type 1 chartists optimistically (pessimistically) buy (sell) assets when prices are above (below) the fundamental value. The orders placed by type 2 chartists are captured by

$$D_t^{C,2} = \begin{cases} +c^{2,a} & if \;\; P_t - F > 0 \\ +c^{2,b} & if \;\; P_t - F < 0 \end{cases}. \tag{3}$$

In a bull market, their buying orders amount to $c^{2,a} > 0$ while in a bear market, their selling orders total $c^{2,b} > 0$.

Fundamentalists bet on a convergence between prices and fundamental values. The orders placed by type 1 fundamentalists are expressed as

$$D_t^{F,1} = \begin{cases} +f^{\,1,a}(F - P_t) & if \;\; F - P_t > 0 \\ +f^{\,1,b}(F - P_t) & if \;\; F - P_t < 0 \end{cases}, \tag{4}$$

while the orders placed by type 2 fundamentalists are denoted by

$$D_t^{F,2} = \begin{cases} +f^{\,2,a} & if \;\; F - P_t > 0 \\ +f^{\,2,b} & if \;\; F - P_t < 0 \end{cases}. \tag{5}$$

The reaction parameters $f^{\,1,a}$, $f^{\,1,b}$, $f^{\,2,a}$ and $f^{\,2,b}$ are all positive. Note that both types of fundamentalists submit buying (selling) orders when the market is undervalued (overvalued).

Apparently, one key characteristic (and novel) feature of this framework is that type 2 agents always trade fixed amounts of assets while type 1 agents increase their orders linearly with the observed mispricing. Moreover, the agents' trading intensity depends on whether the market is in a bull or a bear state. Eight parameters are therefore required to describe the behavior of the four different groups of speculators.

Nevertheless, the model's dynamical system can conveniently be expressed using the following definitions: $s_R = 1 + c^{1,a} - f^{1,b}$, $s_L = 1 + c^{1,b} - f^{1,a}$, $m_R = c^{2,a} - f^{\,2,b}$ and $m_L = f^{\,2,a} - c^{2,b}$. Combining (1)–(5) and expressing the model in terms of deviations from fundamental values, $\widetilde{P}_t = P_t - F$, yields the discontinuous one-dimensional map

$$\widetilde{P}_{t+1} = \begin{cases} s_R\widetilde{P}_t + m_R & if \;\; \widetilde{P}_t > 0 \\ s_L\widetilde{P}_t + m_L & if \;\; \widetilde{P}_t < 0 \end{cases}. \tag{6}$$

Moreover, by using $x' = \widetilde{P}_{t+1}$ and $x = \widetilde{P}_t$, the following is finally obtained:

$$x' = T(x) = \begin{cases} f_L(x) = s_L x + m_L & if \;\; x < 0 \\ f_R(x) = s_R x + m_R & if \;\; x > 0 \end{cases}, \tag{7}$$

which comprises a family of piecewise linear maps.

Of course, the dynamics of (7) depend on the size of the four (aggregated) slope and offset parameters. There are a number of interesting scenarios, a few of which have already been covered in [5]. However, there is no empirical evidence on the size of these parameters and thus it is worthwhile (and fascinating) to study more of them. The main focus of this chapter is on $s_R < 0 < s_L < 1$. Accordingly, in the bear market the aggressiveness of type 1 fundamentalists is "slightly" higher than the aggressiveness of type 1 chartists (such that $0 < s_L < 1$), while in the bull market it is "much" higher (and such that $s_R < 0$). Moreover, $m_L > 0$ and $m_R > 0$ mean that type 2 fundamentalists dominate type 2 chartists in the bear market, and vice versa in the bull market. Note also that $m_L > m_R$ indicates that the dominance of type 2 fundamentalists over type 2 chartists in the bear market may be regarded as larger than the dominance of type 2 chartists over type 2 fundamentalists in the bull market. Of course, $m_L < m_R$ implies the opposite. As will be pointed out in more detail in Section 3, we additionally require in the latter case that the distance between m_L and m_R, and thus the "difference in dominance", is limited, i.e. we assume that $m_L \geq x_R^*$, where $x_R^* = m_R/(1 - s_R)$ is the unique fixed point of the model.

To be able to appreciate our results, let us also put these new cases into perspective with the two (main) cases explored so far. In [5] we analyzed scenarios in which type 1 chartists are always dominated by type 1 fundamentalists while simultaneously type 2 chartists always dominate type 2 fundamentalists (or the other way around). In this contribution, we depart from this kind of symmetry; now, a dominance of one trader type over the other and the level of dominance may depend on economic circumstances, that is, whether the market is in a bear or a bull state. It is interesting to investigate how the departure from this kind of symmetry may affect the dynamics of the model. Is such a twist sufficient to destroy the model's potential to generate complex endogenous price dynamics? As we will see, the opposite holds. Our analysis illustrates that the corresponding map still gives rise to intricate (price) dynamics and thus that the results derived in [5] may be regarded as robust.

3. Some Properties of the Model

The family of maps we consider is given in (7). The restrictions on the parameters we impose in this chapter are:

$$s_R < 0 < s_L < 1 \ , \ m_L \gtreqless m_R \ , \ m_{L,R} > 0 \tag{8}$$

so that we have an increasing straight line for $x < 0$ and a decreasing straight line for $x > 0$. The shape of the map (7) is shown in Fig. 1a,b.

Hence, since we limit the branch on the left to a positive slope and less than one, we have no equilibrium on the left, and the iterated points are pushed to the right, where a negative slope exists. In case of an unstable fixed point, the generic trajectory is necessarily forced to return (after a finite number of turns around the unstable fixed point) to the left, where an increasing sequence will start again. Thus the dynamics are always bounded in a natural way: they can never explode (diverge). The different regimes which can occur under (7) and (8) are visualized in Fig. 1a,b from which we can conclude that:

(i) either the left branch ends above the right one, $m_L \geq m_R$ (as in Fig. 1a), and the map is continuous in the case of $m_L = m_R$ and discontinuous otherwise;

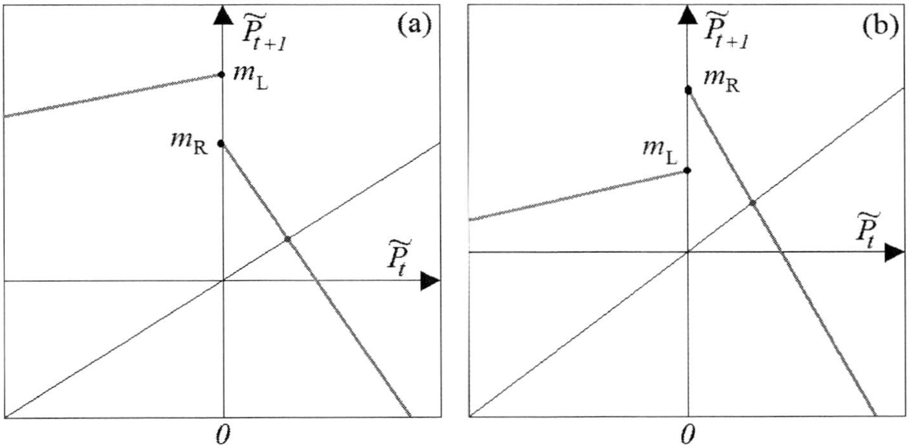

Figure 1. The two cases under analysis.

(ii) or the left branch ends below the right one, yet remains above the fixed point $x_R^* \leq m_L < m_R$ (as in Fig. 1b);

(iii) or the left branch ends below the fixed point, $0 < m_L < x_R^* (< m_R)$.

To keep this chapter concise, we limit our analysis to cases (i) and (ii). As we shall see, the dynamics occurring in the continuous case are the same as those which may occur for a decreasing jump when $m_L > m_R$. That is, the continuous case can only be considered a particular one in class (i) given above. Hence, since our results are totally generic and depend on all of the parameters of the model, the equations giving the border collision bifurcation curves and the flip bifurcations curves of the cycles occurring in the continuous case are the same as those detected for the discontinuous case, with the particular choice of parameters $m_L = m_R$.

Due to the simplicity of the model, it is quite easy to determine the eigenvalue associated with a certain cycle. In fact, a periodic orbit with period $k = p+q$ with p points on the L side and q points on the R side, necessarily has eigenvalue $\lambda = s_L^p s_R^q$. Moreover, we shall see that the cases (i) and (ii) defined above, all of the cycles that may be stable necessarily have a negative eigenvalue, so that they can only have a bifurcation with eigenvalue $\lambda = -1$, which in our piecewise linear map is always a degenerate flip bifurcation. A degenerate flip bifurcation of a k-cycle is such that at the bifurcation value (when the eigenvalue is equal to -1), the map possesses an interval filled with cycles of period $2k$ (with the $k-$cycle in between). This is also a border collision bifurcation (for the cycle at the boundary of the interval), meaning that it is generally not known what occurs after a degenerate flip bifurcation. In our model, the degenerate flip bifurcation of the fixed point is followed by a unique stable $2k-$cycle in case (i), and by chaotic dynamics in case (ii).

Let us start with the equilibrium of our model: the fixed point that comes from the function on the right side. From $f_R(x_R^*) = x_R^*$, a fixed point $x_R^* > 0$ is given by:

$$x_R^* = \frac{m_R}{1 - s_R} \tag{9}$$

which is attracting for $-1 < s_R < 0$. A degenerate flip bifurcation occurs when $s_R = -1$, which means that at the bifurcation value all of the points of interval I :

$$I = [f_R{}^2(0), f_R(0)] = [0, m_R] \tag{10}$$

are cycles of period 2 (except for the fixed point). After the bifurcation, only one cycle of period 2 may or may not be left. A 2−cycle must necessarily be of symbol sequence LR. The two periodic points can be easily found, solving for $f_L \circ f_R(x) = x$, which gives the periodic point on the R side, and solving for $f_R \circ f_L(x) = x$, which gives the periodic point on the L side, so that we obtain

$$x_0 = \frac{s_R m_L + m_R}{1 - s_L s_R} < 0 \ , \ x_1 = \frac{s_L m_R + m_L}{1 - s_L s_R} > 0 \tag{11}$$

which, when existing, is stable for $-1 < \lambda_2 = s_R s_L < 0$. Its existence is associated with the condition given by the numerator of x_0 (as the denominators are always positive), that is: $s_R < -\frac{m_R}{m_L}$ and the border collision bifurcation leading to its existence is $s_R = -\frac{m_R}{m_L}$ yielding $x_0 = 0$, while the second possible border collision bifurcation associated with $x_1 = 0$ can never occur (since under our assumptions on the parameters we always have $(s_L m_R + m_L) > 0$.

We can therefore immediately see that in the continuous case, when $m_L = m_R$, the BCB of the 2−cycle reduces to $s_R = -1$ and thus corresponds to the degenerate flip bifurcation of fixed point x_R^*. While in the discontinuous case, when $m_L > m_R$, the BCB of the 2−cycle is associated with a value $-1 < s_R < 0$ to which an attracting fixed point corresponds. This implies a region of coexistence of the stable fixed point with the stable 2−cycle (born by border collision bifurcation). Thus, keeping the values of parameters m_L and m_R fixed, a 2−cycle will be left at the degenerate flip bifurcation of the fixed point, attracting if $-1 < \lambda_2 = s_R s_L < 0$ or repelling if $s_R s_L < -1$. However, in our assumptions $(0 < s_L < 1)$ for $m_L > m_R$ only a stable 2−cycle can occur.

In Fig. 2a we represent the generic shape of the two-dimensional bifurcation diagram in the slopes (s_R, s_L) for $m_L \geq m_R$ and an enlarged portion in Fig. 2c shows the region of coexistence of the stable fixed point with the stable 2−cycle. The shape of the map T and of its second iterate T^2 in this region is shown in Fig. 2d for $m_L = 3 > m_R = 2$, $s_R = -0.95$ (so that the fixed point is stable), and $s_L = 0.7$. When these two periodic orbits coexist, the basin of attraction of the fixed point x_R^* is bounded by the discontinuity point and its rank-1 preimage on the right side, i.e. $\mathcal{B}(x_R^*) =]0, -m_R/s_R[$, while the other real initial conditions converge to the 2−cycle. Note also that defining $T(0) = m_L$ this point converges to the 2−cycle while defining $T(0) = m_R$ this point converges to the stable fixed point.

On the other hand in the discontinuous case with $m_L < m_R$, the BCB of the 2−cycle is associated with a value $s_R = -\frac{m_R}{m_L} < -1$, so that when the flip bifurcation of the fixed point occurs (at $s_R = -1$), a 2−cycle cannot exist and, the behavior is complex, as we can argue from the bifurcation diagram in Fig. 3.

As stated above, our results are generally valid regardless of the value of the parameters, under the restriction given in (8). In order to simplify the exposition, our figures are related to a fixed value $m_R = 2$, which can be any positive value, and $m_L = 3$, $m_L = 1$, which can be substituted with any value $m_L \geq m_R$, $x_R^* \leq m_L < m_R$, respectively. The same qualitative figures and bifurcations are obtained, as described in the following sections,

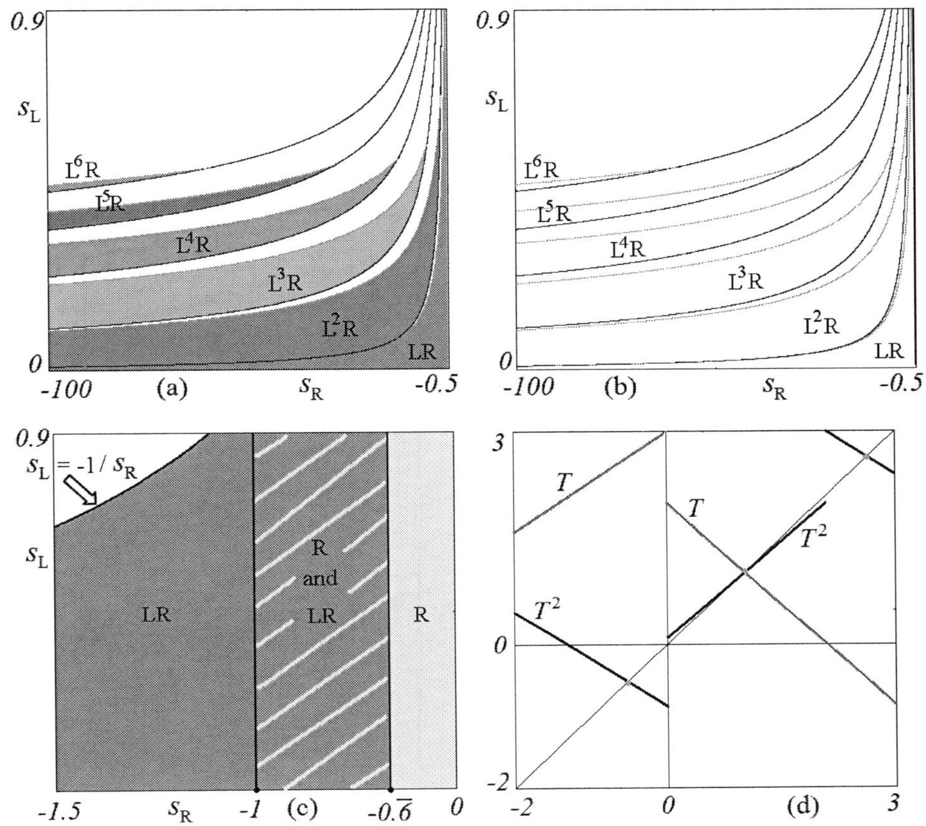

Figure 2. Two dimensional (s_R, s_L) bifurcation diagram in (a) and related BCB curves in (b), at $m_L = 3$ and $m_R = 2$. The enlarged portion for $-1.5 < s_R < 0$ is shown in (c) where the coexistence region occurs for $-1 < s_R < -m_R/m_L = 0.\overline{6}$. In (d) the shape of the map and of its second iterate are presented.

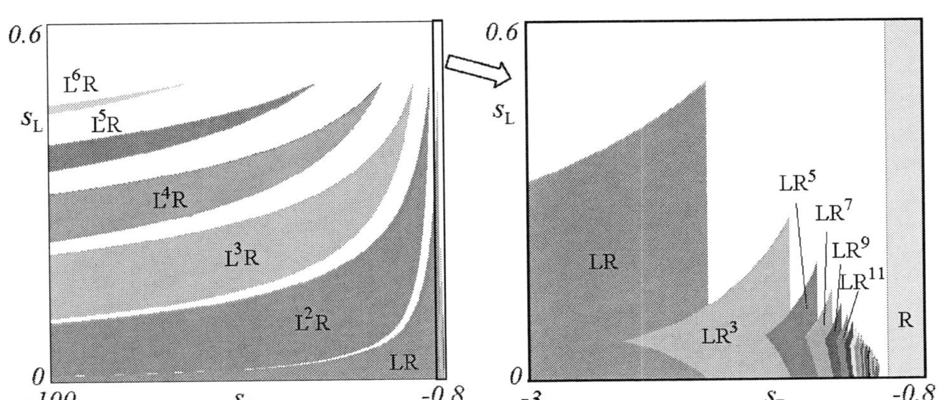

Figure 3. Two-dimensional orbit diagram at $m_L = 1$ and $m_R = 2$.

where we shall analyze what kind of dynamics occur in the model when fixed point x_R^* is unstable, and in particular the structure of chaotic trajectories.

Fig. 3 represents the generic shape of the two-dimensional bifurcation diagram in slopes (s_R, s_L) in case (ii), when $x_R^* \leq m_L < m_R$. We can see that there are two typical scenarios. An increasing sequence of periodicity regions of $k-$cycles for any integer $k = 1, 2, 3...$, described in Section 4 (of type $L^k R$, with period increment by 1). In the enlargement between the periodicity region of the fixed point on the R side, x_R^*, and the periodicity region of the $2-$cycle, there is an infinite sequence of periodicity regions of stable $2p-$cycles, of even periods only, which we call period increment, with increment 2 (of type LR^k, with period increment by 2), as described in Section 5.

In case (i), when $m_L \geq m_R$, as shown in Fig. 2a, the region of (coexistence) of the stable fixed point leads directly to a stable $2-$cycle, and for low values of the slope s_R only stable cycles of type $L^k R$, with period increment 1, exist.

The white regions in Fig. 2a and Fig. 3a represent parameter combinations at which chaotic dynamics occur, thus in both cases wide parameter regions with chaos exist. The chaotic regime in these kinds of maps is associated with *cyclical chaotic intervals*, and chaos is called *robust* (see [13]) because it is persistent with respect to parameter variations. Although the different kinds of cyclical chaotic intervals occurring in our model are not investigated in this chapter, we shall note a peculiarity: the underlying structure associated with the unstable cycles of period $L^k R$ also influences the chaotic trajectories. We provide some typical numerical examples in the following sections.

4. Maximal Cycles $L^k R$

In this Section we describe the BCB curves involved in the period increment scenario where the period increases by one. Let us call x_0 the point of the cycle immediately to the left of the discontinuity point $x = 0$. Then the periodic point x_0 of the orbit of symbol sequence $L^k R$ can be obtained by looking for the fixed point of the function ${f_L}^{k-1} \circ f_R \circ f_L(x)$, that is, by solving for ${f_L}^{k-1} \circ f_R \circ f_L(x) = x$, where the $2-$cycle is obtained again for $k = 1$. We have:

$${f_L}^{k-1} \circ f_R \circ f_L(x) = s_L^k s_R x + s_L^{k-1}(s_R m_L + m_R) + m_L \frac{1 - s_L^{k-1}}{1 - s_L}$$

so that we get:

$$x_0 = \frac{s_L^{k-1}}{1 - s_L^k s_R}[(s_R m_L + m_R) + m_L \phi_{k-1}^L] \ , \ \phi_k^L = \frac{1 - s_L^k}{(1 - s_L) s_L^k} \tag{12}$$

and setting $x_0 = 0$, we obtain the BCB curve of equation:

$$BCB_{L^k R} \ : \ s_R = -\phi_{k-1}^L - \frac{m_R}{m_L} \tag{13}$$

which bounds the existence region of these cycles of period $(k+1)$, given by $s_R < -\phi_{k-1}^L - \frac{m_R}{m_L}$. Moreover, it is a complete existent region. It cannot be followed by a second BCB curve leading to the disappearance of the cycle because, as we have seen for the cycle of period 2, we always have $x_1 = f_L(x_0) > 0$ for any such cycle, so that it can never merge with the boundary $x = 0$. It follows that it can only be attracting or repelling before or after the degenerate flip bifurcation occurs, when its eigenvalue $\lambda(L^k R) = s_L^k s_R$ bifurcates. Thus the equation of the flip bifurcation curve of an existent $(k+1)-$cycle is given by $\lambda(L^k R) = s_L^k s_R = -1$, that is:

$$s_R = -1/s_L^k \tag{14}$$

For increasing values of k, up to 6, the BCB curves given in (13) are drawn in black in Fig. 2b, while the flip bifurcation curves given in (14) are drawn in red.

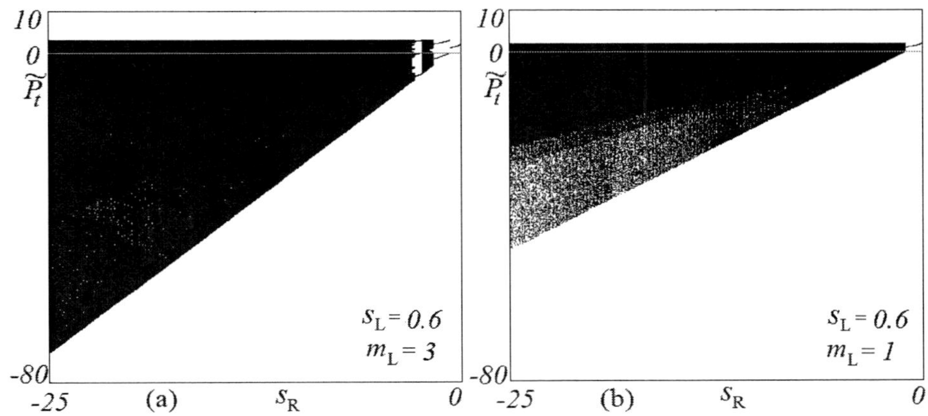

Figure 4. Bifurcation diagrams.

Figs. 4a and 5a show a one-dimensional bifurcation diagram at $s_L = 0.6$ and $s_L = 0.4$, respectively, in case (i), while Figs. 4b and 5b show the analogous situation for case (ii). As we can see, the degenerate flip bifurcations occurring in Fig. 5 are always followed by cyclical chaotic intervals, which become a one-piece chaotic interval (after a short interval in the parameter).

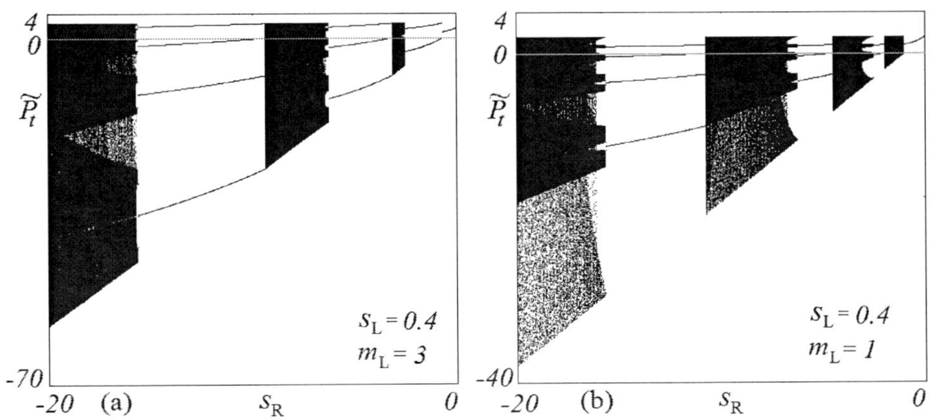

Figure 5. Bifurcation diagrams.

The kind of chaotic dynamics that may occur differ significantly from the usual chaotic trajectories, where we can have an unpredictable number of iterations on both sides. Here, depending on the slopes of the functions, we have always a limited number of points in each region, so that the chaotic structure is in some sense predictable, depending on the slopes. For example, we can always have only one point on the L side for small slopes of s_R in absolute value (Fig. 6a), or we can always have only one point on the R side for very high slopes of s_R (Fig. 6c), and intermediate situations otherwise (as in Fig. 6b).

We have described the equations of the BCB leading to the appearance of cycles with symbol sequence $L^k R$ and have seen that a second BCB curve does not exist. This is the only possible dynamic behavior when $m_L \geq m_R$, as *when the fixed point is unstable*, the fate of point $f_R(0) = m_R$ is the same as that of $f_L(0) = m_L \geq m_R$. Hence we notice in such regimes that the definition of the map in the discontinuity point, $T(0) = m_R$ or $T(0) = m_L$, is irrelevant, as both cases lead to the same attracting set, i.e. we get the same kind of dynamics.

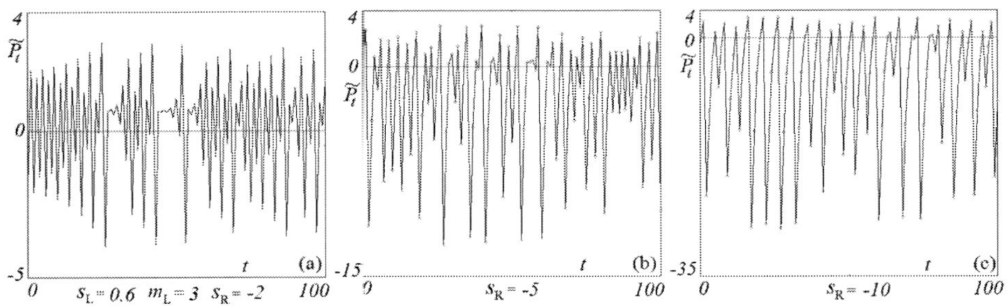

Figure 6. Price versus time.

This kind of dynamic behavior can also exist when $x_R^* \leq m_L < m_R$ for parameters in the left region with respect to the 2−cycle, i.e. for $s_R \leq -\frac{m_R}{m_L}$. The price versus time trajectories in the chaotic regime are also similar, depending on the slopes. An example is given in Fig. 7 for $m_L = 1 < m_R$. We can always only have one point on the L side for small slopes of s_R in absolute value (Fig. 7a), or we can only always have one point on the R side for very high slopes of s_R (Fig. 7c), and intermediate situations otherwise (as in Fig. 7b).

While for $x_R^* \leq m_L < m_R$ and $s_R > -\frac{m_R}{m_L}$ as shown in the enlarged part of Fig. 3, we can have a different dynamic behavior, with periodicity regions that overlap, giving well-known regions with *two coexisting attracting cycles,* and the two different definitions of the map in the discontinuity point converge to two different cycles (with a period which differs by 2), as proved in the next section.

5. Maximal Cycles LR^k

As stated above, the iterations may clearly behave differently when $x_R^* \leq m_L < m_R$, as in such a case, also when the fixed point is unstable, the two points $f_L(0) = m_L$ and $f_R(0) = m_R$ may have a different dynamic behavior. This is not a new phenomenon.

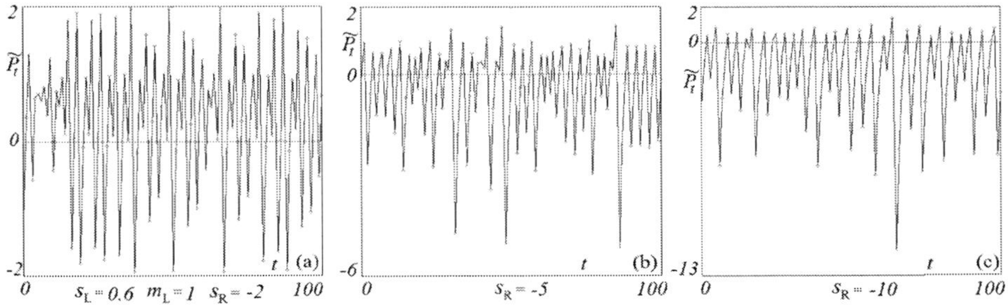

Figure 7. Price versus time.

Indeed, when $x_R^* \leq m_L < m_R$, we can have not only cycles of the kind L^kR (when $s_R \leq -\frac{m_R}{m_L}$), but also cycles with symbol sequence LR^k (when $s_R > -\frac{m_R}{m_L}$). The reason for this is immediately clear when we look at the graph in Fig. 1a: point $f_L(0) = m_L$ may be much less than m_R and close to the unstable fixed point x_R^* so that several applications of function $g(x)$ on the R side are necessary before reaching the L side. Moreover, as we shall see below, the coexistence of two stable cycles of symbol sequence LR^k and LR^{k+2} is allowed in suitable regions for any odd $k \geq 1$. To find the conditions leading to the existence of these new kinds of cycles, let us call x_0 the point of the cycle which is immediately to the left of discontinuity point $x = 0$. Then the periodic point x_0 of the orbit of symbol sequence LR^k can be obtained by looking for the fixed point of the function $f_R^k \circ f_L(x)$, that is, solving for $f_R^k \circ f_L(x) = x$. We have:

$$f_R^k \circ f_L(x) = s_R^k(s_Lx + m_L) + m_R\frac{1 - s_R^k}{1 - s_R}$$

so that we obtain:

$$x_0 = \frac{s_R^k}{1 - s_R^k s_L}[m_L + m_R\phi_k^R] \ , \ \phi_k^R = \frac{1 - s_R^k}{(1 - s_R)s_R^k} \tag{15}$$

and setting $x_0 = 0$ we obtain the BCB curve of equation:

$$BCB_{LR^k}^l \ : \ m_L + m_R\phi_k^R = 0. \tag{16}$$

We denote this by $BCB_{LR^k}^l$ because at the border collision periodic point x_0 of the cycle collides with discontinuity point $x = 0$ from the left. In the parameter plane (s_R, s_L) of Fig. 8, such curves are vertical lines of equation $s_R = const.$, where the constant value is determined from the equations in (16).

We also notice that such a BCB curve $BCB_{LR^k}^l$ leads to a cycle with periodic point $x_1 = f_L(x_0) > x_R^*$. In fact by assumption, we have $f_L(0) = m_L \geq x_R^*$ at the bifurcation value and thus the existent cycle starts with periodic point $x_1 = f_L(x_0) > x_R^*$. This implies that periodic point x_1 may be mapped on the L side after an even number of applications of function $g(x)$, so that *such cycles only exist when* k *is an odd number,* and period $(k + 1)$ is even. Moreover, it is obvious that such cycles only exist as long as another border collision occurs, due to periodic point x_{k-1} (*which implies* $k > 1$) merging with discontinuity point

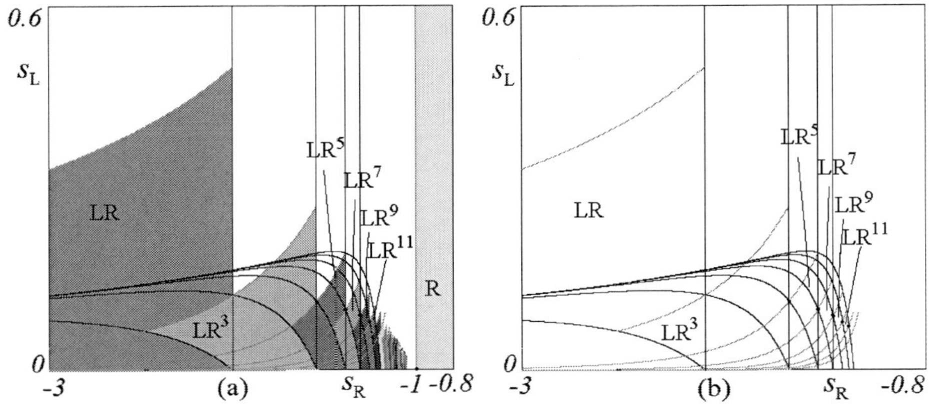

Figure 8. Two-dimensional orbit diagram.

$x = 0$. Equivalently, the cycle exists as long as periodic point x_k merges with the maximum value $f_R(0) = m_R$. That is to say, $x_{k-1} = 0$ iff $x_k = m_R$ iff $x_0 = f_R(m_R)$. Thus we have the equation of the second BCB curve, obtained by equation $x_0 = m_R(1 + s_R)$, that is:

$$\frac{s_R^k}{1 - s_R^k s_L}[m_L + m_R\phi_k^R] = m_R(1 + s_R) \tag{17}$$

which leads to:

$$BCB^r_{LR^k} \; : \; s_L = \frac{1}{s_R^k} - \frac{m_L}{m_R(1 + s_R)} - \frac{\phi_k^R}{(1 + s_R)}. \tag{18}$$

We call this $BCB^r_{LR^k}$ because at the border collision periodic point x_{k-1} of the cycle collides with discontinuity point $x = 0$ from the right. A few BCB curves on both sides, from (16) and (18), are shown in black in Fig. 8 (the $BCB^l_{LR^k}$ are the vertical lines).

We have noticed above that such bifurcation curves $BCB^r_{LR^k}$ only exist for $k > 1$, since for $k = 1$ we have the 2−cycle, whose periodic point x_1 can only collide the fixed point x^*_R, as already mentioned in Section 3.

We can see from Fig. 8a that the cycles determined here may be stable or unstable. Stability is associated with the related eigenvalue. We know this must be negative, because we have an odd number of periodic points in the R region, so that $\lambda(LR^k) = s_L s_R^k < 0$, and its flip bifurcation occurs at $\lambda(LR^k) = s_L s_R^k = -1$, that is:

$$s_L = -1/s_R^k. \tag{19}$$

The related flip bifurcation curves are shown in red in Fig. 8.

Fig. 8 also emphasizes that the numerically calculated flip bifurcation curves always intersect at the same point of two BCB curves. That is: each curve $BCB^l_{LR^k}$ and $BCB^r_{LR^{k+4}}$ intersects exactly at a point belonging to the flip bifurcation curve of cycle LR^{k+2}, *which proves that two stable cycles at most can coexist.* This property can be easily verified from the related equation. In fact, by using the relation

$$\phi_{k+1}^{R} = \phi_{k}^{R} + \frac{1}{s_{R}^{k+1}}$$

after some algebra it follows that $\phi_k^R = -\frac{m_L}{m_R}$ from (16) and $s_R^k = -\frac{1}{s_L s_R^2}$ from (19) for cycle LR^{k+2} identically satisfy the equation of $BCB^r_{LR^{k+4}}$.

The relevant result in this regime is that a stable cycle may not be the only existent cycle, i.e. may be not globally attracting, as we have seen that we can have a stable cycle and also several unstable cycles placed on the basin boundary of the stable one. Moreover, in particular regions we have the *coexistence of two stable cycles.*

6. Conclusion

In this chapter we considered a piecewise linear discontinuous map with one increasing branch on the L side and a decreasing branch on the R side, both having positive offsets, and representing interactions between heterogeneous traders in a financial market. We determined the border collision bifurcation curves leading to the existence of stable cycles in two qualitatively different regimes for the values of the jump. In case (i), for $m_L \geq m_R$, only stable cycles of symbolic sequence $L^k R$ can exist, whose BCB curves are given in Section 4. In case (ii), for $x_R^* \leq m_L < m_R$ there are all the stable cycles LR^k for $s_R \leq -\frac{m_R}{m_L}$. In region $-\frac{m_R}{m_L} < s_R < -1$ there are overlapping periodicity regions for stable cycles of even periods only, of type LR^k, whose BCB curves were determined in Section 5. Some regions have still not been explored, and several parameter constellations for the models considered here have been left for further studies.

Finally, let us reflect the dynamic properties of our model from an economic point of view. As is well known, actual financial markets are quite volatile, occasionally displaying severe bubbles and crashes. Our model obviously has the potential to replicate such features, at least in a qualitative manner. Besides fixed point dynamics, we also find periodic or chaotic motion (and some intriguing examples are given in Figures 6 and 7 with strongly fluctuating prices and erratic switches between bull and bear markets episodes). Moreover, there may even be coexisting attractors, and the types of bifurcations we observe imply that even a tiny shift in one of the behavioral parameters may significantly affect the variability of prices and thus the efficiency of financial markets. Given the threat originating from actual financial markets for the real economy, it is apparently very important to understand the main drivers of such dynamics. Our study ultimately illustrates that even quite simple behavioral models in which market participants follow well-established trading patterns can be useful to improve our basic understanding of what is going on in these systems.

It goes without saying that more work is required in this area. Here we studied a situation where our discontinuous map consists of two linear pieces. The next natural step would be to extend the analysis and explore models which contain three or more linear pieces.

References

[1] Tramontana, F., Gardini, L., Dieci, F., & Westerhoff, F. (2009). The emergence of "Bull and Bear" dynamics in a nonlinear 3d model of interacting markets. *Discrete Dynamics in Nature and Society*, Article ID 310471, 30 pages, doi:10.1155/2009/310471.

[2] Tramontana, F., Gardini, L., Dieci, F., & Westerhoff, F. (2009). Global bifurcations in a three dimensional financial model of "bull and bear" interactions. In C. Chiarella, G. I. Bischi & L. Gardini, (Eds.), *Nonlinear Dynamics in Economics, Finance and Social Sciences*(pp. 333–352) Springer-Verlag.

[3] Day, R. (1982). Irregular growth cycles. *The American Economic Review* **72** (3), 406–414.

[4] Day, R. (1994). *Complex Economic Dynamics*. Cambridge, USA: MIT Press.

[5] Tramontana, F., Gardini, L., & Westerhoff, F. (2009). On the complicated price dynamics of a simple one-dimensional discontinuous financial market model with heterogeneous interacting traders. *submitted for publication*

[6] Nusse, H. E., & Yorke, J. A. (1992). Border-collision bifurcations including period two to period three for piecewise smooth systems. *Physica D,* **57**, 39–57.

[7] Nusse, H. E., Ott, E., & Yorke, J. A. (1994). Border-collision bifurcations: An explanation for observed bifurcation phenomena. *Physical Review E,* **49**, 1073–1076.

[8] Banerjee, S., Karthik, M. S., Yuan, G., & Yorke, J. A. (2000). Bifurcations in One-Dimensional Piecewise Smooth Maps - Theory and Applications in Switching Circuits. *IEEE Trans. Circuits Syst.-I: Fund. Theory Appl., 47* (3), 389–394.

[9] Maistrenko, Y. L., Maistrenko, V. L., & Chua, L. O. (1993). Cycles of chaotic intervals in a time-delayed Chua's circuit. *International Journal of Bifurcation and Chaos,* **3** (6), 1557–1572.

[10] Maistrenko, Y. L., Maistrenko, V. L., Vikul, S. I., & Chua, L. O. (1995). Bifurcations of attracting cycles from time-delayed Chua's circuit. *International Journal of Bifurcation and Chaos,* **5** (3), 653–671.

[11] Maistrenko, Y. L., Maistrenko, V. L., & Vikul, S. I. (1999). On period-adding sequences of attracting cycles in piecewise linear maps. *Chaos, Solitons & Fractals,* **9** (1), 67–75.

[12] Day, R., & Pianigiani, G. (1991). Statistical dynamics and economics. *Journal of Economic Behavior and Organization,* **16**, 37–84.

[13] Banerjee, S., Yorke, J. A., & Grebogi, C. (1998). Robust chaos. *Physical Review Letters,* **80**, 3049–3052.

INDEX

D

E

F

G

H

I

J

K

L

M

N

O

P

R

S

T

U

V

W

Y

Z